Agricultural R&D in the Developing World

Agricultural R&D in the Developing World: Too Little, Too Late?

Edited by
Philip G. Pardey, Julian M. Alston, and Roley R. Piggott

International Food Policy Research Institute
2033 K Street, N.W.
Washington, D.C.

International Food Policy Research Institute
2033 K Street, N.W.
Washington, D.C. 20006-1002
U.S.A.
Telephone +1-202-862-5600
www.ifpri.org

How to cite this book: Pardey, P. G., J. M. Alston, and R. R. Piggott, eds. *Agricultural R&D in the developing world: Too little, too late?* Washington, DC: International Food Policy Research Institute.

Library of Congress Cataloging-in-Publication Data

Agricultural R&D in the developing world : too little, too late? / edited by Philip G. Pardey, Julian M. Alston, and Roley R. Piggott.
   p.   cm.
Includes bibliographical references and index.
ISBN 0-89629-756-X (alk. paper)
   1. Agriculture—Economic aspects—Developing countries.   2. Agricultural innovations—Developing countries.   3. Agriculture—Research—Developing countries.   I. Title: Agricultural R and D in the developing world.   II. Pardey, Philip G.   III. Alston, Julian M.   IV. Piggott, Roley.
HD1410.6.D44A47   2006
331.1—dc22   2006006804

Dedicated to Derek Edward Tribe, 1926–2003,
who, as the first executive director of Australia's Crawford Fund,
believed passionately in and worked tirelessly for
the support of international agricultural research.

We still have not developed a set of successful public programs for investing in agricultural research and technology in poor countries . . . the investment in general is woefully inadequate both in the manner in which it is being accomplished and in the amounts spent for this purpose.

—Theodore W. Schultz, What ails world agriculture? *Bulletin of the Atomic Scientists,* January 1968. Reprinted in V. W. Ruttan, A. D. Waldo, and J. P. Houck, *Agricultural policy in an affluent society.* New York: W. W. Norton and Company, 1969, pp. 299–300.

Contents

Tables

Figures

Foreword

This book was conceived as a companion to the 1999 volume *Paying for Agricultural Productivity*, published by Johns Hopkins University Press in conjunction with IFPRI. That volume dealt with investments, institutions, and policy processes regarding agricultural R&D in developed countries. This book addresses the same set of issues for the developing countries, and the relationship of those countries to the richer parts of the world where the preponderance of agricultural innovation still takes place. It also reviews developments within the Consultative Group on International Agricultural Research (CGIAR), along with the changing roles of international research generally, in light of the substantial shifts in science funding and policy (as well as in the science itself) that are taking place throughout the world.

The book combines new evidence with economic theory and an economic way of thinking about science policy—highlighting the developing-country aspects—as well as a set of in-depth, comparative country studies. These country studies take us well beyond generalities, providing insights into the important changes taking place within these countries and others they represent. The countries covered include the largest developing countries—China and India—as well as a range of richer and poorer, and more- and less-developed countries, representing most parts of the globe.

The evidence and ideas presented in the book are disquieting. Over the past several decades, at least, spillovers of agricultural technology from rich countries to poor countries demonstrably increased productivity and food security for many parts of the developing world. As the authors document, however, recent developments in both the developed and developing worlds mean that poor countries may no longer be able to depend as they have in the past on spillovers of new agricultural technologies and knowledge from richer countries, especially advances related to enhanced productivity of staple foods.

As a consequence of these changes, simply maintaining their current agricultural R&D policies may leave many developing countries as agricultural technology orphans in the decades ahead. Developing countries may have to become more self-reliant and perhaps more dependent on one another for the collective benefits of agricultural R&D and technology. Some of the more advanced developing countries like South Korea, Brazil, China, and India seem to be gaining ground, with productive and self-sustaining local research sectors taking hold. However, other parts of the developing world, as illustrated in this book by reviews of agricultural R&D in Zambia, Bangladesh, and Indonesia, are merely regaining lost ground or slipping further behind. Aside from a handful of larger countries, many developing countries, especially in Africa, are facing serious funding and institutional constraints that inhibit the effectiveness of local R&D. Together, these factors may lead to serious food deficits.

The information assembled here and the lessons learned in this volume argue for refocusing attention on agricultural R&D as an instrument for long-run economic development to help avert a continuation of the chronic hunger and malnutrition that afflict all too many people around the world. These lessons will pay off if they help revitalize multinational engagement and investment in the global public benefits of international agricultural research.

Joachim von Braun
Director General, IFPRI

Acknowledgments

T he research giving rise to this volume took place under the auspices of the Agricultural Science and Technology Indicators (ASTI) initiative, an undertaking to stay abreast of agricultural R&D trends worldwide led by staff located at the International Food Policy Research Institute (IFPRI).

Initial funding for this work was provided by the Ford Foundation. Additional support was obtained from funding provided to IFPRI by the U.S. Agency for International Development (USAID). This was supplemented by significant general support from the International Science and Technology Practice and Policy (InSTePP) center and the Department of Applied Economics at the University of Minnesota; the University of California Agricultural Issues Center and the Department of Agricultural and Resource Economics at the University of California, Davis; and the Faculty of Economics, Business and Law at the University of New England, Australia.

The editors acknowledge with gratitude the outstanding assistance of Mary Jane Banks, Sue Pohlod, Louise Letnes, and the staff in the Communications Division at IFPRI who helped turn our chapter files into a coherent book manuscript. We also received extensive and excellent comments from Stanley Wood and two anonymous reviewers, and helpful guidance from IFPRI's Publication Review Committee. Finally, we owe a big debt of gratitude to the authors of the country chapters, who worked willingly with us through multiple rounds of revisions.

Chapter 1

Introduction and Overview

Julian M. Alston, Philip G. Pardey, and Roley R. Piggott

In the early 21st century, the science of agriculture has started to shift gears, just as it did 100 years ago. At the beginning of the 20th century, Charles Darwin's theory of evolution, the pure-line theory of Wilhelm Johannsen, and the rediscovery of Gregor Mendel's laws of heredity contributed to the rise of plant breeding, while Louis Pasteur's germ theory of disease and the development of vaccines opened up lines of research in the veterinary sciences. The next epoch in agricultural technology will also have fundamental biological science at its foundation. Today, scientists armed with new molecular biologies involving genomics, proteomics, recombinant DNA, and supporting informatics technologies are delving deeper into the genetics of life, with potentially profound and pervasive implications for agriculture worldwide.

The context in which that science will take place has evolved and shifted as well. The public purpose in agricultural R&D is less focused and more closely scrutinized than it was a century ago; the general public seems less trusting of some areas of science, and perhaps of some scientists (National Science Board 2002); and marked changes are taking place in the intellectual property regimes relating to the genetic resources used in agriculture and the technologies used to transform them (Boettiger et al. 2004; Pardey, Koo, and Nottenburg 2004). Complacency has crept in too. Some question the need for continued public funding at recent levels, suggesting that the world's food problems are being solved or constrained by things other than R&D, or that the private sector will do the job (see Runge et al. 2003). Others see a scientific apartheid taking shape, with large parts of the developing world being left behind or denied the prospects science has to offer for growth, development, and prosperity (Serageldin 2001).

The world's agricultural economy was transformed remarkably during the 20th century. The agricultural productivity growth that fueled this change was generated primarily by agricultural R&D financed and conducted by a small group of rich countries—especially the United States, but also Japan, Germany, and France. In an increasingly interdependent world, both rich and poor countries have depended on agricultural research conducted in the private and public laboratories of these few countries, even if they have not contributed to financing the activity.

But now the rich-country research agendas are shifting. In particular, they are no longer as interested in simple productivity enhancement. Dietary patterns and other priorities change as incomes increase. Food-security concerns are still pervasive among poor people, predominantly in poor countries. In rich countries we see a declining emphasis on enhancing the production of staple foods and an increasing emphasis on enhancing certain attributes of food (such as growing demand for processed and so-called functional foods) and on food production systems (such as organic farming, humane livestock production systems, localized food sources, and "fair trade" coffee). In addition to growing differences between rich and poor countries in consumer demand for innovation, research agendas may diverge because of differences in producer and processor demands. Farmers in rich countries are demanding high-technology inputs that often are not as relevant for subsistence agriculture (such as precision farming technology or other capital-intensive methods). As well as differences in value-adding processes to serve consumer demands, differences in farm production technologies are emerging to serve the evolving agribusiness demands for farm products with specific attributes for particular food, feed, energy, medical, or industrial applications.

As rich-country research responds to these changing patterns of demand, the emphasis of the science is shifting in ways that could undermine the international spillovers that contributed significant past gains in food production throughout poorer countries. These spillovers are not generally well understood, and their importance is underappreciated (Alston 2002).

Other aspects of agricultural science policy, and the context in which research is done, are changing as well. In particular, the rise of modern biotechnology and enhanced intellectual property rights (IPR) regimes mean that technologies that were once freely accessible will be less accessible in the future. Moreover, the new technologies may not be as portable as in the past. Biotech companies, which are mostly located in the rich countries—particularly in the United States—emphasize technologies that are applicable at home. These and other factors limit incentives for companies to develop technologies for less-developed countries (Bradford et al. 2004). Hence some fear that less-developed countries will become technological orphans, abandoned by their former private- and public-sector benefactors in rich countries (see, for example, Pinstrup-Andersen and Cohen 2001).

In *Paying for Agricultural Productivity*, Alston, Pardey, and Smith (1999) documented the changing institutions and investments in agricultural R&D in a selection of rich countries.[1] In many countries, toward the end of the 20th century public and private roles shifted, and support for public agricultural research slowed, especially for near-market, applied, productivity-enhancing research. Slower-growing, stagnant, or shrinking public agricultural research funds are increasingly being diverted toward environmental objectives, food quality and safety, and so on. Who, then, will do the research required to generate sustenance for a growing world population when—at least for another century—virtually all population growth will occur in the poorer parts of the world?

The purpose of this volume is to document the changing institutions and investments in agricultural R&D in less-developed countries, in part to form a companion volume to *Paying for Agricultural Productivity* by providing a more complete global picture of the issues. A more important purpose is to take stock of what is happening in less-developed countries. This task is especially compelling if, as seems likely, these countries will have to become more self-reliant in developing crucial new agricultural technologies.

In Chapter 2 we set the scene for the chapters that follow. We introduce some economic principles for government intervention in agricultural research, along with detailed data on the evolving patterns of agricultural research spending around the world. Chapters 3 through 11 cover nine countries, including the most important among the less-developed countries, in terms of total investment in agricultural R&D.[2] The case-study countries include a reasonable representation of countries from Asia, Latin America, and Africa. Some basic features of the economies of these countries (plus the United States for comparison), are summarized in Table 1.1, including measures of their overall size, structure, economic policies and performance, and institutional infrastructure; and measures of the key features of their agricultural sectors, such as primary products, agriculture's share of GDP and the workforce, and agroecological attributes.

The chapters document the history and current status of the national agricultural research systems (NARSs) in terms of policies, institutions, investments, and achievements. The case studies cover a geographically dispersed area (South Africa and China, for example) and diverse farming systems (such as Brazil vs. Korea), yet some common themes emerge.

In addition to these country-specific chapters, Chapter 12 addresses the collective multinational effort to provide agricultural R&D through international

Table 1.1   Profiles of case-study countries

Indicator	Bangladesh		Brazil		China		Colombia	
Economy-wide indicators								
Population (2003, millions)	138.1		176.6		1,288.4		44.6	
Urbanized (2003, percent of total population)	27		83		39		76	
GDP (2003, billions)								
Current international dollars	244.4		1,375.8		6,446.0		298.8	
Current U.S. dollars	51.9		492.3		1,417.0		78.7	
GDP per capita (2003)								
Current international dollars	1,770		7,790		5,003		6,700	
Current U.S. dollars	376		2,788		1,100		1,765	
Growth in GDP per capita (1993–2003, percent per annum)	3.1		1.1		7.7		0.4	
Trade shares, 2002								
Value of exports in GDP (percent)	14		15		29		20	
Value of imports in GDP (percent)	19		13		26		21	
Communications (per 1,000 people)								
Telephone mainlines, 2002	5		223		167		179	
Mobile phones, 2003	10		264		215		141	
Internet users, 2003	2		82		63		54	
Road density, 1999 (km per km^2)	1.59		0.20		0.14		0.11	
Percentage of roads paved, 1999	10		6		22		14	
Economic freedom index, 2005	3.95		3.25		3.46		3.21	
Ranking (out of 161)	141		90		112		88	
Trade policy	5		4		4		4	
Property rights	4		3		4		4	
Corruption perceptions index, 2004	1.5		3.9		3.4		3.8	
Corruption perceptions (ranking out of 145)	145		59		71		60	
Agricultural indicators								
Agricultural value-added, 2001								
Current international dollars (bilions)	52.6		78.6		852.0		37.7	
Percent of GDP	24		6		16		14	
Population actively engaged in agriculture, 2004 (percent of total)	52		15		64		18	
Top five agricultural products by value	Rice	64	Beef and veal	22	Pig meat	17	Beef and veal	19
(average 2001–03, percent of total)	Beef and veal	4	Soybeans	13	Rice	10	Cow milk	18
	Goat milk	3	Chicken meat	11	Hen eggs	6	Chicken meat	9
	Potatoes	3	Sugarcane	8	Maize	4	Coffee	8
	Pimento	3	Cow milk	8	Wheat	4	Sugarcane	7

India	Indonesia	South Africa	South Korea	Zambia	United States
1,064.4	214.7	45.8	47.9	10.4	290.8
28	44	59	84	40	78
3,078.0	721.5	474.1	861.0	9.1	10,923.4
600.6	208.3	159.9	605.3	4.3	10,948.6
2,892	3,361	10,352	17,975	875	37,563
564	970	3,491	12,637	413	37,650
4.3	1.6	0.7	4.4	−0.6	2.1
15	36	34	35	24	10
16	29	30	34	29	14
40	37	107	489	8	646
25	87	364	701	22	543
17	38	58	610	6	551
0.85	0.20	0.30	0.88	0.90	0.69
57	57	20	75	22	59
3.53	3.54	2.78	2.64	3.40	1.85
118	121	56	45	106	12
5	2	2	3	3	2
3	4	3	2	3	1
2.8	2.0	4.6	4.5	2.6	7.5
90	133	44	47	102	17
658.5	109.6	13.2	30.3	1.8	198.6
25	17	3	4	22	2
58	46	8	8	67	2
Rice 18	Rice 37	Beef and veal 16	Pig meat 17	Maize 15	Maize 17
Buffalo milk 11	Coconuts 6	Maize 14	Rice 15	Beef and veal 16	Beef and veal 16
Wheat 8	Palm oil 6	Chicken meat 12	Cow milk 7	Cassava 10	Cow milk 11
Cow milk 7	Maize 5	Cow milk 8	Hen eggs 6	Hen eggs 7	Chicken meat 10
Sugarcane 4	Cassava 4	Grapes 5	Beef and veal 6	Chicken meat 7	Soybeans 10

(continued)

Table 1.1   (continued)

Indicator	Bangladesh	Brazil	China	Colombia
Area of agricultural land (avg 1999–2001, thousand km²)	91	2,619	5,496	457
Percentage of total land area	70	31	59	44
Percentage of agricultural land irrigated	46.2	1.1	9.9	2
Percentage of agricultural land arable and permanently cropped	93.4	25	27.2	.6
Percentage of agricultural land permanently pastured	6.6	75	72.8	90.4
Agroecological attributes (percent of ag)				
Temperate				
Irrigated and mixed irrigated	0	0	18.8	0
Rainfed	0	0	35.3	0
Moderate cool tropics	0	15.0	38.7	30.9
Warm tropics and subtropics				
Irrigated and mixed irrigated	56.6	1.1	1.0	10.9
Sloped rainfed	2.0	18.0	1.7	22.0
Flat rainfed	41.4	65.9	4.5	36.1

Sources: Data for population (total and urbanized), GDP, GDP per capita, growth in GDP per capita, trade shares, telephone mainlines, mobile phones, Internet usage, road density, proportion of roads paved (except for China), and agricultural value-added are from World Bank 2005. Data for China's proportion of roads paved are from CIA 2005. Data for the economic freedom index are from Miles et al. 2005. Data for the corruption perception index are from Transparency International 2005. Data for population actively engaged in agriculture are from Table A.3 in FAO 2005a. Data for quantity of agricultural production by value are from FAO 2005b, weighted by commodity-specific international prices averaged over the 1989–91 period from unpublished FAO data files. Shares of agricultural area in total and in a given agroecology are calculated from data and digitized maps underlying Wood et al. 2000.

Notes: GDP per capita in current U.S. dollar units was calculated from respective GDP and population data in World Bank 2005. The growth in GDP per capita was calculated by taking the average of the difference in natural logs for GDP per capita (in constant

agricultural research centers, emphasizing the Consultative Group on International Agricultural Research (CGIAR) system. Chapter 13 presents a synthesis of the main themes and issues from the case studies, and directions for policy change to address these issues.

The Audience

This book has been written primarily for those who make policy and allocate resources for agricultural research and extension, and the policy analysts and development specialists who advise them: specifically, strategic decision makers and their advisers in international agencies, national governments, and public or private agricultural research and extension organizations. These decision makers must gauge

India	Indonesia	South Africa	South Korea	Zambia	United States
1,807	445	996	20	353	4,122
61	25	82	20	47	45
30.3	10.8	1.5	60	0	5.4
94	74.8	15.8	95	15	43.2
6	25.2	84.2	5	85	56.8
0	0	0	43.4	0	5.6
0	0	0	56.4	0	66.7
5.2	0.5	77.4	0.2	5.1	22.5
47.9	27.7	2.2	0	0	0.7
8.7	32.2	3.3	0	18.6	1.6
38.3	39.5	17.1	0	76.2	2.9

local currency units) over the years 1993 to 2003. The proportion of paved roads for China was calculated from respective data within CIA 2005. Internet usage figures for Brazil, South Africa, and the United States are 2002 (not 2003) data. The economic-freedom index ranges from 1 (most free) to 5 (most economically repressed); the general index is constructed from subratings based on trade policy, fiscal burden of government, government intervention in the economy, monetary policy, capital flows and foreign investment, banking system and finance, wages and prices, property rights, regulation, and informal market; the highest-ranking country is Hong Kong, with an index of 1.35. The corruption perceptions index ranges from 0 (highly corrupt) to 10 (highly clean); the highest-ranking country is Finland, with an index of 9.7. Agricultural land includes arable, permanently cropped, and permanently pastured land. International dollars are obtained by currency conversion using purchasing power parity (PPP) indexes, which compare prices across a broader range of goods and services than conventional exchange rates.

the adequacy and appropriateness of research activities for which they are responsible and build the new institutions for R&D that will facilitate sustained growth and development in the decades ahead. The information should also be of interest to students and scholars who seek to know what has happened in agricultural R&D and why, and to understand the consequences in ways that may lead to better-informed policy choices. Understanding the histories of public agricultural research institutions and the forces of change that confront each system, and learning from the changes made to address these external forces, will provide a basis for formulating public agricultural R&D policies that are both politically feasible and economically worthwhile. Beyond these primary audiences, the material in this book should also be accessible and of interest to farmers, food processors, wholesalers, retailers, environmentalists, scientists, and all who have a direct stake in, or are affected by, the agricultural research system, as well as those generally interested in development and development economics.

Notes

The authors thank Steven Dehmer, Ulrike Wood-Sichra, and Kate Sebastian for their exceptional help in assembling and processing the data reported in this chapter.

1. See also Alston, Pardey, and Taylor (2001) and Pardey and Beintema (2001).

2. The most significant deficiency in country coverage is that we do not include any of the countries of the former Soviet Union.

References

Alston, J. M. 2002. Spillovers. *Australian Journal of Agricultural and Resource Economics* 48 (3): 315–346.

Alston, J. M., P. G. Pardey, and V. H. Smith, eds. 1999. *Paying for agricultural productivity.* Baltimore: Johns Hopkins University Press.

Alston, J. M., P. G. Pardey, and M. J. Taylor, eds. 2001. *Agricultural science policy: Changing global agendas.* Baltimore: Johns Hopkins University Press.

Boettiger, S., G. Graff, P. G. Pardey, E. van Dusen, and B. D. Wright. 2004. Intellectual property rights for plant biotechnology: International aspects. In *Handbook of plant biotechnology,* ed. P. Christou and H. Klee. Chichester, U.K.: John Wiley and Sons.

Bradford, K. J., J. M. Alston, P. G. Lemaux, and D. A. Sumner. 2004. Challenges and opportunities for horticultural biotechnology. *California Agriculture* 58 (2): 68–71.

CIA (Central Intelligence Agency of the United States). 2005. *The world factbook.* http://www.cia.gov/cia/publications/factbook/. Accessed May 2005.

FAO (Food and Agriculture Organization of the United Nations). 2005a. *FAO statistical yearbook.* Volume 1. Rome.

———. 2005b. FAOSTAT database. http://faostat.fao.org. Accessed September 2005.

Miles, M. A., E. J. Feulner, and M. A. O'Grady. 2005. *2004 index of economic freedom.* Washington, D.C.: The Heritage Foundation; New York: The Wall Street Journal.

National Science Board. 2002. Science and technology: Public attitudes and public understanding. Chapter 7 in *Science and engineering indicators 2002.* Vol. 1. Washington, D.C.: U.S. Government Printing Office.

Pardey, P. G., and N. M. Beintema. 2001. *Slow magic: Agricultural R&D a century after Mendel.* IFPRI Food Policy Report. Washington, D.C.: International Food Policy Research Institute.

Pardey, P. G., B. Koo, and C. Nottenburg. 2004. Creating, protecting, and using crop biotechnologies worldwide in an era of intellectual property. *Minnesota Journal of Law, Science & Technology* 6 (1): 213–252.

Pinstrup-Andersen, P., and M. J. Cohen. 2001. Rich and poor country perspectives on biotechnology. Chapter 3 in *The future of food: Biotechnology markets in an international setting,* ed. P. G. Pardey. Washington, D.C.: International Food Policy Research Institute.

Runge, C. F., B. Senauer, P. G. Pardey, and M. W. Rosegrant. 2003. *Ending hunger in our lifetime: Food security and globalization.* Baltimore: Johns Hopkins University Press.

Serageldin, I. 2001. Changing agendas for agricultural research. Chapter 2 in *Agricultural science policy: Changing global agendas,* ed. J. M. Alston, P. G. Pardey, and M. J. Taylor. Baltimore: Johns Hopkins University Press.

Transparency International. 2004. Transparency International corruption perceptions index 2004. http://www.transparency.org/cpi/2004/dnld/media_pack_en.pdf. Accessed May 2005.

Wood, S., K. Sebastian, and S. J. Scherr. 2000. *Pilot analysis of global ecosystems: Agroecosystems.* Washington, D.C.: World Resources Institute.

World Bank. 2005. World development indicators. http://www.worldbank.org/data/onlinedatabases/onlinedatabases.html. Accessed May 2005.

Chapter 2

Developing-Country Perspectives on Agricultural R&D: New Pressures for Self-Reliance?

Julian M. Alston and Philip G. Pardey

This chapter provides a conceptual and empirical context for the case studies in Chapters 3 through 12. First, we briefly discuss the nature of market failures in agricultural research—both among firms within a country, and among nations—and the roles for government intervention in general. Next, we consider the distinguishing features of less-developed countries and what they might imply for R&D policy. We also discuss the important role of agricultural R&D and technology spillovers among nations, and the past dependence of the world's poorest countries on their richer neighbors. Next, we document the longer-term global story of institutions and investments in agricultural R&D, emphasizing the great importance of past achievements in agriculture and recent changes that leave grounds for concern about the prospects for the next 20 years and beyond. In the light of these facts, we contemplate the prospects for the future and the implied need to reinvent international collective action in agricultural R&D and reinvest in the associated global public goods institutions.

The presentation of facts and ideas here is brief, in recognition of both space limitations and the availability of the more complete treatments upon which much of this discussion draws. The in-principle arguments about the economics of agricultural R&D policy are based on Chapter 2 in *Paying for Agricultural Productivity*, by Alston and Pardey (1999); our discussion of trends in research funding borrows heavily from Pardey et al. (2006) and Chapter 3 in *Paying for Agricultural Produc-*

tivity, by Pardey, Roseboom, and Craig (1999). We refer readers interested in a more complete treatment to these source documents; however, our contribution involves more than simply taking that material and summarizing it. In considering the specific perspective of less-developed countries, we reinterpret and tailor the ideas and arguments, and bring to bear different facts.

Policy Principles

Alston and Pardey (1999) laid out the case for government intervention in agricultural R&D and relevant principles for the determination of the appropriate form and extent of intervention. These arguments are useful for contemplating past and prospective policy changes. The key idea is that incomplete or ineffective property rights over inventions can lead to market failure in agricultural R&D, which means that inventors are unable to fully appropriate the returns to their research investments. Market failures in research can happen at the level of firms within a state or country, states within a country, or among countries—in any context where the distribution of benefits from adopting the results does not closely match the distribution of the costs incurred in doing the research.

Market failure leads to private-sector underinvestment in agricultural R&D, a phenomenon that can account for the consensus in the empirical literature dealing with different commodities and different countries, that agricultural R&D has been, on average, a highly profitable investment from society's point of view (Alston et al. 2000). In turn, this outcome suggests that research may have been underfunded, and that current government intervention may be inadequate.[1]

This is not to say that the amount of government spending necessarily should increase. Changes in government intervention can take many forms. Some commentators propose increasing R&D funding from general government revenues, but this is only one possible alternative. Governments can also change the incentives for others to increase their investments in private or public R&D (as well as influence what research is done, by whom, and how effectively). A premise that government intervention is inadequate implies simply that the nature of the intervention ought to change so as to stimulate either more private investment or more public investment. Policy options available to the government for stimulating private funding or performance of agricultural R&D include

- improving intellectual property protection;

- changing institutional arrangements to facilitate collective action by producers, for instance, by establishing levy arrangements; and

• encouraging individual or collective action through the provision of subsidies (or tax concessions) or grants in conjunction with levies.

Intellectual property rights are applicable or enforceable only for certain types of inventions, and they have the disadvantage that privately optimal prices may exceed socially optimal prices.[2] Commodity-specific levy arrangements are most applicable for commodity-specific R&D of a relatively applied nature (as implemented in Australia, Colombia, and Uruguay, for instance), although more general agricultural R&D could be funded by a more general agricultural levy (as in the Netherlands). In cases where the fruits of invention can be only partially appropriated, a case can be made for partial support from general government revenues through subsidies or matching grants in conjunction with commodity levies, as used in the Australian R&D corporations (see, for example, Alston, Freebairn, and James 2004). To some extent, questions about how to finance agricultural R&D can be separated from who conducts the research, what research is undertaken, and how the R&D process is managed. It is useful to consider these elements as separate issues, but inevitably they become intertwined.

In addition to efficiency gains from increasing the total R&D investment, the government can also intervene with a view to improving the efficiency with which resources are used within the R&D system. Changes over time in economic circumstances imply changes in R&D institutions. Some research activities that were once clearly perceived as the province of the government have become part of the private domain. Examples include much applied work into the development and evaluation of new agricultural chemicals and new plant varieties.

Both in one country over time, and among different countries at the same time, circumstances differ in ways that call for different policies and institutional arrangements. Policies must be suited to the setting. Some restructuring or consolidation of agricultural R&D institutions, in some instances on a geographic basis, is warranted by the changing nature of the research being undertaken; its focus relative to agriculture, agribusiness, and the environment; and the spatial and economic applicability of the results, as well as the changing nature of economies of size, scale, and scope in research. In addition to changes in the organization of research institutions, there is also scope for more economic rationalism in the processes for managing research and allocating research resources and in the structure of incentives for scientists.

Distinctive Features of Less-Developed Countries

These general notions about market failure and options for government action apply generally, but with different specific implications as cases change. Less-developed countries tend to differ from more-developed countries in some systematic ways. In particular, for a number of reasons, the phenomenon of private-sector neglect and national underinvestment in agricultural R&D is likely to be more pronounced in less-developed countries than in developed ones. Why is this so, and what does it imply?

First, less-developed countries are commonly characterized as having a comparatively high incidence of incomplete markets, resulting from high transaction costs and inadequate property rights, which in turn may be attributable to inadequate infrastructure and defective institutions, among other things. To the extent that they exist, information problems, high transport and communications costs, poorly functioning credit markets, and the like, combined with the limited education of some farmers, are likely to make it harder to capitalize on new inventions. In rich countries, we might discount the issues of risk and capital costs as disincentives to investment in invention, but in less-developed countries these factors might take on a greater importance, especially if capital markets do not function well—for whatever reason.

Second, the types of technology often suited to less-developed country agriculture have hitherto been of the sort for which appropriability problems are more pronounced—types that have been comparatively neglected by the private sector even in the richest countries. In particular, until recently, private research has tended to emphasize mechanical and chemical technologies, which are comparatively well protected by patents, trade secrecy, and other intellectual property rights; and the private sector has generally neglected varietal technologies except where the returns are appropriable, as for hybrid seed (see Olmstead and Rhode 2002). In less-developed countries, the emphasis in innovation has often been on self-pollinating crop varieties and disembodied farm management practices, which are the least appropriable of all. The recent innovations in rich-country institutions mean that private firms are now finding it more profitable to invest in plant varieties; the same may be true in some less-developed countries, but not all countries have made comparable institutional changes.[3]

Third, in many less-developed countries, prices have been distorted by policies in ways that diminish incentives and opportunities for farmers to adopt new technologies (see Schultz 1978; Alston and Pardey 1993; and Sunding and Zilberman 2001).[4] Only when we achieve a reasonable rate of inventor appropriability of the returns to the technologies that are applicable in less-developed countries, combined with an economic infrastructure that facilitates adoption of those technologies, can we expect a significant private-sector role to emerge.

Accepting that markets may fail, for whatever reason, we have to consider the possibility that governments in less-developed countries also might fail—in this case, fail to correct the underinvestment in agricultural research—for both economic and political reasons. For instance, and as a fourth factor accounting for their low rates of investment in agricultural R&D, government revenues may be comparatively expensive, or have a comparatively high opportunity cost in less-developed countries. This can be so because it is comparatively expensive to raise government revenues through general taxation measures.[5] And many less-developed countries are characterized by underinvestment in a host of other public goods, such as transportation and communications infrastructure, schools, and hospitals, as well as agricultural science (Runge et al. 2003), which might also have high social rates of return.

Fifth, there are political factors to consider. In rich countries, agriculture is a small share of the economy, and any individual citizen bears a negligible burden from financing a comparatively high rate of public investment in agricultural R&D (for instance, in the United States, the public expenditure of US$3.8 billion on agricultural R&D in 2000 amounted to less than US$14 per person per year). The factors that account for high rates of general support for agriculture in the industrialized countries can also help account for the comparatively high intensity of public agricultural research. In many less-developed countries, where agriculture represents a much greater share of the total economic activity, and where per capita incomes are much lower, a meaningful investment in public agricultural research may have a much more appreciable impact on individual citizens. This burden is felt immediately, whereas the payoff it promises may take a long time to come and will be much less perceptible when it does.

Finally, even many of the rich countries of the world have not had very substantial private or public agricultural science industries. Why should we expect the poorest countries of the world to act like the richest of the rich in this regard?[6] The lion's share of the public (as well as private) investment in agricultural science has been undertaken by a small number of countries; and these have been the countries that have also undertaken the greatest share of scientific research, more generally. Typically, these have been the large economic powerhouses, especially the United States. Differences in per capita income, the total size of the economy, and comparative advantages in science (reflecting not just wealth but also the nature of the society) may all have influenced the international distribution of the burden of agricultural R&D investments.

It might not make economic sense for small, poor, agrarian nations to spend their comparatively scarce intellectual and other capital resources in agricultural science on their own behalf in a world in which other countries can do it so much more effectively.[7] And in the past it has been an effective strategy for many nations to free-ride on the efforts of a few others in agricultural R&D. Both inadvertent technology spillovers and international initiatives such as the CGIAR and bilateral agricultural R&D development aid might have crowded out some national investments in agricultural R&D in less-developed countries.[8]

An important consideration is economies of size, scale, and scope in research, which influence the optimal size and portfolio of a given research institution. In some cases the "optimal" institution may efficiently provide research for a state or region within a nation, but for some kinds of research the efficient scale of institutions may be too great for an individual nation (see, for example, Byerlee and Traxler 2001). Many nations may be too small to achieve an efficient scale in any of the relevant elements of their agricultural R&D interests, except perhaps in certain types of adaptive research. A particular problem for efficiency in agricultural science, especially for many smaller countries, is that there are few effective institutions for financing and organizing research on a multinational basis when the research is applicable across multiple countries, and individual countries are too small to achieve efficient scale (see Chapter 12 in this volume).

Technology Spillovers: Past, Present, and Future

The history of agricultural development shows that agricultural technology need not be home-grown; over the years it has been bought, borrowed, and stolen. For instance, in the late 18th century, Thomas Jefferson, risking the death penalty, smuggled rice seeds out of Italy in the lining of his coat to encourage cultivation of the crop in South Carolina. Agricultural innovations move across borders, both by design and by accident. These technology spillovers imply both international market failures and a case for multinational government action to correct them, paralleling the intranational arguments presented above.

R&D spillovers among geopolitical entities arise when research conducted by one state (or nation) confers benefits on other states (or nations) that are able to adopt the results. Such spillovers have two kinds of implications for research policy. First, they add complications to already awkward policy questions that arise when research is being conducted and funded by state and national governments—such as how much and what mix of research should be undertaken, who should pay for it, who should do it, and what institutional arrangements should be put in place. Second, and perhaps more important, they introduce an additional dimension to incentive problems. The fundamental economic basis for the government support of agricultural research is incomplete appropriability of research benefits by inventors. Research and technology spillovers among research providers within a state can be addressed (at least in principle) by state-government policy, but state-government policy cannot effectively address spillovers across state boundaries.

Similarly, federal-government policy might address spillovers among research providers in different states within a nation, but national-government policy cannot effectively address spillovers among nations.

Alston (2002) reviewed the evidence of agricultural R&D spillovers, with emphasis on the international dimension. The main findings can be stated simply. First, intranational and international spillovers of public agricultural R&D results are very important. In the small proportion of studies that have taken them into account, spillovers were responsible for a sizable share—in many cases, more than half—of total measured agricultural productivity growth and the corresponding research benefits. Second, spillovers can have profound implications for the distribution of research benefits between consumers and producers and thus among countries, depending on their trade status and capacity to adopt the technology. Third, it is not easy to measure these impacts, and the results can be sensitive to the specifics of the approach taken, but studies that ignore interstate and international spillovers are likely to obtain seriously distorted estimates of the returns to agricultural research. Finally, because spillovers are so important, research resources have been misallocated both within and among nations. In particular, international spillovers contribute to a global underinvestment in agricultural R&D that existing public policies have only partly succeeded in correcting.[9] The stakes are large because the benefits from agricultural technology spillovers are worth many times more than the investments that give rise to them.

This volume examines spillovers from a less-developed-country perspective. It is important to note the important role of spillins to the world's poorest countries of technologies from industrialized countries (especially the United States, but also the United Kingdom, France, and others), both individually and through their collective action via the CGIAR. Until recently, much of the successful innovative effort in most of the world's poorer countries applied at the very last stage of the process—selecting and adapting crop varieties and livestock breeds for local conditions using materials developed elsewhere. Only a few larger countries, such as Brazil, China, and India, were able to achieve much by themselves at the more upstream stages of the research and innovation process, even for improved crop technologies for which conventional breeding strategies are widely applied. Until recently that strategy was reasonable, given an abundant and freely accessible supply of suitable materials, at least for the main temperate-zone food crops. Changes in the emphasis of rich-country research, combined with new intellectual property rules and practices and an increased use of modern biotechnology methods, have already begun to spell a drying up of the public pool of new varieties. In addition, and as set out in detail in Chapter 12, the other main source of varietal materials— the CGIAR—has changed its emphasis and is scaling back its role in providing finished material or advanced breeding lines.[10] The reduction in spillovers from these traditional sources means that less-developed countries will have to find new ways of meeting their demands for new varieties.

Research Spending Patterns

The public and private roles in agricultural science have changed, reflecting changing economic conditions in the broader economy as well as in agriculture. Changes have also occurred in institutional arrangements, such as intellectual property rights, and in public attitudes and perceptions. Although many elements of the changes have been common to various countries, reflecting common influences at work, there have been some important divergences among countries as well—especially between the richest and the poorest countries. Pardey et al. (2006) document these changes.

General Trends

Over the last two decades of the 20th century, worldwide public investments in agricultural research increased by 51 percent in inflation-adjusted terms, from an estimated $15.2 billion (in 2000 international dollars) in 1981 to around $23 billion in 2000 (Table 2.1).[11] During the 1990s, for the first time, developing countries as a group undertook more of the world's public agricultural research than the developed countries, but with the Asian and Pacific region and China accounting for more of the developing-country total, and Sub-Saharan Africa losing market share.

What the regional totals fail to reveal is that public spending was concentrated in only a handful of countries. The United States, Japan, France, and Germany accounted for two-thirds of the $10.2 billion of public research done by rich countries in 2000, about the same as two decades before. Similarly, four of the developing countries among those included in this book—China, India, Brazil, and South Africa—spent almost 50 percent of the developing world's public agricultural research money in 2000, up from 37 percent in 1981.

Despite this pattern of strong longer-term growth in spending since the 1970s, for many parts of the world the rapid and quite pervasive growth in spending during the 1970s and early 1980s gave way to a dramatic slowdown during the 1990s. In the rich countries, public investment actually shrank by 0.58 percent annually between 1991 and 2000, compared with an increase of 2.3 percent per year during the 1980s. Spending in Africa grew by only 0.82 percent per year in the 1990s—a much slower rate than during the 1980s (1.25 percent per year). This slowing reflects a longer-run trend: rapid growth in spending in the 1960s gradu-

Table 2.1   Global public agricultural-research spending, 1981–2000

Expenditures (million 2000 international dollars)	1981	1991	2000
Developing countries	6,904	9,459	12,819
Sub-Saharan Africa	1,196	1,365	1,461
China	1,049	1,733	3,150
Asia and Pacific	3,047	4,847	7,523
Latin America and the Caribbean	1,897	2,107	2,454
Middle East and North Africa	764	1,139	1,382
Developed countries	8,293	10,534	10,191
Total	15,197	19,992	23,010
Annual growth rates (percent per year)	**1981–91**	**1991–2000**	**1981–2000**
Developing countries	3.04	2.90	3.14
Sub-Saharan Africa	1.25	0.82	0.99
China	4.76	5.04	4.86
Asia and Pacific	4.33	3.92	4.19
Latin America and the Caribbean	1.13	2.06	2.01
Middle East and North Africa	4.12	1.87	3.35
Developed countries	2.27	−0.58	1.10
Total	2.63	1.20	2.11

Source: Agricultural Science and Technology Indicators (ASTI) data underlying Pardey et al. 2006.

Note: Data are provisional estimates and exclude Eastern Europe and countries of the former Soviet Union.

ally gave way in the 1980s and beyond to debt crises, curbs on government spending, and waning donor support for agriculture in general, and agricultural R&D in particular, during the 1990s. In fact, if large countries like Nigeria and South Africa are excluded, spending for Africa overall actually declined by 2.5 percent per year during the 1990s (Beintema and Stads 2004). Spending in Asia grew by an average of 3.9 percent per year during the 1990s, compared with 4.3 percent annually during the previous decade. Growth slowed in the Middle East and North Africa as well.

China and India are exceptions. Growth in spending during the 1990s averaged 5.04 percent per year in China and 6.37 percent per year in India. Things look a little better in Latin America, too, with spending growing 2.06 percent per year from 1991 to 2000, compared with about half that rate during the previous decade. But the recovery in Latin America seems fragile and is not distributed evenly throughout the region. Public research in countries like Brazil (with public spending approaching a billion dollars a year, a considerably larger commitment than in any of the developed countries besides the United States and Japan) and Colombia did better in the early 1990s but suffered cutbacks in the later part of the decade. Many of the poorer (and smaller) countries have failed to experience any sustained growth in funding for the past several decades.

Research Intensities

Turning now from absolute to relative measures of R&D investments, in 2000, developed countries as a group spent $2.36 on public agricultural R&D for every $100 of agricultural output, a sizable increase over the $1.41 they spent per $100 of output two decades earlier (Table 2.2). Since 1981, research intensities have risen for the developing countries as a group, but unevenly. Despite having gained a greater absolute share of the developing world's total agricultural research spending, China's agricultural research intensity in 2000 was no greater than in 1981. In other words, China's research spending grew, but its agricultural sector grew just as quickly. Although public research throughout the rest of Asia and Latin America appears to have grown in intensity during the last decade of our data, Africa lost considerable ground, with research intensities now lower than in the 1970s.

Other research-intensity ratios are also revealing. Rich countries spent nearly $700 per agricultural worker, more than double the corresponding 1981 ratio. Poor countries spent just $10.21 per agricultural worker in 2000, substantially less than double the 1981 figure. These differences are perhaps not surprising. A much smaller share of the rich-country workforce is employed in agriculture, and the absolute number of agricultural workers declined more rapidly in rich countries than it did in the poor ones. Agricultural research spending per capita rose, too, by an average of only 9 percent for developed countries (from $10.91 per capita in 1981 to $11.92 in 2000) and 29 percent in developing countries (from $2.12 per capita in 1981 to $2.73 in 2000). Notably, per capita research spending (in terms of both total population and agricultural workers) declined in Africa, the only region of the world where this occurred.[12]

Private and Public Research Roles

By the mid-1990s, roughly one-third of the $36.9 billion total investment in agricultural research worldwide was by private firms, including those involved in providing farm inputs and processing farm products (Table 2.3). But little of this private research took place in developing countries. The overwhelming majority ($12.6 billion, or 91 percent of the global total) was conducted in developed countries. In the less-developed countries, where public funds are still the major source of support, the private share of research was just 8.3 percent. (Public funds remain a significant source of support in rich countries, too, accounting for about 45 percent of their total funding in 2000).

Although more than one-half of the world's public R&D dollars are spent in developing countries, only one-third of the public plus private research spending occurs there. In addition, the research-intensity gap between rich and poor countries is wide and growing. As we saw, in 2000, public research intensity was four

Table 2.2 Global public agricultural research-intensity ratios, 1981–2000

Region/country	Expenditures as a percentage of AgGDP			Expenditures per capita (2000 international dollars)			Expenditures per economically active member of agricultural population (2000 international dollars)		
	1981	1991	2000	1981	1991	2000	1981	1991	2000
Developing countries	0.52	0.50	0.53	2.1	2.3	2.7	7.0	8.3	10.2
Sub-Saharan Africa	0.84	0.79	0.72	3.1	2.7	2.3	11.2	10.5	8.2
China	0.41	0.35	0.40	1.0	1.5	2.5	2.5	3.5	6.2
Asia and Pacific	0.36	0.38	0.41	1.3	1.7	2.4	3.8	5.2	7.6
Latin America and Caribbean	0.88	0.96	1.16	5.5	6.6	5.9	45.1	50.5	60.7
Middle East and North Africa	0.61	0.54	0.66	3.2	3.6	3.7	19.2	27.3	30.2
Developed countries	1.41	2.38	2.36	10.9	13.0	11.9	316.5	528.3	691.6
Total	0.79	0.86	0.80	3.8	4.2	4.1	15.1	17.2	18.1

Source: Agricultural Science and Technology Indicators (ASTI) data underlying Pardey et al. 2006.

Note: Data are provisional estimates and exclude Eastern Europe and countries of the former Soviet Union.

Table 2.3   Private and public agricultural R&D investments, circa 2000

Region	Expenditures (million 2000 international dollars)			Shares (percent)		
	Public	Private	Total	Public	Private	Total
Developing countries	12,909	1,108	14,089	91.6	8.4	100
Developed countries	10,191	12,577	22,767	44.8	55.2	100
Total	23,100	13,756	36,856	62.7	37.3	100

Source: Agricultural Science and Technology Indicators (ASTI) data underlying Pardey et al. 2006.
Note: Data are provisional estimates. Combining estimates from various sources resulted in unavoidable discrepancies in the categorization of "private" and "public" research. For example, in Asia data for private spending included nonprofit producer organizations, whereas in Latin America and elsewhere we included research done by nonprofit agencies under public research when possible.

times higher in rich countries than in poor ones; if total private and public spending is considered, the gap grows to more than eightfold, with rich countries spending about $5.27 on agricultural R&D per $100 of agricultural GDP.

Research Knowledge

The eightfold difference in total research intensities is an indication of the present gap in generating new technologies between rich and poor countries. However, a more meaningful measure of a country's technological capacity and a better account of cross-country differences in agricultural productivity is the size of the accumulated stock of knowledge—not merely the amount of investment in current research and innovative activity—it provides. Science is a cumulative endeavor. Innovations beget new ideas and further rounds of innovation, which ultimately add to the cumulative stock of knowledge.

The current stock of knowledge and the contribution of past research spending to that stock is sensitive to the types of science being done, the institutional structures surrounding the science, and the economic context. Some science spending makes persistent and even perpetual contributions to the changing stock of locally produced knowledge; the same spending in societies ravaged by wars, institutional instability, and outright collapse may have a much more ephemeral effect.

The sequential and cumulative nature of scientific progress and knowledge is starkly illustrated by crop improvement. It typically takes seven to ten years of breeding to develop a uniform, stable, and superior crop variety; but today's breeders build on an accumulation of knowledge. Because breeding lines from earlier research are used to develop new varieties, research of the distant past is still feeding today's research.

Providing adequate funding for research is thus only part of the story. Putting in place the policies and practices to accumulate innovations and increase the stock of knowledge is equally important and almost universally unappreciated. Discoveries and data that are improperly documented or inaccessible (and effectively exist only in the mind of the researcher) are lost from the historical record when researchers retire from science. These "hidden" losses seem particularly prevalent in cash-strapped research agencies in the developing world, where inadequate and often irregular amounts of funding limit the functioning of libraries, data banks, and genebanks, and hasten staff turnover.

Political instability can lead to catastrophic losses, too. Civil strife and wars cause an exodus of scientific staff, or at least a flight from practicing science. Many of Uganda's scientific facilities, for example, were in shreds when its civil war ended in the early 1980s. It is hard to imagine that today's Congo once had perhaps the most sophisticated scientific infrastructure in colonial Africa, comparable to the facilities and quality of staff found in most developed countries at the time.

Figure 2.1 represents financial measures of the stock of scientific knowledge based on research performed in the United States (assuming a baseline rate of depreciation of the knowledge stock of 3 percent per annum) and Africa (for which we show both a 3 percent baseline depreciation rate and a rate of 6 percent per year,

Figure 2.1   African and American stocks of research knowledge, 1995

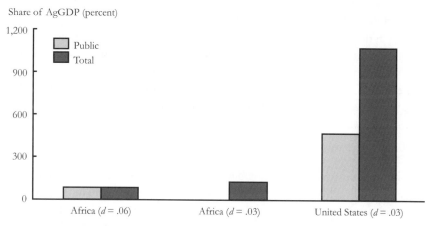

Source: Pardey and Beintema 2001.

Note: *d* indicates depreciation rate. The lag time relating innovations, I_t, to present and past research expenditures, R_{t-s}, was taken to be ten years for both regions, so the stock of knowledge for year *t*, K_t, was formed as $K_t = (1-d) K_{t-1} + I_t$, where *d* is the rate of knowledge depreciation and $I_t = \sum_{j=0}^{10} R_{t-j}$.

which is perhaps more realistic given the instability and lack of infrastructure for R&D throughout much of the region). Knowledge stocks in 1995—representing a discounted accumulation of research spending from 1850 for the United States and 1900 for Africa—were expressed as percentages of 1995 agricultural GDP to normalize for differences in the sizes of the respective agricultural sectors. The accumulated stock of knowledge in the United States was about 11 times the amount of agricultural output produced in 1995. In other words, for every $100 of agricultural output, there existed a $1,100 stock of knowledge to draw upon. In Africa, the stock of knowledge in 1995 was actually less than the value of African agricultural output that year. The ratio of the U.S. knowledge stock relative to U.S. agricultural output in 1995 was nearly 12 times higher than the corresponding amount for Africa. If a depreciation rate of 6 percent instead of 3 percent is used, the gap in American and African ratios is more than 14-fold.

Policy Implications

Agricultural R&D for less-developed countries is at a crossroads. The close of the 20th century witnessed changing policy contexts, fundamental shifts in the scientific basis for agricultural R&D, and shifting funding patterns for agricultural research in rich countries. These changes imply a need to rethink national policies in less-developed countries and reconsider multinational approaches in order to determine what types of activities to conduct through the CGIAR and similar institutions and how to organize and finance them.

Even though there is no evidence to suggest that the world can afford to reduce its rate of investment in agricultural research, and every indication that we should invest more, we cannot presume that the rich countries of the world will play the same roles as in the past. In particular, countries that in the past relied on technological spillovers from the North may no longer have that luxury available to them in the same ways or to the same extent. This change can be seen as involving three elements:

- The types of technologies being developed in the rich countries may no longer be as readily applicable to less-developed countries as they were in the past: the agenda in richer countries is shifting away from areas like yield improvement in major crops to other crop characteristics and even to nonagricultural production concerns like health and nutrition and the environment.

- Applicable technologies developed in richer countries may not be as readily accessible because of intellectual-property protection of privately owned technologies: many biotech companies have little or no interest in developing technologies for less-developed country applications; and even where they have such technologies available, they are often not interested in pursuing potential markets in less developed countries, for a host of reasons.

- Those technologies that are applicable and available are likely to require more substantial local development and adaptation, which call for more sophisticated and more extensive forms of scientific research and development than in the past: for instance, more advanced skills in modern biotechnology or conventional breeding may be required to take advantage of enabling technologies or simply to make use of less-finished lines that must be tailored to local production environments.

In short, different approaches may have to be devised to make it possible for less-developed countries to achieve equivalent access and tap into technological potentials generated by rich countries, and, in many instances, less-developed countries may have to extend their own R&D efforts upstream to more fundamental areas of the science.

Finally, it must be remembered that agricultural R&D is a slow business. As Pardey and Beintema note (2001, p. 2): "It is the accumulation of results over the long haul that accounts for the differences in agricultural productivity observed around the world." In contemplating their evidence on stocks of knowledge, it can be seen that the imbalance between the North and the South is very much greater than the annual flows alone reveal. The tail end of the 20th century saw some evidence of a partial catching up, but the current prospects could spell a dangerous shift toward falling farther behind—and the long-term, dire consequences may not become apparent for some time to come.

Notes

1. One explanation for this government failure is that, just as in the case of private market failure, when the distributions of benefits and costs of government-funded research are not closely aligned, incentives are distorted. If taxpayers in a country bear all of the cost of research that benefits a select group of producers, they have attenuated incentives to fund the amount of research that will maximize net national benefits, particularly if some of the producers who benefit are foreigners.

2. Many research outputs have public-good characteristics to some extent, implying socially optimal prices that may not allow for the recovery of costs. In the case of a "pure public good," one that is nonrival in consumption and non-price-excludable, the socially optimal price is zero (to achieve marginal social benefits equal to marginal social cost and thereby maximize net national benefits). Furthermore, patents and the like confer monopoly privileges, which result in prices above marginal cost, even for rival goods. See Lindner (1993, 2003).

3. Innovations in intellectual property rights regimes and biosafety protocols are seen as critical determinants of appropriability of returns to new crop and livestock technologies, but not all nations have gone as far as the United States in these respects. See Boettiger et al. 2004 for more discussions on these points.

4. The fact that the more-developed countries have distorted prices in the opposite direction is a double-edged sword for the less-developed countries. On the one hand, richer countries are encouraged to produce and innovate more rapidly, further depressing prices faced by less-developed-country producers. On the other hand, as recipients of technology spillovers, the world's poorer producers have also benefited from an enhanced rate of technological development in the North.

5. A dollar of government spending costs society more than a dollar. For every dollar of government revenue, at least a dollar has been taken from someone as taxes (maybe someone living in a different place and time from those where research benefits will be realized). The marginal and average excess burden of taxation rises with increases in the price responsiveness of supply and demand (that is, elasticities) and the size of the tax rate; the total excess burden rises with the square of the tax rate. It follows that a small tax on an agricultural commodity must have a very small total, average, and marginal excess burden (regardless of the elasticities of supply and demand for such a small tax rate) compared with general taxation measures. To this amount, we can add the costs of enforcement, collection, and disbursement of the funds, the costs of compliance, and the social costs associated with market responses to the (dis)incentive effects of taxation (see, for example, Fox 1985; Fullerton 1991; and Alston and Pardey 1996, Chapter 7).

6. As noted by Pardey et al. (2006), investment in the sciences is generally much more concentrated in rich countries (which accounted for about 82 percent of global investment in all the sciences in the mid-1990s, with about 35 percent of that total occurring in the United States alone) than is agricultural R&D (in which rich countries conduct 63 percent of all agricultural R&D and 44 percent of the world's publicly funded agricultural research). Moreover, the geographical concentration of particular classes of agricultural research—for instance, research into agricultural chemicals or machinery—is even greater than that of agricultural R&D in general.

7. As demonstrated by Maredia and Byerlee (2000), it has made economic sense for many less-developed countries to emphasize adapting research results from other countries rather than to participate directly in upstream research activities. Their results indicated that only 41 out of the total of 69 wheat-improvement programs operating in their sample of 39 developing countries could economically justify maintaining fully fledged wheat-breeding programs. For the remaining 28 programs, it would have made sense to restrict the scope of research to screening and selection roles—presuming that varieties from which to select and screen would continue to be available from other national and international sources.

8. Beintema and Stads (2004) found that donor contributions accounted for 35 percent of spending on agricultural R&D for the principle research agencies in a sample of 23 African countries in 2000.

9. There have also been private actions to address these international market-failure problems, including the efforts of philanthropic organizations like the Ford, Rockefeller, and, more recently, McKnight foundations to fund international collaborative research; multinational companies that operate in multiple markets; and private nonprofit entities like CAMBIA in Canberra, Australia, and the Donald Danforth Plant Science Center in St. Louis, Missouri, which conduct research in rich countries that is targeted to the agricultural concerns of poor countries.

10. Norman Borlaug, a winner of the Nobel Peace Prize and previously head of the wheat improvement program at the International Center for Maize and Wheat Improvement (CIMMYT),

pioneered a shuttle-breeding technique wherein two crops of wheat were planted each year (one in northern Mexico, the other in the southern part of the country) to accelerate the turnaround of successive crop generations when breeding improved wheat varieties. A dramatic illustration of the CGIAR's present financial plight is that, for the first time in almost three decades, CIMMYT could afford to plant only one breeding cycle in 2003.

11. All these data involve conversions from local currency units to U.S. dollar equivalents, using purchasing power parities rather than market exchange rates to account for cross-country price differentials. See Pardey, Roseboom, and Craig 1992 for details.

12. Roe and Pardey (1991) provide a political-economy perspective on these various research-intensity ratios.

References

Alston, J. M. 2002. Spillovers. *Australian Journal of Agricultural and Resource Economics* 48 (3): 315–346.

Alston, J. M., and P. G. Pardey. 1993. Market distortions and technological progress in agriculture. *Technological Forecasting and Social Change* 43 (3/4): 301–319.

———. 1996. *Making science pay: The economics of agricultural R&D policy.* Washington, D.C.: American Enterprise Institute.

———. 1999. Principles for agricultural R&D policy. Chapter 2 in *Paying for agricultural productivity,* ed. J. M. Alston, P. G. Pardey, and V. H. Smith. Baltimore: Johns Hopkins University Press.

Alston, J. M., J. W. Freebairn, and J. S. James. 2004. Levy-funded research choices by producers and society. *Australian Journal of Agricultural and Resource Economics* 48 (1): 33–64.

Alston, J. M., C. Chan-Kang, M. C. Marra, P. G. Pardey, and T. J. Wyatt. 2000. *A meta-analysis of the rates of return to agricultural R&D: Ex pede Herculem.* IFPRI Research Report No. 113. Washington, D.C.: International Food Policy Research Institute.

Beintema, N. M., and G.-J. Stads. 2004. *Investing in Sub-Saharan African research: Recent trends.* 2020 Africa Conference Brief 8. Washington, D.C.: International Food Policy Research Institute.

Boettiger, S., G. Graff, P. G. Pardey, E. van Dusen, and B. D. Wright. 2004. Intellectual property rights for plant biotechnology: International aspects. In *Handbook of plant biotechnology,* ed. P. Christou and H. Klee. Chichester, UK: John Wiley and Sons.

Byerlee, D., and G. Traxler. 2001. The role of technology spillovers and economies of size in the efficient design of agricultural research systems. Chapter 9 in *Agricultural science policy: Changing global agendas,* ed. J. M. Alston, P. G. Pardey, and M. J. Taylor. Baltimore: Johns Hopkins University Press.

Fox, G. C. 1985. Is the United States really underinvesting in agricultural research? *American Journal of Agricultural Economics* 67 (November): 806–812.

Fullerton, D. 1991. Reconciling recent estimates of the marginal welfare cost of taxation. *American Economic Review* 81: 302–308.

Lindner, R. K. 1993. Privatising the production of knowledge: Promise and pitfalls of agricultural research and extension. *Australian Journal of Agricultural Economics* 37 (3): 205–225.

———. 2003. Access issues for plant breeders in an increasingly privatized world. Paper presented at the Australian Agricultural and Resource Economics Society annual conference, Fremantle, Western Australia, February.

Maredia, M. K., and D. Byerlee. 2000. Efficiency of research investments in the presence of international spillovers: Wheat research in developing countries. *Agricultural Economics* 22 (1): 1–16.

Olmstead, A. L., and P. W. Rhode. 2002. The red queen and the hard reds: Productivity growth in American wheat, 1800–1940. *Journal of Economic History* 62 (4): 929–966.

Pardey, P. G., and N. M. Beintema. 2001. *Slow magic: Agricultural R&D a century after Mendel.* IFPRI Food Policy Report. Washington, D.C.: International Food Policy Research Institute.

Pardey, P. G., J. Roseboom, and B. J. Craig. 1992. A yardstick for international comparisons: An application to national agricultural research expenditures. *Economic Development and Cultural Change* 40 (2): 333–349.

———. 1999. Agricultural R&D investments and impacts. Chapter 3 in *Paying for agricultural productivity,* ed. J. M. Alston, P. G. Pardey, and V. H. Smith. Baltimore: Johns Hopkins University Press.

Pardey, P. G., N. M. Beintema, S. Dehmer, and S. Wood. 2006. *Agricultural research: A growing global divide?* IFPRI Food Policy Report. Washington, D.C.: International Food Policy Research Institute (draft version).

Roe, T. L., and P. G. Pardey. 1991 Economic policy and investment in rural public goods: A political economy perspective. Chapter 1 in *Agricultural research policy: International quantitative perspectives,* ed. P. G. Pardey, J. Roseboom, and J. R. Anderson. Cambridge, U.K.: Cambridge University Press.

Runge, C. F., B. Senauer, P. G. Pardey, and M. W. Rosegrant. 2003. *Ending hunger in our lifetime: Food security and globalization.* Baltimore: Johns Hopkins University Press.

Schultz, T. W. 1978. On economics and politics of agriculture. In *Distortions in agricultural incentives,* ed. T. W. Schultz. Bloomington: Indiana University Press.

Sunding, D., and D. Zilberman. 2001. The agricultural innovation process: Research and technology adoption in a changing agricultural sector. Chapter 4 in *Handbook of agricultural economics,* Vol. 1a, ed. B. L. Gardner and G. C. Rausser. Amsterdam: Elsevier.

Chapter 3

China: An Unfinished Reform Agenda

Shenggen Fan, Keming Qian, and Xiaobo Zhang

Introduction

Agricultural production in China has grown rapidly—relative to other countries—over the past four decades. Much of this growth can be attributed to investments in agricultural research by national and regional governments combined with policy reform and increased use of inputs.[1] After 50 years of development, the Chinese agricultural research system is now arguably the largest in the world, employing over 50,000 senior scientists and spending more than US$3.8 billion in 2002 (measured in 1995 international dollars).[2] However, the system is currently facing a dilemma. Chinese agricultural production is becoming increasingly dependent on new technologies generated by research, especially as agricultural land and other natural resources become more limiting factors. The quantity of agricultural land—and high-quality land in particular—will only decline further in the future with rapid industrialization and urbanization. At the same time, a national policy introduced in the mid-1980s has encouraged research institutes to become finan-cially self-supporting. As a result, on the positive side, research has become more integrated with economic development because research institutes have sought financial support by selling their services. On the negative side, however, areas of research not easily commercialized, including significant aspects of agricultural research, face financial problems as governments at various levels reduce funding for R&D.

The objectives of this chapter are to review the evolution of the organizational structure, institutional management, and financing of the Chinese agricultural research system and to explore reform options to promote future agricultural growth and food security and reduce poverty. We first review the trend in agricultural production and productivity growth in Chinese agriculture, using newly available data and new aggregation methods. We then discuss the institutional and policy environment of the Chinese agricultural R&D system. Next, we analyze major issues in the provision and financing of agricultural R&D in China. This analysis is followed by two case studies: one of a national research institute, and the other of a provincial institute. Finally, we offer some policy choices regarding reform of the existing system in light of emerging challenges in the 21st century.

Production and Productivity in Chinese Agriculture

Over the past several decades, and particularly since 1978, the Chinese economy has performed spectacularly well. Per capita gross domestic product (GDP) grew at 6.2 percent per year from 1952 to 2002. Prior to 1978, the growth rate was only 3.4 percent, but between 1978 and 2002 it jumped to 8.2 percent per year (*China Statistical Yearbook,* various years). The economy has also undergone dramatic and continuing structural change.

In 1952, agriculture accounted for more than half the national GDP, while urban industry and services accounted for 21 and 29 percent, respectively (Table 3.1). The Chinese economy was largely agrarian. By 2002, however, agriculture had declined to around 15 percent of GDP—a rapid decline of about two-thirds of

Table 3.1   China: Structural change in the economy, 1952–2002

Indicators	1952	1960[a]	1970	1980	1990	2000	2002
Share of GDP (percent)							
Agriculture	50.5	*23.4*	38.0	30.1	27.1	15.9	15.4
Industry	20.9	*44.5*	35.6	48.5	41.6	50.9	51.1
Service	28.6	*32.1*	26.5	21.4	31.3	33.2	33.5
Share of employment (percent)							
Agriculture	83.5	*82.1*	80.8	68.7	60.1	50.0	50.0
Industry	7.4	*7.9*	10.2	18.2	21.4	22.5	21.4
Service	9.1	*9.9*	9.0	13.1	18.5	27.5	28.6
Per capita GDP (1995 U.S. dollars)							
Official 1995 exchange rate	46.31	58.3	94.6	144.0	341.7	804.5	924.2
Purchasing power parity[b]	203.6	256.4	415.6	632.9	1,501.9	3,536.1	4,062.1
Exports as percentage of GDP	4.0	4.1	2.5	4.7	16.1	23.1	25.7
Imports as percentage of GDP	5.5	2.9	2.5	5.4	13.9	20.8	23.3

Sources: National Statistical Bureau, various years, for all data, except per capita GDP converted with purchasing power parities (PPPs), which was obtained from World Bank 2004.

Note: Percentages do not always sum to 100 given rounding errors.

[a]Italicized data for 1960 are 1962 values.

[b]Purchasing power parity, or PPP, is an index used to reflect the purchasing power of currencies by comparing prices across a broader range of goods and services than conventional exchange rates.

Figure 3.1. China: Yield of major grain crops, 1949–2000

Metric tons per hectare

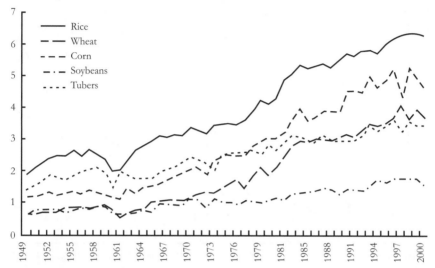

Source: National Statistical Bureau, various years.
Note: Rice is measured as paddy rice.

a percentage point per year. Labor shifts among sectors have been striking. In 1952, more than 80 percent of the national labor force was in agriculture, only 6 percent in urban industry, and 10 percent in the urban service sector. By 2002, less than half the labor force was engaged in agricultural activities; more than 21 percent worked in the industrial sector and 29 percent in the service sector.

Agricultural production has grown at a much faster pace in China than in most other countries for the past 50 years. The yield of rice, the staple of the Chinese diet, has increased from 1.9 tons to 6.3 tons per hectare, a rate of increase of 2.24 percent per year (Figure 3.1). The yield of wheat, another important crop in China, grew even faster, from 0.6 to 3.9 tons per hectare, or 3.4 percent per year. Overall agricultural production grew by 3.3 percent per year from 1952 to 1997 (Figure 3.2). Growth in grain output and production value has been much higher than the population growth over the same period, so that the amount and value of output per capita has increased.[3]

A large proportion of this growth can be attributed to productivity improvement, which in turn comes primarily from new technologies released by the national agricultural research system. Over the period 1952 to 1997, growth in productivity

Figure 3.2   China: Agricultural production and productivity growth, 1952–97

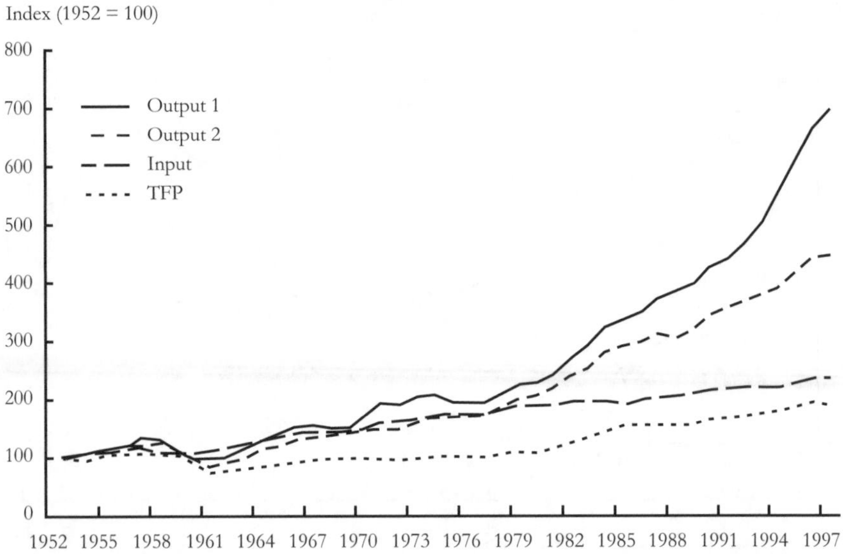

Index (1952 = 100)

Sources: National Statistical Bureau, various years; Fan and Zhang 2002.
Notes: Output 1 is the official production index reported by the National Statistical Bureau in various issues of China's statistical yearbooks. Fan and Zhang (2002) argue that the National Statistical Bureau may have overreported agricultural production growth in China by using the constant price index in the aggregation, in addition to overreporting the meat and fisheries output. Output 2 is Fan and Zhang's reconstructed production index using the Tornqvist–Theil index and an adjusted meat and fisheries output. Input is the index of total input aggregated using the Tornqvist–Theil approach. TFP is the total factor productivity index, the ratio of total output (output 2) to total input, both constructed using the Tornqvist–Theil index.

accounted for an estimated 47 percent of total production growth in agriculture (Fan and Zhang 2002). Prior to 1979, increased input use accounted for 95 percent of the growth in output, while productivity improvement accounted for only 5 percent. But after 1979, productivity growth accounted for 71 percent of the production growth, while increased input use accounted for less than 30 percent.[4] This trend indicates that future growth in agricultural production will rely on continued productivity improvements.

The Institutional and Policy Environment

One of the distinguishing characteristics of agricultural research in China is the dominance of public research conducted in national and provincial academies, prefectural institutes of agricultural sciences, and agricultural universities. Related county-level activities deal with technology transfer issues, such as demonstration trials, farmer education, and other extension-related work. Private agricultural research is minimal, although private agricultural research and development initiatives have begun to emerge in recent years.

Like many other sectors of the economy, the Chinese agricultural research system underwent substantial reforms in the last decade of the 20th century. The objectives (or at least the stated intentions) of these reforms were to make the system more efficient and more responsive to the needs of the agricultural sector in particular, and to the development of the economy more generally, while reducing the core public funding provided to research institutes in the context of increasing demand for government funds. These reforms resulted in the emergence of non-governmental funding for agricultural research. In terms of the ownership of R&D institutes and sources of funding, it is useful to distinguish between five types of agricultural research institutions in China: traditional publicly funded and managed research institutes, development firms owned by public agricultural research institutes, government-owned agribusiness firms, shareholder companies, and multinational companies.

Public-Sector Research Institutes

Public-sector research institutes still form the backbone of the Chinese agricultural research system, despite the rapid emergence of other types of research institutions. Public agricultural research at the national level is conducted mainly within academies and institutes under the Ministry of Agriculture, complemented by the research efforts of various institutes under the administrative control of other ministries. Provincial agricultural academies conduct research targeted primarily at local circumstances. At the prefectural level, the emphasis is on applied and adaptive research and development. The principal research entity is the prefectural agricultural research institute, which is generally administered by the prefectural government. Research at this level is important given the relatively large size of prefectures in China.

The Chinese system is highly decentralized in terms of both management and funding (Table 3.2). Based on 2002 data, only about 12 percent of the scientists and engineers (excluding university personnel) are employed by national institutes. A large proportion of researchers (49 percent) work in institutes administered and often largely financed at the provincial level, while the remaining 39 percent work in prefectural institutes. There is a marked disparity in the average size of the institutes: the national institutes employ an average of 70 scientists per institute, the provincial institutes half this number, and prefectural institutes just 19 scientists

Table 3.2 China: Vertical structure of agricultural research institutes, 1989 and 2002

Category	National	Provincial	Prefectural	Total	National	Provincial	Prefectural	Total
Number of institutes	56	423	620	1,099	59	429	608	1,096
Number of staff (total)	13,590	65,124	46,562	125,276	11,641	45,086	35,622	92,349
Number of scientists and engineers	5,676	17,827	10,161	33,664	4,114	16,458	11,355	31,927
Scientists and engineers per institute	101.36	42.14	16.39	30.63	69.73	38.36	18.68	29.13
Research expenditures (million yuan, 1999 prices)	270	985	654	1,909	1,378	2,923	1,408	5,759
Research expenditure per staff member (yuan, 1999 prices)	19,868	15,125	14,046	15,238	118,375	64,832	39,526	62,361
Research expenditure per scientist or engineer (yuan, 1999 prices)	47,569	55,253	64,364	56,707	334,954	177,604	123,998	180,380

Source: Ministry of Agriculture, various years.

Note: Data pertain to the nonuniversity institutes within the Ministry of Agriculture system only.

per institute. The average spending per staff member at the national level for 2002 was about 120,000 yuan, roughly double the provincial level and triple the prefectural level. These data are generally consistent with the notion of larger, more scientist-intensive institutes at the national level that focus on pre-technology rather than site-specific research. Provincial and prefectural institutes are generally smaller, less scientist-intensive, and involved in more localized, adaptive research and technology development activities.

A distinctive aspect of the agricultural research system in China is that research is institutionally separated from education and extension. The Chinese Academy of Agricultural Sciences (CAAS) falls under the administrative jurisdiction of the Ministry of Agriculture; provincial academies are under the jurisdiction of parallel departments in provincial governments. Prior to 2000, there were seven key national agricultural universities (China [formerly Beijing], Nanjing, Shenyang, Northwest, Central, South, and Southwest), also under the jurisdiction of the Ministry of Agriculture. Provincial agricultural universities were managed by their respective provincial governments. But in 2000, the management of all agricultural universities was transferred to the education system. At the national level, three key agricultural universities—China, Nanjing, and Central—are under the jurisdiction of the Ministry of Education, while provincial agricultural universities or colleges come under the supervision of the provincial department of education. Extension is the responsibility of the Department of Agriculture, with very little involvement by provincial agricultural universities or academies of agricultural sciences. This system contrasts sharply with the U.S. land-grant system, which integrates educational, research, and extension activities. The separation between research, education, and extension has inhibited the integration of technology generation and transfer activities into Chinese agriculture.

Development Firms Owned by Public Agricultural Research Institutes

Increasing demand for agricultural research funding strained government budgets in the mid-1980s. Moreover, the government was dissatisfied with the performance of the agricultural research agencies. Overstaffing, compartmentalization, lack of coordination, and duplication of research efforts left the impression that agricultural research was an expensive and not very effective form of government investment. In particular, the government was concerned about the weak linkage between research and the needs of producers and the low rate of technology adoption.

In March 1985, the Communist Party's Central Committee called for an overhaul of the Chinese R&D system. Many reforms were proposed in the official government document titled "Decision on the Reform of the Science and Technology Management System," and a similar decision was promulgated by the State Council in 1987. Since then there have been about 40 government decisions, regulations, and laws involving reforms of the science and technology system. The main initiatives spelled out in the 1985 and 1987 government documents included changing the basis by which research institutes were funded, encouraging the commercialization of technology and the development of technology markets, and rewarding individual scientists based on their performance. The overriding purpose of the reforms was to make the science sector more responsive to rapidly changing market and economic realities. The principal reform was to modify the funding mechanism in ways that encouraged research institutes to establish contacts with technology users and to conduct research and development that would directly support agricultural enterprises. The direct allocation of funds, consisting almost entirely of block grants to research institutes, was replaced by a mixed system of block grants supplemented with mechanisms whereby institutes competed for project funding from the government and international donors, while also marketing various services directly to farmers and others.

After the 1985 reforms, many research institutes began establishing commercial enterprises or firms. However, the impact of these commercial endeavors on Chinese agricultural innovation has been mixed. At first, these firms were not independent legal entities. Moreover, their businesses were not necessarily related to their research but were developed opportunistically, involving any business or commercial activity that seemed likely to generate revenues. For example, the Institute of Taihu and the Institute of Lixiahe in Jiangsu province, both well known in China for their excellent research programs, produced mineral water and manufactured spare parts for automobiles, respectively. Many institutes at the Chinese Academy of Agricultural Sciences own restaurants, grocery stores, and commercial office complexes, but a lack of capital and management skills resulted in low profits and exposed many research institutes to significant business risks, which they are generally ill equipped to handle. An example was the China National Rice Research Institute in Hangzhou, which began manufacturing monosodium glutamate in 1988. It eventually lost more than 10 million yuan and was saddled with many legal and financial problems. The factory recently went bankrupt.

Another limitation was that many researchers were inexperienced in extension or in dealing with farmers about commercial issues. Those who are active and successful in their research resent the diversion because it detracts from their research time, whereas those prepared to become involved in the transfer of research technology often receive little or no financial reward for their efforts. This separation between research and extension remains unresolved, although the commercial activities and spin-offs of many public research institutes have, in part, substituted for the lack of formal links between extension and research.

Finally, many farmers were either unable or unprepared to pay for technology. In some cases, where high-quality seed or propagation material of perennial crops such as fruit trees was offered, payment was less of a problem, but where the advice or technology was related to an activity regarded as public-good research, farmers expected it to be provided free of charge.

Since the mid-1990s, based on the experience of the previous five to ten years, many public agricultural research institutes have focused their business activities on research-related industries (such as seed, chemicals, vaccines, and so on) to strengthen their competitiveness. They have also begun to set up legally independent companies to avoid direct exposure to risk. The operations of the parent institutes and their associated commercial businesses have become more clearly separated. For example, the seed company of the Institute of Vegetables and Flowers (IVF) at the Chinese Academy of Agricultural Science (CAAS) was established in 1990. Scientists at IVF are responsible for developing and field-testing new varieties. As promising new parent lines for hybrid vegetable seeds are developed, they are made available to the seed company of IVF, which then conducts demonstrations in targeted markets, produces hybrid seeds, and finally markets them. Since 1990, the seed company has earned more than 10 million yuan annually, and about 90 percent of the revenue has been returned to the IVF. The IVF allocates 10 percent of this income to the breeders as a bonus, and the balance is used to cover general research and operational costs.

These commercial enterprises have not only been instrumental in transferring and commercializing technology developed by their parent institutes, as was expected and encouraged by the government, but have also generated substantial revenues to help underwrite the operations of their parent institutes. In 2000, 73 companies at CAAS generated 120.5 million yuan in profit, complementing 243.4 million yuan in core funding from the central government.

Agribusiness Firms Owned by Governments

Revenue-generating businesses include state-owned seed, agricultural, food, chemical, and machinery enterprises. In the former planned economy, these companies received technologies free of charge from the public agricultural research institutes. Since the 1985 reforms, many public research institutes have opted to commercialize their own research and generate income to subsidize their costs, leading to significant awareness of the intellectual property rights (IPR) aspects of agricultural R&D (Koo et al. 2003). Consequently it has become increasingly difficult for agribusinesses to freely access technologies from the public research institutes. In response, some large state-owned companies have negotiated research contracts with public research institutes to license the use of their technologies (involving various up-front, lump-sum payments or per-unit fees based on subsequent sales), while others have opted to develop their own in-house R&D capacities.

An absence of data means that the total R&D investment made by state-owned agribusiness is unknown. A case study of the Chinese seed industry (Qian 1999) indicated that no improved varieties were developed by companies prior to 1985. In contrast, in 1999, 86 improved varieties were released by state-owned and private companies, although these accounted for less than 2 percent of the total varieties released.

Shareholder Companies

Shareholder companies aligned with agricultural technologies have emerged rapidly in recent years. Most of these companies grew out of the development firms founded by public research institutes or agribusiness firms owned by governments. As they grew, many were listed on the stock market to mobilize operating capital. For example, the former Technology Development Company, a very successful development firm owned by the Hunan Academy of Agricultural Sciences, became a listed company in 2000 and mobilized about 700 million yuan from shareholders. The former national livestock company and the fisheries company (both previously owned by the Ministry of Agriculture) also became listed companies in 2000, with a majority holding retained by the government. These three companies each invested several million yuan in agricultural R&D in 2000.

The central government designated 151 of the country's largest agricultural companies as leading companies in agriculture in 2000, most of which were shareholder companies. The government gave these companies preferential policy treatment, including tax exemptions and low-interest loans, conditional on their investing a certain portion of their revenue in agricultural R&D.

Multinational Companies

According to Rozelle, Pray, and Huang (1999), technology flows through multinational firms have led to rapid gains in productivity and output in China's agricultural sector.[5] These firms may play a larger role in the future, given China's recent entry into the World Trade Organization (WTO). For example, modern technology has been introduced in the poultry industry by importing parental genetic stock and breeding materials and by the introduction of superior animal feed milling and mixing methods, coupled with the development of improved poultry genetics.

But the insecure nature of property rights in China means that much potential remains to be realized from the involvement of multinational companies. Various laws and regulations are in place to protect property rights, but their enforcement is weak (Koo et al. 2003). So far, most of the plant breeding and screening research by foreign firms has been on hybridized vegetables and sunflower seeds, because these varieties are hard to duplicate as long as the hybrid parents are kept confidential. In addition, these seeds are not monopolized by the state-owned seed companies; in contrast, the sale of seeds for principal food crops (especially hybrid rice and maize, in which seed quality is difficult to assure) has been strictly limited to the state-owned seed companies, although these restrictions have been relaxed recently. Large private seed companies are now able to market seed varieties that they have developed or acquired.

The weak enforcement of intellectual property rights is a major concern for corporations with duplicable technologies. Profitable markets have developed for some pesticide firms whose products contain active ingredients that are complex and difficult to duplicate, while other pesticides are readily copied (some illegally) and sold at low prices. Transnational corporations that can prevent technology loss by technical means do so; but agrochemicals are widely reported to be reverse engineered. Even when technology can be protected and market demand is high, fragmented retailing and wholesaling networks limit market penetration (Rozelle, Pray, and Huang 1999).

Provision and Financing of Agricultural R&D

Spending on Agricultural Research

Research expenditures. The amount of investment in agricultural research was quite modest during the first five-year plan (1953–57), averaging 130 million 1999 yuan, although the national government actively promoted the establishment of a number of agricultural research institutes (Table 3.3). This was followed by the Great Leap Forward, a program by which the government sought to jump-start the development process through the mass mobilization of people and financial resources in large public-works endeavors. As a consequence of these policies, the investment by the central government throughout the Chinese economy ballooned to unrealistic and unsustainable levels, with expenditures on agricultural research more than doubling in just three years, beginning in 1958. The ensuing policy readjustments, instigated in 1961, reduced 1962 agricultural research expenditures to less than 50 percent of those prevailing just two years earlier.

From this lower level, public investment in agricultural research in China steadily increased until the Cultural Revolution, which began in 1966. Research expenditures again contracted sharply, and the earlier growth in research personnel ceased. Not until 1972 did the system return to a more stable and balanced pattern

Table 3.3 China: Public investment in agricultural research, 1953–2002

Period	Agricultural research expenditures (million constant 1999 yuan per year)	Number of scientists	Expenditures per scientist (constant 1999 yuan per scientist year)	Share of total government spending (%)	Share of total R&D expenditures (%)	Share of total government spending in agriculture (%)	As a percentage of total AgGDP (%)
1953–57	130	NA	NA	NA	NA	1.49	0.07
1958–60	896	140,789	6,366	0.38	10.17	3.25	0.55
1961–65	766	102,498	7,469	0.56	10.24	3.90	0.41
1966–76	1,158	99,657	11,621	0.45	9.93	4.53	0.36
1977–85	2,429	80,278	30,257	0.56	10.34	5.24	0.44
1986–90	3,085	57,564	53,598	0.51	11.90	6.16	0.38
1991–94	3,808	61,545	61,876	0.54	14.29	6.14	0.39
1995–2000	4,590	83,424	55,016	0.53	12.06	8.42	0.34
2002	7,837	53,461	146,491	0.36	9.75	5.46	0.49

Sources: Fan and Pardey 1992, 1997; National Statistical Bureau, various years; and State Science and Technology Commission, various years. See Appendix Table 3A.1 for annual data.

Note: NA indicates data are not available.

of growth. Particularly since 1979, the central government has made a fairly sustained effort to strengthen the nation's agricultural research capacity, with real expenditures growing at 4.8 percent per year over the ensuing decade. However, expenditures failed to grow further during the first half of the 1990s and did not begin to grow again until 1998. This recent surge in spending reflected a refocused attention on food security concerns and a new thrust directed more generally to high-end technology, including biotechnologies relevant to agriculture. For example, the investment in agricultural biotechnology research increased from 16 million yuan in 1986 to 92 million yuan in 1999 (in 1999 prices), with an annual growth rate of 14 percent per year (Huang et al. 2001). This growth rate was three to four times higher than the growth in overall agricultural research expenditures during the same period.

Share in total government expenditures. Agricultural research expenditure as a percentage of total government expenditure was relatively low in the 1950s, ranging from 0.11 percent during 1953–57 to 0.38 percent during 1958–60. Since then it has been quite constant, peaking at 0.56 percent during 1977–85. Expenditure on agricultural research as a percentage of total national R&D expenditure was also quite constant, except during 1966–76 and in 2002, when it was at its smallest for the past several decades. Overall, China's share of total R&D spending directed toward agriculture has fluctuated between 10 to 14 percent. In contrast, research expenditure as a percentage of government spending on agriculture has generally increased over time, from about 1.49 percent during the years 1953 to 1957 to 8.42 percent for the years 1995 to 2000. This indicates that, within the agricultural sector, the government has placed increasing emphasis on research and development. The recent decline in agricultural R&D as a share of government spending on agriculture reflects a more rapid increase in government spending on agriculture relative to the growth in government spending on agricultural R&D.

Research intensity. Agricultural research intensity (ARI) ratios, expressing expenditure on public sector agricultural research as a proportion of the value of agricultural product, are commonly used indicators of the support to national agricultural research systems (NARSs). China's agricultural research-intensity ratio (0.55 percent) was above the less-developed country (weighted) average of 0.47 percent in the early 1960s (Pardey, Roseboom, and Anderson 1991). Even during the Cultural Revolution, China maintained a respectable official level of investment in agricultural research. Since then, the ratio has decreased, reflecting an extraordinarily rapid growth in agricultural output and a generally slower growth in agricultural

R&D spending. By the late 1990s, the latest period for which comparative data are available, China's ARI (0.34 percent in 1995–2000) was about half the developing country average (0.62 percent in 1995) and roughly one-eighth of the developed-country average for public research (2.64 percent in 1995). In 2002, China's ARI jumped to 0.49 percent, reflecting a 35 percent increase in agricultural research expenditures since 2000, as against a 5.7 percent increase in agricultural GDP. This rapid increase in agricultural research investment reflects the government's intention of using science and technology as a means of increasing food security and improving agricultural productivity and efficiency under an increasingly open and internationally competitive agricultural trade regime.

Funding Mechanism and Sources of Agricultural Research

Funding Mechanisms

The State Planning Commission finalizes the annual budgets for all ministerial spending at the national level. It also authorizes the disbursement of central government funds to the various ministries, as well as to the State Science and Technology Commission (SSTC). The SSTC is in turn responsible for allocating the science and technology funds at its disposal to the various agricultural and nonagricultural ministries and national research agencies such as the Chinese Academy of Science (CAS) and, to a limited extent, the Chinese Academy of Agricultural Science (CAAS). At these upper levels of government, allocation procedures are largely driven by precedent and political considerations. Within the respective ministries and agricultural research agencies (such as CAAS), there are currently no formally established or transparent mechanisms for setting research priorities and allocating funds. Project funds that support labor and operational costs have been increasingly allocated through competitive funding mechanisms. For example, funds from the National Natural Sciences Foundation, National Social Sciences Foundation, National Young Scientists Foundation, and other government funding agencies are allocated based on peer reviews.

Funding mechanisms at the provincial and prefectural levels parallel those at the national (or, in Chinese parlance, state) level. Some national funds flow to local government agencies, in some instances from the national to the provincial institutes in support of collaborative research activities. But because government financing within China is highly decentralized, the funds available to provincial and prefectural planning commissions are principally generated through locally administered public financing instruments (for example, taxes on industry and commerce, agricultural land taxes, and resource extraction taxes).

Funding for most research institutes consists of both core and project funds. Core funds, which are mainly used for salaries, are allocated to various organizations by central and local finance departments at the various levels of government, on the recommendations of their counterpart Science and Technology Commissions.

Funding Sources

Prior to the mid-1980s, government funds were the dominant source of support for agricultural research, and even in 1987 they still accounted for more than 70 percent of the total agricultural research expenditures (Table 3.4). Since the reforms of the mid-1980s, research institutes have been encouraged to generate income by providing services to other units or by fulfilling assigned research tasks. Part of these earnings may be retained for use as science and technology research funds by the research units that generate them. As a result, the government's share of total funding has declined dramatically, and development income (meaning income earned from commercial activities) has become almost as important as core government funding. In 1999, only about half the total funding for the system was from the government. Almost 45 percent was income generated by research institutes from services and commercial activities that increasingly draw on the

Table 3.4   China: Income source shares for agricultural research institutes

Year/level	Government	Development[a]	Loans	Other	Total
1987					
National	86.2	12.8	0.2	0.8	100
Other	66.7	26.5	4.2	2.6	100
Total	70.5	23.9	3.4	2.2	100
1993					
National	68.1	26.2	3.4	2.3	100
Provincial	45.2	44.1	7.3	3.4	100
Prefectural	42.8	39.2	13.8	4.2	100
Total	47.1	40.2	9.1	3.6	100
1999					
National	52.2	45.7	2.1	0.0	100
Provincial	51.0	43.3	5.7	0.0	100
Prefectural	43.4	46.8	9.8	0.0	100
Total	48.5	44.9	6.6	0.0	100
2002					
National	64.0	31.4	0.6	4.0	100
Provincial	59.5	28.9	2.9	8.7	100
Prefectural	59.5	27.0	8.1	5.4	100
Total	60.7	29.0	3.7	6.6	100

Source: Ministry of Agriculture, various years.

Note: The data for the national level cover Ministry of Agriculture institutes only; forestry and universities are excluded.

[a] Represents self-generated funds, largely from the sale of goods and services.

technologies arising from R&D. It is likely that an even greater share of the funds available for agricultural R&D will come from such sources, given the incentives to underreport such funding: for example, an institute associated with a national academy such as CAAS must pay a proportion of its self-generated income (perhaps up to 30 percent) to the academy. Development income is often used by research institutes to subsidize researchers' salaries and other benefits, although it is rarely used directly for research.

In recent years the government has ratcheted up its support to science and technology, partly because of improvements in the overall budget situation and partly because it has placed a higher priority on science-based growth strategies. And, perhaps more important, policymakers have begun to realize the public-good dimensions of agricultural research. Consequently, in 2002, government funding jumped to more than 60 percent of the total income received by agricultural research institutes, while the share of development income declined to 29 percent.

Allocation of Research Funds among Subsectors

China has given top priority to crop research, particularly in grain crops, for the past several decades. In 2002, China spent 51 percent of total agricultural research resources on crop research, declining from a peak of 65 percent in 1989 (Table 3.5). This trend is consistent with the changing contribution of crops to total production value (54 percent in 2002). Livestock research accounts for only about 10 percent of total research resources, but the sector accounts for almost 30 percent of the total production value. The fisheries sector accounts for about 7 percent of total research resources but more than 10 percent of the total production value. On the other hand, the forestry sector accounts for only 3.7 percent of total production value but double that in terms of its share of research resources. Based on congruence between the share of research expenditures and the value of the respective sector, there appears to be a substantial overinvestment in forestry research and underinvestment in the livestock and fisheries sectors. Although a more careful study is needed to make definitive conclusions, it appears that China needs to invest more in livestock and fishery research. This shift will be particularly important in the future, as these two subsectors will be the major sources of growth in agricultural production.

Institutional Case Studies

The Chinese Academy of Agricultural Sciences

Founded in 1957, CAAS is the national academy engaged in agricultural R&D, excluding forestry and fisheries. It constitutes the largest and arguably most impor-

Table 3.5   China: Shares of research expenditures among subsectors, 1987–99, 2002

Year	Crop	Forestry	Animal husbandry	Fisheries	Water conservancy	Other	Total
1987	52	13	9	9	10	7	100
1988	54	10	13	9	9	5	100
1989	65	9	8	6	6	6	100
1990	55	11	10	7	9	8	100
1991	52	10	15	8	9	6	100
1992	51	10	16	7	10	6	100
1993	50	9	15	7	11	8	100
1994	50	8	16	7	11	8	100
1995	53	8	15	7	10	7	100
1996	56	9	13	7	11	4	100
1997	58	10	8	7	12	5	100
1998	58	10	9	8	11	4	100
1999	58	9	10	7	10	6	100
2002	51	10	8	6	10	15	100

Sources: Ministry of Agriculture, various years.

Note: National-level data cover Ministry of Agriculture institutes only; forestry and universities are excluded.

tant agricultural R&D institution in China. To a large extent, the structure and performance of CAAS reflect the government's policies on research in general and are therefore indicative of the future of Chinese agricultural research.

This section reviews key aspects of the reforms of CAAS by analyzing the changes in organizational structure, human resource management, funding sources, research priorities, and development and commercial activities.

Organizational structure. CAAS is administratively affiliated with the Ministry of Agriculture (MOA) but is largely influenced by the R&D policy of the Ministry of Sciences and Technology (MOST). In terms of bureaucratic hierarchy, the president of CAAS is ostensibly equivalent to the vice minister of the MOA, but CAAS has no direct administrative control over the provincial academies of agricultural sciences. CAAS is an independent legal entity, consisting of 8 departments at its headquarters, 1 graduate school, 1 publishing house, and 39 institutes (15 located in Beijing and 24 in various provinces across China).

All the institutes under CAAS are independent legal entities, operating autonomously in terms of fund-raising, staff recruitment, and daily operations, but the director general and deputy director general of each institute are appointed by CAAS headquarters. A typical institute has 1 director general, 2 to 4 deputies, 4 management offices—administration, human resources, research management, and development—and 8 to 15 research divisions.

Table 3.6   China: Composition of CAAS personnel, 1994–2001

Year	Research staff	R&D management staff	Business staff	Support staff	Retirees	Total
1994	3,340	1,136	927	1,598	2,878	9,879
1995	3,239	1,073	1,563	NA	3,119	8,994
1996	3,351	982	1,187	1,339	3,442	10,301
1997	3,602	1,089	1,283	1,193	3,978	11,145
1998	3,265	904	1,086	1,137	4,010	10,402
1999	3,018	961	1,436	1,208	4,597	11,220
2000	3,133	982	1,534	945	4,581	11,175
2001	3,003	949	1,428	1,037	4,962	11,379

Source: Chinese Academy of Agricultural Sciences, various years.
Note: NA indicates data are not available.

Human resources. Table 3.6 presents the personnel structure of CAAS during the period 1994 to 2001. The total number of personnel increased slightly, with reductions occurring in the number of research, management, and support staff. Notably, the business staff increased markedly, and the number of retirees soared from 2,878 to 4,962 in the period observed. Over time, as in most Chinese public institutes, these retirees have taken a larger share of the CAAS payroll and become a significant budgetary burden.[6]

Although the total number of staff fell, the number with higher degrees rose. Staff holding Ph.D.s increased from 136 in 1994 to 371 in 2001 (Table 3.7). The number holding bachelor's and master's degrees also grew in proportion to the total number of R&D staff.

Table 3.7   China: Education levels of CAAS personnel, 1994–2001

Year	R&D staff	Ph.D. degrees	M.Sc. degrees	Bachelor's degrees	College
1994	6,074	136	732	922	2,808
1995	5,873	149	728	920	2,774
1996	5,650	204	711	911	2,482
1997	5,884	220	754	978	2,613
1998	5,306	245	688	924	2,269
1999	5,187	292	669	961	2,193
2000	5,060	338	704	1,007	2,090
2001	4,989	371	683	1,006	2,072

Source: Chinese Academy of Agricultural Sciences, various years.

Table 3.8   China: Allocation of CAAS research expenditure, 1994–2001

Year	Basic research	Applied research	Experimentation and development	Other	Total
Constant 1994 yuan (thousands)					
1994	7,390	17,463	6,533	4,694	36,080
1996	5,918	24,334	10,670	6,937	47,859
1997	6,336	32,554	13,480	11,057	63,427
1999	11,371	44,003	14,423	17,825	87,622
2000	16,806	49,840	34,571	23,160	124,377
2001	26,062	59,598	40,820	32,165	158,645
Percentage					
1994	20	48	18	13	100
1996	12	51	22	14	100
1997	10	51	21	17	100
1999	13	50	16	20	100
2000	14	40	28	19	100
2001	16	38	26	20	100

Source: Chinese Academy of Agricultural Sciences, various years.

Note: Data for 1995 and 1998 were not available. Percentages do not always sum to 100 given rounding errors.

Research priorities. CAAS's mandate is to undertake basic, so-called basic applied, and applied research and development of strategic importance to China. In reality, however, most of the research is quite applied. Table 3.8 shows CAAS's research orientation as reflected by its expenditures between 1994 and 2000. Even in real terms, CAAS expenditures have grown remarkably. Evaluated in 1994 constant prices, total spending increased from 36.08 million yuan in 1994 to 158.65 million yuan in 2000. Although the proportions of CAAS spending directed to other types of research expenditure have increased, applied and developmental research (Table 3.8, data columns 2 and 3) still dominate, accounting for almost two-thirds of the CAAS total.

Development activities. Managerial and support staff numbers were cut by 27 percent between 1994 and 2001 as a direct consequence of reforms. Most of these staff were transferred to development or commercial activities, and the income generated from these activities accounted for a larger share of the total income. The number of staff engaged in development and commercial activities rose from 927 to 1,428 over the same period, accounting for 9 percent of total staff. The income from development and commercial activities increased by 56.5 percent to a total of 23.94 million yuan in 2001 (1994 prices).

Most of the commercial undertakings took the form of spin-off companies rather than revenue-raising efforts through technology licensing or royalty arrangements.

Table 3.9   China: CAAS funding sources, 1994–2001

Year	Government sources		Nongovernment sources	
	Constant 1994 yuan (millions)	Share (%)	Constant 1994 yuan (millions)	Share (%)
1994	192.37	71.21	51.26	18.97
1995	207.10	70.51	63.92	21.76
1996	235.38	69.17	80.50	23.14
1997	270.49	66.83	113.53	28.05
1998	182.58	54.57	130.77	39.09
1999	263.68	51.64	237.29	46.47
2000	270.70	51.04	251.77	47.47
2001	400.76	55.73	313.16	43.55

Source: Chinese Academy of Agricultural Sciences, various years.

Note: Shares do not sum to 100 percent because a third category, bans, is not shown.

As of 2001, there were 72 companies operating within CAAS, with each of the academy's institutes operating about two enterprises. As previously mentioned, these companies are closely linked with their parent institutes, making use of institute staff to commercialize and market the research products of the respective institutes. A share of the profits reverts to the parent institute to subsidize salaries and operational costs. In 2001, the 72 companies generated about 42 percent of CAAS's total revenue. The companies not only generate revenues to supplement public funding but also promote the application of research more relevant to on- and off-farm production needs.

Funding sources. Between 1994 and 2001, public funding for CAAS more than doubled, from 192.37 million to 400.76 million yuan (Table 3.9). Nongovernment funding increased fivefold, from 51.26 million yuan to 313.16 million yuan, most of which was generated through commercial activities. The proportion of government funding decreased from 71.2 percent to 55.7 percent, while nongovernment funding increased from 19 percent to 43.6 percent. As the advancing reforms intended, CAAS could no longer rely on public funding alone, and it seems the reforms have effectively diversified the academy's funding channels.

Research output. A key question is whether the diversification in funding sources and implementation of new incentive systems have adversely affected research productivity. China has yet to develop an evaluation system to assess the performance of the research institutes. Table 3.10 provides some indications of the general status of CAAS's research output. The volume of published science and technology papers

Table 3.10 China: CAAS research output, 1994–2001

Year	Published research papers		Published books	Patents	
	Total	Published abroad		Applications	Authorizations
1994	2,327	206	89	NA	NA
1995	2,835	258	110	NA	NA
1996	2,784	217	131	16	5
1997	2,742	181	123	15	12
1998	2,562	185	104	39	18
1999	2,842	198	211	26	21
2000	2,668	206	145	32	18
2001	2,396	174	167	39	26
1994–2001	21,156	1,625	1,080	167	100

Source: Chinese Academy of Agricultural Sciences, various years.
Note: NA indicates data are not available.

increased only slightly between 1994 and 2000. By 2001, the number of published scientific papers totaled 21,156, including 1,625 published abroad. In contrast, the number of published books has increased dramatically, but in China books are generally not refereed or peer-reviewed and hence are much easier to publish than refereed papers. In the current performance-evaluation system, books are ranked at least as high as refereed articles.

The number of patent applications in China grew steadily between 1994 and 2001. Since 1996, CAAS has submitted more than 167 patent applications to the National Patent Agency, indicating, perhaps, that CAAS researchers are coming to appreciate the implications of protecting intellectual property when commercializing innovations. Each year during this period the CAAS's research projects won about 10 national prizes, 20 regional or local prizes, and more than 50 provincial and ministry prizes.

In summary, in the eight years up to 2001, tracking the number of publications or patent approvals produced no clear indication that research productivity at CAAS has been materially affected by the changed circumstances.

The Jiangsu Provincial Academy of Agricultural Science

Jiangsu is one of the most advanced provinces in China in terms of agricultural production and research. The Jiangsu Academy of Agricultural Science (JAAS) is the largest of the provincial agricultural academies, with more than 2,000 full-time employees in 1998 (Qian, Zhu, and Fan 1997). Because Jiangsu has been a pioneer of efforts to reform China's agricultural research and development system, it is an interesting institution to study in terms of the R&D changes taking place.[7]

Institutional aspects. JAAS is a comprehensive public agricultural research institution directly administrated by the Jiangsu Provincial Government. Founded in 1932, it was originally named the National Agricultural Research Institute (NARI) because Nanjing was the national capital at the time. The early organizational structure largely mimicked the Soviet system of the 1950s, but China's transition from a planned to a market economy brought about a demand for institutional change in the agricultural R&D sector. Beginning especially in the early 1980s, the provincial agricultural R&D system in Jiangsu underwent a series of substantial reforms.

In 1982, the provincial government introduced guidelines for reform titled "Opinion on Strengthening Agricultural R&D" (see Wang 2000). The guidelines called for research institutes located at headquarters to focus on projects broadly relevant to the ecology of the province, leaving the regional institutes to focus on more localized, adaptive research. Since then, funds have been reallocated to reflect this intent.

Based on further guidelines in 1985 from the central government for reform of the science and technology sector, the Jiangsu Provincial Government enacted a decree in 1988 to change the system of performance appraisal and promotion. Under the old system, promotions were largely determined by duration of service, whereas now—with a view to providing incentives and enhancing productivity—they are based on performance. Institutions like JAAS proposed detailed guidelines for performance evaluations. For example, single-authored journal articles carry greater weight for evaluation purposes than coauthored articles. Performance evaluation and ranking have profound implications for employees in China: they can affect all aspects of a researcher's life. Public research institutions continue to carry the responsibility for providing employees and retirees with benefits, including housing subsidies, retirement pensions, and medical care, and they allocate such benefits largely according to seniority. Consequently, a senior fellow may be eligible for a three-bedroom apartment, while a fellow may only qualify for a two-bedroom apartment. Naturally this system creates great incentives for researchers to seek promotion through publishing journal articles, preferably as a single or lead author.

Publishing scientific articles is one metric of research output; generating technologies that are commercially successful is another. In 1993, the State Science and Technology Commission and State Reform Commission proposed new guidelines in the wake of financial decentralization under the title "Some Opinions on Staff Management, Structural Adjustment, and In-Depth Reform" (see Wang 2000). The document recommended that research institutions respond to market signals by producing outputs with more immediate economic consequences. The document also encouraged research institutes to generate revenues from development

Table 3.11 China: Composition of JAAS personnel, 1988–98

Year	Research staff	Support staff	Business staff	Retirees	Total Excluding retirees	Total Including retirees
1988	1,105	1,691	164	743	2,960	3,703
1989	1,058	1,653	201	774	2,912	3,686
1990	1,067	1,649	216	839	2,932	3,771
1991	1,104	1,584	219	854	2,907	3,761
1992	1,131	1,573	179	914	2,883	3,797
1993	1,137	1,466	165	1,078	2,768	3,846
1994	1,216	1,412	214	1,148	2,842	3,990
1995	1,206	1,404	230	1,207	2,840	4,047
1996	1,163	1,387	240	1,277	2,790	4,067
1997	1,084	1,381	264	1,357	2,729	4,086
1998	1,114	1,259	393	1,447	2,766	4,213
Percentage change, 1988–98	0.8	−25.5	139.6	94.8	−6.6	13.8

Source: Jiangsu Academy of Agricultural Sciences, various years.

and other commercial activities. The original aim of this reform was to subsidize R&D with revenues from businesses, but many institutes passed on their development revenues to staff members, leaving little for R&D. Nevertheless, commercialization has become a major feature in Jiangsu's agricultural R&D system.

Personnel. Several features are apparent from Table 3.11. First, the number of JAAS research staff changed little between 1988 and 1998: numbers rose from 1,105 in 1988 to 1,216 in 1994, then dropped to 1,114 in 1998. Second, responding to policy reforms, the number of managerial and support staff was cut by about 26 percent. At the same time, the number of employees involved in activities generating business income more than doubled, from 164 to 393. Third, with an aging population of researchers, the number of retirees rose from 743 to 1,447.

Excluding retirees, the total number of full-time employees at JAAS was 2,766 in 1998, a decline of 6.6 percent from 1988. Including retirees, however, the number of staff on the payroll increased by 13.8 percent from 3,703 to 4,213, with researchers accounting for only 26.4 percent of the 1998 total.

Funding and expenditures. Core government funding increased more than threefold from 1988 to 1998, from 9.2 million to 37.7 million yuan, evaluated at 1988 constant prices (Table 3.12). Project funding fluctuated around 4.5 million yuan for the first half of the 1990s, then increased significantly in 1997 and 1998.

Table 3.12 China: Major JAAS revenue and expenditure shares, 1988–98

Category	1988	1989	1990	1991	1992	1993	1994	1995	1996	1997	1998
Major revenues (constant 1988 yuan, millions)											
Core	9.2	8.9	9.6	10.3	11.1	10.6	18.9	19.7	22.8	29.5	37.7
Project funding	4.9	5.4	6.0	4.1	4.7	4.2	4.1	4.0	4.8	6.3	8.0
Net development income	1.1	2.3	2.9	3.8	4.6	5.3	5.7	6.2	10.1	12.8	14.2
Major expenditures (constant 1988 yuan, millions)											
Wages	10.2	8.9	9.8	13.1	11.9	15.7	17.4	16.8	23.4	29.8	35.4
R&D	6.4	4.1	4.5	9.2	5.4	7.1	2.3	2.3	4.3	10.6	12.2
Development	10.3	5.7	5.2	11.1	13.0	24.3	22.4	20.4	44.1	47.0	47.1

Source: Jiangsu Academy of Agricultural Sciences, various years.

With increased commercialization, net income from business activities rose sharply, from 1.1 million to 14.2 million yuan over the same period.

In terms of expenditure, core funding was used largely to finance wages; hence the two sets of data show similar upward trends between 1988 and 1998, in response to the growth of retiree numbers. JAAS expenditure declined from 6.4 million yuan in 1988 to 2.3 million yuan by 1995, then soared to 12.2 million yuan by 1998, when the government pumped significant new funding into the agricultural R&D system following the large spike in grain imports in 1994 and 1995. Development expenditures increased markedly, from 10.3 million to 47.1 million yuan. Because of the incentive mechanisms that directly link staff incomes—particularly staff bonuses—with business revenues, researchers, managerial staff, and support staff all benefit from profit-making research activities.

In line with the national trend toward decentralizing government services, JAAS became increasingly dependent on funding from within the province rather than from the central government (Figure 3.3). In 1988, state funding accounted for over 70 percent but by 1998 dropped to less than 50 percent. Because Jiangsu is one of the richest provinces, it was able to supplement its shrinking share of state

Figure 3.3   China: JAAS funding sources, 1988–98

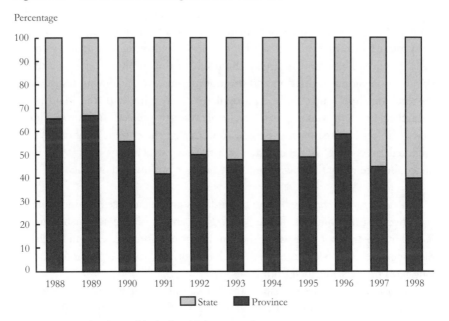

Source: Jiangsu Academy of Agricultural Sciences, various years.

Table 3.13 China: Average size of JAAS research projects, 1988–98

Year	Research funding per capita	Number of researchers per project
1988	5.8	2.5
1989	3.9	2.2
1990	4.3	1.7
1991	8.3	1.6
1992	4.8	1.6
1993	6.2	1.6
1994	1.9	1.6
1995	1.9	1.5
1996	3.7	1.6
1997	9.8	1.5
1998	10.9	1.4

Source: Jiangsu Academy of Agricultural Sciences, various years.

funding. But in many poorer provinces, agricultural research institutions face more severe budget restrictions (Fan, Zhang, and Zhang 2004).

Size of research projects. Table 3.13 indicates the scale of research activities through funding per researcher and the average number of researchers per project. Because the total number of full-time researchers remained relatively stable, funding per researcher closely correlates with total funding, decreasing dramatically from 1988 to 1995 and increasing thereafter. The average number of researchers per project fell from 2.5 in 1988 to 1.4 in 1998, indicating minimal researcher collaboration. This trend is largely the result of the emphasis on first authorship in professional evaluation and promotion; however, achieving results with far-reaching significance will be particularly challenging with the majority of researchers now undertaking such small-scale research projects. In informal interviews with researchers, most expressed concern that the current incentive system inhibited larger-scale cooperative research projects, which are perceived as more uncertain in terms of funding, promotion and recognition, and outputs.

Research performance. Changes in funding sources and incentive mechanisms also affect research outputs (Table 3.14). The benefits of sole authorship are reflected in the dramatic increase in the number of published papers and books. At the same time, large peer-reviewed research outputs, indicative of more significant, long-term projects, declined from 70 to 42.

Awards, and royalties for papers and books, can serve as an intermediate indicator of the productivity of research staff. Figure 3.4 plots research productivity based

Table 3.14 China: JAAS research output, 1988–98

Year	Papers	Books	Other peer-reviewed outputs		Prizes[c]		Model demonstration plots[d]
			Evaluated variety[a]	Prize-winning[b]	State 1 and 2	Province 1 and 2	
1988	546	2	70	76	1	14	535
1989	636	14	68	82	3	5	675
1990	674	18	111	75	1	21	1,018
1991	648	17	57	97	2	10	661
1992	619	20	75	71	5	18	859
1993	701	17	43	69	4	9	709
1994	581	15	55	59	0	10	1,207
1995	608	21	48	43	2	5	685
1996	497	27	36	80	1	15	846
1997	605	15	44	65	5	12	761
1998	652	21	42	75	3	13	709

Source: Jiangsu Academy of Agricultural Sciences, various years.

[a] Indicates released crop varieties subject to evaluation.

[b] Indicates that the research output has won a peer-reviewed prize.

[c] Includes class 1 and class 2 prizes awarded by state and provincial agencies.

[d] Represents the number of demonstration plots established for side-by-side comparisons of new and old crop varieties or to demonstrate new agricultural technologies to farmers.

on labor and investment input. The first indicator is output value per researcher, and the second is output value per 1,000 yuan of input. Both indicators show that productivity has changed little during the survey period despite the increase in overall funding to JAAS.

Given that one of its original purposes was to supplement government funds for R&D, commercialization has been successful. However, research output (at least to the extent revealed by publication and related measures) has changed little, suggesting that the commercial revenues have not significantly increased the funds used for R&D, as originally envisioned.

A Prospective Look at China's Research Reforms

Agricultural research has played a key role in meeting the national food demand and reducing poverty, as many studies have shown (Alston et al. 2000; Fan 2000; Fan, Zhang, and Zhang 2004). However, much remains to be achieved. China's demand for agricultural products will continue to expand (in terms of both the quantity and quality of products and shifts in the composition of food, feed, and

Figure 3.4   China: Publication performance of JAAS researchers, 1988–98

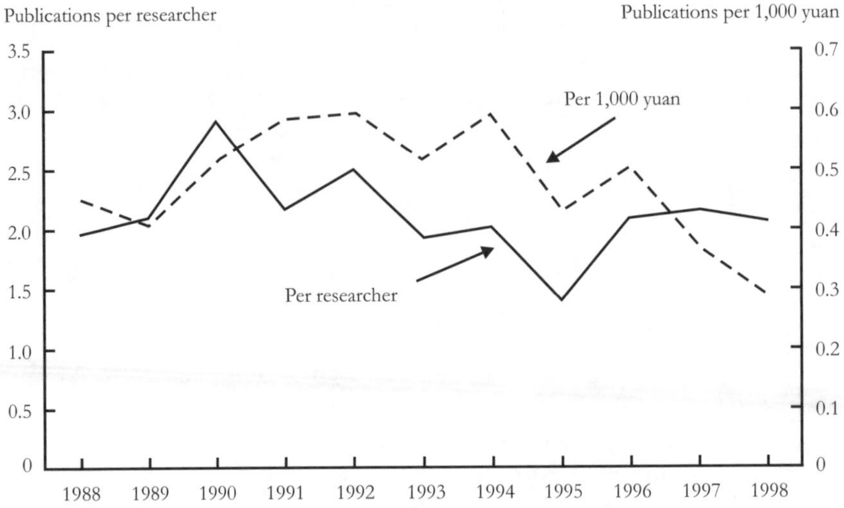

Publications per researcher   Publications per 1,000 yuan

Source: Compiled by authors.

fiber demands) in ways that remain heavily reliant on improvements in productivity. How China's agricultural research system responds to these demands will be critical; so will the research policies that can help or hinder these developments.

Increasing Public Investment in Agricultural Research

A further increase in investment in agricultural R&D is needed. Despite its comparatively rapid overall growth, China's agricultural R&D spending—relative to the size of the agricultural sector it serves—lags well behind that of many other countries. But do significant scale and scope economies go unrealized as a result of the parallel national, provincial, and prefectural systems? As of 2002, agricultural research expenditure as a percentage of agricultural GDP averaged around 0.50 percent, well below the corresponding developed-country average and even lower than in most developing countries (which averaged 0.62 percent). Various evidence shows that agricultural research investment not only yields high economic returns but also significantly reduces rural poverty and regional income inequality (Fan 2000). Moreover, according to recent evidence, agricultural research has contributed to a large drop in urban poverty by lowering food prices (Fan, Fang, and Zhang 2003). Absent agricultural research, China would have many more urban poor today. Finally, increased agricultural research investment is one of the most efficient ways to solve China's long-term food-security problem (Huang, Rozelle, and Rosegrant 1999). All these factors suggest that increased investment in agricultural research is a "win–win–win" (growth–poverty and equity–food security) national development strategy.

Reforming the Public Research Institutes

After more than 15 years of reform, the Chinese public agricultural research system now faces new challenges. The coexistence of public research and commercial activities has played an important role in mobilizing resources to support agricultural research and in enhancing the link between agricultural research and those who ultimately use its outputs. As the system evolves, however, these symbiotic activities are often in conflict because public agricultural research aims to provide public goods and carry out basic, strategic, and not-for-profit research, whereas revenue-generating businesses provide private goods and engage in commercial activities. Hence, the two operations would likely benefit from even more distinct and separate institutional arrangements. A more focused, efficient, and effective research system is urgently needed to achieve the multiple goals of agricultural growth, food security, and poverty reduction. The commercial activities, which are not always compatible with these goals, need to be hived off from the public research agencies.

On the one hand, the government should increase its investment in public research; on the other, the current public research institutes need further reform. The major (and interrelated) problems currently confronting most of the research institutes are overstaffing, the heavy financial burden imposed by retirees, the lack of an effective incentive system, and lack of coordination between national and regional research institutes.

To avoid overstaffing, all research and administrative positions should be created on the basis of need, and all positions should be filled though public announcements and open competition. Redundant staff should be encouraged to retire and provided assistance in seeking employment elsewhere. The reform of the agricultural research system should be considered in the larger social and financial context. These challenges are largely similar to the problems of the state-owned enterprises (SOEs). Hence, some of the future reforms required for research are likely to proceed in step with the overall economic and institutional reforms of China's SOEs. Several schemes to reform the Chinese pension system have been proposed. For example, current and newly hired staff could be required to contribute a share of their salary to a retirement account, while contributions for retired staff could be covered by government funds. Incentive structures for researchers should be performance based. Promotion and annual salary increases should be based on more rigorous performance assessment.

The current organizational structure for agricultural research strictly parallels the country's administrative system rather than being based on agroecological or other relevant considerations. In Gongzhuning City, Jinglin Province, for example, the provincial academy of agricultural sciences and a prefectural agricultural research institute both carry out R&D on maize. Similar duplications exist in almost all provinces in China. If research resources are to be allocated more efficiently and appropriately across agroecological zones, professional linkages and coordination between institutes at different levels must be improved. One solution would be to merge institutes with similar mandates within agroecological zones—particularly within cities.

Private versus Public Research

In recent years, the focus has been on privatizing the funding for publicly performed research rather than privatizing research per se. Several factors have contributed to this trend. A high proportion of the agricultural research carried out by the Ministry of Agriculture's agencies is directed toward production. But if China continues to develop as it has over the past decade, the demand for agricultural technologies will increasingly move off-farm. Further increases in the use of off-farm inputs in agriculture, such as fertilizers, pesticides, and machinery, will stimulate increased demand for new technologies and know-how aimed at the input supply sector. Rising per capita incomes are resulting in a rapid increase in the demand for processed agricultural products; this in turn will stimulate the demand for postharvest technologies related to the storage, processing, packaging, and marketing of agricultural produce. China's existing research capacity in input supply and, particularly, postharvest technology is embryonic. Private research could fill much of this gap, given that much of the required technological and market development is more amenable to private initiatives.

Considering the increasing fiscal constraints facing the Chinese national agricultural research system, multinational agribusiness and R&D firms can be called upon to play a greater role in the growth of Chinese agriculture. But this will not happen spontaneously. A number of significant policy and administrative changes are needed to improve the environment for these firms before they are likely to play a larger role. These include strict and transparent enforcement of IPR protection for agrochemicals, veterinary pharmaceuticals, plant and animal genetics and biotechnology, and other agricultural technologies, to reassure investors that theft of proprietary technology will not be tolerated. The legal framework is in place, but its enforcement remains uncertain (Koo et al. 2003). The restrictions on foreign direct investment in improving grain, oilseed, and cottonseed varieties also need to be removed. These restrictions have hindered investment and technology transfer and prevent Chinese farmers from accessing the newest internationally developed seed varieties. The current policy also requiring that Chinese partners must have a majority share in domestic marketing enterprises makes transnational firms reluctant to manufacture high-technology products because they cannot control product distribution. Firms that manufacture agricultural inputs need the opportunity to market their products directly to farmers. Market competition would improve distribution efficiency.

Regulations dealing with foreign direct investments by transnational firms should be more transparent. Domestic taxation schedules, import tariffs, and foreign exchange rules are adequately defined. However, application and approval procedures are complex, requiring separate negotiations with officials in each province in which investment and operations are proposed. There is also a problem of changing the rules after investments have been made: while such changes may be necessary for equity or other reasons, provision should be made for grandfathering the foreign enterprises over an adjustment period.

The Chinese agricultural research system has experienced dramatic change over the past several decades and now represents one of the world's largest public agricultural R&D institutions. For the past 15 years, the system has also pursued an aggressive reform agenda and has achieved substantial success. However, further reforms are still required to transform the system into a modern and efficient powerhouse propelling Chinese agriculture into the new century.

Appendix Table 3A.1   China: Agricultural research expenditures, 1961–2002

Year	Current prices (million yuan)	1999 prices (million yuan)	1999 prices (million international dollars)
1961	199.3	630.9	336.5
1962	142.3	456.2	243.3
1963	190.8	623.6	332.5
1964	247.3	802.9	428.2
1965	276.0	876.7	467.6
1966	254.7	822.9	438.9
1967	157.4	505.2	269.4
1968	151.9	481.3	256.7
1969	245.3	807.6	430.7
1970	303.2	1,025.5	546.9
1971	280.7	943.2	503.0
1972	365.4	1,227.9	654.8
1973	350.6	1,176.5	627.4
1974	351.7	1,177.4	627.9

(continued)

Appendix Table 3A.1 (continued)

Year	Current prices (million yuan)	1999 prices (million yuan)	1999 prices (million international dollars)
1975	408.6	1,384.1	738.1
1976	399.9	1,357.2	723.8
1977	425.0	1,426.9	761.0
1978	546.2	1,809.7	965.1
1979	641.3	2,051.9	1,094.2
1980	667.5	2,057.7	1,097.3
1981	639.4	1,926.8	1,027.5
1982	657.1	1,983.8	1,057.9
1983	827.9	2,473.2	1,318.9
1984	990.6	2,821.3	1,504.5
1985	1,077.4	2,785.8	1,485.6
1986	1,140.5	2,819.2	1,503.5
1987	1,126.5	2,650.4	1,413.4
1988	1,476.4	3,098.0	1,652.1
1989	1,703.9	3,286.0	1,752.4
1990	1,627.6	2,970.3	1,584.0
1991	1,862.1	3,183.8	1,697.9
1992	2,357.7	3,736.0	1,992.4
1993	2,809.9	3,887.0	2,072.9
1994	3,596.7	4,149.5	2,212.9
1995	4,049.8	4,128.2	2,201.5
1996	4,450.2	4,283.0	2,284.1
1997	4,145.4	3,957.2	2,110.3
1998	4,804.1	4,698.7	2,505.8
1999	4,895.0	4,895.0	2,610.4
2000	5,841.5	5,787.0	3,086.1
2001	NA	NA	NA
2002	7,958.6	7,837.0	4,179.4

Sources: Data compiled by authors from Fan and Pardey 1992, 1997; State Statistical Bureau, various years; and State Science and Technology Commission, various years.
Note: Expenditures include spending by relevant institutes from all levels of governments and agricultural research spending in the universities. NA indicates data are not available.

Notes

The authors thank Philip Pardey for his encouragement and detailed comments on various draft versions of this chapter. They are also grateful to Mary Jane Banks for her excellent editorial and formatting assistance. Many research staff participated in carrying out the surveys reported in the two institutional case studies described in the chapter. They include Wang Feiji, Qian Guxia, Qu Changhong, and Liu Yan, all from the Chinese Academy of Agricultural Sciences; Wang Qin from the Jiangsu Province Bureau of Science and Technology; and Li Guangmin and Yang Jinshen from Hebei Academy of Agricultural Sciences. The authors acknowledge financial support from the Natural Science Foundation of China (Approval No. 70525003).

1. The impact of and returns to research investment in Chinese agriculture have been measured by numerous scholars, including Huang and Rozelle (1996); Fan and Pardey (1997); Huang, Rozelle, and Rosegrant (1999); Fan (2000); and Fan, Zhang, and Zhang (2004).

2. The U.S. system spends more in total (that is, from both public and private sources) on agricultural R&D but employs fewer scientists. Measured in terms of new knowledge and technologies produced versus resources committed to research, the U.S. system is most likely considerably larger.

3. The population growth rate was 1.6 percent per year between 1952 and 2000.

4. The contribution of productivity increases comes from technical change, technical efficiency improvement, and allocative efficiency improvement.

5. Rozelle, Pray, and Huang (1999) argue that foreign technology transfer has played a key role in promoting agricultural productivity for the past several years and can continue to do so, given greater transparency in government regulations and greater security in property rights generally and, specifically, those applying to technologies.

6. Unlike most developed countries, China has yet to develop national pension and social-security systems; thus the institutes are required by the government to provide a pension, housing, and medical care coverage to all their retirees.

7. A survey of all research institutes at the Jiangsu Academy of Agricultural Sciences (JAAS) was conducted jointly by IFPRI, CAAS, and JAAS in August and September 2000. The survey, which included 15 provincial and 9 regional institutes for the period 1988–98, compiled details on personnel, expenditures, funding sources, and research achievements. The 15 provincial research units consisted of the headquarters, research center, training center, veterinary institute, horticulture institute, food institute, modernization institute, grain crop institute, fertilizer institute, genetic institute, vegetable institute, plant protection institute, cash crop institute, and information institute. The 9 regional institutes were Xuzhou, Huaiyin, Taihu, Yanjiang, Yanhai, Lixiahe, Zhenjiang, Nanjing, and Lianyungang.

References

Alston, J. M., C. Chan-Kang, M. C. Marra, P. G. Pardey, and T. J. Wyatt. 2000. *A meta-analysis of the rates of return to agricultural R&D: Ex pede Herculem.* IFPRI Research Report No. 113. Washington, D.C.: International Food Policy Research Institute.

Chinese Academy of Agricultural Sciences. Various years. *Agricultural science and technology indicators of CAAS.* Beijing: Chinese Academy of Agricultural Sciences, Department of Sciences and Technology Management.

Fan, S. 2000. Research investment and the economic returns to Chinese agricultural research. *Journal of Productivity Analysis* 14 (92): 163–180.

Fan, S., and P. G. Pardey. 1992. *Agricultural research in China: Its impact and institutional development.* International Service for National Agricultural Research, The Hague.

———. 1997. Research, productivity, and output growth in Chinese agriculture. *Journal of Development Economics* 53: 115–137.

Fan, S., and X. Zhang. 2002. Production and productivity growth in Chinese agriculture: New national and regional measures. *Economic Development and Cultural Change* 50 (4): 819–838.

Fan, S., C. Fang, and X. Zhang. 2003. Agricultural research and urban poverty: The case of China. *World Development* 31 (4): 733–741.

Fan, S., L. Zhang, and X. Zhang. 2004. Investment reforms and poverty in rural China. *Economic Development and Cultural Change* 52 (2): 395–422.

Huang, J., and S. Rozelle. 1996. Technological change: Rediscovering the engine of productivity growth in China's agricultural economy. *Journal of Development Economics.* 49 (2): 337–369.

Huang, J., S. Rozelle, and M. W. Rosegrant. 1999. China's food economy to the twenty-first century: Supply, demand, and trade. *Economic Development and Cultural Change* 47 (4): 737–766.

Huang, J., S. Rozelle, C. Pray, and Q. Wang. 2001. Plant biotechnology in the developing world: The case of China. Paper presented at the International Conference on Rural Investment, Growth, and Poverty Reduction, Beijing, November 5–6, 2001.

Jiangsu Academy of Agricultural Sciences. Various years. Unpublished finance and budget documents, Department of Sciences and Technology Management.

Koo, B., P. G. Pardey, K. Qian, and Y. Ziang. 2003. *The economics of generating and maintaining plant variety rights in China.* Environment and Production Technology Discussion Paper No. 100. Washington, D.C.: International Food Policy Research Institute.

Ministry of Agriculture. Various years. *Agricultural science and technology statistical materials.* Beijing: Ministry of Agriculture.

National Statistical Bureau. Various years. *China statistical yearbook.* Beijing: China Statistical Press.

Pardey, P. G., J. Roseboom, and J. R. Anderson. 1991. Regional perspectives on national agricultural research. Chapter 7 in *Agricultural research policy: International quantitative perspectives,* ed. P. G. Pardey, J. Roseboom, and J. R. Anderson. Cambridge, U.K.: Cambridge University Press.

Qian, K. 1999. To share IPR of plant germplasm together with public and private sector and farmers: Analysis of social welfare and incentives to innovation. Report to the Drafting Groups of the National People's Congress for China Seed Law, Beijing. Mimeo.

Qian, K., X. Zhu, and S. Fan. 1997. *Analysis of research priorities in Jiangsu agricultural research: The case of rice, wheat, rapeseed, and cotton.* Beijing: China Agricultural Science and Technology Press.

Rozelle, S., C. Pray, and J. Huang. 1999. Importing the means of production: Foreign capital and technologies flows in China's agriculture. Paper presented at the International Agricultural Trade Consortium Conference, San Francisco, June 25–26.

State Science and Technology Commission. Various years. *China statistical yearbook on science and technology.* Beijing: China Statistical Press.

Wang, Q. 2000. Incentive mechanisms and agricultural R&D performance in China. Paper presented at workshop "Public Investment in Chinese Agriculture," funded by the Australian Centre for International Agricultural Research (ACIAR), Wuxi, China, November 1–4.

World Bank. 2004. *World development report 2004.* Washington, D.C.

Chapter 4

Indonesia: Coping with Economic and Political Instability

Keith O. Fuglie and Roley R. Piggott

Introduction

Broad Characteristics of the Indonesian Economy

Indonesia is a Southeast Asian archipelago consisting of some 17,500 equatorial islands (6,000 of which are inhabited) stretching in an east–west direction over 5,000 kilometers. It has a land area of 1.83 million square kilometers; in 2000 this supported a population of 203.5 million (the fourth largest in the world), which is growing at about 1.4 percent per annum. While the overall population density is about 111 persons per square kilometer, 59 percent of the population lives on the island of Java, which has a population density of 944 persons per square kilometer. The overall ratio of urban to rural population was about 40:60 in 1999 (22:78 in 1980).

The Asian financial crisis that began in 1997 affected Indonesia severely: its economy shrank by around 15 percent between 1997 and 1998. Since then, modest growth has resumed, but at substantially lower growth rates than those recorded in the decades prior to the crisis. The global rankings published in the *World Development Report for 1999* (World Bank 2001) placed Indonesia 143rd of 206 economies in terms of real gross national product (GNP) per capita.

The extent of structural changes in the Indonesian economy between 1965 and 2003 is shown in Table 4.1. The population doubled. Real GDP increased by about 900 percent and real per capita income by about 440 percent. Large changes have occurred in the sectoral shares of GDP, with agriculture's share declining from

Table 4.1   Indonesia: Structural changes in the economy, 1965–2003

Indicator	1965	1975	1985	1995	2000	2003
Population (millions)	104.6	132.6	163.0	192.8	206.3	214.7
Gross domestic product (billions of 1999 international dollars)	75.2	148.4	285.8	588.9	609.7	680.9
Percentage of GDP						
Agriculture	56.0	30.2	23.2	17.1	17.2	16.6
Mining, oil, and gas	31.4	36.3	40.9	41.1	36.7	39.9
Manufacturing	8.4	9.8	16.0	24.1	24.9	24.7
Services	4.2	23.7	19.9	17.7	21.2	18.9
Percentage of employment						
Agriculture	69.2	61.6	54.7	44.0	45.3	46.3
Manufacturing	6.9	8.4	9.3	12.6	13.0	12.0
Other	23.9	30.1	36.1	43.4	41.8	41.7
Per capita income (1999 international dollars)	719	1,120	1,753	3,055	2,956	3,172
Exports as percentage of GDP	5.5	24.0	22.2	26.3	42.9	31.2
Imports as percentage of GDP	5.4	21.0	20.4	27.6	33.5	25.7

Source: World Bank 2005.

Note: Percentages do not always sum to 100 given rounding errors.

nearly 60 percent to only 17 percent, accompanied by significant increases in the shares of the services sector (now the dominant sector, with a 40 percent share in 2003), manufacturing (25 percent), and mining, oil, and gas (19 percent). Similar trends have occurred in sectoral employment shares, with agriculture's share declining from nearly 70 percent to 46 percent. The intensity of international trade has increased, with the share of exports in GDP growing from 5.5 percent in 1965 to 26 percent in 2003, and imports as a percentage of GDP growing from 5.4 percent in 1965 to 25.7 percent in 2003.

Broad trends in the agricultural economy from the early 1960s to the early 2000s are shown in Table 4.2. Real agricultural GDP has increased; food-crop production dominates the sector, accounting for half of the total. However, the relative importance of crop production (and of food crops in particular) has declined, and the relative importance of livestock, forestry, and fisheries production has increased. Indonesia possesses the world's second largest area of tropical forest (after Brazil) and among the largest saltwater and coastal fishing grounds.

Rice production dominates the food-crop sector, and production increased fourfold between the early 1960s and the early 2000s, mainly as a result of yield increases. The increased use of modern varieties and fertilizer has been important in securing higher yields. Rice remains the staple food and is of great political importance. After rice, cassava is the next most important food crop, closely followed by maize. Nonfood "estate" crops, such as rubber, oil palm, sugarcane, and cacao, are

Table 4.2 Indonesia: Trends in agriculture, 1961–2003 (annual averages)

Indicator	1961–65	1971–75	1981–85	1991–95	2001–03
Agricultural GDP (millions of 1999 international dollars)	39,049	45,911	60,319	88,689	110,385
Agricultural research (millions of 1999 international dollars)	NA	110.6	208.1	230.1	233.3
Percentage of AgGDP					
Food crops	65.1	59.9	61.8	55.8	50.7
Nonfood crops	17.3	17.1	15.8	16.6	15.5
Livestock	6.6	7.1	9.9	11.4	12.8
Forestry	3.0	10.3	5.7	6.9	6.3
Fisheries	8.0	5.7	6.8	9.3	14.7
Rice output (million tons of paddy rice)	12.4	21.2	35.8	47.5	51.3
Livestock (million head)	10.5	9.9	12.0	16.2	17.4
Total cropland (million hectares)[a]	17.6	18.9	26.0	32.2	39.3
Java and Madura	9.0	8.8	7.0	7.1	7.1
Other islands	8.6	10.0	19.6	25.1	32.2
Number of farm households (millions)	12.2	14.4	19.5	21.7	24.9
Java and Madura	7.9	8.7	11.6	11.8	13.6
Other islands	4.3	5.7	7.9	9.9	11.3
Average size of farm[b] (hectares)	1.1	1.0	1.0	0.8	0.8
Java and Madura	0.7	0.6	0.6	0.5	0.4
Other islands	1.7	1.5	1.6	1.2	1.3
Agricultural research spending (1999 international dollars)					
Agricultural research per farm	NA	7.7	10.7	10.6	9.4
Agricultural research per capita	NA	0.9	1.3	1.2	1.1
Agricultural research as percentage of AgGDP	NA	0.2	0.3	0.3	0.2
Rice yield (kilograms per hectare)	1,761	2,542	3,786	4,352	4,465
Irrigated cropland (percent)[c]	15.2	16.1	17.9	22.8	23.5
Fertilizer use (kilograms per hectare)	6.9	22.7	63.3	73.9	74.3
Agricultural wage (kilograms of rice per day)[d]	1.1	2.7	3.7	4.1	5.9
Agricultural exports as percentage of AgGDP	NA	NA	NA	24	31
Agricultural imports as percentage of AgGDP	NA	NA	NA	16	21

Sources: Agricultural GDP, shares of AgGDP, and agricultural trade are from BPS, *Statistical Yearbook of Indonesia* (annual issues, 1961–95). Rice output, livestock numbers, rice yield, and fertilizer use are from FAO 2005. Cropland, irrigated cropland, and agricultural wages are from van der Eng 1996. Farm numbers and landholdings are from agricultural census for 1963, 1973, 1983 (BPS 1985), 1993 (BPS 1995), and 2003 (BPS 2004). Research expenditures include expenditures by the Agency for Agricultural Research and Development (AARD) and the estate-crop research institutes of the Indonesian Planters Association for Research and Development (IPARD). AARD conducted forestry research until 1982 and fisheries research until 2000. Sources for research expenditures for AARD institutes: 1974–83 from Pardey, Eveleens, and Abdurachman 2000 (Table Appendix 2); 1984–85 from AARD 1991; 1986–92 from AARD 1992b; 1993 from AARD 1994; 1994–95 from AARD 1997; 1996–98 from AARD 1999b; 1999–2000 from AARD 2003. Sources for research expenditures by IPARD institutes: 1974–83 from Pardey, Eveleens, and Abdurachman 2000 (Table Appendix 2); 1984–85 government contribution from Pardey, Eveleens, and Abdurachman 2000, and member contribution from AARD 1990; 1986–88 from AARD 1992b; 1989–2000 from R. Sumitro, personal communication, 2001. A major source of funds (around 75 percent in 1998) for IPARD institutes is product sales, but these data are available only from 1989 onward. Revenue from product sales was estimated for 1974–88 using a constant revenue per scientist ratio (1989–2000 average in constant 1999 rupiahs).

Notes: Percentages do not always sum to 100 given rounding errors. NA indicates data are not available.

[a]Includes land in annual (paddy, garden, and upland crops) and perennial (estate) crops. Only data for 2001 and 2002 were available for estimating average agricultural land during 2001–3.

[b]Represents farm household landholdings and does not include land in perennial or estate crops.

[c]Represents percentage of cropland planted to annuals receiving irrigation at least part of the year.

[d]Represents wages of male plantation workers on Java.

becoming an increasingly important component of Indonesia's agricultural sector.[1] Livestock production is also growing rapidly in response to the rising demand for animal protein, commensurate with rising per capita incomes.

Although little new land is available for cropping on Java, there has been a steady increase in the area of land cropped on other islands. Total agricultural cropland (including land in perennial or estate crops) grew from 17.6 million hectares in the early 1960s to 37.4 million hectares by 2002. According to the Indonesian agricultural census (done every ten years since 1963), the number of farm households steadily increased nationwide between 1963 and 2003. The agricultural census also reports landholdings by farm households (these estimates mainly refer to annual cropland and exclude land in perennial crops, even though smallholders are major producers of most estate crops). According to census figures, the average farm size has been decreasing, to about 0.4 hectares per household in Java and 1.3 hectares per household outside Java.

Spending for agricultural research was very low in the 1970s, but real spending per farm and per capita had doubled by the 1980s. Nevertheless, Indonesia ranks near the bottom among Asian countries in agricultural research spending relative to agricultural GDP (Pardey, Roseboom, and Fan 1998).

The Indonesian Agriculture Success Story

Much has been written about Indonesia's success in raising agricultural production, particularly rice, over the past three decades. Indonesia went from being the world's largest rice importer in the mid-1960s to becoming nearly self-sufficient by the mid-1980s (Jatileksono 1987). But agricultural growth in Indonesia has not been limited to rice. Since Indonesia adopted a more outward orientation in 1985, its exports of agricultural commodities have grown substantially. Agricultural exports as a share of agricultural GDP increased from 16 percent in 1985 to nearly 30 percent a decade later (Erwidodo 1999). By the mid-1990s, Indonesia emerged as the world's second largest exporter of rubber and oil palm and the third largest exporter of cacao and coffee. The value of shrimp exports also grew dramatically over this period, surpassing everything but rubber as an agricultural export earner. Imports of agricultural products grew at an even more rapid rate (Erwidodo 1999).

Table 4.3 elaborates on some of the data provided in Table 4.2, tracing the major changes in agricultural production and input use in Indonesia between 1961 and 2000.[2] Quantities produced are shown in million metric tons of "rice equivalents" in value terms, meaning that commodity prices are normalized on the price of rice in a given year. The average growth in agricultural production over this period was 2.9 percent per annum, with total output rising from 50.5 million metric tons per year in the early 1960s to 137.1 million metric tons per year by the

Table 4.3 Indonesia: Changes in agricultural production and input use, 1961–2000

Production/inputs	Average quantity (millions of tons of rice equivalents)				Average annual growth rate (percent)			
	1961–65	1971–75	1981–85	1991–95	1961–67	1968–92	1993–2000	1961–2000
Agriculture outputs, total	50.50	65.60	94.46	137.12	0.66	4.04	1.04	2.90
Crop and animal outputs, total[a]	35.34	48.93	75.63	112.75	1.11	4.72	1.20	3.44
Food crops, all	19.73	28.74	45.91	62.33	1.20	5.01	0.43	3.48
Rice, paddy	12.39	21.18	35.77	47.50	1.74	5.50	0.75	3.94
Cassava	2.48	2.42	2.79	3.39	-0.51	1.94	0.16	1.20
Maize	1.69	1.75	2.71	4.33	9.71	7.68	2.54	6.94
Horticultural crops, all	3.21	4.51	5.55	8.68	2.72	3.52	4.20	3.54
Fruits, all	1.43	2.04	2.86	3.81	2.43	3.49	5.69	3.78
Vegetables, all	1.78	2.47	2.68	4.87	2.97	3.90	3.89	3.75
Nonfood crops, all	9.05	11.10	16.38	27.18	0.63	4.32	2.67	3.41
Cane sugar	0.84	1.17	1.96	2.93	1.35	5.59	-4.12	2.95
Rubber	1.68	1.93	2.38	3.45	0.41	2.85	1.80	2.26
Palm oil	0.19	0.38	1.24	4.37	2.59	12.75	10.16	10.65
Animal products, all	3.34	4.57	7.79	14.56	1.48	5.66	0.67	4.00
Meat	3.04	4.18	6.67	12.41	1.62	12.63	3.87	3.75
Milk and eggs	0.30	0.39	1.12	2.15	0.14	8.15	3.46	5.95
Fish products, all	2.91	3.89	6.42	11.12	4.61	4.41	4.27	4.41
Forest products, all	12.26	12.78	12.41	13.25	-1.49	0.74	-3.54	-0.48
Agricultural inputs								
Cropland (million hectares)	17.55	18.91	26.02	32.25	0.52	2.34	1.93	1.97
Area harvested (million hectares)	17.52	19.62	22.66	28.35	0.81	2.43	0.99	1.88
Irrigated cropland (million hectares)	2.42	2.66	3.31	4.56	1.44	2.34	0.30	1.78
Agricultural labor (million workers)	28.61	31.70	37.55	46.01	0.70	1.66	1.04	1.39
Fertilizer (million tons/year)	0.12	0.43	1.67	2.46	1.65	16.04	0.13	10.56
Agricultural machinery (million horsepower)	0.07	0.16	0.19	0.58	7.45	14.31	5.88	11.52
Animals (million head of stock)	14.00	13.59	18.41	30.99	-0.01	3.37	-0.26	2.10

Source: These data are from Fuglie (2004), who analyzed agricultural productivity growth in Indonesia from 1961 to 2000.

Notes: The first four columns show average annual figures for the first half of each decade from the 1960s to the 1990s. The second four columns report growth rates for each series over the entire period of this study (1961–2000) and during three periods of Indonesia's agricultural development.

a Net of seed and feed.

early 1990s. Rice production itself grew by nearly 4 percent per annum. Average annual growth rates for animal and fish products also exceeded 4 percent during these four decades.

In Table 4.3 we also show the performance of Indonesia's agriculture during three periods: 1961–67, a period of political and economic instability in Indonesia; 1968–91, when agricultural output and productivity grew rapidly); and 1993–2000, when agricultural productivity growth appeared to stagnate. During the first period, agricultural output grew by only 0.7 percent per year, but this growth was mostly resource-based and correlated closely with the increase in agricultural land and labor. Productivity growth played a major role in accelerating agricultural growth, which increased by more than 4 percent per annum during the second period. The third period includes the Asian financial crisis that began in 1997. The El Niño phenomenon also caused a significant drought in 1997–98, which caused crop production to fall. Overall growth in agricultural output since 1993 has averaged about 1 percent per year, roughly matching the rate of growth in agricultural resource use, a pattern which suggests that there was once again little or no improvement in overall agricultural productivity. Further, although the Asian financial crisis and El Niño had strong negative effects on the Indonesian agriculture sector, a slowdown in agricultural productivity growth is evident even before these events.

The intensification of agricultural growth between 1968 and 1992 was broad-based, affecting not only food-crop production but also horticulture, estate crops, and livestock production. Between 1968 and 1992, when productivity growth accelerated, annual growth rates in production exceeded 4 percent for rice, maize, nonfood crops, animal products, and fish products. During these years, yield improvements from Green Revolution technologies (especially new varieties and fertilizers) were particularly important in rice and, to a lesser degree, in maize and other crops. From 1993 to 2000 agricultural production growth fell to 1.0 percent per year. The animal subsector, which relies heavily on imported feed, was particularly hard hit by the Asian financial crisis and the resultant devaluation of the rupiah.

Much of the growth in production that occurred between 1961 and 2000 can be accounted for by increases in conventional inputs, such as cropland, labor, and fertilizers. However, for long-term sustainability of growth in agriculture, productivity gains are more important. In Table 4.4 we show estimates of a total factor productivity (TFP) index developed by Fuglie (2004). This index shows that TFP grew by about 0.77 percent per annum in the early 1960s but then increased to 2.56 percent per annum between 1968 and 1992. The drop in TFP between 1993 and 2000 reflects a number of factors, including a drought-induced decline in crop production, an economic recession, fewer workers exiting agriculture, and expansion of cropland into more marginal areas. It appears that once the initial gains of

Table 4.4   Indonesia: Agricultural productivity growth, 1961–2000

Indicator	Average annual growth rate (percent)			
	1961–67	1968–92	1993–2000	1961–2000
Total outputs (crop and animal)	1.25	4.79	1.12	3.49
Total inputs	0.48	2.24	1.19	1.75
Total factor productivity	0.77	2.56	–0.07	1.74
Labor productivity (output per worker)	0.33	2.95	0.07	1.96
Land productivity (output per unit of cropland)	0.78	2.38	–0.93	1.45
Land area per worker	–0.45	0.60	1.02	0.52
Food crop output per capita	0.18	4.04	–0.39	2.54
Rice output per capita	0.97	3.70	–0.35	2.45

Source: These data are from Fuglie 2004. See source note to Table 4.3 for more details.

the Green Revolution were exhausted, public and private investment in agriculture were not sufficient to sustain the supply of new technology to the sector.

Table 4.4 also shows changes in some indicators of food security (food and rice output per capita) and partial productivity (output per worker and output per unit of cropland). Indonesia's success in enhancing food security is illustrated by the impressive growth in per capita food production (an average of 2.54 percent per annum from 1961 to 2000). Per capita food production has fallen since 1993, however. Within the agricultural sector, output per worker grew by nearly 2 percent, and output per unit of cropland increased by 1.45 percent per year from 1961 to 2000. Cropland per worker employed in agriculture continued to expand throughout the 1970s, 1980s, and 1990s, with virtually all the expansion occurring outside Java.

The acceleration of growth in TFP from the 1970s corresponds to the period in which investment in agricultural research in Indonesia was substantially increased. But a number of other factors also contributed to the increase: investments in irrigation, improvements in the quality of the agricultural labor force (through rural education), agricultural price policies, government-led food-crop "intensification" programs, and trade and investment liberalization (Jatileksono 1996; van der Eng 1996; Erwidodo 1999). Between 1970 and 2003, government development expenditures for agriculture first increased and then declined relative to agricultural GDP (Table 4.5).[3] Government expenditures for agriculture also declined as a share of total development expenditures, especially after 1989. Expenditures on fertilizer subsidies accounted for a large share of public expenditures for agriculture throughout much of this period, although the fertilizer subsidy was eliminated after 1999.

These national averages above mask important regional differences, especially between land-scarce Java and relatively land-abundant islands like Sumatra,

Table 4.5 Indonesia: Government development expenditures for agriculture, 1970–2003 (million 1999 international dollars)

	Total development expenditures	Development expenditures for agriculture and natural resources					Agricultural shares (percent)		
Year	for all sectors	Total	Agriculture and forestry	Irrigation	Fertilizer subsidy	Environment	Agriculture's share of total development expenditures	Agricultural development expenditures as a share of AgGDP	AgGDP as a share of total GDP
1970	3,485	955	486	400	69	NA	27.4	2.1	47.2
1971	4,886	1,164	849	300	14	NA	23.8	2.5	44.8
1972	4,890	1,246	777	395	73	NA	25.5	2.7	40.2
1973	5,516	1,240	635	347	259	NA	22.5	2.5	40.1
1974	5,699	1,671	952	286	433	NA	29.3	3.8	32.7
1975	10,933	5,986	3,089	344	2,554	NA	54.8	13.2	31.7
1976	13,765	3,865	2,013	518	1,335	NA	28.1	8.2	31.1
1977	17,863	4,027	2,454	640	933	NA	22.5	7.8	31.1
1978	17,133	3,460	2,090	928	441	NA	20.2	6.5	30.5
1979	15,195	3,166	1,997	679	491	NA	20.8	5.9	28.1
1980	18,217	3,967	1,952	902	567	545	21.8	7.7	24.8
1981	24,311	6,199	3,546	880	1,165	608	25.5	11.1	25.3
1982	26,889	6,569	3,395	1,018	1,439	717	24.4	10.8	26.3
1983	24,960	5,898	2,835	980	1,425	658	23.6	9.3	26.4
1984	30,675	5,443	2,581	846	1,418	598	17.7	8.6	22.7
1985	29,523	8,575	4,343	1,379	2,170	682	29.0	12.9	23.1

Year									
1986	31,305	6,049	2,574	1,402	1,373	700	19.3	8.5	24.1
1987	20,951	4,282	2,072	601	1,174	435	20.4	5.9	23.3
1988	21,936	7,159	4,062	884	1,750	463	32.6	9.0	24.1
1989	25,781	4,764	2,761	1,109	421	473	18.5	5.7	23.6
1990	27,025	6,400	3,944	987	543	926	23.7	7.8	21.5
1991	29,125	5,310	2,906	1,388	476	540	18.2	6.6	19.7
1992	34,070	5,883	3,171	1,629	515	569	17.3	6.8	19.5
1993	35,851	5,497	2,909	1,715	274	599	15.3	6.3	18.5
1994	36,625	5,453	2,846	1,629	385	594	14.9	5.7	17.3
1995	40,549	5,211	1,308	2,229	1,077	597	12.9	5.1	17.1
1996	34,991	4,627	1,342	2,483	174	629	13.2	4.3	16.7
1997	38,828	4,765	1,398	2,502	201	664	12.3	4.4	16.1
1998	22,859	3,195	902	1,559	326	409	14.0	3.0	18.1
1999	35,864	8,014	3,955	2,523	1,123	412	22.3	7.1	19.4
2000	37,275	4,290	2,196	1,650	0	444	11.5	4.1	19.4
2001	53,390	3,017	1,355	1,359	0	303	5.7	2.8	20.4
2002	56,358	3,278	1,506	1,507	0	265	5.8	2.9	21.4
2003	70,658	3,813	1,803	1,816	0	195	5.4	3.4	22.4

Sources: Expenditures for 1970–92 from Government of Indonesia 1974, 1979, 1984, 1989, 1995; expenditures for 1993–2003 from BPS, *Statistical Yearbook of Indonesia* (annual issues, 1970–2003); rupiahs were converted to international dollars using a purchasing power index from World Bank 2005; and the GDP deflator is from International Monetary Fund 2001.

Notes: NA indicates data are not available. Development expenditures do not include routine expenditures for government personnel or capital maintenance.

Kalimantan, and Sulawesi. Differences in regional agricultural productivity changes are discussed in Booth 1988 and van der Eng 1996. This is an important topic for future research on agricultural productivity in Indonesia.

Estimates of productivity growth in Indonesian agriculture are limited because the environmental costs of agricultural development have not been taken into account. Growth in agricultural land area, forest, and fish production have come at some cost to environmental resources, including land degradation, loss of forest habitat, and a decline in water quality, none of which have so far been incorporated into agricultural productivity measurements for Indonesia.

Reality Check: The 1997–98 Crisis

Events since 1997 have afforded a somber reminder of Indonesia's vulnerable food-security situation. A combination of drought, forest fires, the Asian financial crisis, and political upheaval adversely affected the production and distribution of food crops (especially rice) and animal products and exposed large segments of the population to food insecurity. Rice imports reached an all-time high of 4 million metric tons in 1998, more than double the peak level in the 1960s (Kasryno, Nataatmadja, and Rachman 1999). Stringer (1999, pp. 169–70) describes the combination of adverse events and their consequences as follows:

> Indonesia's current socioeconomic crisis has dramatically reversed decades of rapid economic growth, steady progress in poverty reduction, and substantial improvements in food security. Before the crisis began in August, 1997, Indonesia was frequently cited as one of the highest performing Asian economies with per capita GDP growth in the top 10 percent of all developing countries. Since the crisis however, the rupiah's value has dropped precipitously, inflation has soared and GDP has fallen an estimated 14 percent in 1998 (World Bank 1998). The country's poor and those facing food insecurity are especially vulnerable to the falling incomes, increasing food prices, decreases in real wages and rising unemployment and underemployment brought on by these crisis induced events.
>
> Indonesia's capacity to address the crisis has been greatly complicated by forest fires, drought, floods and a sharp decline in crude oil prices. . . . Estimates of the economic damage to Indonesia's logging and timber industries, (excluding environmental and health costs) are set at more than U.S.$900 million (Tay 1998). . . .
>
> A prolonged drought throughout 1997/98 reduced export crop production and, more importantly for the country's food security objectives, contributed to a large drop in paddy production. Initial estimates suggest

that the 1998 paddy crop is nearly 10 percent below the 1996 production level (FAO 1998; CBS 1999). . . .

Around one-third of the country's population spends 70 percent or more of their total expenditures on food (SUSENAS 1996). Thus, the collapsing demand, rising unemployment, falling food production, increasing food prices and rapidly expanding numbers of malnourished stress the fundamental role agriculture must play in revitalizing the economy.

The crises during the late 1990s led to major changes in agricultural policy in Indonesia. Most important was the reduction in barriers to agricultural trade, including reduction or elimination of tariffs and the elimination of the import monopoly of BULOG (the state trading agency) on major food items such as rice, wheat, and soybeans. Another important result of the crises was that budget austerity measures reduced public spending on agriculture. The long-standing fertilizer subsidy was discontinued in 1999. Funding for agricultural research and extension was also reduced in real terms.

Not all effects of the Asian financial crisis were deleterious for Indonesian agriculture. The resulting devaluation of the rupiah led to a general improvement in the farm–nonfarm terms of trade, as prices of tradable commodities rose faster than prices of nontradable goods and services. Cacao producers in Sulawesi, for example, experienced a windfall as prices in rupiah rose fivefold in a matter of months (Ruf and Cerad-Tera 1999). With the end of the 1997–98 drought, agricultural production in Indonesia recovered in 1999 and 2000. In fact, the value of agriculture to the wider economy was demonstrated by its ability to absorb nonfarm labor displaced by the economic crisis. As a result, unemployment and poverty rates did not increase as much as predicted in some early projections (Manning 2000).

Various policymakers have highlighted the need for an increased agricultural R&D effort to improve Indonesia's food security and meet other long-run development goals. H. S. Dillon, director of the Center for Agricultural Policy Studies in Jakarta, has commented that one of the reasons for the slowdown in technological progress in Indonesian agriculture in recent years (especially when compared with other land-constrained Asian states) is "persistent underfunding of the public sector R&D effort" and claims that "a substantial increase in the real expenditures on agricultural R&D is warranted, given the potential economic and social payoffs likely to result from raising smallholder productivity" (Dillon 1999, p. 12). He is also critical of various features of the Indonesian agricultural research system, including the highly fragmented nature of the agricultural R&D effort, the limited involvement of universities, weak linkages between Indonesia's own R&D effort

Table 4.6   Indonesia: Ministry of Agriculture expenditures by function, 1994–99 (million 1999 international dollars)

Function	1994	1995	1996	1997	1998	1999
Secretary general						
Main office	30.6	219.4	63.2	13.3	32.9	8.5
Regional offices	114.5	119.8	287.0	131.4	187.1	90.6
Quarantine	10.2	10.7	18.2	12.6	12.3	8.5
Foreign office	0.7	0.8	0.8	0.9	0.6	0.9
Mass guidance	108.4	74.1	49.2	42.7	27.2	25.8
Research and development	125.1	131.2	125.5	126.5	76.7	65.7
Education and training	70.5	73.0	70.7	70.9	42.9	41.5
Agribusiness development	0.0	4.8	7.9	7.8	4.5	5.0
Subtotal secretary general	459.9	633.7	622.7	627.7	384.1	322.2
Inspectorate general	4.8	5.2	5.1	4.8	2.9	0.0
Director general, food crops	277.3	243.7	153.0	131.6	76.3	60.7
Director general, plantation	240.7	198.4	118.5	104.3	65.5	0.0
Director general, livestock	84.9	43.9	47.8	49.5	28.8	16.7
Director general, fisheries	122.1	86.0	80.6	72.0	41.9	26.8
Total	1,189.7	1,211.0	1,027.8	989.8	599.4	440.5
Share of total for R&D (percent)	10.5	10.8	12.2	12.8	12.8	14.9

Source: M. Gunawan, personal communication 2003.

Notes: Expenditures include routine and development expenditures. Rupiahs were converted to international dollar denominated currency units using purchasing power parity (PPP) indexes from World Bank 2005.

and those of international R&D providers, disruption of research efforts in the Agency for Agricultural Research and Development (AARD) resulting from a 1995 internal reorganization, and weak intellectual property rights for agricultural technologies.

Recent trends in Ministry of Agriculture (MOA) expenditures for agriculture are shown in Table 4.6. Between 1994 and 1999, routine and development expenditures by MOA declined from $1.19 billion to $440 million in real terms (constant 1999 international dollars). The precipitous decline in public spending on agriculture was part of overall government austerity measures needed to meet a commitment to the International Monetary Fund (IMF) to reduce deficit spending. MOA's spending on agricultural research fell by about half, in real terms, over this period even though research grew as a share of all agricultural expenditures.

Planning for Increased Agricultural Productivity: Challenges and Constraints
Many of the science and technology issues confronting Indonesia's agricultural sector apply to the economy as a whole, such as the need to establish technology competence to effectively absorb new technology from abroad, and to increase international competitiveness through increased productivity rather than low wages.

These issues have featured prominently in Indonesia's science and technology policy (Hill 1995). Agricultural R&D policy has the additional goals of providing food security, reducing rural poverty, and maintaining the quality of natural resources.

While Indonesia substantially increased its science and technology capacity in the 1980s and 1990s, it still remains behind many Asian countries in several important aspects. By the late 1980s, Indonesia's spending for all R&D was less than 0.2 percent of GNP, lower than that of most other countries of Southeast Asia and far below that of industrialized countries such as Japan and Korea (UNESCO 2001). Public spending for education was also low by Asian standards, despite the rapid expansion of the educational system. The enrollment ratio for tertiary education (11.3 percent in 1996), though only half that of Thailand, was in the middle range for developing countries in Asia, as was the share of tertiary students enrolled in science and technology fields (UNESCO 2001).

The State Ministry for Research and Technology (RISTEK) has responsibility for coordinating R&D policy in Indonesia but has little control over the allocation of research expenditures. RISTEK operates a number of competitive grant and other programs for funding research, especially for universities. Budgets for government research institutions are allocated either through ministries or directly to nondepartment agencies. The most important nondepartment research institutions include the Agency for Assessment and Application of Technology (BPPT) for industrial technology, the Indonesian Institutes of Sciences (LIPI) for basic sciences, the Central Statistics Agency (BPS), the National Nuclear Energy Agency (BATAN), and the National Institute for Aeronautics and Space (LAPAN). But agriculture remains the highest priority for government-supported research. AARD in the Ministry of Agriculture is the largest government research agency in Indonesia, with more than 3,000 researchers (Table 4.7). Together with IPARD (estate crops), FORDA (forestry), and the Center for Fisheries, Research and Development (previously part of AARD but transferred to the newly formed Ministry for Marine Resources and Fisheries in 2001), AARD has had by far the largest number of research staff of any government research institution.

The policy direction for agricultural research in Indonesia is articulated in AARD's strategic plans. The 1999–2004 strategic plan describes the main "constraints and challenges" facing the Indonesian agricultural sector. The summary below draws heavily on AARD 1999a (pp. 23–30):

- The industrial and service sectors have not absorbed surplus labor from the agricultural sector to the degree previously anticipated. At the same time, urban migration has occurred as a result of factors such as increased land

Table 4.7 Indonesia: Major government research institutions, 1997

Institution	Affiliation	Research focus	Number of research staff
Agency for Assessment and Application of Technology	Nondepartment agency	Industrial technologies	2,078
Indonesian Institute of Sciences	Nondepartment agency	Basic sciences	1,591
Central Statistics Agency	Nondepartment agency	Statistics	1,842
National Nuclear Energy Agency	Nondepartment agency	Nuclear energy	1,344
National Institute of Aeronautics and Space	Nondepartment agency	Aeronautics and space	480
National Coordination Agency for Survey and Mapping	Nondepartment agency	Mapping	194
Agency for Agricultural Research and Development	Ministry of Agriculture	Crops, livestock, and fisheries	3,008
Indonesian Research Institutes for Estate Crops	Indonesian Planters Association for Research and Development (Ministry of Agriculture coordination)	Estate crops (oil palm, rubber, sugar, tea, coffee, cacao, quinine)	296
Forestry Research and Development Agency	Ministry of Forestry	Forestry	417
Agency for Public Works Research and Development	Ministry of Public Works	Infrastructure	495
Center for Oil and Gas Technology Research and Development	Ministry of Energy and Mineral Resources	Oil and gas	343
Center for Mineral Technology Research and Development	Ministry of Energy and Mineral Resources	Mining	145
Agency for Health Research and Development	Ministry of Health	Health	326
Agency for Education Research and Development	Ministry of National Education	Education	267

Sources: Data refer to the number of research staff with university degrees (B.Sc., M.Sc., or Ph.D.) in 1997 (except for the Ministry of Energy and Mineral Resources data, which are for 1995). Number of scientists at Agency for Agricultural Research and Development from AARD 1997. Number of scientists at Indonesian Research Institutes for Estate Crops from IFPRI 2004. Number of scientists at Ministry of Energy and Mineral Resources from RISTEK 1996, and at all other research institutes from RISTEK 1998.

fragmentation, low agricultural-sector wages, and limited rural employment opportunities. Investments are needed in rural areas to provide employment opportunities. Agricultural development will require increased commercialization of agriculture in the form of agribusiness development and value-adding activities.

• While population growth remains high and rice is still the favored food staple, self-sufficiency is threatened by climatic variability, pest and disease outbreaks, and unstable market forces. Moreover, the land area available for rice has diminished, especially on Java, where land is being converted to industrial development and housing. Rice yields have leveled out. More irrigated land and use of inherently less productive land for rice are needed. At the same time, food production and consumption need to be diversified.

• Land fragmentation will remain a problem until industrialization draws enough small landholders out of agriculture to enable "extensification" of agricultural production. Farming systems research that allows for efficient agricultural production on small landholdings is needed.

• Rural financial institutions have not performed well in providing capital to agriculture. Better incentives are needed for these institutions to mobilize capital for agriculture.

• Future policy must capitalize on the competitive advantage of different agro-ecological zones. This entails a focus not only on cultivation techniques but also on farming systems, integrated pest management, and reduction in post-harvest losses.

• More practical farm-management skills are needed, including decisionmaking tools and bookkeeping methods that normally accompany the transition from subsistence to commercial agriculture.

• Increased environmental awareness is important not only to maintain the resource base but also to allow Indonesia to be competitive in international markets.

Elsewhere in the strategic plan, attention is drawn to water scarcity as a potential impediment to increased agricultural output. One of the challenges will be to develop agricultural technology and plant varieties that are more efficient in water use. Another will be the development of on-farm and multifarm strategies for water management.

Finally, reference must be made to the political situation since the fall of the New Order government in 1998. One outcome of this situation (and, to some extent, the cause) has been a demand for greater democracy and public participation in decisionmaking. Decisions about agricultural R&D activity will need to be increasingly decentralized, in the sense of taking account of farmers' wishes and perceived needs. This shift will entail a greater research emphasis on farming systems and less on commodity production.

Financing and Provision of Agricultural R&D

A Brief History of Agricultural Research in Indonesia

Agricultural research in Indonesia dates back to the establishment of tropical botanical gardens by Dutch colonial authorities in the early 1800s. The purposes of these gardens were to collect and study tropical plant species and introduce new export commodities to the colonies. The most prominent was the botanical garden in Bogor, West Java, established in 1817. During the 19th century, the garden accommodated a large number of specialists and made considerable contributions to fundamental studies in tropical botany, but scientists gave scant attention to the practical problems of farming (Oudejans 1999).

Applied agricultural research was stimulated by plantation owners who demanded solutions to immediate crop management and disease problems. Plantation growers, producing mainly for export, could profit from an expansion of supply and, through their associations, had the means to fund commodity-oriented research. Sugarcane planters were among the first to establish a research station, in East Java in 1887, followed by planters of coffee and cacao in 1901, tea in 1902, tobacco in 1907, and rubber in 1916. Most of these experiment stations remained relatively small, usually with fewer than 10 senior scientists. An exception was the sugar research station, which, by the 1920s, had a staff of 35 Europeans and more than 200 Indonesians (Oudejans 1999). Sugar scientists made significant technical advances, such as discovering a method for sexually crossing sugarcane that allowed breeders to develop disease-resistant varieties. These advances led to dramatic increases in sugar yield in the early years of the 20th century (Pray 1991).

Government-supported agricultural research was given a firmer footing with the establishment of a Department of Agriculture in 1905 under the leadership of Melchior Treub. Treub was a highly regarded Dutch scientist who sought to organize the new department along the lines of the U.S. Department of Agriculture, which at that time placed a heavy emphasis on research. The new department was mainly concerned with plantation crops, although an experiment station for rice and secondary food crops was established near Bogor in 1907. The commitment to food-crop research was insufficient to boost crop yields significantly, and in the 1920s and 1930s rice production lagged behind population growth, forcing Indonesia to import food staples.

Agricultural research in Indonesia was severely disrupted by World War II (1942–45), the War of Independence (1945–49), and a steadily deteriorating economy during the 1950s and early 1960s. Many foreign-owned plantations were nationalized during this period. A subsequent sharp decline in plantation production curtailed support for the plantation-supported experiment stations. The decrease in numbers of scientific and technical personnel engaged in agricultural research was not reversed until the late 1960s.

The New Order government of President Suharto, which came to power in 1965–66, set improved macroeconomic policies and established food self-sufficiency as a national priority. Funding for agricultural research was gradually increased. To improve the coordination of agricultural research, a new Agency for Agricultural Research and Development (AARD) was established within the Ministry of Agriculture in 1974. AARD was given overall responsibility for food, forestry, and fisheries research. In 1979, the Indonesian Planters Association for Research and Development (IPARD), a consortium of state-owned and private estates that supports research on estate crops, was brought under AARD's oversight. In 1983, forestry research was spun off from AARD into the newly established Ministry of Forestry, and in 2001 fisheries research was transferred from AARD to the new Ministry of Marine Affairs and Fisheries. AARD continues to have responsibility for crop and livestock research, agricultural economics research, agricultural resources research, and, through IPARD, estate-crops research.

Overview of the Institutional Structure of Agricultural Research

In Indonesia, the central government is the primary source of funds for agricultural research (Fuglie 1999). The international donor community has played a major role in supporting agricultural research in Indonesia, especially during the 1980s and early 1990s, when Indonesia's capacity in agricultural research was greatly expanded (Pardey, Eveleens, and Abdurachman 2000). Most government expenditures for agricultural research are directed toward commodities important to smallholders. Research institutes for estate and export commodities are largely funded through contributions by large growers. In-house research by private companies in Indonesia is growing but remains limited (Pray and Fuglie 2002).

The principal role of universities in agricultural research has been to train the scientific and technical personnel employed in government research institutes and the private sector. University scientists also engage in research activities when special project funding can be obtained. Funding for university research may come from AARD, the Ministry of Research and Technology, international donors, the private sector, or other sources.

International agricultural research centers play an important role in Indonesia's agricultural research system. Indonesia hosts the headquarters of the Center for International Forestry Research (CIFOR) and the Southeast Asia regional offices of the World Agroforestry Centre (formerly ICRAF) and the International Potato Center (CIP). The United Nations Centre for Alleviation of Poverty through Secondary Crops' Development in Asia and the Pacific (CAPSA), and the ASEAN-funded Southeast Asia Regional Center for Tropical Biology (BIOTROP) are also located in Indonesia. AARD has cooperative research arrangements with several other international agricultural research centers—including the Asian Vegetable Research and Development Center (AVRDC), the International Maize and Wheat Improvement Center (CIMMYT), the International Livestock Research Institute (ILRI), and International Rice Research Institute (IRRI)—and agricultural research institutes in Japan, Europe, North America, and Australia.

In the 1990s, AARD research institutes and agricultural universities began to explore new ways of self-financing at least part of the costs of agricultural research. Although government policy so far does not allow government agencies to retain funds raised through product sales, AARD established a semi-autonomous foundation in 1999, the Intellectual Property and Technology Transfer Management Office (IPTTMO), to help commercialize AARD innovations. This office has responsibility for patenting and licensing AARD innovations to private firms. IPTTMO has the legal authority to retain earnings from technology licensing. Between 1998 and 2001, IPTTMO had obtained 36 patents on AARD inventions (AARD 2003), mostly for machinery innovations, animal vaccines, and feed additives.

Intellectual property rights (IPR) for inventions and creative works are relatively new to Indonesia and remain poorly enforced. A national patent law was enacted in 1991 and amended in 1997 and 2001 to bring it into compliance with the World Trade Organization's agreement on Trade-Related Aspects of Intellectual Property (TRIPs). In 1997, Indonesia signed the international Patent Cooperation Treaty. IPR for agricultural innovations were strengthened by the 1997 amendments to the patent law, which eliminated a provision barring plant and animal patents, and by the passage of plant breeders' rights legislation in 2001.

The principal funders and performers of agricultural research in Indonesia are shown in Figure 4.1. We estimate that total spending for agricultural research in

Figure 4.1   Indonesia: Funding channels for agricultural research, 1998–99

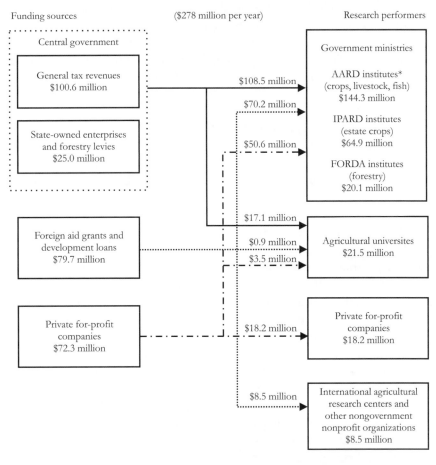

Funding sources   ($278 million per year)   Research performers

Central government

General tax revenues
$100.6 million

$108.5 million

$70.2 million

Government ministries

AARD institutes*
(crops, livestock, fish)
$144.3 million

IPARD institutes
(estate crops)
$64.9 million

State-owned enterprises
and forestry levies
$25.0 million

$50.6 million

FORDA institutes
(forestry)
$20.1 million

$17.1 million

Foreign aid grants and
development loans
$79.7 million

$0.9 million

$3.5 million

Agricultural universites
$21.5 million

Private for-profit
companies
$72.3 million

$18.2 million

Private for-profit
companies
$18.2 million

$8.5 million

International agricultural
research centers and
other nongovernment
nonprofit organizations
$8.5 million

Sources: Government finance and expenditures from AARD 2000; FORDA 1997; R. Sumitro, personal communication 2001. University expenditures based on IPB 2000. Private expenditures from Pray and Fuglie 2002.
Notes: Figures are in 1999 international dollars and are estimates only.
*In 2001, fisheries research moved from AARD to the Ministry of Marine Affairs and Fisheries.

Indonesia in 1998–99 was about $278 million in 1999 international dollars. The central government provided about $126 million from tax revenues, contributions of state-owned estates for estate-crop research, and forest concession levies. Foreign assistance (especially in the form of loans from the World Bank and the Asian Development Bank) provided another $80 million. Private companies conducted about $18 million of their own research and purchased about $50 million of planting materials and other technology products from estate-crop research institutes. These earnings are used to support research on estate crops. Government institutes were the largest research performers, conducting $229 million worth of research. Research at agricultural universities is estimated to be $21.5 million. International agricultural research centers performed at least $8.5 million worth of research in Indonesia.

Organizational Changes in Public Agricultural Research

As described above, public agricultural research in Indonesia has undergone several reorganizations since the establishment of AARD in 1974. These reorganizations reflect the growing capacity and widening agenda in agricultural research. Figure 4.2 shows the organization of agricultural research within government ministries as of 2001. More than 70 percent of agricultural scientists were housed in AARD, with the rest distributed among IPARD, FORDA, and the fisheries institutes.

AARD underwent a major internal reorganization in 1995 to decentralize its agricultural research efforts. Some regional substations of the Central Food Crop Research Center (CRIFC) were upgraded and given mandates to lead research on specific commodities. In addition, technology assessment centers were established in each province to link research, extension, and on-farm testing of new technologies. These changes reflected the steadily growing research capacity of the regional substations, increased emphasis on other commodities once rice self-sufficiency was approached in the mid-1980s, and concern that linkages between research and extension were inadequate to move technology into the hands of small farmers quickly. These provincial-level assessment institutes for agricultural technology may eventually be transferred to provincial government control as part of the trend toward decentralization of Indonesian government services.

Research linkages between AARD and both the universities and the private sector have recently been strengthened with the support of loans from the World Bank and the Asian Development Bank (ADB). The ARMP-II (World Bank) and PAATP (ADB) projects set aside special funds for collaborative research projects between AARD scientists and universities, international centers, and private companies. Foreign and private partners are required to provide matching funds. Through these projects, AARD raised 684 million rupiah and IPARD 845 million rupiah in matching contributions from private companies in 2001 (AARD 2001).

Since the 1980s the government of Indonesia has made a concerted effort to expand national capacity in biotechnology research. In 1988, the government designated three institutions as "centers of excellence" for biotechnology research: the University of Indonesia in Jakarta for medical applications, the Agency for the

Figure 4.2   Indonesia: Organization of agricultural research within government ministries, 2001

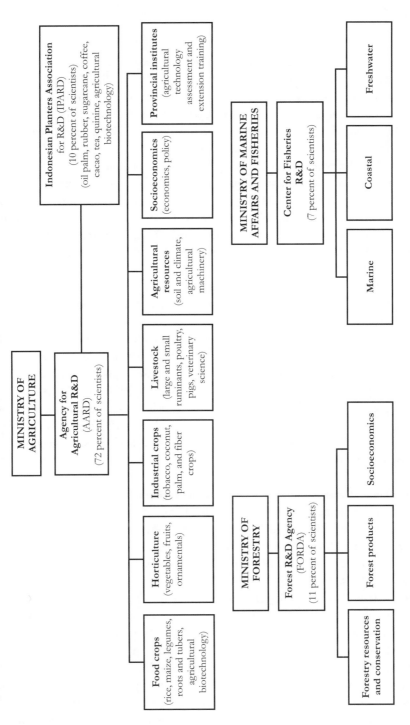

Source: Compiled by authors.

Assessment and Application of Technology (BPPT) for industrial applications, and AARD for agricultural applications. In 1993, the Center for Research and Development of Biotechnology at the Indonesian Institute of Sciences (LIPI) was assigned as a second center of excellence for agricultural biotechnology (Moeljopawiro 1999). Agricultural biotechnology research within AARD is concentrated at the Center for Agricultural Biotechnology and Genetic Resources in Bogor.[4]

AARD has relied heavily on foreign-funded special projects to develop its agricultural biotechnology research capacity, such as the Rockefeller Foundation's Rice Biotechnology Network, led by IRRI; the USAID-funded project on Agricultural Biotechnology for Sustainable Productivity, led by Michigan State University; and World Bank loan funds (Fagi and Herman 1998). Falconi (1999) reported that in 1997 AARD spent US$6.0 million (18.7 million in international dollars) on agricultural biotechnology research. Falconi estimated that about 85 percent of agricultural biotechnology research was done by government research institutes, 11 percent at universities, and 4 percent in the private sector. Food crops received the greatest share of these resources.

Several applications of biotechnology to agriculture have been under development, including cell and tissue culture for plant propagation, marker-selected breeding, the use of monoclonal antibodies for disease diagnosis, and the development of genetically modified crops (Moeljopawiro 1999). In 1997, the Ministry of Agriculture issued biosafety regulations for field-testing genetically modified organisms. In 2001, several hundred hectares of a *Bacillus thuringiensis* cotton variety developed by Monsanto were grown in Indonesia, the first genetically modified organism approved for commercial use in the country.

Funding and Staffing of Public Agricultural Research

Over the past three decades, Indonesia has significantly boosted its capacity in agricultural research. When AARD was formed in 1974, only seven of its agricultural scientists held Ph.D. degrees. By 2003, the education status of agricultural scientists employed at AARD, IPARD, and fisheries had increased to 355 Ph.D.s, 1,095 M.Sc.'s, and 2,187 with bachelor's degrees, not including research staff for forestry (Table 4.8). Research expenditures also increased in real terms, from around $100 million in 1974 to $270 million in 2003 (constant international dollars), although funding per scientist declined. The sharp increase in the number of AARD scientists between 1994 and 1995, especially at the B.Sc. level, reflects an internal reorganization that amalgamated certain agricultural extension and research functions when provincial assessment institutes for agricultural technology were formed. But, despite this rapid growth, expenditures for agricultural research in Indonesia as a percentage of agricultural GDP and as a percentage of total government expenditure still ranked near the bottom of those for developing countries in Asia (Pardey, Roseboom, and Fan 1998). Furthermore, the economic and political crises of the late 1990s took their toll on agricultural research, with real expenditures falling from $283 million in 1997 to $202 million in 2000. Research expenditures began to recover after 2000 and were nearly back to precrisis levels by 2003.

Setting Priorities for Agricultural Research

The selection of agricultural research projects for the allocation of development funds at AARD institutes involves a series of screening steps that start with the individual scientist and move up the AARD hierarchy to the AARD Secretariat. For example, a proposal on rice breeding would first be cleared by the Rice Research Institute at Sukamandi, West Java, then forwarded to the Central Research Institute for Food Crops in Bogor and finally to the AARD Secretariat in Jakarta. Evaluations at each step are mostly internal, although since 1999 AARD has also used external reviewers from universities and other government science institutes. The principal criterion used by AARD is quality of research.

Proposals approved by the AARD Secretariat are forwarded to the National Planning Agency (BAPPENAS), where they are evaluated for their contribution to economic development goals and their potential economic value. However, formal benefit–cost analysis is generally not used. Valuation is based largely on the importance of the commodity to Indonesia's agriculture. Consideration is given to economic value, food security, poverty, and the geographic focus of the research.

Agricultural research in Indonesia has received substantial financial support through loan projects from the World Bank and Asian Development Bank. These loans typically require the government to provide matching funds from current revenues. The Ministry of Finance has a role in evaluating and approving all government loan projects. In addition, the Ministry of Finance evaluates research project budgets against standard cost guidelines for land, labor, travel, materials, and so on.

Since the national elections in 1999, the Indonesian House of Representatives (DPR) has become active in establishing government policies and budget priorities. Cabinet ministers and directors of government agencies must increasingly provide justification for their budgets and programs to legislators. This trend has added a new dynamic in mobilizing domestic support for agricultural research.

Sources of Funds for Agricultural Research

Financial support for public research in Indonesia comes from a number of sources, including the central government budget, special assessments on commodity groups, foreign assistance, and funds raised by the research stations themselves through product sales, technology licenses, and contract research.

Table 4.8 Indonesia: Agricultural research funding and staffing, 1974–2003

| | Agricultural research expenditures | | | Number of agricultural scientists (SY) | | | | Expenditure per scientist | |
| | Million current rupiahs | Million 1999 rupiahs | Million 1999 international dollars | Ph.D. | M.Sc. | B.Sc. | Total | Million 1999 rupiahs per SY | Constant 1999 international dollars per SY |
Year									
1974	8,417	197,061	104.13	NA	NA	NA	NA	NA	NA
1975	10,516	221,430	117.01	11	33	294	338	655.118	346,182
1976	16,199	295,508	156.15	25	34	383	442	668.571	353,291
1977	17,954	289,135	152.79	28	39	500	567	509.939	269,465
1978	21,030	309,475	163.54	29	40	513	582	531.745	280,988
1979	23,005	253,383	133.89	35	51	632	718	352.902	186,483
1980	36,269	304,962	161.15	46	143	704	893	341.502	180,459
1981	43,545	331,530	175.19	48	151	714	913	363.121	191,883
1982	48,188	345,917	182.79	55	172	843	1,070	323.287	170,833
1983	66,766	419,493	221.67	68	249	934	1,251	335.326	177,195
1984	75,539	439,259	232.12	92	271	1,040	1,403	313.085	165,443
1985	77,656	433,014	228.82	115	311	1,074	1,500	288.676	152,544
1986	91,397	510,129	269.57	143	342	1,486	1,971	258.817	136,766
1987	99,471	480,945	254.14	157	432	1,254	1,843	260.958	137,897
1988	96,020	411,777	217.59	176	475	1,420	2,071	198.878	105,092
1989	88,861	346,455	183.08	193	505	1,633	2,330	148.693	78,573
1990	109,927	397,859	210.24	242	645	1,543	2,430	163.728	86,518
1991	121,079	402,675	212.78	241	651	1,549	2,441	164.963	87,171
1992	141,415	446,361	235.87	251	678	1,677	2,606	171.282	90,510
1993	138,971	402,872	212.89	271	719	1,727	2,717	148.278	78,354
1994	172,061	462,809	244.56	281	761	1,741	2,783	166.299	87,877
1995	188,632	462,503	244.40	305	823	2,184	3,312	139.645	73,792

1996	217,261	489,371	258.60	320	821	2,163	3,304	148.115	78,268
1997	268,238	536,722	283.62	320	820	2,164	3,304	162.446	85,841
1998	393,385	449,092	237.31	332	816	2,246	3,393	132.359	69,942
1999	387,072	387,072	204.54	341	813	2,327	3,481	111.196	58,759
2000	418,922	382,134	201.93	346	849	2,489	3,684	103.728	54,813
2001	484,865	399,253	210.98	348	908	2,426	3,682	108.434	57,299
2002	539,394	414,466	219.01	347	953	2,321	3,620	114.493	60,501
2003	708,028	510,639	269.84	355	1,095	2,187	3,637	140.401	74,192

Sources: Research expenditures for AARD institutes: 1974–83 from Pardey, Eveleens, and Abdurachman 2000 (Table Appendix 2); 1984–85 from AARD 1991; 1986–92 from AARD 1992b; 1993 from AARD 1994; 1994–95 from AARD 1997; 1996–98 from AARD 1999b; 1999–2003 from AARD 2003. Research expenditures for IPARD institutes: 1974–83 from Pardey, Eveleens, and Abdurachman 2000 (Table Appendix 2); 1984–85 government contribution from Pardey, Eveleens, and Abdurachman 2000, and member contribution from AARD 1990; 1986–88 from AARD 1992b; 1989–93 from R. Sumitro, personal communication 2001; 1994–2003 from IFPRI 2004. A major source of funds for IPARD institutes is derived from product sales (around 75 percent in 1998), but these data are only available from 1989 onward. Revenue from product sales was estimated for 1974–88 using a constant revenue-per-scientist ratio (1989–2000 average in constant 1999 rupiah). Research staff for AARD institutes: 1975–86 from Pardey, Eveleens, and Abdurachman 2000 (Table Appendix 6); 1987 from AARD 1987b; 1988 from AARD 1989; 1989 from AARD 1990; 1991 from AARD 1991; 1992 from AARD 1992b; 1993 from AARD 1993; 1994 from AARD 1994; 1995 from AARD 1995; 1996 from AARD 1996; 1997 from AARD 1997. Data for 1998 are an estimated average of data for 1997 and 1999; 1999 is from AARD 1999b; 2000 from AARD 2000; 2001 from AARD 2001; 2002 from AARD 2002; 2003 from AARD 2003. Research staff for IPARD institutes: 1975–93 from Evenson et al. 1994 (Table A1.5); 1994–2003 from IFPRI 2004.

Notes: Research expenditures and staff are for AARD and IPARD (estate crops) institutes. AARD included forestry research until 1982. During 1999 and 2000, industrial crop-research institutes were temporarily transferred to the Ministry of Forestry, and their expenditures and staff were not reported in AARD publications (they were transferred back to AARD in 2001). After 2000, fisheries research was transferred from AARD to the newly formed Ministry of Fisheries and Marine Resources. To keep coverage consistent, the numbers in this table have been adjusted to include the industrial crop institutes during 1999 and 2000 and fisheries research for the years 2001 through 2003. The 1974–99 fiscal years are from April to March; 2000 fiscal year is from April–December only. 2001–3 fiscal years are from January to December. SY indicates science years. Rupiahs were converted to international dollar denominated currency units using purchasing power parity from World Bank 2005; the GDP price deflator is from International Monetary Fund 2001. NA indicates that data are not available.

In times of financial austerity, the government's development budgets may be sharply reduced, while routine budgets remain largely unaffected. Development budgets for agricultural research have been relatively unstable: between 1986–90 and 1998–2000 the agricultural research development budget was cut by more than 60 percent in real terms from the years immediately preceding (Table 4.9). Foreign loans and grants played a major role in stabilizing research funds during these periods. In the late 1980s, the U.S. government provided significant grant assistance for AARD. In the late 1990s and early 2000s, the World Bank and the Asian Development Bank provided large loans for agricultural research. The loan programs have been particularly crucial for supporting the strengthening of the provincial assessment institutes for agricultural technology.

The main sources of funds for agricultural research differ significantly among commodities. Government revenues supplemented with foreign loans and grants make up the bulk of AARD's budget for crops and livestock. For forestry research, government revenues provide about one-third of the annual budget; most of the remainder comes from the forestry sector through a special assessment on forest concessions.

Research on estate crops is mainly financed by the plantation sector itself. IPARD's semi-autonomous status allows estate-crop research institutes to keep revenues from product sales. Further, members of IPARD contribute funds for research on estate crops.[5] These two sources fund about 95 percent of plantation research in Indonesia. Government contributions account for only about 5 percent. In part because of the different mechanisms for financing agricultural research and the special status of IPARD,[6] scientists working at the plantation-crop research institutes are significantly better funded than researchers at AARD. In 1996, research expenditures per scientist at IPARD institutes were about four times higher than at AARD institutes.

Research at universities is funded mainly from government sources, including competitive grant programs. In 1998–99, Bogor Agricultural University (IPB) raised over 10 billion rupiah to support research projects. About 80 percent of this was from government research funds, 16 percent from the private sector, and the remainder from foreign sources (IPB 2000).[7]

A small but growing share of agricultural research in Indonesia is conducted by private companies (Table 4.10). Such research is estimated to have increased from $6.6 million to $18.2 million between 1985 and 1996 (in constant 1999 international dollars). Privately owned rubber and oil palm plantations conduct some in-house research outside the IPARD system; they spent about $6 million for research in 1996. Private seed companies began breeding activities in Indonesia in the late

Table 4.9   Indonesia: Sources of funding for agricultural research at AARD and IPARD, 1974–2003
(million 1999 international dollars)

| Year | Government of Indonesia | | Estates | Foreign | Total |
	Routine	Development			
1974	11.0	47.5	25.3	20.4	104.2
1975	15.2	54.6	27.5	19.7	117.0
1976	15.8	78.4	27.8	34.2	156.2
1977	18.6	62.0	27.4	44.7	152.7
1978	21.3	73.7	28.7	39.8	163.5
1979	17.2	57.1	26.3	33.3	133.9
1980	20.0	66.1	30.5	44.5	161.1
1981	24.1	67.5	33.9	49.8	175.3
1982	24.1	72.5	34.8	51.3	182.7
1983	23.7	57.9	38.9	101.2	221.7
1984	23.3	58.5	44.3	106.0	232.1
1985	27.9	66.2	62.0	72.7	228.8
1986	33.8	33.0	72.3	130.5	269.6
1987	29.0	5.4	62.1	157.7	254.2
1988	29.0	8.1	60.3	120.2	217.6
1989	29.1	15.0	68.4	70.7	183.2
1990	31.7	17.8	89.9	70.9	210.3
1991	34.8	45.4	80.6	52.0	212.8
1992	40.2	52.8	83.1	59.8	235.9
1993	42.5	58.8	76.6	35.0	212.9
1994	57.3	70.4	74.2	42.6	244.6
1995	65.3	76.5	84.2	18.4	244.5
1996	68.2	77.7	73.9	38.8	258.6
1997	71.0	77.4	89.8	45.4	283.6
1998	41.1	27.2	67.9	101.0	237.2
1999	47.6	36.1	50.6	70.2	204.5
2000	46.1	21.4	47.9	86.5	201.9
2001	56.1	34.6	42.5	77.7	210.9
2002	57.5	46.9	47.7	67.0	219.0
2003	62.4	64.5	54.0	89.0	269.9

Sources: Sources of funds for AARD institutes: 1974–83 from Pardey, Eveleens, and Abdurachman 2000 (Table Appendix 2); 1984–85 from AARD 1991; 1986–92 from AARD 1992b; 1993 from AARD 1994; 1994–95 from AARD 1997; 1996–98 from AARD 1999b; 1999–2003 from AARD 2003. AARD funding amounts have been adjusted to include industrial crop institutes during 1998–99 and fisheries institutes during 2001–3, years for which funding for these institutes is not recorded in AARD publications. Sources of funds for IPARD institutes: 1974–83 from Pardey, Eveleens, and Abdurachman 2000 (Table Appendix 2); 1984–85 government contribution from Pardey, Eveleens, and Abdurachman 2000 and member contribution from AARD 1990; 1986–88 from AARD 1992b; 1989–93 from R. Sumitro, personal communication 2001; 1994–2003 from IFPRI 2004. A major source of funds for IPARD institutes is product sales (around 75 percent in 1998), but these data are only available from 1989 onward. Revenue from product sales was estimated for 1974–88 using a constant revenue-per-scientist ratio (1989–2000 average in constant 1999 rupiahs).
Note: Rupiahs were converted to international dollar denominations using purchasing power parity (PPP) indexes from World Bank 2005; the GDP price deflator is from International Monetary Fund 2001.

Table 4.10 Indonesia: Private agricultural research, 1985 and 1996

Research focus	Expenditure (million 1999 international dollars)		Number of companies doing research	
	1985	1996	1985	1996
Crop breeding	0.0	2.1	0	6
Crop protection	2.6	7.2	1	6
Plantations	2.0	6.0	3	4
Animals	2.0	3.0	3	3
All	6.6	18.2	7	19
Percentage of all agricultural research	3.125	7.003		
Percentage of agricultural GDP	0.010	0.018		

Source: Pray and Fuglie 2002.

Note: Rupiahs were converted to international dollar denominations using purchasing power parity (PPP) indexes from World Bank 2005.

1980s, mainly in hybrid corn and vegetables, but annual research expenditures were only $2.1 million by the mid-1990s. Chemical companies conduct crop-protection research for screening and registering new pesticides. At least one multinational chemical company operated a research station in Indonesia for screening new chemical compounds under tropical conditions. Research on animal production was conducted mainly by large integrated poultry producers. As a share of total agricultural research conducted in Indonesia, private research increased from 3.1 percent to 7.0 percent between 1985 and 1996. Thus, private research, while still relatively small-scale, grew more rapidly than public research. Private research also grew relative to the size of the Indonesian agricultural sector.

Allocation of Agricultural Research Funds

Detailed information on the allocation of scientific resources for agriculture in Indonesia is presented in Table 4.11. Commodity institutes generally have about twice as many M.Sc.s as Ph.D. holders. However, the institutes that focus on biotechnology (one for food crops and one for estate crops) employ more Ph.D.s The provincial assessment institutes for agricultural technology (AIATs) have a relatively large number of staff with only bachelor's degrees, many of whom work in extension training. Most of the growth in AARD research staff since 1995 has occurred in the AIATs.

We used the allocation of scientists among commodity-oriented institutes to develop some parity ratios for research resource allocation in Indonesia. We define the parity ratio as the number of scientist years (SY) per billion international dollars of value-added production for a commodity group. Parity ratios provide a rough first approximation for assessing the allocation of research resources among

Table 4.11 Indonesia: Number of agricultural researchers by institution, 1997

Institution	Number of scientists per institution			
	Ph.D.	M.Sc.	B.Sc.	Total
AARD centers and institutes				
Food Crops Research Center	8	13	22	43
Biotechnology	34	22	71	127
Rice	14	24	55	93
Legumes and root crops	7	37	47	91
Corn and cereals	9	32	62	103
Swamp crops	6	24	44	74
Total food crops research	78	152	305	535
Horticultural Research Center	3	4	14	21
Vegetables	9	16	37	62
Fruits	4	9	43	56
Ornamentals	8	18	34	60
Total horticultural research	24	47	125	196
Animal Research Center	1	3	9	13
Animal production	40	40	56	136
Veterinary science	10	26	28	64
Total animal research	51	69	93	213
Fisheries Research Center	4	5	13	22
Saltwater fish	14	27	55	96
Freshwater fish	5	27	57	89
Coastal water fish	3	20	60	83
Total fisheries research	26	79	185	290
Industrial Crops Research Center	5	10	28	43
Medicinal plants	13	32	77	122
Tobacco and fiber crops	6	20	62	88
Coconut and palms	2	17	26	45
Total industrial crops research	26	82	208	316
Agricultural machinery	1	7	36	44
Soil and climate	14	50	95	159
Agricultural socioeconomics	20	45	57	122
Assessment Institutes for Agricultural Technology (AIAT)	27	167	793	987
AARD Secretariat and planning	9	29	66	104
AARD library and information	0	11	31	42
Total AARD institutes	276	738	1,994	3,008
IPARD institutes (plantation crops)				
Oil palm	11	31	46	88
Rubber	17	41	57	115
Sugar	16	29	67	112
Coffee and cacao	8	17	17	42
Tea and quinine	4	15	21	40
Biotechnology and agribusiness	10	8	14	32
Total estate crops (IPARD)	66	141	222	429
Forestry institutes (FORDA)	30	117	339	486
Total agriculture	372	996	2,555	3,923

Sources: Scientists at AARD institutes from AARD 1997. IPARD scientists from R. Sumitro, personal communication 2001. Forestry scientists from FORDA 1997.

Note: Fisheries research was transferred from AARD to the Ministry of Marine Affairs and Fisheries in 2001.

Table 4.12 Indonesia: Parity ratios for agricultural research by commodity group, 1997

Commodity group	Value-added (billion dollars per year)	Number of scientists (SY) in 1997				Parity ratio (SY per billion dollars)
		Ph.D.	M.Sc.	B.Sc.	Total SY	
Nonfood crops	17.5	88	221	396	705	40.4
Forestry	12.8	30	117	339	486	38.0
Fisheries	13.7	26	79	185	290	21.2
Livestock	13.7	51	69	93	213	15.6
Food crops	38.1	78	152	305	535	14.0
Horticulture	18.8	24	47	125	196	10.4
Total	126.0	297	685	1,443	2,425	19.2

Sources: Value-added for commodity crops is from Warr and Azis 1997. Scientists at AARD and IPARD institutes from AARD 1997.
Notes: Value-added is averaged over 1989–93 in 1999 international dollars. SY indicates scientist years.

commodities. It should be kept in mind that equal parity among commodities may not be economically or socially optimal (Ruttan 1982).

For all agriculture research, there was an average of 19 SY per billion dollars in value-added in the agricultural sector. The parity ratio for research on nonfood crops (estate and industrial crops) was double the average, at 40 SY per billion dollars in value added. Research on food crops, livestock, and horticulture received the least attention, with only 10–15 SY per billion dollars in value added. Also, funding per scientist at IPARD institutes (estate crops) is substantially higher than funding per scientist at AARD institutes, further widening the gap in parity among commodity groups. The disparity in parity ratios between research on estate crops versus other crop and livestock commodities reflects both the longer history of estate-crop research in Indonesia and the ability of these institutes to finance research through commodity sales and producer contributions.

Accountability and Impact of Agricultural Research

The investment in agricultural R&D has brought significant benefits to the Indonesian economy. One indicator of its effectiveness is the release and dissemination of new crop varieties. Between 1969 and 2003, at least 668 new crop varieties were released in Indonesia (Table 4.13). About one-quarter of the new releases were high-yielding rice varieties. Improved rice varieties had been disseminated to nearly two-thirds of rice-growing areas by 1991 (mostly to wetland rice areas). New varieties of soybean and maize were also widely disseminated in the 1980s. Another indicator of the benefits from research is the increased rate of growth in total factor productivity in crop and livestock agriculture during the 1970s and 1980s (Fuglie 2004).

Measurement of the economic value of research outcomes has so far not entered into the formal evaluation of agricultural research in Indonesia. Only a few studies have been carried out on the economic impact of agricultural research. Salmon (1991) estimated that rice research expenditures between 1965 and 1977 achieved an annual internal rate of return of 151 percent. Evenson et al. (1997) estimated rates of return to research for eight food crops (1968–92), six vegetable crops (1982–92), and six fruit crops (1982–92). They found a significant correlation between the level of research investments and the rate of productivity growth for most of these commodities. Estimated rates of return to research exceed 100 percent for wetland rice, dryland rice, maize, soybeans, sweet potatoes, all six vegetable crops, and three out of the six fruit crops included in the study. Only research on cassava and mangoes showed no impact. The high rates of return to research reflected the very low level of research investment relative to commodity value. Thus, any positive statistical association found between research and productivity would necessarily result in a high marginal rate of return to research (Evenson et al. 1997).

One limitation of the returns-to-research studies is that they probably did not fully account for the contributions of research conducted outside the country. Indonesian agriculture has been able to benefit significantly from technologies developed elsewhere and introduced through public and private channels. Indonesia's growing capacity to conduct agricultural research has undoubtedly enhanced its ability to acquire and disseminate new technologies developed elsewhere. But in some cases introduced technologies required little government-supported research. Several of the first releases of new rice varieties, for example, were varieties developed by IRRI in the Philippines. In 1991, one major IRRI variety (IR36) occupied about one-third of the wetland rice growing area in Indonesia (AARD 1992a). Pray and Fuglie (2002) identified several areas where the private sector played a major role in transferring technologies to Indonesia, including new clones of oil palm and rubber from Malaysia, hybrid vegetable and hybrid maize varieties, and hybrid poultry and integrated poultry production systems. The private sector also played a major role in the rapid expansion of coastal shrimp farming in the early 1990s, based on technology developed in Taiwan (World Bank et al. 2002).

The return-to-research studies have been influential in strengthening financial support for agricultural research within the Indonesian bureaucracy and the foreign-aid community. In the late 1990s, the Asian Development Bank and the World Bank financed several loans to expand and strengthen Indonesian agricultural research.

Table 4.13 Indonesia: Number of crop varieties released, 1969–2003

Crop	1969–73	1974–78	1979–83	1984–88	1989–93	1994–98	1999–2003	Total	Area under improved varieties in 1991 (percent)
Food crops									
Rice	4	18	26	27	21	11	42	149	65
Maize	1	1	7	6	11	13	13	52	44
Soybeans	—	1	4	5	15	7	14	46	66
Groundnuts	—	—	5	1	9	3	5	23	
Mungbeans	—	—	5	3	3	4	2	17	
Sweet potatoes	—	2	—	2	3	3	6	16	
Cassava	—	2	—	1	3	4	2	12	
Sorghum	3	—	1	3	2	—	2	11	
Other legumes	—	—	—	1	4	5	—	10	
Wheat	—	—	—	—	2	—	—	2	
Total food crops	8	24	48	49	73	50	86	338	
Horticulture									
Potatoes	—	—	2	1	1	—	9	13	
Vegetables	—	—	—	16	—	8	28	52	
Fruits	—	—	—	22	19	37	39	117	
Ornamentals	—	—	—	—	—	—	45	45	
Total horticulture	0	0	2	39	20	45	121	227	

Nonfood crops								Total
Sugarcane	—	—	—	2	31	—	NA	33
Rubber	—	—	—	—	1	11	NA	12
Coffee	—	—	—	—	2	3	1	6
Tea	—	—	—	5	—	—	NA	5
Cacao	—	—	—	—	—	4	NA	4
Oil palm	—	—	—	—	1	—	NA	1
Coconut	—	—	1	4	3	—	—	8
Tobacco	—	—	1	1	—	—	2	4
Fiber crops	—	—	—	3	7	2	5	17
Spice and nut crops	—	—	—	4	7	—	2	13
Total nonfood crops	—	0	2	15	52	20	10	103
Total number of varieties released	8	26	54	103	145	115	217	668

Sources: Varieties released between 1969 and 1995 reported in AARD 1995; data for 1996 through 1999 from AARD 1999b; data for 2000 through 2003 from AARD 2003. Estimates of area under improved varieties from AARD 1992a for rice and soybean and CIMMYT 1994 for maize.

Note: A dash indicates no varieties released in this period. NA means data not available.

The evidence on previous rates of return to research were cited in the loan pro-posals and helped convince bank officials that agricultural research was likely to be a high-payoff investment for Indonesia.

Concluding Observations

Indonesia represents a case where agricultural R&D expanded rapidly from almost nil in the last 30 years of the 20th century, but where R&D investment still remains low relative to the size of the country's agriculture. The initial focus on increasing the production of rice in order to enhance national food security was highly successful, but this effort apparently stalled by the 1990s. A major goal of the current R&D effort is to diversify growth to other commodities and farming systems. To that end, the agricultural R&D system has greatly increased the num-ber of commodities, problem areas, and geographical locations in which it con-ducts research. However, the expansion of the scope of the system in the face of chronic underfunding has resulted in fragmentation and lack of continuity in many agricultural research endeavors.

The Indonesian agricultural research system actually has several distinct com-ponents, each with different modes of financing and operations. The largest component of the system is AARD, which is financed primarily from general gov-ernment revenues and foreign aid. Foreign assistance has been critical in counter-balancing the instability in the government development budget for agricultural research. AARD is attempting to diversify its sources of financing to include rev-enue from technology licensing and other product sales. But, given weak enforce-ment of intellectual property rights and restrictive government regulations on the use of revenues earned by public institutions, technology sales are unlikely to become a significant source of funds for AARD in the near term.

A second component of the system is IPARD, which has responsibility for estate crops. Although IPARD is nominally under AARD's wing, it functions largely autonomously and is almost entirely self-financed. IPARD has been more successful than AARD in mobilizing financial support for research, and research intensity for estate crops is considerably higher than for food crops and livestock. An important issue facing IPARD is how it addresses the needs of small producers of estate crops. The productivity of smallholders is far below that of the large estates (AARD 1992a). IPARD's willingness and ability to develop effective delivery sys-tems for small farms will have a major impact on productivity growth in estate-crop production in Indonesia.

Forestry and fisheries research, once part of AARD, now constitute separate components of the system, falling under the jurisdiction of separate ministries.

Forestry research receives about two-thirds of its funding from the forestry sector itself and appears to be relatively well funded. Since fisheries research was separated from AARD in 2001, it has remained relatively small and reliant on government revenue for most of its funding. It is too early to judge how its new status will affect its financing, policies, and impact.

The other components of the agricultural R&D system in Indonesia include the agricultural universities, the private sector, and the international agricultural research centers. Universities have significant intellectual capacity for research but rely primarily on winning competitive grants and other projects from the Ministry for Research and Technology and other government sources. Private-sector research is still relatively small-scale and focused on a few commodities such as estate crops, hybrid crops, poultry, and pesticide utilization. AARD has had relatively good linkages with international agricultural research centers, especially IRRI's rice breeding program. In the 1980s two international centers with mandates for natural resources research (CIFOR and ICRAF) established a significant presence in Indonesia. Linkages among AARD, universities, and private companies were strengthened through special funds established as part of loans projects from the World Bank and ADB. But it is too early to evaluate the effectiveness (and sustainability) of these initiatives.

The Indonesian government has made a concerted effort to build capacity in agricultural biotechnology research. Its strategy has been to concentrate this capacity in a limited number of research institutes. At the same time, its biotechnology resources have been allocated across a large number of commodities and technologies. It has also established a regulatory system for field testing and approving genetically modified organisms for commercial use. By 2001 a few hundred hectares of genetically modified cotton developed by the private sector were grown commercially in Sulawesi.

Like much of the Indonesian central government, the agricultural research system faces a major challenge in adjusting to the new political climate brought about by the political and economic crises that have engulfed the country since 1997 and led to the change of government in 1998. One consequence of the crises was that public investment in agriculture, including agricultural research, fell significantly in real terms. To maintain and enhance its viability and impact, the agricultural research system will need to increase its base of support in the national parliament and among civil society at large. AARD responded early to the need for greater decentralization of government services by establishing agricultural research and extension training centers in each province. Most of the growth in AARD staff since 1995 has been in the provincial centers. A major question facing these centers is whether provincial governments will be willing and able to assume a larger role in supporting them financially. The agricultural research system will need to find new and creative means to increase its financial base and stability.

Notes

The authors thank Edi Abdurachman, Achmad Fagi, Memed Gunawan, Jonny Holbert, Faisal Kasryno, Sukendra Mahalaya, Philip Pardey, Effendi Pasandaran, Gert-Jan Stads, Rahdi Sumitro, and two anonymous reviewers for their helpful contributions to this study.

1. This chapter follows the crop classifications of the Indonesian Ministry of Agriculture. Oil palm, rubber, sugarcane, coffee, tea, and cacao are classified as estate crops, even though smallholders play a major role in the production of these crops (and are in fact the major producers of rubber, coffee, and cacao). Other nonfood crops are classified as industrial crops: these include coconut, other palms, tobacco, spices, and fiber crops.

2. For longer-run assessments of productivity changes in Indonesian agriculture, see Booth 1988 and van der Eng 1996. Geertz 1963 provides the classic treatment of changes in indigenous agricultural production in Indonesia (especially Java) from precolonial times to the 1950s.

3. The government of Indonesia classifies its expenditures into "routine" expenditures, for salaries and capital maintenance, and "development" expenditures, for everything else.

4. AARD's first laboratory for agricultural biotechnology was established in 1989 with financial support from Japan. In 1995, AARD created the Research Institute for Food Crop Biotechnology (RIFCB) to house its growing biotechnology research capacity. In 2001, AARD's crop and livestock biotechnology research was amalgamated into the newly formed Center for Agricultural Biotechnology and Genetic Resources.

5. Estate-crop research was funded by a cess (tax) on commodity exports until the early 1980s. Now contributions are apportioned among IPARD members in proportion to their total sales. IPARD is composed of 14 state-owned plantation enterprises and 4 to 5 large private plantations (R. Sumitro, personal communication 2001). IPARD has research stations for oil palm, rubber, sugarcane, coffee, tea, and cacao.

6. For example, the salaries of scientists working at the plantation crop institutes, which are not subject to civil service rules, are substantially higher than those of civil servants of similar grade.

7. Agricultural research by Indonesian universities has not been systematically assessed or studied. For this study, we examined the profile of research expenditures for Bogor Agricultural University (IPB) for 1998–99 and simply multiplied these figures by three to obtain an estimate for agricultural research by all universities in Indonesia. IPB has by far the largest agricultural research program of universities in Indonesia. The financing of education and research activities at several national universities (including IPB) is now being significantly changed as these universities acquire autonomous status. One implication is that routine government support will decline and universities will have greater flexibility (and a greater need) to be financially self-sufficient.

References

AARD (Agency for Agricultural Research and Development). 1987–90. *Organisasi dan data kepegawaian, sarana/prasarana, serta anggaran* (Organization, staffing, facilities and budget). Jakarta: Ministry of Agriculture.

————. 1991. *Buku Saku: Organisasi, sumberdaya dan program penelitian, 1991* (Pocket book: Organization, resources and research program, 1991). Jakarta: Ministry of Agriculture.

————. 1992a. *Five years of agricultural research and development in Indonesia, 1987–1991: The accomplishment and the contributions.* Jakarta: Ministry of Agriculture.

————. 1992b. *Statistik penelitian pertanian: Organisasi, sumberdaya dan program penelitian, 1992* (Agricultural research statistics: Organization, resources and research program, 1992). Jakarta: Ministry of Agriculture.

————. 1993–97. *Pocket book: Organization, resources and research program.* Jakarta: Ministry of Agriculture.

————. 1995–97. *Statistik penelitian pertanian: Sumberdaya, program dan hasil penelitian* (Agricultural research statistics: Resources, program and research results). Jakarta: Ministry of Agriculture.

————. 1999a. *Strategic plan: Agency for agricultural research and development, 1999–2004.* Jakarta: Ministry of Agriculture.

————. 1999b. *Statistik penelitian pertanian: Sumberdaya, program dan hasil penelitian, 1999* (Agricultural research statistics: Resources, Program and research results, 1999). Jakarta: Ministry of Agriculture.

————. 2000–03. *Statistik penelitian pertanian: Sumberdaya, program dan hasil penelitian,* (Agricultural research statistics: Resources, Program and research results). Jakarta: Ministry of Agriculture.

Booth, A. 1988. *Agricultural development in Indonesia.* Sydney: Allen and Unwin.

BPS (Badan Pusat Statistik). 1961–2000. *Statistical Yearbook of Indonesia.* Jakarta.

————. 1985. *Sensus pertanian 1983: Analisa pendahuluan hasil pendaftaran rumahtangga* (Agricultural census 1983: Analysis of the preliminary results of the household survey). Jakarta.

————. 1995. *Sensus pertanian 1993: Analysis profil rumah tangga pertanian* (Agricultural census 1993: Profile analysis of agricultural households). Jakarta.

————. 2004. *Sensus pertanian 2003: Angka nasional hasil pendaftaran rumah tangga* (Agricultural census 2003: National total results of the household survey). Jakarta.

CIMMYT (International Maize and Wheat Improvement Center). 1994. *1993/94 world maize facts and trends.* Mexico City.

Dillon, H. S. 1999. Agroindustry on the road to economic recovery in Indonesia: National strategies with dynamic internal markets and changing regional trade context. Paper presented at the AAEA International and Industry Preconference, Nashville, Tennessee, August 6–7.

Erwidodo. 1999. *Effects of trade liberalization on agriculture in Indonesia: Institutional and structural aspects.* Working Paper Series 41. Bogor: United Nations Regional Co-ordination Centre for

Course Grains, Pulses, Roots and Tuber Crops in the Humid Tropics of Asia and the Pacific (CGPRT Centre).

Evenson, R. E., E. Abdurachman, B. Hutabarat, and A. C. Tubagus. 1994. Economic impacts of agricultural research in Indonesia. Economic Growth Center, Yale University, New Haven, Conn.

————. 1997. Contribution of research on food and horticultural crops in Indonesia: An economic analysis. *Ekonomi dan Keuangan Indonesia* 45 (4): 551–578.

Fagi, A. M., and M. Herman. 1998. Current status of agricultural biotechnology research in Indonesia. In *Agricultural biotechnology in international development,* ed. C. L. Ives and B. M. Bedford. Wallingford, U.K.: CAB International.

Falconi, C. A. 1999. *Agricultural biotechnology research capacity in four developing countries.* ISNAR Briefing Paper 42. The Hague: International Service for National Agricultural Research.

FORDA (Forestry Research and Development Agency). 1997. *Laporan tahunan 1996–97* (Annual report 1996–97). Jakarta: Badan Penelitian dan Pengembangan Kehutanan (Forestry Research and Development Agency), Ministry of Forestry.

Fuglie, K. O. 1999. Investing in agricultural productivity in Indonesia. *Forum Penelitian Agro Ekonomi* 17 (2): 1–16.

————. 2004. Productivity growth in Indonesian agriculture, 1961–2000. *Bulletin of Indonesian Economic Studies* 40 (2): 209–225.

Geertz, C. 1963. *Agricultural involution: The process of ecological change in Indonesia.* Berkeley: University of California Press.

Government of Indonesia. 1974, 1979, 1984, 1989, 1995. August 15 Presidential address to the Republic of Indonesia. Jakarta.

Hill, H. 1995. Indonesia's great leap forward? Technology development and policy issues. *Bulletin of Indonesian Economic Studies* 31 (2): 83–123.

IFPRI (International Food Policy Research Institute). 2004. Agricultural science and technology indicators survey for Asia and the Pacific. IFPRI, Washington, D.C. Draft.

International Monetary Fund. 2001. *International Financial Statistics Yearbook 2001.* Washington, D.C.

IPB (Bogor Agricultural University). 2000. *Laporan tahunan IPB, tahun anggaran 1998/1999* (IPB annual report for 1998/1999). Bogor: IPB.

Jatileksono, T. 1987. *Equity and achievement in the Indonesian rice economy.* Jakarta: Gadjah Mada University Press.

————. 1996. Major policy instruments for food and agriculture in Indonesia. Paper presented at the Conference on Food and Agricultural Policy Challenges for the Asia-Pacific, Philippine Institute for Development Studies, Manila, October 1–3.

Kasryno, F., H. Nataatmadja, and B. Rachman. 1999. Agricultural development in Indonesia entering the 21st century. In *Indonesia's economic crisis: Effects on agriculture and policy responses,* ed. P. Simatupang, S. Pasaribu, S. Bahri, and R. Stringer. Adelaide, Australia: Centre for International Economic Studies, University of Adelaide.

Manning, C. 2000. Labour market adjustments to Indonesia's economic crisis: Context, trends and implications. *Bulletin of Indonesian Economic Studies* 36 (1): 105–136.

Moeljopawiro, S. 1999. Managing biotechnology in AARD: Priorities, funding and implementation. In *Managing agricultural biotechnology: Addressing research program needs and policy implications,* ed. J. I. Cohen. Wallingford, U.K.: CAB International.

Oudejans, J. H. M. 1999. *Studies on IPM policy in SE Asia.* Wageningen, the Netherlands: Wageningen Agricultural University.

Pardey, P. G., W. M. Eveleens, and E. Abdurachman. 2000. Indonesian agricultural research and extension. International Service for National Agricultural Research, The Hague.

Pardey, P. G., J. Roseboom, and S. Fan. 1998. Trends in financing Asian and Australian agricultural research. In *Financing agricultural research: A source book.* The Hague: International Service for National Agricultural Research.

Pray, C. E. 1991. The development of Asian research institutions: Underinvestment, allocation of resources, and productivity. In *Research and productivity in Asian agriculture,* ed. R. E. Evenson and C. E. Pray. Ithaca, N.Y.: Cornell University Press.

Pray, C. E., and K. O. Fuglie. 2002. *Private investment in agricultural research and international technology transfer in Asia.* Bogor: Published jointly by the International Potato Center, Rutgers University, and the Economic Research Service of the U.S. Department of Agriculture.

RISTEK (State Ministry for Research and Technology). 1996. *Direktori lembaga-lembaga penelitian Indonesia* (Directory of Indonesian research institutions). 2nd ed. Tangerang: RISTEK and National Research Council.

———. 1998. *Data statistik tenaga RISTEK Oktober 1997* (Statistics on Research and Technology Staff, October 1997). Jakarta.

Ruf, F., and Y. Cerad-Tera. 1999. The impact of the economic crisis on Indonesia's cacao sector. In *Indonesia's economic crisis: Effects on agriculture and policy responses,* ed. P. Simatupang, S. Pasaribu, S. Bahri, and R. Stringer. Adelaide, Australia: Centre for International Economic Studies, University of Adelaide.

Ruttan, V. W. 1982. *Agricultural research policy.* Minneapolis: University of Minnesota Press.

Salmon, D. C. 1991. Rice productivity and the returns to rice research in Indonesia. In *Research and productivity in Asian agriculture,* ed. R. E. Evenson and C. E. Pray. Ithaca, N.Y.: Cornell University Press.

Simatupang, P. 1999. Toward sustainable food security: The need for a new paradigm. In *Indonesia's economic crisis: Effects on agriculture and policy responses,* ed. P. Simatupang, S. Pasaribu, S. Bahri, and R. Stringer. Adelaide, Australia: Centre for International Economic Studies, University of Adelaide.

Stringer, R. 1999. The impacts of Indonesia's economic crisis on food crops and food security. In *Indonesia's economic crisis: Effects on agriculture and policy responses,* ed. P. Simatupang, S. Pasaribu, S. Bahri, and R. Stringer. Adelaide, Australia: Centre for International Economic Studies, University of Adelaide.

UNESCO (United Nations Education, Scientific and Cultural Organization). 2001. Science and technology indicators database. http://unescostat.unesco.org/statsen/statistics. Accessed November 2001.

van der Eng, P. 1996. *Agricultural growth in Indonesia: Productivity change and policy impact since 1880.* Basingstoke, U.K.: Macmillan.

Warr, P. G., and M. Azis. 1997. *Database from WAYANG: General equilibrium model of the Indonesian economy.* Canberra: Australian National University.

World Bank. 1998. Indonesia in crisis: A macroeconomic update. Washington, D.C.

———. 2001. *World development report 2000/2001.* Washington, D.C.

———. 2005. *World development indicators online.* https://publications.worldbank.org/subscriptions/WDI. Accessed July 11, 2005.

World Bank, NACA (Network of Aquaculture Centres in Asia-Pacific), WWF (World Wildlife Fund), and FAO. 2002. Shrimp farming and the environment. Synthesis report. http://www.enaca.org/shrimp. Accessed 2002.

Chapter 5

Korea: Growth, Consolidation, and Prospects for Realignment

Jung-Sup Choi, Daniel A. Sumner, and Hyunok Lee

Introduction

The Great King Sejong initiated an active agricultural research and development (R&D) policy in Korea about 570 years ago. Famous for many scholarly and scientific achievements, including the creation of the Korean phonetic alphabet, he founded a national scholarly institute, known as the "Hall of Worthies," encouraging the most talented scholars in the country to conduct a variety of research activities (Eckert et al. 1990). Sejong's focus was on efforts to improve the welfare of the common people, including the promotion of agriculture to secure an adequate food supply. One part of his agricultural R&D effort was to transfer relatively advanced agricultural techniques used in the southern provinces to the north, where farmers were still using Chinese techniques that were not well suited to Korean conditions. King Sejong sent out officials from Seoul to study advanced agricultural technology and prepared a manual, "Straight Talk on Farming," designed to help advisers and farmers suit their agricultural practices to the agronomic and climatic conditions on the peninsula. Based on survey data, the king reported that the average farming household in the province around Seoul could produce "several times" more using better farming methods. Recognizing the importance of climate to farmers, the crown prince invented a rain gauge, which ranks among the major technological achievements of the period. Every village in the country was required to report rainfall and the amount of rain absorbed into the soil (Eckert et al. 1990). Despite this impressive start, for many reasons, Korean agricultural R&D, Korean agricultural progress, and the Korean economy all languished for much of the next 500 years.

While the ancient history of Korean agricultural R&D is a fascinating and understudied topic, this chapter reviews agricultural R&D policy in South Korea over recent decades. Our working definition of agricultural research and development is conditioned by the available data. It includes efforts to improve farm and related technology and practices by systematic investigation and dissemination of information and products that embody new knowledge. These efforts include all branches of the social, physical, and biological sciences and engineering. We devote most of our attention to research but include information on the formal agricultural extension system as well. We focus on agriculture, including both crop and livestock commodities, but much of the available data include forestry and fisheries in the totals for R&D funding and expenditures. We discuss further limitations on available information below. Before characterizing the R&D system, we attempt to place this information in context by discussing South Korean agriculture and agricultural policy.

Unfortunately, we have been unable to include information about agricultural R&D in North Korea. North Korea does conduct some agricultural research, but no reliable public data are available to describe the system or the extent of the efforts. We know of no systematic study of North Korean agricultural R&D. (Analyses of aspects of the North Korean economy and agriculture include Kim, Lee, and Sumner 1998 and Noland, Robinson, and Scatasta 1997).Therefore we concentrate on South Korea, and in what follows we use the terms *Korea* and *South Korea* interchangeably.

Overview of South Korean Agriculture in Recent Decades

South Korea's rapid economic transformation over the past several decades has been called an economic miracle (Lucas 1993). Per capita income grew from less than US$300 in 1971 to almost US$10,000 in 2000 (in 2000 dollars). In recognition of this transformation, South Korea became a member of the OECD in 2000. By many measures, South Korea is no longer a less-developed country. However, economic growth in Korea has been mostly associated with expansion of the industrial and service sectors. Agriculture has also modernized, but the vulnerable conditions in agriculture, including lagging per capita incomes, have caused Korea to continue to claim developing-country status before the WTO in negotiations on agriculture. Nonetheless, the rapid growth in the rest of the economy has shaped South Korean agricultural policy and changes in agricultural production.

Table 5.1   Korea: Patterns in agriculture, 1970–2000

Year	1970	1975	1980	1985	1990	1995	2000
Farm population (thousand)	14,422	13,244	10,827	8,521	6,661	4,851	4,032
Farm share of population (percent)	44.7	37.5	28.4	20.9	15.5	10.8	8.5
Land per farm household (hectares)	0.9	0.9	1.0	1.1	1.2	1.3	1.4
Total cultivated area (thousand hectares)	3,264	3,144	2,765	2,592	2,409	2,197	2,098
Percentage of cultivated area							
Rice	36.9	38.7	44.6	47.7	51.6	48.1	51.1
Barley	22.4	22.6	12.0	9.2	6.6	4.0	3.2
Soybeans	9.0	8.7	6.8	6.0	6.3	4.8	4.1
Wheat	3.0	1.4	1.0	0.1	0.0	0.1	0.0
Corn	1.4	1.0	1.3	1.0	1.1	0.8	0.8
Vegetables	7.9	8.0	13.6	14.1	13.2	18.3	18.4
Fruits	1.8	2.4	3.6	4.2	5.5	7.9	8.2
Meat production (thousand metric tons)	165	225	424	590	775	1,059	1,189
Percentage of meat production							
Beef	22.4	31.1	21.9	20.0	12.3	14.6	18.0
Pork	50.3	44.0	56.4	58.6	65.5	60.3	60.1
Poultry	27.3	24.9	21.7	21.4	22.2	25.0	22.0
Imports as percentage of total consumption							
Rice	6.9	5.4	4.9	0.0	0.0	1.0	2.0
Barley	0.0	8.0	42.4	36.3	2.6	33.0	53.1
Soybeans	13.9	14.2	64.9	77.5	79.9	90.1	93.6
Wheat	84.6	94.3	95.2	99.6	99.95	99.7	99.9
Corn	81.1	91.7	94.1	95.9	98.1	98.9	99.1
Beef	0.0	0.0	6.9	3.9	47.5	48.6	47.2
Pork and poultry	0.0	0.0	1.8	0.9	0.5	5.6	11.9

Source: MAF, various years.

Production Changes and Commodity Distribution

To provide an overview of South Korean agriculture, Table 5.1 presents summary statistics for the past three decades at five-year intervals. These data provide a context for the discussion of agricultural R&D and allow us to better understand the degree to which agriculture has been transformed.

As recently as 1970, almost 45 percent of the population lived on farms (the U.S. farm population, by comparison, was then less than 4 percent of the population). Three decades later, only 8.5 percent of the population lives on farms. The farm population fell from about 14.4 million to about 4 million as the national population rose from about 32 million to almost 50 million. For the same period, agricultural gross national product (GNP) as a percentage of total GNP declined from 27 percent to about 5 percent. The lower share of GNP indicates persistent income differences between farm and urban households and also some degree of part-time farming.

The average farm area grew during these three decades, but relatively slowly (increasing only 50 percent over a period in which income doubled every six years), and remains small, at less than 1.5 hectares per farm household. Most agricultural land in South Korea is cultivated. Pasture is relatively unimportant. The cultivated area has declined dramatically with urbanization and a rapid reduction in grain production. Since 1970, the share of land used for barley, soybeans, wheat, and corn has declined from about 36 percent to about 8 percent. These declines are all the more dramatic when we consider that the total cultivated areas declined by one-third. The area under fruit and vegetable production grew from less than 10 percent of the total cultivated area to almost 27 percent.

Rice has long been the staple of the Korean diet, and annual per capita consumption is more than 100 kilograms per person. Rice is also the mainstay of South Korean agriculture, as it has been for centuries. Indeed, the rice share of cultivated area actually grew from about 37 percent in 1970 to about 50 percent by 1985 and has remained stable since then. Rice also generates about 50 percent of total crop revenue and about 30 percent of total agricultural GDP, and it is cultivated on about 80 percent of crop farms (MAF, various years).

Along with rapid growth in per capita incomes has come rapid development of the South Korean livestock industry. Table 5.1 shows a sevenfold increase in meat production over three decades, with a gradual increase in the share of pork in the mix of meat production.

Commodity Policy and Trade

Agricultural policies in Korea have been directed toward two main objectives: self-sufficiency in rice and higher rural incomes. The dominance of rice in Korean agriculture was maintained mainly through high import barriers that allowed domestic prices to exceed border prices by a factor of four or five. Relatively tight import controls and high tariffs also applied to many other commodities, such as beef, citrus, and other horticultural crops. The most important goal of domestic agricultural policy was farm income support, and the main instruments were commodity procurement programs, input subsidies, and (to a lesser extent) loan subsidies.

Rice issues have dominated not only trade policy in agriculture but also domestic agricultural policy. Rice continues to account for more than 90 percent of the total aggregate measure of support for South Korean agriculture as calculated for implementation of the Uruguay Round Agriculture Agreement (URAA) (USDA 1999). The major instrument of the internal rice support program has been government procurement of a portion of national rice production. Each year the congress sets a government purchase price and a procurement target. Historically, the government price has been about 20 percent above the market price. The right to sell to the government is allocated to individual farmers through a kind of quota system. Under this system, the quantity procured by the government accounted for about 20 percent of the total crop. The government uses the rice it buys for military and other government purposes, or sells it back into the market at prevailing market prices. This program has been evolving rapidly.

The ban on rice imports was lifted and other barriers were lowered in 1995 as Korea began to comply with the URAA. The minimum-access provisions of the URAA required Korea to gradually expand imports of rice from 1 percent of base-period domestic consumption in 1995 to 4 percent by 2004. The minimum-access quantities themselves have been too small to have any measurable impact on the domestic market, especially as imports have been administered to favor the importation of rice for processing (Choi and Sumner 2000).

South Korean import data in Table 5.1 reflect the tight import controls on rice, the gradual relaxation of barriers for meat, soybeans, and barley, and the openness to importation of the other grains. South Korea is a major importer of agricultural products despite high protection for rice and several other commodities.

Agricultural Productivity Growth

In keeping with the goal of achieving self-sufficiency in rice, one major undertaking included the introduction of the high-yielding but low-quality variety *Tongil*. First introduced in 1975 with an intense government campaign, by 1985 it occupied half the total rice area. However, *Tongil* rice disappeared rapidly in the early 1990s, as incomes and demand for quality increased and government rules were relaxed.

In response to high price incentives and R&D efforts (discussed in detail in the following sections), rice yields increased by about 50 percent in three decades. Per-hectare yields of milled rice rose from 3.3 tons in 1970 to 5.0 tons in 2000. The annual rate of total factor productivity growth for rice from 1993 through 1997 was between 7 and 8 percent (Kwon and Lee 2001). Yet, despite yield and other productivity growth, the cost of producing rice has remained high. Korean production costs are about five times higher than those in California, which produces a similar quality of japonica rice (Cooperative Extension Service, University of California, Davis 1998). Implicit land rental costs account for 42 percent of production costs in Korea, and labor accounts for another 24 percent (Kwon and Lee 2001). Relatively high wages compared with most other Asian rice-producing countries, and high labor-to-land ratios compared with the United States and Australia, contribute to high costs relative to other major rice-growing regions. Of course, the very high land prices reflect high domestic prices relative to nonland variable costs.

Partial productivity measures also show rapid growth for other commodities over the past 30 years. For example, crop yields have increased rapidly, and milk yield grew from 5.0 metric tons per head in 1970 to 7.9 metric tons per head in 2000. Overall, the total real value of agricultural output grew by 110 percent over the 30-year period because of both productivity growth and a shift across commodities, while both land and labor use declined substantially. Real output per unit of land increased by 260 percent, and real output per unit of labor increased by 450 percent between 1970 and 2000.

South Korean Agriculture in Transition

The URAA stimulated many changes in South Korean agriculture. For the first time, the Korean rice industry has faced international competition. This shift in policy has had ramifications throughout agriculture as farmers attempt to improve productivity and search for commodities that may be competitive with imports. Some adjustments have been aimed at improving productivity in rice farming. The Korean government initiated a series of efforts to improve institutional arrangements in areas such as farmland ownership, domestic rice subsidy programs, marketing and distribution arrangements, and cooperatives. In 1992, Korea also began a decade-long rural restructuring project that allocated $40 billion to farmers and rural areas. This infusion of public resources into agriculture was significant. However, the most important impetus for transition came from individuals' anticipation of market opening and adjustments to meet that challenge (Sumner, Lee, and Hallstrom 1999). We now turn to how R&D fits into this picture of Korean agriculture in rapid transition.

Institutional Arrangements for Agricultural R&D

The modern Korean agricultural R&D system is about 40 years old. There have been a number of changes over time, but the basic structure has remained in place. Agricultural research and development follows many of the familiar patterns of funding and performance seen in other countries. However, compared with most other OECD members, the South Korean institutions are relatively new, and the R&D situation, as with much else in South Korean agriculture, has been evolving rapidly.

Public funding for agricultural research now follows three channels:

1. The Office of the Prime Minister provides funding through research councils that support the basic staff and core expenditures of the government-supported research institutions.

2. Specific ministries, mainly the Ministry of Agriculture and Forestry (MAF), and administrations, mainly the Rural Development Administration (RDA), support their own intramural research institutions and provide project funds for government-supported institutes, universities, and private research institutions.

3. Science funds not tied directly to agriculture are provided to universities and public and private research institutions for more-basic research.

The RDA is the largest source of public funding for agricultural R&D. It was created in 1962 and is a separate, autonomous unit within MAF. MAF, together with the Ministry of Maritime Affairs and Fisheries, sets general directions for agricultural R&D, then MAF and RDA request funds for the research budget, and the Planning and Budget Agency modifies the request and coordinates the overall Korean government budget.

Government research institutions in agriculture, forestry, and fisheries include 46 national and public research institutions and 4 government-supported research institutions (Ministry of Science and Technology 2001). RDA, the largest R&D agency in the agricultural sector, operates 10 intramural research institutes. When the RDA was established in 1962, it had 12 intramural research institutes; this number reached 19 by the early 1990s but fell back to 12 with reform in 1994. The most significant consolidation in 1994 was the creation of the National Institute of Agricultural Science and Technology through the merger of 4 independent institutes (the Institute of Agricultural Science, the Agricultural Chemicals Research Institute, the Agricultural Genetic Engineering Institute, and the National Sericulture Entomology Research Institute).

South Korean data distinguish between units of the government that are under the direct supervision of a specific ministry, such as the intramural institutes under the RDA, and other publicly funded units that are collectively known as public nongovernmental enterprises. Before 1999, each institute had belonged to the corresponding ministry. Since then, government-supported research institutes have been placed under the Office of the Prime Minister rather than under individual ministries. This reform was designed to enhance the independence of the institutes, encourage joint research, and facilitate the sharing of information among institutes. Under the new system, each government-supported institution competes with external research institutions, such as universities or private research bodies, for project funds other than basic salaries and basic costs, which are provided by the government. The Korea Rural Economic Institute, the Korean Maritime Institute, the Food Research Institute, and the Korean Research Institute of Bioscience and Biotechnology all report to the Office of the Prime Minister.

Figure 5.1 Korea: Distribution of research funds from the special tax for agricultural and rural development

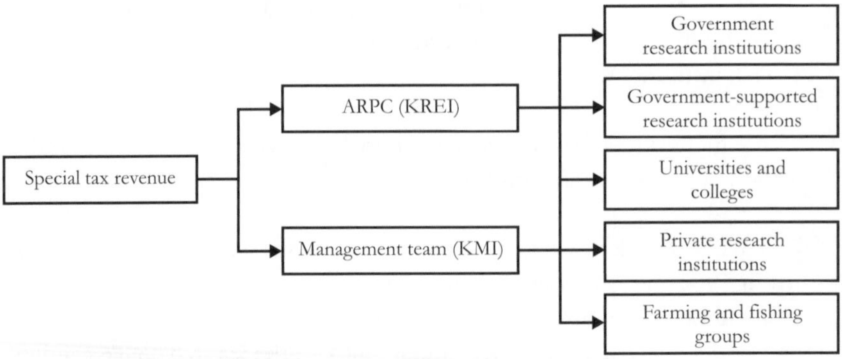

Source: Compiled by authors.

MAF provides some research funds directly to the research entities that are separate from RDA's budget. MAF's research fund is allocated competitively, and the government-supported research institutes win the largest share of these grants. Since 1994, MAF has provided additional competitive research grants drawn from the special tax for agricultural and rural development, administered by the Agricultural R&D Promotion Center (ARPC), an affiliate of the Korea Rural Economic Institute.[1] Figure 5.1 shows the flow of funds from the 1994 special tax.

The Ministry of Maritime Affairs and Fisheries now guides research policy for fisheries and maintains the Korea Maritime Institute (KMI), which also funds competitive grants. The Forestry Administration, within MAF, operates two intramural research institutes.

Rural and agricultural extension services have been provided primarily by the RDA rather than by universities or by state or local governments. The extension service was introduced in the late 1950s to promote the dissemination of agricultural production technology. RDA took over the extension role when it was established in 1962. The rate of adoption of modern agricultural practices was very low throughout the 1960s and 1970s, and extension was an important tool for increasing productivity. Because the government's focus during this period was on increasing rice self-sufficiency, the extension service concentrated on disseminating new high-yielding varieties and other high-productivity technology. The extension service still accounts for a major part of the RDA budget. Figure 5.2 illustrates the basic organization of agricultural extension in South Korea.

**Figure 5.2   Korea: Rural extension organizations—Rural Development
Administration, 2000**

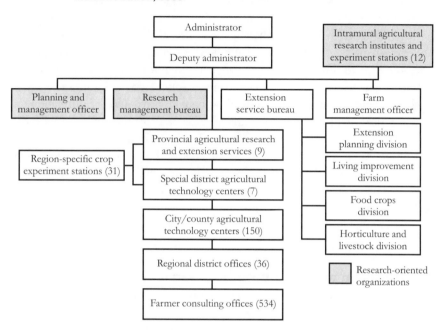

Source: Compiled by authors.
Note: Figures in parentheses indicate number of stations, centers, offices, or services.

The National Agricultural Cooperative Federation (NACF) has also exerted a significant influence on agricultural R&D. NACF operates as a major marketing cooperative, but it is also a farm input supplier, a financial institution, and an insurance company. It has been a powerful political force and has had quasi-governmental authority in implementing farm programs. NACF also operates an agricultural college and has performed extension services. However, NACF has not been as influential in extension as RDA.

The role of universities in Korean agricultural R&D resembles that of institutions in Australia and several European countries more closely than that of universities in the United States. The total number of universities conducting agricultural research is not available, but about 35 university research institutes are devoted to agriculture, forestry, or fisheries (Ministry of Science and Technology 2001). University funding for agricultural research is limited, staff teaching loads are high, and support for research must be garnered from relatively short-term grants. As is discussed below, there have been some increases recently in the competitive funds available from government sources for university research related to agriculture, but these funds remain small relative to the funding for government researchers.

Private companies are important in certain parts of the formal R&D effort, but we have relatively little information about their work; thus they are necessarily underrepresented in the discussion that follows. Overall, companies in the agriculture, forestry, and fisheries sectors operate ten formal research institutes (Ministry of Science and Technology 2001). Companies account for a significant share of the total formal outlays on agricultural R&D—about 16 percent. (For information on private agricultural R&D in other parts of Asia, see Pray and Fuglie 2001.) Individual farms and small local entrepreneurs devote much effort to innovation in agriculture. As farm size, crop mix, costs of labor, and other aspects of agriculture have changed rapidly, farmers have invested in, developed, and adopted innovations. Such innovation requires sustained investment of resources, but unfortunately such R&D on farms is difficult to measure, and we have not been able to document it thoroughly.

The Provision of Agricultural R&D Services

This section reviews evidence on budget trends and a number of other characteristics of Korean R&D providers. Because of data limitations, we focus more on government and university providers than on the private sector.

Expenditures of R&D Providers

Agricultural R&D in Korea is performed by several types of research organizations: government agencies and government-supported research institutions, public and private universities and colleges, and private companies, including cooperatives.

Table 5.2 provides shares of R&D expenditures by research provider from 1995 to 2000. Since 1995 the university and college share has grown from about 12.1 percent to almost 20.8 percent of the total, while the share of companies has fallen from 17.5 percent to 12.6 percent. Government R&D organizations and government-sponsored institutes have conducted the bulk of the research every year, ranging from 70.4 percent in 1995 to 63.7 percent in 1999 before increasing to 66.6 percent in 2000. Company data are not available prior to 1995, so it is not possible to calculate comparable shares for earlier years.

Table 5.3 contains more detail on R&D expenditures since 1978 for government and university research. Table 5.3 provides the data in Korean won; Appendix Table 5A.1 converts data to international dollars using a purchasing power parity exchange rate. The data are complete for government and government-supported research institutes for this period and provide information on university

Table 5.2   Korea: R&D expenditures on agriculture, forestry, and fisheries by type of research entity, 1995–2000 (percent)

Year	Government institutes	Universities and colleges	Companies	Total
1995	70.4	12.1	17.5	100
1998	67.4	17.3	15.3	100
1999	63.7	20.1	16.2	100
2000	66.6	20.8	12.6	100

Source: Ministry of Science and Technology and Korea Institute of S&T Evaluation and Planning 2001.

expenditures from 1978 to 1988 and from 1995 to 2000. R&D expenditures, expressed in real terms using the GDP deflator, have risen substantially. The bulk of research has always been conducted at national and public research institutes, especially the RDA. The government-supported institutes, which have more autonomy from MAF, have accounted for an important part of the research expenditures. Over the period shown in Table 5.3, the share of government research done by the national and public institutes has fluctuated, but it remained around 15 percent before declining to about 11.5 percent for the last three years in our series.

University expenditures grew from about 13.5 billion won for the 1978–79 average to about 35 billion won in 1988, while R&D expenditures in government research institutes were comparatively stagnant in real terms. (We find the huge measured drop in public university expenditures from 1978 to 1979 inexplicable and therefore use an average of the two years.) Overall, the share of research expenditures by universities doubled from about 10 percent of the (noncompany) total during the 1978–79 average to about 20 percent in 1988.

The decade from 1988 to 1997 saw very rapid overall growth in university and government research, with university expenditures remaining a relatively constant proportion. Reflecting URAA initiatives, government expenditures doubled in real terms from 1991 to 1993 and continued to grow gradually thereafter. Even the financial crisis of 1998 did not curtail research substantially.

Research Orientation
It is always difficult to classify R&D projects. Classification into "applied" versus "basic" research or "development" efforts is to some degree arbitrary. Here we report the classifications used by the institutions themselves. The research expenditures by public research institutions in agriculture, forestry, and fisheries in 2000 suggest that about half of all research is applied. The remaining half is divided almost evenly between basic and development research. Government-supported agricultural research institutions spend a higher proportion of their funds on development research than do the national and public research institutions (Ministry

Table 5.3　Korea: R&D expenditures on agriculture, forestry, and fisheries by type of research entity, 1978–2000 (billion 1999 won)

Year	Research institutes			Universities and colleges			Companies			Total
	Total	National and public	Government-supported	Total	National and public	Private	Total	Government-invested	Private	
1978	107.4	99.6	7.8	21.0	18.1	2.9	NA	NA	NA	128.4
1979	150.0	129.8	20.2	6.6	4.3	2.3	NA	NA	NA	156.6
1980	114.6	95.5	19.1	12.5	10.7	1.8	NA	NA	NA	127.1
1981	93.0	74.7	18.3	7.7	7.1	0.7	NA	NA	NA	100.7
1982	112.9	95.3	17.6	18.3	14.6	3.7	NA	NA	NA	131.2
1983	93.0	86.2	6.8	15.8	11.9	3.9	NA	NA	NA	108.8
1984	107.9	87.9	20.0	23.1	17.9	5.3	NA	NA	NA	131.0
1985	106.2	88.2	18.0	21.3	17.6	3.7	NA	NA	NA	127.5
1986	118.8	99.9	18.9	36.5	29.4	7.1	NA	NA	NA	155.3
1987	133.1	113.9	19.2	32.1	23.5	8.5	NA	NA	NA	165.2
1988	136.3	115.1	21.2	35.4	30.1	5.3	NA	NA	NA	171.7
1989	142.7	121.2	21.5	NA	NA	NA	NA	NA	NA	NA
1990	166.6	130.8	35.8	NA	NA	NA	NA	NA	NA	NA
1991	166.7	132.2	34.5	NA	NA	NA	NA	NA	NA	NA
1992	202.0	168.6	33.4	NA	NA	NA	NA	NA	NA	NA
1993	327.2	290.1	37.1	NA	NA	NA	NA	NA	NA	NA
1994	293.8	252.2	41.6	NA	NA	NA	NA	NA	NA	NA
1995	335.5	296.9	38.6	57.7	35.1	22.7	83.5	8.0	75.5	476.7
1996	346.5	299.0	47.5	86.5	44.0	42.5	NA	NA	NA	433.0
1997	372.3	321.9	50.4	83.2	45.1	38.1	97.1	8.3	88.8	552.6
1998	336.3	295.4	40.9	86.5	52.5	34.0	76.1	10.5	65.6	498.9
1999	309.9	278.4	31.5	102.8	65.9	36.9	83.1	12.5	70.7	495.8
2000	330.4	287.9	42.5	103.4	65.2	38.2	62.7	NA	NA	496.5

Source: Ministry of Science and Technology and Korea Institute of S&T Evaluation and Planning 2001.

Notes: Data were converted to 1999 won using a GDP deflator. NA indicates data not available.

of Science and Technology 2001). We have no information on how the Korean classification system compares in practice with those in other countries.

Consistent with national agricultural policy, research on rice has been the central focus of agricultural R&D in South Korea. As a result, a number of high-yielding cultivars have been developed. In 2000, 99.2 percent of all paddy land was planted to cultivars developed by RDA (Rural Development Administration 2000). Research on rice, however, declined as a share of total research in the 1990s. Research on nonrice crops, including fruits and vegetables, specialty crops, livestock, and flowers, has increased (J. Park et al. 2000).

The amount of research devoted to each commodity may also be observed from an analysis of research papers written by the RDA staff. In 1958, about 53 percent of these research papers were devoted to grains (37 percent to rice and another 16 percent to other grains). This percentage fell to about 33 percent in 1970 and then rose back to about 45 percent in 1980 and 1990 (Table 5.4). It declined to about 40 percent by 1995 and to 31 percent by 1998. Considering rice alone, the share of research papers increased from about 21 percent in 1970 to 30 percent in 1980 before falling back to about 17 percent in 1998. The continuing high publication share for nonrice grains is puzzling, given the unimportance of those crops in South Korean agriculture. It may be driven by three factors: the relevance of research on other grains to rice applications; a prevalence of researchers trained in an era when other grains were more important; and the fact that many researchers have studied in places such as the United States or Australia, where other grains are important, and thus their early publications relate to these other crops. There is considerable variability in some of the data on other crops, but two other trends stand out in Table 5.4. First, the share of publications on livestock research dropped substantially, from a high of almost 35 percent in 1970 to less than 20 percent in 1998. Second, the share of publications devoted to vegetable crop research increased from about 6 percent in 1970 to 15.5 percent in 1998.

Table 5.4   Korea: Percentage of RDA research papers by commodity group, 1970–98

Year	Rice	Grains	Specialty crops	Vegetables	Fruits	Livestock	Flowers	Forestry	Other
1970	21.1	11.5	1.9	5.8	12.0	34.6	3.8	0.0	9.3
1980	30.3	15.2	4.3	8.7	4.3	26.1	4.3	0.0	6.8
1990	26.0	20.0	7.3	7.3	4.0	22.7	5.3	2.0	5.4
1995	21.5	18.1	5.1	14.7	11.0	20.9	4.0	0.6	4.1
1998	17.0	13.7	8.2	15.5	9.5	19.5	8.6	0.3	7.7

Sources: Complied by authors from Rural Development Administration 1999 and S. Park et al. 2000.

Another indicator of the current orientation of R&D in Korea is the distribution of ARPC funds. About half of these funds are allocated to projects classified as "advanced technology," with a quarter allocated to overtly applied projects in the field or projects involving farmers; the final quarter goes to projects classified only as "national priority." The precise meanings of these categories are difficult to discern, but the general thrust is that at least half these funds are allocated to relatively basic research efforts as opposed to field studies (MAF 1999).

Agricultural R&D Personnel Qualifications and Orientation

The total number of researchers and other staff at government agricultural research institutions in South Korea has changed little since 1978. The total number of staff was about 4,546 in 1978 and grew to 5,108 by 2000. However, the proportions of staff in each job classification changed substantially. In 1978 there were 0.72 technicians and 0.87 support staff per researcher. By 1999 those ratios had fallen to 0.5 technicians and 0.33 support staff per researcher (Ministry of Science and Technology 2001).

Between 1978 and 2000, however, there were large shifts in the reported numbers in each classification. Some of these changes likely occurred as a part of institutional reorganizations. For example, the total reported staff increased from 5,597 in 1992 to 8,184 in 1993. This change is consistent with the increase in R&D expenditures for those years, shown in Table 5.3. However, personnel data show that the staff numbers declined to 6,399 in 1994. By 1996 the total number of staff had fallen by another 20 percent, with the number of researchers accounting for about half the decline. Another drop of about one-sixth of the total staff occurred in 1997, but on this occasion most of the staff cuts were in the technician category. Expenditures grew during this period; even allowing for real salary increases and additional budgets for supplies and equipment, it is difficult to understand how the staff reductions are consistent with the expenditure increases. Thus, reported staff numbers do not seem to reflect reductions in the actual amount of research effort.

Table 5.5 summarizes the share of researchers, including support staff, across research institutions for 2000. These data show that university and college researchers account for a significantly higher share of total research personnel than of total R&D expenditures (Table 5.3). This disparity reflects the part-time nature of academic research and a relative lack of research facilities.

In 1978 only about 5 percent of researchers held Ph.D.s and another 15 percent held master's degrees. By 1999, 38 percent of researchers held Ph.D.s, and another 49 percent held master's degrees (Ministry of Science and Technology 2001).

Table 5.5   Korea: Agricultural researchers by type of research entity, 2000

Type of research entity	Number of researchers	Percentage of total researchers
Government research institutes	5,108	53.3
Universities and colleges	3,255	34.0
Companies	1,216	12.7
Total	9,579	100.0

Source: Ministry of Science and Technology and Korea Institute of S&T Evaluation and Planning 2001.

Data on numbers, broad topics, and qualifications of agricultural researchers in colleges and universities and in companies are provided in Table 5.6. Universities and colleges had 3,255 staff members who devoted some time to agricultural research in 2000. Of these, two-thirds were classified as crop agriculture and forestry researchers, and another 20 percent, approximately, as animal husbandry researchers. About two-thirds of these researchers have Ph.D.s, and almost all the rest have master's degrees. One concern with the data on university and college researchers is that we do not know the extent of their research commitment. For example, we do not know what portion of their time these individuals devote to research relative to teaching and other responsibilities. Nor do we know how their research is directed to specific topics.

Of 1,216 company researchers, about two-thirds work in crop agriculture and forestry, with another one-sixth in animal husbandry. However, only 15 percent of the company researchers have Ph.D.s, and only about half have any type of graduate degree. These differences in qualifications suggest significant differences in the nature of academic and company research.

Table 5.6   Korea: Education levels of agricultural researchers in universities and companies, 2000

Research focus	Ph.D.	M.Sc.	B. Sc.	Other	Total
Universities and colleges					
Agriculture and forestry	1,490	560	140	41	2,231
Animal husbandry	430	121	8	13	572
Fisheries and marine	273	37	5	0	315
Other	99	34	1	3	137
Total	2,292	752	154	57	3,255
Companies					
Agriculture and forestry	116	294	382	28	820
Animal husbandry	30	96	73	2	201
Fisheries and marine	6	10	18	1	35
Other	7	30	88	35	160
Total	159	430	561	35	1,216

Source: Ministry of Science and Technology and Korea Institute of S&T Evaluation and Planning 2001.

As noted earlier, the extension service in Korea has been a branch of the RDA for about four decades. The number of extension personnel was relatively stable (between 6,000 and 8,000) from 1965 through 1997. The size of the extension staff doubled from 1963 to 1965 as the result of a presidential intervention. President Park, who took an active personal interest in rural issues and food security, decided that about 3,000 individuals who had been employed under contract to distribute *Tongil* rice varieties to farmers should be incorporated into the extension service. This shift more than doubled the number of extension workers in a two-year period. However, in 1997, most extension workers employed by the central government were transferred to local government appointments. The number of extension workers dropped from 6,839 in 1997 to 5,545 in 1998 and 5,032 in 1999, a 27 percent decrease in two years (Rural Development Administration 1998, 1999, and 2000; KREI 1999).

Funding of Agricultural R&D in Korea

Funding for agricultural R&D in Korea has grown dramatically in both nominal and real terms over three decades, but with some fluctuations. Research institutions evolved significantly in the 1990s as substantial new resources were added.

Agricultural R&D Intensity

We do not have a complete history of total R&D expenditures for South Korea because data on research by companies are limited. However, using the data from Table 5.3 together with agricultural GDP data, we find that agricultural R&D intensity has grown rapidly for many years. The sum of university and government R&D was 0.68 percent of agricultural GDP in 1988, growing to 1.68 percent by 1995 and to 1.82 percent in 1997. This measure of research intensity has changed little since. Government agricultural R&D has also grown rapidly. In particular, from 1992 to 1995, in response to the pressure created by URAA, government agricultural R&D rose from 0.81 percent to 1.44 percent of agricultural GDP.

Table 5.7 shows two measures of relative intensity of agricultural R&D since 1994. Total R&D expenditures have risen from about 9 trillion won in 1994 to over 14 trillion won in 2000 (in 1999 prices). After a dip during the financial crisis in 1998, total R&D expenditures jumped by 2.9 trillion won in 2000. Agricultural R&D followed a similar pattern, except that the dip in 1998 was less severe, and expenditures actually declined in 2000 even in nominal terms. Agricultural R&D remained at around 4.5 percent of total R&D (except in 1996) before falling to 3.5 percent in 2000. This percentage is far less than the share of agriculture in the South Korean economy. Agriculture, forestry, and fisheries accounted

Table 5.7 Korea: Agricultural R&D expenditure and research intensity, 1994–2000 (1999 prices)

Year	R&D expenditure on agriculture, forestry, and fisheries			Gross domestic product of agriculture, forestry, and fisheries			Total R&D expenditure	
	Billion won	Million U.S. dollars	Percentage of total R&D expenditure	Billion won	Million U.S. dollars	Percentage of total R&D expenditure	Billion won	Million U.S. dollars
1994	414.4	349	4.4	25,037.0	21,060	1.7	9,366.8	7,879
1995	476.7	401	4.6	25,865.2	21,757	1.8	10,456.0	8,795
1996	433.0	364	3.7	26,053.8	21,916	1.7	11,597.2	9,755
1997	552.6	465	4.4	25,072.4	21,090	2.2	12,595.1	10,595
1998	499.0	420	4.5	21,621.5	18,187	2.3	11,152.8	9,381
1999	512.4	431	4.3	24,481.5	20,593	2.1	11,921.8	10,028
2000	496.6	418	3.5	24,241.3	20,391	2.0	14,065.3	11,831

Source: Ministry of Science and Technology and Korea Institute of S&T Evaluation and Planning 2001.

Note: Data were converted to 1999 won using a GDP deflator, and to U.S. dollars using a 1999 purchasing power parity (PPP) exchange rate ($1=1,188.82 won).

for 6.2 percent of the national earnings in 1995 and 4.6 percent in 2000. As a share of the labor force, agriculture is even more important. Agriculture accounted for 12.4 percent of the labor force in 1995 and 10.9 percent of the labor force in 2000.

One interpretation of these figures is that Korea has underinvested in agricultural research relative to other sectors of the economy. However, such a conclusion would be premature without information on the actual or prospective rates of return to investments in agricultural R&D relative to R&D in other parts of the economy. There are two reasons why agricultural R&D may offer lower rates of return than R&D in other sectors for a given level of current intensity. First, given the difficulty in appropriation of benefits from agricultural R&D oriented to farm production, there is an in-principle case for much of this research to be supported by public funds. However, government funding makes it harder to link funding to performance relative to investments by private firms for their own expected profit. Thus, even though the *potential* payoff may be higher, the *realized* payoff to agricultural R&D may be lower, and the lower research intensity follows as an appropriate consequence. These theoretical arguments notwithstanding, evidence generally supports the view that public agricultural R&D has a comparatively high payoff (Alston et al. 2000). Second, because the payoff to R&D investments is achieved only with a significant time lag, it may be more appropriate to compare R&D investments now to the projected future size of the agricultural economy. That is, investments in R&D in 2005 are likely to be applied in Korea in 2010 or later. This makes the relative research intensity measures misleading for industries in which the projected relative shares are changing rapidly.

Agricultural R&D Funding Sources and Flows

Data on company funding of R&D are not available, but Table 5.3 provides the data on company performance of R&D, and we believe that almost all of those funds spent by private research institutions were provided by private companies themselves. Also, recent data show that little company funding now flows to government institutions (Ministry of Science and Technology 2001).

The composition of funding for government agricultural research institutions had one major fluctuation in the past 30 years. From 1984 to 1996 a significant share of the cost of the research performed by these organizations was covered by private funds. Private support for research at government institutions grew from almost nothing in the early 1980s to between 10 and 20 percent for a decade before declining gradually to almost zero again by 1997 (Ministry of Science and Technology 2001).

MAF, RDA, and ARPC are now the three main agricultural funding agencies for agricultural R&D projects. In addition, the Ministry of Maritime Affairs and Fisheries and the Ministry of Finance and Economy provide funds to the R&D institutions with mandates in the corresponding areas.

MAF finances mainly policy-oriented R&D in agriculture. Previously the research funds from MAF were available solely to government-supported research institutions such as the Korea Food Research Institute (KFRI) and the Korea Rural Economic Institute (KREI), but these funds are now allocated through competitive grants among government-supported research institutions, universities and colleges, and private companies. Most of the RDA's research budget is allocated to ten intramural research institutions under RDA. However, a small share is distributed to other public and private research institutions and to universities and colleges in the form of long-term joint research projects with RDA. The Forestry Administration mainly provides research funds to its own research arms—the Forestry Research Institute and the National Arboretum. Forestry research is also conducted by the KREI. The Ministry of Maritime Affairs and Fisheries research funds are made available to the Korea Ocean Research and Development Institute and the KMI.

As noted above, the significant changes in agricultural R&D policy that took place in 1992 and 1994 were motivated by international trade issues. As it became clear that the URAA would create some additional pressure to import, the Korean government responded with substantial new agricultural R&D funding. Two new programs were initiated, with the stated goals of strengthening agricultural competitiveness and improving the quality of rural life. The Agricultural and Rural Structural Improvement Program, which ran from 1992 to 1998, devoted 33,400 billion won to R&D. Of this total, about 6 percent each was devoted to forestry and fisheries, about 35 percent was devoted to rice, and about 12 percent to livestock R&D. Only 4 percent of the funds were devoted to horticulture (MAF 2000). This allocation can be understood as a response to the real threat that potential imports might pose for domestic rice production, but it was not consistent with the ever-growing importance of horticulture in Korean agriculture. Given that Korean rice prices are about four times higher than border prices, R&D could do little to protect domestic rice production and land prices that rely on high domestic prices if the border were opened significantly. Competitiveness is different for significant parts of the Korean horticultural industry. Given the premium on freshness, the uniqueness of the Korean market, and the high cost of transportation, R&D has the potential to help some segments of the Korean horticultural industry to compete effectively with imports.

The second response to the URAA was the special tax for rural and agricultural development, which was scheduled to provide about $45 billion won for R&D until 2004. The agricultural research fund is managed by the ARPC. With the establishment of the Ministry of Maritime Affairs and Fisheries in 1997, the fisheries section of ARPC was transferred to an R&D Management Team for Fisheries under the Korea Maritime Institute. These funds are allocated to government-supported research institutions, private research institutions, and universities and colleges.

Interestingly, the ARPC was created as a unit under KREI in 1995 and is staffed and managed mainly by economists. The idea behind this institutional arrangement, under which the allocation of scientific R&D funds was explicitly the role of economics staff, was to tie the allocations of R&D funds more directly to the economic issues of importance to agriculture in Korea (KREI 1997). Furthermore, one might expect that formal economic principles and analysis would play a more significant role in the allocation of funds. However, it is not clear that such approaches are in fact used in the allocation process. The procedures used by ARPC seem to be much the same as other peer-reviewed competitive research programs.

Summary and Conclusion

The Rural Development Administration is both the largest funder and the largest provider of Korean Agricultural R&D and extension. Rice-related technological development continues to receive substantial research resources. Over the past 30 years, with strong financial and political support, the RDA bred a number of high-yielding rice cultivars that have been widely used in Korea.

More recently, in response to URAA, the government created a new funding source and a new agency, APRC, for agricultural R&D. The special tax for rural development funds was scheduled to end in 2004 but was recently extended until 2014. Many countries, including the United States, have responded to competitive pressures in agriculture with additional commodity subsidies and attempts to increase protection. Faced with WTO limits on direct subsidies and with declining border protection, Korea opted to devote substantial new resources to R&D and other productivity-enhancing public-good investments.

The additional funds available through ARPC provided universities and the private sector an expanded opportunity to participate in agricultural research. A growing problem, however, is coordination in setting research goals and priorities. This issue applies in most countries, and is probably even more troublesome in places such as the United States, where much agricultural R&D is funded by states and performed by individual universities.

As Korea grapples with the lack of international competitiveness of some important industries, it must look to rapid changes in farm size, the commodity mix on farms, demographic and human capital transformations, and innovative technologies. Obviously, these issues are not unique to Korea, but Korea may be ahead of most other countries in facing these questions in the context of an incredibly rapid transformation of the economy. By all accounts, Korean farm leaders expect the border to open, and they expect major changes.

Given the major adjustments facing Korean agriculture, the potential payoff for some new R&D investments is less clear. R&D investments must be applicable to those commodities, farm sizes, organizations, and regions that are likely to remain viable for 5 or 10 years from the time of the investments. Careful economic analysis may show that R&D investments would have a higher payoff if they ignored some of the productivity concerns of hundreds of thousands of small rice farms that might be already gone by the time research results were available for adoption. Furthermore, given terrain that makes tiny plot sizes the only possibility in much of the country, the payoff might also be higher for R&D investments that focused mainly on regions of the country that are likely to remain in commercial agriculture. It may be counterproductive to dilute the Korean R&D budget by investing in marginal areas that are unlikely to remain in agriculture and can never be made competitive in rice production. The challenge is how to maintain a political consensus to support agricultural R&D if it opts to neglect parts of the country and many of the current farms.

The objective of a more productivity-based R&D policy may be achieved by tying agricultural R&D funding measures to broader funding for aid in the transition out of farming or to shifts to other commodities. A budget for aid to rural areas and residents could be made broadly available, with self-selection into various arms of a program that included agricultural R&D, aid for rural schooling and other human capital development, and aid for rural nonfarm infrastructure. This effort could smooth the process of adjustment to more open markets for farm commodities and mitigate losses for some commodities and regions.

The transition facing Korean agriculture suggests that, more than in most countries, effective R&D investment policy must be developed in the context of economic analysis of the effects of changes in other economic policy that affect agriculture. Korean officials recognize this fact, but implementation remains a challenge.

Appendix Table 5A.1 Korea: R&D expenditures on agriculture, forestry, and fisheries by research entity, 1978–2000 (million 1999 international dollars)

Year	Research institutes			Universities and colleges			Companies			Total
	Total	National and public	Government-supported	Total	National and public	Private	Total	Government-invested	Private	
1978	90.4	83.8	6.6	17.7	15.2	2.4	NA	NA	NA	108.0
1979	126.2	109.2	17.0	5.6	3.7	1.9	NA	NA	NA	131.8
1980	96.4	80.3	16.1	10.5	9.0	1.5	NA	NA	NA	106.9
1981	78.3	62.9	15.4	6.5	5.9	0.6	NA	NA	NA	84.8
1982	94.9	80.1	14.8	15.4	12.3	3.1	NA	NA	NA	110.3
1983	78.2	72.5	5.7	13.3	10.0	3.3	NA	NA	NA	91.5
1984	90.8	74.0	16.8	19.4	15.0	4.4	NA	NA	NA	110.2
1985	89.3	74.2	15.1	17.9	14.8	3.1	NA	NA	NA	107.2
1986	99.9	84.0	15.9	30.7	24.8	5.9	NA	NA	NA	130.6
1987	119.9	95.8	16.1	27.0	19.8	7.2	NA	NA	NA	138.9
1988	114.7	96.8	17.9	29.7	25.3	4.4	NA	NA	NA	144.4
1989	120.1	102.0	18.1	NA	NA	NA	NA	NA	NA	NA
1990	140.2	110.1	30.1	NA	NA	NA	NA	NA	NA	NA
1991	140.2	111.2	29.0	NA	NA	NA	NA	NA	NA	NA
1992	169.9	141.8	28.1	NA	NA	NA	NA	NA	NA	NA
1993	275.2	244.0	31.2	NA	NA	NA	NA	NA	NA	NA
1994	247.1	212.1	35.0	NA	NA	NA	NA	NA	NA	NA
1995	282.2	249.8	32.4	48.6	29.5	19.1	70.2	6.7	63.5	401.0
1996	291.5	251.5	40.0	72.8	37.0	35.8	NA	NA	NA	364.3
1997	313.1	270.7	42.4	70.1	37.9	32.0	81.7	7.0	74.7	464.9
1998	282.9	248.5	34.4	72.8	44.2	28.6	64.0	8.8	55.2	419.7
1999	260.7	234.2	26.5	86.5	55.4	31.1	70.0	10.5	59.5	417.2
2000	278.0	242.2	35.8	87.0	54.8	32.2	52.7	NA	NA	417.7

Source: Ministry of Science and Technology and Korea Institute of S&T Evaluation and Planning 2001.

Notes: Data were converted from Korean won to U.S. dollars using a 1999 purchasing power parity (PPP) exchange rate ($1=1,188.82 won). NA indicates data not available.

Note

1. The special tax for agricultural and rural development (first introduced in 1995 for a 10-year period but now extended to 2014) is a tax earmarked for agricultural development, the enhancement of agricultural competitiveness, and the improvement of rural living conditions and rural welfare. It was implemented as a surtax or surcharge on a number of existing taxes such as income tax, corporate tax, and import tariffs. The surcharge is typically in the range of 20 percent, such that if the income tax rate, for example, is 30 percent, the special tax constitutes a further 6 percent. The total annual revenue target for the tax is around 1,500 billion won (about US$1.5 billion).

References

Alston, J. M., C. Chan-Kang, M. C. Marra, P. G. Pardey, and T. J. Wyatt. 2000. *A meta-analysis of the rates of return to agricultural R&D: Ex pede Herculem.* IFPRI Research Report No. 113. Washington, D.C.: International Food Policy Research Institute.

Choi, J. S., and D. A. Sumner. 2000. Opening markets while maintaining protection: Tariff rate quotas in Korea and Japan. *Agricultural and Resource Economics Review* (29) 1: 91–102.

Cooperative Extension Service, University of California, Davis. 1998. Sample costs to produce: Rice, Sacramento Valley, 1998. University of California, Davis.

Eckert, C. J., K. B. Lee, Y. I. Lew, M. Robinson, and E. W. Wagner. 1990. *Korea old and new: A history.* Seoul: Ilchockak Publishers for Korea Institute, Harvard University.

Kim, W. K., H. Lee, and D. A. Sumner. 1998. Assessing the food situation in North Korea. *Economic Development and Cultural Change* 46 (3): 519–537.

KREI (Korea Rural Economic Institute). 1999. *Fifty years of agricultural policy.* 3 vols. Seoul: Ministry of Agriculture and Forestry.

Kwon, O. S., and H. Lee. 2001. Productivity improvement in Korean rice: Parametric and nonparametric analysis. University of California, Davis. Mimeo.

Lucas, R. E. 1993. Making a miracle. *Econometrica* (61) 2: 251–272.

MAF (Ministry of Agriculture and Forestry). Various years, 1994–2001. *Agricultural statistical yearbook.* Seoul: MAF.

———. 1999. *Plan for agricultural science and technological development.* Seoul: MAF.

———. 2000. *White paper on the agricultural and rural structural improvement program, 1992–1998.* Seoul: MAF.

Ministry of Science and Technology. 2001. *2000 science and technology annual.* Seoul: Ministry of Science and Technology.

Ministry of Science and Technology and Korea Institute of S&T Evaluation and Planning. 2001. *Report on the survey of research and development in science and technology, 1971–2000.* Seoul: Ministry of Science and Technology.

Noland, M., S. Robinson, and M. Scatasta. 1997. Modeling economic reform in North Korea. *Journal of Asian Economics* 1 (8): 15–38.

Park, J. K., S. I. Oh, S. J. Yoon, D. K. Suh, C. S. Kang, S. H. Lee, S. W. Paik, S. H. Paik, E. S. Lee, Y. K. Lee, C. Y. Kang, S. S. Kim, and T. J. Kim. 2000. *A study on the establishment of agricultural technology assessment system.* Seoul: Rural Development Administration.

Park, S. W., D. S. Lee, S. I. Oh, and J. H. Kim. 2000. *Situation and policy direction for scientific technology in agriculture toward the 21st century.* Seoul: Korea Rural Economic Institute.

Pray, C. E., and K. Fuglie. 2001. *Private investment in agricultural research and international technology transfer in Asia.* USDA Agricultural Economic Report No. 805. Washington, D.C.: U.S. Department of Agriculture.

Rural Development Administration. 1998. *Annual report for agricultural extension, 1998.* Seoul: Ministry of Agriculture and Forestry.

———. 1999. *Annual report for agricultural extension, 1999.* Seoul: Ministry of Agriculture and Forestry.

———. 2000. *Annual report for agricultural extension, 2000.* Seoul: Ministry of Agriculture and Forestry.

Sumner, D. A., H. Lee, and D. G. Hallstrom. 1999. Implications of trade reform for agricultural markets in northeast Asia: A Korean example. *Agricultural Economics* 21: 309–322.

USDA (U.S. Department of Agriculture). 1999. Economic Research Service, Website Briefing Room. South Korea Agricultural Policy. http://www.econ.ag.gov/briefing/region/korea/policy.htm. Accessed December 1999.

Chapter 6

Bangladesh: Uncertain Prospects

Raisuddin Ahmed and Zahurul Karim

Introduction

Bangladesh is one of the most impoverished countries in the world. Agriculture remains the primary source of income for about 60 percent of the population. Agricultural growth therefore holds the key to the nation's pervasive poverty. So formidable are resource limitations, the climatic and environmental conditions, and the complexity of the country's agricultural institutions that the pace of agricultural growth rests heavily on gains in productivity, especially those gains arising from research and development. Bangladesh's achievements in agriculture and rural development have been significant since independence in 1971, and research and development have played a vital role in this achievement.

This chapter focuses on the evolution of research policies and institutions, the priority given to agricultural research in resource allocation, the impact of agricultural research on productivity, and a vision for the future role of research.

Generally, *research and development* means not only the generation of applicable knowledge or superior products, but also the transfer of such knowledge or products to potential users. In this chapter, however, the term refers specifically to the generation and development of knowledge or products to usable forms; we exclude extension and other activities associated with the transfer of research results.

Structural Background

Agriculture and the Economy

The transformation of Bangladesh's economy, measured by changes in the sectoral shares of gross domestic product (GDP), is shown in Table 6.1. This structural

Table 6.1   Bangladesh: Structural change in the economy, 1975–2004

Indicators	1975	1985	1995	2000	2004
Share of gross domestic product (percent)					
Agriculture	62.0	41.8	30.9	27.8	21.0
Industry	11.6	16.0	17.6	18.2	24.0
Manufacturing	7.0	9.9	9.6	9.9	16.0
Construction and mining of mineral resources	4.6	6.1	7.0	8.6	8.0
Services	26.4	42.2	51.5	54.0	55.0
Share of employment (percent)	111.6	116.0	116.6	118.5	126.0
Agriculture	78.0	72.0	NA	62.5	60.3
Industry	8.0	9.0	NA	12.0	12.7
Services	14.0	19.0	NA	25.5	27.0
Per capita income (1995 U.S. dollars)	147.0	190.0	240.0	272.0	380.0
Exports as a percentage of gross domestic product	2.9	7.4	14.2	16.1	18.0
Imports as a percentage of gross domestic product	8.1	18.3	22.5	23.1	26.0

Sources: Sector shares are from World Bank, Bangladesh Country Operations Division 1996; 2000 estimates are updated from World Bank, Bangladesh Country Operations Division 1996 using BBS Labour Force Surveys and Planning Commission documents, various years. Employment statistics are calculated from data in the labor surveys of 1977, 1979, and 1993, using intercensus trend factors, and hence are less reliable than the other data in the table. The 2004 statistics are author compilations of data obtained in connection with a public expenditure review in preparation for the World Bank (Ahmed and Mudahar 2006 forthcoming).

Notes: NA indicates not available. Shares of GDP do not sum to 100 percent because categories overlap. For example,

change clearly indicates a rapid movement away from an agriculture-dominated economy. Agriculture's share of GDP declined from 62 percent in 1975 to 21 percent in 2004, but agriculture's share of total employment has not declined as quickly. The declining share of agriculture in GDP should not be construed to reflect a diminishing role of agriculture in the overall growth of the economy or in poverty reduction. Notably, the service sector has expanded at an unusually rapid pace at this stage of economic transformation. Much of the growth in the services sector relates to the marketing and processing of agricultural products resulting from rapid commercialization and diversification in agriculture.[1] Another feature of the structural change is the extent of openness of the economy, as measured by the international trade components (exports and imports) in GDP. The sum of exports and imports constituted only 11 percent of GDP in 1975 but climbed to about 44 percent in 2004.

Poverty

Food poverty, measured by counting the number of persons consuming less than 2,212 calories per day, is especially high in Bangladesh. Most estimates from 1983–84 through 1991–92 suggest that about 50 percent of the overall population could not afford a diet meeting the caloric norm (see Ahmed, Haggblade, and

Chowdhury 2000 for a summary). Recent estimates, however, show that the average incidence of poverty might have declined slightly, to about 45 percent, between 1996 and 2000 (Sen and Mujeiri 2000). Most analysts agree that the great majority of the poor live in rural areas and that more than half the rural population live below the poverty line, compared with about one-third of urban dwellers.

Population, Land Use, and Farm Structure

In 2003, the population of Bangladesh was estimated to be 138 million, inhabiting an area of just over 50,000 square miles—of which about 22.3 million acres (69 percent of total land area) are cultivated land (FAO 2005). Competition for the use of land for agriculture, urbanization, homesteads, and infrastructure is intense; from 1983–84 through 1995–96, the cultivated area declined by 12 percent (BBS 1996). The average farm size fell from 2.26 to 1.69 acres. Because land is cultivated repeatedly within a year, the cropping intensity averages 170 percent. Rice is the dominant crop, occupying about 73 percent of the cropped area in 1996. Notwithstanding the country's large and still-growing population, the rate of population growth has fallen over time, from an average of 2.3 percent annually between 1975 and 1985 to 1.8 percent between 1985 and 1995. Since then, the annual growth rate is estimated to be 1.7 percent (World Bank 2005).

Agroecological Environment

Except for the hilly regions in the northeast and southeast, the country is mainly flat, formed at the deltaic confluence of the Ganges and the Brahmaputra and Meghna river systems. The river system, topography, rainfall, and soil types all interact to shape conditions for agricultural production. Devastating floods, severe drought, and occasional tidal ingression of saline water are quite common in Bangladesh.

Rainfall and topography are, however, two critical factors in agriculture. The normal rainfall is 2,500 millimeters per year, mostly occurring from May through September, and its distribution is more crucial in Bangladesh than the annual average. Topography generally determines how much natural protection a particular area has from floodwater. Forty percent of the cultivated land is normally inundated under 90 or more centimeters of water in peak rainy months.

Evolution of Research Institutions and Policies

The agricultural research institutions and organizations in Bangladesh are the product of a process that began in the colonial era, particularly during the years 1910 to 1940, when the British government in India introduced limited home rule, allowing participation of natives in governance (Pray 1979, 1980). Thus, the 1928 Royal Commission on Agriculture was instrumental in the establishment of the Bengal Department of Agriculture, which made some concerted efforts to establish regional experimental stations, research centers for jute and rice, and an agricultural college in Dhaka (Alim and Sen 1969).

During the Pakistani era (1947–71), a number of significant milestones enlarged the scope of agricultural research:

- A rice research institute was established in 1968, consolidating the earlier entities established for research on rice

- Commodity-specific research institutes were established, such as the Jute Research Institute, the Tea Research Institute, the Sugarcane Research Institute, and the Forest Research Institute

- The Atomic Energy Commission was encouraged to conduct research on the application of nuclear science to agricultural research, and the Institute of Nuclear Agriculture was set up in Mymensingh

- Research on other crops (such as vegetables, fruits, pulses, oilseeds, and wheat) was organized under the Bangladesh Agriculture Research Institute

- Earlier soil research units were regrouped under the Soil Research Institute

- An agricultural university was established in Mymensingh

Since independence, efforts have focused mainly on strengthening the effectiveness and expanding the scope of agricultural research. The first task of the new Bangladesh government in this regard was to organize a research council to coordinate and monitor various institutes and to enhance resources for efficient research.

The creation of the Bangladesh Agricultural Research Council (BARC) in 1973 was a strategic step to enhance efficiency in research management. Initially BARC was conceived as a body to coordinate discrete research institutes under the ministries of agriculture, livestock, fisheries, and forestry; but through a number of legal enactments, particularly one in 1996, BARC has become the cornerstone institution responsible not only for coordination but also for the preparation and implementation of an agricultural research strategy that maintains the administrative autonomy of individual institutes. BARC has developed a master plan for research and human development and unified incentive structures, initiated review processes for various institutes, and introduced a grant mechanism for specific research projects. The names of individual institutes under BARC, their functions, staff strength, and extent of staff attrition are shown in Table 6.2.

The table clearly indicates that research on crops dominates the national agenda, reflecting an early development policy preoccupation with achieving food-grain self-sufficiency and expanding jute exports. The research institutes are generally organized with a central research hub for each institute and a large number of sub-stations located around the country, with the intent of tailoring research to various agroecologies. The implications of the last column in Table 6.2 will become clear when we discuss human resources for research.

NGOs and the Private Sector

Of a total of about 7,000 nongovernmental organizations (NGOs) in the country, about 1,500 are involved in agriculture, providing credit for employment- and income-generating activities and information on agricultural technology. The NGOs do little research but are involved in development programs for livestock, fisheries, sericulture, apiculture, and forestry. These activities are believed to have made significant changes in rural society, particularly in the landless communities.

Bangladesh has virtually no private institutions for agricultural research. To strengthen the incentives for private participation in research, the government enacted legal provisions for patent rights almost a century ago (in 1911), to be followed by trademark protection legislation in 1940 and a copyright act, which came into force in November 2000.[2] Although patents for nonagricultural innovations have been registered (there were 59 applications by residents in 2001, with 21 granted as of May 2003), none have been registered for seeds, crop varieties, plant types, or any other agricultural technologies.

Sources of information on private agricultural research are limited mostly to personal experiences before 1986, when a survey was conducted under a project organized jointly by the University of Minnesota and Rutgers University. The survey reports that there was little private agricultural research undertaken in Bangladesh (Pray 1987), and what there was mostly involved transferring technologies from elsewhere rather than generating new innovations locally. The most effective program was the Bangladesh Tobacco Company's applied research involving adaptive trials of imported Virginia and burley tobacco. Several pesticide companies had small R&D programs, and the largest pump manufacturer did some research on pump designs. Finally, one company was conducting trials on different varieties of vegetables.

Table 6.2 Bangladesh: Description of research institutes, 2001

Institute name	Acronym	Year of inception	Ministerial affiliation	Primary functions	Average number of scientists, 1995–2000	Scientific staff attrition, 1995–2000
Bangladesh Agricultural Research Institute	BARI	1970	Agriculture	Crop research, with the exception of rice, tea, sugarcane, and jute	700	230
Bangladesh Rice Research Institute	BRRI	1970	Agriculture	Rice research	230	58
Bangladesh Jute Research Institute	BJRI	1958	Agriculture	Jute research (various aspects)	200	8
Bangladesh Sugarcane Research Institute	BSRI	1973	Agriculture	Sugarcane breeding	75	9
Bangladesh Tea Research Institute			Commerce	Tea research	36	35
Bangladesh Institute of Nuclear Agriculture	BINA	1972	Atomic Energy Commission	Application of nuclear science to agriculture	107	2
Bangladesh Fisheries Research Institute	BFRI	1984	Fisheries	Fish culture (various aspects)	65	1
Bangladesh Livestock Research Institute	BLRI	1984	Livestock	Cattle and poultry research	35	1
Bangladesh Forest Research			Forest	Forestry (various aspects)	100	27
Soil Resource Development Institute	SRDI	1986	Agriculture	Soil and fertility research and monitoring (various aspects)	454	4

Source: BARC 2001.
Note: Number of scientists excludes research managers.

To update the 1986 survey, IFPRI and BARC sought information on private-sector agricultural R&D during September–October 2001 and February–March 2002. It appears that the scope and intensity of private-sector R&D has expanded somewhat. However, as in the mid-1980s, most of this private activity involves the importation of new technology rather than local innovation. Pesticide companies, poultry producers, fish farmers, and certain NGOs are importing a host of technologies, ranging from seeds to plant-growth regulators. Some of these importers are making efforts to fit these agricultural techniques into domestic production practices. A couple of large commercial poultry farms, for example, are importing chicks from the Netherlands, along with complementary modern technologies for controlling disease on their farms. A number of NGOs are also involved in small-scale adaptive research and dissemination of modern agricultural technology. In addition, food processing enterprises, which are increasing rapidly both in number and volume of business, are involved in R&D pertaining to packaging materials, quality of processed products, and storability of products, particularly those meant for the export market.

Even though private investors are gradually coming forward to invest in agricultural R&D, the total effort of the private sector is still small. Why is this the case? The Minnesota–Rutgers study speculated that the small size of the modern agricultural input and processing sector and government policies are responsible. The binding constraints, the report argues, are underdeveloped agriculture and government intervention in industries. While few would disagree with this broad conclusion, there are other reasons too. Risk is a formidable constraint. Other barriers include weak demand for new innovations from the large number of small and semisubsistence farmers, perceived competition from government research, and the demise of big business conglomerates.

Public Resources for Agricultural Research

To what extent should public resources be invested in agricultural research? This is a complex question with no straightforward answer, not least because resource-allocation decisions are ultimately made by politicians, not economists. Beyond the equi-marginal, benefit–cost investment principle espoused by economists (see, for example, Alston, Norton, and Pardey 1998), various rules of thumb have been used to guide the allocation of funds to agricultural R&D. The 1974 UN World Food Conference suggested that developing countries should aim for a 1985 target of allocating 0.5 percent of AgGDP to agricultural research (United Nations 1974, p. 97). The World Bank (1981, p. 8), in a widely quoted statement, asserted that a "desirable [agricultural research] investment target . . . would be an annual expen-

Figure 6.1 Bangladesh: The agricultural research-intensity ratio target

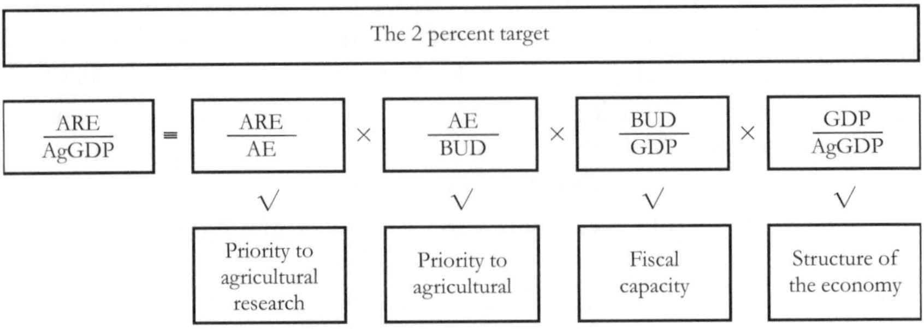

$$\boxed{\frac{\text{ARE}}{\text{AgGDP}}} = \boxed{\frac{\text{ARE}}{\text{AE}}} \times \boxed{\frac{\text{AE}}{\text{BUD}}} \times \boxed{\frac{\text{BUD}}{\text{GDP}}} \times \boxed{\frac{\text{GDP}}{\text{AgGDP}}}$$

| | Priority to agricultural research | Priority to agricultural | Fiscal capacity | Structure of the economy |

Notes: ARE indicates agricultural research expenditures, AgGDP agricultural gross domestic product, AE all agricultural expenditures, and BUD the government budget.

diture (recurrent plus capital) equivalent to about 2 percent of agricultural gross domestic product." Imperfect as this ratio may be, it serves as a reference for judging the adequacy of public resources allocated to agricultural research. However, as Pardey, Kang, and Elliott (1989) pointed out, the ratio of agricultural research expenditure to agricultural GDP is best seen within the broader context of the process of public-resource allocation, as reflected in the identity shown in Figure 6.1.

The identity expresses the ratio of agricultural research expenditure (ARE) to agricultural GDP (AgGDP) as the product of ratios. The first ratio (ARE/AE) is the share of agricultural research expenditure in all agricultural expenditures. It may be taken as the priority given to agricultural research within the agricultural strategy. The second ratio (AE/BUD) is the share of agricultural expenditures in the government budget. We call this the "priority to agriculture." The third ratio (BUD/GDP) is government expenditure's share of gross domestic product. It may alternatively be considered as the "fiscal effort" (which reflects the will of a government to take a role in the economy), the "fiscal burden" (which reflects the weight of the public sector on the economy), or the "fiscal capacity" (which reflects the existence of high-value, easily taxed sectors). The final ratio (GDP/AgGDP) is the inverse of agriculture's share of gross domestic product.[3]

Following the above framework, Bangladesh's public expenditures are analyzed at three stages. First, aggregate public expenditures are examined to indicate the size of the government in relation to the size of the economy (BUD/GDP). Second, the sectoral analysis demonstrates the priority given to agriculture relative to other sectors. Finally, the intrasectoral allocations are examined to show the priority of agricultural research in the budget for agriculture.

Aggregate Public Expenditure

The annual budget has two components: annual development program (ADP) and annual current budget. The current budget is also termed the "revenue budget." The ADP includes project-by-project allocations for the budget year and estimates of expenditures for the previous year for all ministries and agencies. It is the annual phase of implementation of development projects under a five-year plan. Most, but not all, the projects included in the five-year plan are accommodated in the ADP. These projects are supposed to be processed and approved through an inter-ministerial committee organized under the direction of the Planning Commission before they are accommodated in the ADP. ADP can be considered in some measure akin to the public-sector investment budget.

The current budget is meant for general administration, security, and regular functions of the government. The demands for the current budget are first matched against revenue collection, and any surplus from this balancing of current budget and revenue collection (tax and nontax revenue) is available for financing the ADP. The combined demands for ADP and the current budget, when balanced against the total revenue collection, provide an initial indication of the magnitude of deficit financing. Macroeconomic considerations, on the other hand, tend to limit the extent of deficit financing from domestic sources. The deficit is therefore partly financed by foreign aid in the form of commodity grants and project aid, and partly by domestic borrowing from the banking system and nonbank public sources. Foreign financing covered an average of 85 percent of total deficits from 1985 through 1995 (World Bank, Bangladesh Country Operations Division 1996). Currently, about 52 percent of the deficit is financed from foreign sources. Final budget figures result from harmonization among all these fiscal factors. The overall fiscal deficit was about 7.5 percent of GDP in the mid-1980s and declined to about 5.6 percent in the second half of the 1990s. This change reflects reform in the tax structure, improvement in tax collection, and increased reliance on domestic borrowing.

The budget statistics for the years 1976 through 2004 are presented in Table 6.3. The absolute magnitude of annual average total public expenditures, in nominal taka terms, has increased from about Tk. 35 billion in the first period to about Tk. 409 billion in the fifth period—an increase of about 12-fold over 24 years. In terms of dollar-equivalent expenditure, the increase is only about 3-fold, the difference reflecting the effects of depreciation in the country's rate of currency exchange and inflation. In terms of expenditure at 1996 constant prices, the increase is equivalent to about 4.5 percent per annum compared with a rate of growth of GDP of about 5.0 percent per annum. Current expenditure has increased faster than development expenditure: the ratio of development expenditure to total expenditure fell

Table 6.3 Bangladesh: Trends in annual average public expenditure, 1976–2004

Indicators	1976–81	1984–90	1991–95	1995–2000	2001–04
Total expenditure					
Million taka	35,200.0	97,478.6	190,232.2	278,678.0	408,810.0
Million U.S. dollars	2,186.0	3,157.3	4,844.6	6,245.4	6,929.0
Development expenditure					
Million taka	18,135.5	47,110.0	94,892.0	129,650.0	145,786.0
Million U.S. dollars	1,137.3	1,535.1	2,414.8	2,911.6	2,471.0
Current expenditure					
Million taka	13,518.3	50,368.6	95,340.2	149,028.0	263,021.0
Million U.S. dollars	839.3	1,622.2	2,429.8	3,333.8	4,458.0
Ratio (percent)					
Development expenditure/total expenditure	51.5	48.3	49.9	46.5	35.7
Total expenditure/GDP	16.3	16.0	13.6	14.5	13.5
Development expenditure/GDP	10.1	7.9	6.4	8.3	4.8
Current expenditure/GDP	6.2	8.1	7.2	7.7	8.7
Project aid/development expenditure	32.3	56.1	47.1	41.4	37.0

Sources: For expenditures, BBS, various years; for GDP and exchange rates, World Bank 2001 and Ahmed 2002. The 2004 statistics are from the authors compilation of data obtained in connection with a public expenditure review in preparation for the World Bank (Ahmed and Mudahar 2006 forthcoming).

Note: Expenditures and GDP are in current prices.

from 51.5 percent in the first period to 35.7 percent in the fifth period. The increased cost of democratic institutions and defense expenditures are largely responsible for the faster increase in current expenditure.

The ratio of public expenditures to GDP is, perhaps, more meaningful than absolute magnitudes. The ratio of total public expenditure to GDP, an indicator of the size of the government, was 16 percent in the first period, gradually declining to about 14 percent of GDP by the third period and stabilizing at that level thereafter. This modest decrease in the size of the public budget relative to GDP was a consequence of emphasizing a market-oriented strategy of development through reforms. The ratio of development expenditure to GDP declined faster than the ratio of total (development plus current) expenditure to GDP, while the ratio of current expenditure to GDP in fact increased slightly. An interesting aspect of public expenditure, particularly the development expenditure, is the extent of foreign project aid in financing the development budget. In the second half of the 1970s, only about 32 percent of developmental expenditures were financed through project aid. This proportion peaked at 56 percent during the second half of the 1980s. Thereafter, the proportion of project aid dropped to 47 percent in the first half of the 1990s and to 37 percent in the period 2001–04. The low level of project aid during the late 1970s is understandable: foreign aid flows into Bangladesh were limited after the war of independence disrupted relationships with donors. However, the decline in project aid during the 1990s, from its peak in the second half of the 1980s, is not readily understandable. Ostensibly there are at least three reasons for this. First, it is natural to surmise that the proportion of project aid declined during the 1990s, given a worldwide contraction in the supply of foreign aid. However, this was not the case for Bangladesh. Aid commitments from donors continued to increase during this period, and the accumulated foreign aid in the pipeline was $5.7 billion as of June 2000. It is the increasing gap between commitment and utilization that caused the decline in the proportions of project aid during the 1990s. A second possibility, namely that the increasing shift of donor assistance to NGOs caused shortfalls in public-sector project aid, is also not an adequate explanation, as NGOs receive only a small share (about 15 percent) of overall project aid to Bangladesh. A third reason seems the most plausible: namely that a sharply deteriorating trend in governance, buttressed by aid conditionalities, caused a fall in the proportion of foreign-aid dispersals.

Sectoral Distribution of Public Expenditure

The definition of sectors is important when inferring priorities from the sectoral distribution of expenditures. The agricultural sector in the Bangladesh economy is traditionally defined to include crop production, marketing of food (including public food marketing), livestock, fisheries, and forestry production. Economists have tended to include rural institutions and rural infrastructures, as well as flood control and large irrigation development activities, as components of agriculture. This practice gives rise to two definitions of the agricultural sector, one somewhat narrower than the other: the first includes crops, food marketing, livestock, fisheries, and forestry, while the second also includes rural institutions and infrastructure, and water control and development. We present sectoral distributions in which agriculture, rural development and institutions, and flood control and water resources are shown separately.

The sectoral distributions of public expenditure are shown separately for ADP and current expenditures. Typically, limitations in detailed, disaggregated data for the current budget do not allow a straightforward addition of the two budgets at sectoral levels. However, for the agricultural sector, we made a concerted effort to collect detailed, disaggregated data, including data for the current budget, that we present in the intrasectoral analysis of agriculture.

The sectoral shares in the ADP are shown in Table 6.4. The agricultural sector, as traditionally defined, has been losing ground in the development budget: from a 14 percent share during 1976–81, it gradually declined to 4.0 percent during 2001–04. However, using the broader definition of the agricultural sector, inclusive of

Table 6.4   Bangladesh: Average sectoral shares of total annual development program, 1976–2004

Indicator	1976–81	1984–90	1991–95	1995–2000	2001–04
Agriculture	14.0	7.0	5.9	4.7	4.0
Rural development and institutions	3.7	3.4	6.4	8.7	12.3
Flood control and water resources	12.9	12.3	9.1	7.2	4.5
Industry	15.5	8.3	1.4	1.1	2.3
Power	10.7	15.2	12.4	11.0	15.2
Natural resources	3.6	5.2	4.4	3.9	4.2
Transport	15.4	9.4	16.9	18.5	17.4
Communication	3.0	1.9	3.6	2.7	3.5
Physical planning and housing	6.3	3.6	4.7	5.4	6.3
Education and training	4.2	4.9	10.5	12.9	13.5
Health, population control, and family planning	5.8	6.2	8.0	5.9	7.7
Social welfare, women's affairs, and youth development	0.7	0.5	0.9	1.4	1.2
Other	4.2	22.0	15.9	16.7	7.9

Sources: Compiled by the authors from unpublished Government of Bangladesh budget documents and Ahmed 2002. The 2004 statistics are from the authors' compilation of data obtained in connection with a public expenditure review in preparation for the World Bank (Ahmed and Mudahar 2006 forthcoming).

rural institutions and water development, the decline has been less pronounced: an average share of 30.6 percent in 1976–81, declining to 20.8 percent in 2001–04. Notably, the share of ADP spending on rural development and institutions increased from 3.7 percent in the first period to 12.3 percent in the final period.

The share of industry shrank drastically, from 15.5 percent in the first period to only 2.3 percent in the final period. The education share tripled, the social welfare share doubled, and the transport-sector share increased only marginally between the first and the fifth periods. The shares of ADP spending directed toward power increased substantially, and those for communication, natural resources, and health changed only modestly.

These changing spending priorities among sectors are broadly consistent with recent thinking in development economics that emphasizes the important roles of improvements in human resources and increasingly market-oriented development strategies in accelerating growth. In Bangladesh, this thinking on development strategy was enacted through structural reforms that directly affected public spending priorities. Interestingly, spending on health, population control, and communications do not command the priority accorded to education.

Another significant dimension of the distribution of public expenditures among sectors is the extent of project aid in various sectors, perhaps reflecting, in part, the donors' perception of priorities among sectors. The sectoral composition of project aid is shown in Table 6.5. For the agricultural sector, narrowly defined,

Table 6.5 Bangladesh: Project aid as share of annual development program, by sector, 1976–2004

Indicator	1976–81	1984–90	1991–95	1995–2000	2001–04
Agriculture	20.0	52.0	56.2	51.7	43.9
Rural development and institutions	26.0	83.7	62.4	49.2	30.5
Flood control and water resource	23.4	61.0	47.5	55.2	27.5
Industry	53.4	60.8	20.1	22.8	29.0
Power	40.0	74.6	47.8	33.3	43.9
Natural resources	37.2	55.4	58.2	49.4	37.4
Transport	37.2	55.4	58.2	49.4	57.6
Communication	24.0	47.7	31.4	27.3	35.2
Physical planning and housing	24.1	43.2	40.4	39.0	41.4
Education and training	14.0	60.1	47.2	29.7	24.4
Health, population control, and family planning	34.9	61.2	60.0	63.0	62.6
Social welfare, women's affairs, and youth development	12.9	31.4	30.1	24.4	23.1
Other	17.2	29.6	25.4	25.2	24.2

Sources: Compiled by the authors from unpublished Government of Bangladesh budget documents and Ahmed 2002. The 2004 statistics are from the authors' compilation of data obtained in connection with a public expenditure review in preparation for the World Bank (Ahmed and Mudahar 2006 forthcoming).

along with natural resources, power, health, and transport, the average proportions of project aid are higher than the national average for all sectors. From 1976 through 1981, the industry and power sectors received disproportionately large amounts of project aid, but these have fallen drastically, particularly aid for industry.

The sectoral shares in current expenditure are shown in Table 6.6. Unfortunately, current expenditures are not available in sufficiently disaggregated form to reveal longer-run sectoral trends that correspond to the ADP series just discussed. Despite these shortcomings, we can draw some conclusions. The current budget does not exhibit the marked changes in sectoral shares evident in the development budget: in 1990–94, education took the largest share of the current budget, followed closely by defense, then by general administration and debt servicing. Police and justice together accounted for 7.2 percent of the current budget. Given the country's current difficulties with law and order and governance, this share is arguably too low.

Subsidies account for about 5 to 6 percent of the current budget. The share going to food subsidies has declined but still accounts for about 3 percent of the current budget. The subsidy on public enterprises has increased, and it accounted for 2.6 percent of the current budget in 1990–94.

The share of agriculture in the current budget is quite low—barely 4 percent. Given the role of agriculture in the economy and its importance in the development

Table 6.6   Bangladesh: Average sectoral expenditure shares in current budget, 1984–90 and 1990–94

Items of expenditure	1984–90	1990–94
General administration	12.7	14.7
Justice and police	7.4	7.2
Defense	18.4	17.3
Scientific departments	0.5	0.6
Education	16.9	18.4
Health and family planning	5.4	6.0
Social welfare	9.8	7.7
Agriculture	3.8	4.1
Manufacturing and construction	0.6	0.4
Transport and communication	1.7	2.2
Other	1.0	1.0
Debt service	11.5	12.2
Food subsidy	6.5	3.1
Other subsidy	2.0	2.6
Contingency	2.7	2.5

Source: Calculated by authors from World Bank, Bangladesh Country Operations Division 1996.

Note: "General administration" primarily reflects a subsidy to compensate losses to public enterprises. This is not a true picture of the loss because the debt of public enterprises to nationalized commercial banks is not included. Recent data on current budget are available in a different form, that is, by administration division rather than a functional form as in this table. The conversion from administrative to functional forms for all sectors warrants further research.

budget, this small share perhaps reflects the low priority given to agriculture in allocation of the nation's own revenues.

Often in Bangladesh, when a project in the ADP is completed, if its operation thereafter is to be maintained, then the operation must be financed from the current budget. Given that the agriculture sector accounts for such a small share of the current budget, one wonders how agricultural development activities initiated under the development budget are sustained.

Intrasectoral Allocations in Agriculture and Agricultural Research
The analysis of intrasectoral allocations that follows is based on the narrow definition of the agricultural sector and is limited to development expenditures only (Table 6.7). The crop subsector continues to dominate, drawing 69 percent of developmental expenditures in agriculture between 1976 and 1981, a share that declined to 44 percent in the period 2001 to 2004. The food marketing subsector had a 13 percent share in the first period, dropping to 4.4 percent in the final

Table 6.7   Bangladesh: Average subsectoral expenditures in total agricultural development
expenditure, 1976–2004

Subsectors	1976–81	1984–90	1991–95	1995–2000	2001–04
Crops					
Million taka	1,566.6	1,652.1	2,531.5	3,123.0	4,527.5
Percentage	68.6	50.5	45.8	51.5	43.9
Forestry					
Million taka	161.1	443.8	897.0	1,005.7	1,700.0
Percentage	7.1	13.6	16.3	16.6	16.5
Food marketing					
Million taka	294.5	266.5	397.5	355.3	452.5
Percentage	12.9	8.1	7.2	5.8	4.4
Fisheries					
Million taka	179.1	522.2	935.1	703.0	1,330.0
Percentage	7.8	16.0	16.9	11.7	12.9
Livestock					
Million taka	82.0	385.9	761.5	871.9	2,300.0
Percentage	3.6	11.8	13.8	14.4	22.3
Total agriculture (narrow)					
Million taka	2,283.2	3,270.4	5,522.6	6,058.8	1,0310.0
Percentage	100.0	100.0	100.0	100.0	100.0

Sources: Calculated by the authors from data in unpublished Government of Bangladesh budget documents and
Ahmed 2002. The 2004 statistics are from the authors' compilation from data obtained in connection with a public
expenditure review in preparation for the World Bank (Ahmed and Mudahar 2006 forthcoming).

period.[4] This decrease reflects reforms in the public marketing of food. The share of
agricultural spending directed toward fisheries increased from 8 percent in 1976–
81 to about 13 percent by the early 2000s. Similarly, the forestry share increased
from 7 to about 17 percent, and the livestock share from about 3 to about 22 percent. These changes in the subsectoral shares in agriculture broadly reflect shifting
agricultural policy, emphasizing diversification from crop to noncrop agricultural
products as sources of agricultural growth.

Agricultural Research

Table 6.8 shows the proportion of agricultural expenditures devoted to agricultural
research. It appears that only 8.6 percent of agricultural development expenditures
were spent on agricultural research from 1976 through 1981, increasing to 12.5
percent in the period 2001–04.[5] The total agricultural development expenditure
directed to R&D, including rural institutions and water development (that is,
using the broad agriculture definition), was just 3.9 percent during the period
1976–81, dropping to 2.9 percent in the period 2001–04. Adding current expenditures to the development expenditures for agricultural research provides a more

Table 6.8   Bangladesh: Average public expenditure on agricultural research, 1976–2004

Indicator	1976–81	1984–90	1991–95	1995–2000	2001–04
Expenditure (million taka)					
Research development expenditures	195.4	618.6	605.0	968.1	978.0
Research current expenditures	50.6	198.0	254.7	307.6	527.0
Total research expenditures	246.0	816.6	859.7	1,275.7	1,505.0
Research development expenditures as percentage of total development expenditures in agriculture (narrow)	8.6	18.9	11.0	15.8	12.5
Research development expenditures as percentage of total development expenditures in agriculture (broad)	3.9	5.8	3.0	3.6	2.9
Total research expenditures as percentage of agricultural gross domestic product	0.35	0.34	0.27	0.25	0.24
Project aid as percentage of research development expenditures	42.9	55.9	38.2	48.2	38.4

Sources: Calculated from data in unpublished Government of Bangladesh budget documents and information collected from BARC on individual research institutes. The statistics for 2001–04 are from authors' compilation of data obtained in connection with a public expenditure review in preparation for the World Bank (Ahmed and Mudahar 2006 forthcoming).

complete picture of public expenditures. When this total is expressed as a proportion of agricultural GDP, it appears that Bangladesh devotes only a tiny proportion of its resources to agricultural research—0.35 percent during the period 1976–81 and 0.24 percent for the period 2001–04. This figure is well below the 2 percent target considered appropriate for research, and half the 1995 developing-country average (0.62 percent) reported by Pardey and Beintema (2001).

The data show that the share of project aid in total agricultural research expenditures has been volatile. It was 43 percent in the period 1976–81, increasing to 56 percent in the period 1984–90, declining to 38 percent during the first half of the 1990s, and rebounding to 48 percent during the second half of that decade. Compared with the proportions of project aid in total agricultural development expenditures (Table 6.5), it appears that research enjoyed a higher share of project aid during the first two periods but lost ground during the subsequent two periods. The decrease in total research expenditures, combined with a dwindling proportion of foreign aid in the development funds directed to agricultural R&D, could represent a cause for serious concern, especially as Bangladesh has been vigorously championing poverty reduction and improving the competitive strength of its agricultural sector in an increasingly globalized market.

Table 6.9 shows how research expenditures are distributed among various commodity-oriented research institutes. Crop research institutes command a larger

Table 6.9   Bangladesh: Subsectoral shares in expenditures on agricultural research, 1976–2004

Subsector	1976–81	1984–90	1991–95	1995–2000	2001–04
Annual development program (percent)					
Crops	84.65	77.82	84.01	79.57	78.5
Forestry	3.89	4.95	3.34	5.78	7.44
Fisheries	10.85	11.07	7.55	7.77	8.25
Livestock	0.61	6.16	5.10	6.88	5.81
Total	100.00	100.00	100.00	100.00	100.00
Current budget (percent)					
Crops	90.52	85.15	87.67	87.91	85.12
Forestry	4.15	4.14	2.20	3.32	3.50
Fisheries	4.74	7.93	7.34	5.23	7.66
Livestock	0.59	2.78	2.79	3.54	3.72
Total	100.00	100.00	100.00	100.00	100.00
Total research budget (percent)					
Crops	85.80	79.60	85.00	81.60	80.80
Forestry	4.00	4.70	3.10	5.20	6.00
Fisheries	9.60	10.30	7.50	7.20	8.10
Livestock	0.60	5.40	4.40	6.00	5.10
Total	100.00	100.00	100.00	100.00	100.00

Sources: Calculated by authors from unpublished Government of Bangladesh budget documents and information collected from BARC on individual research institutes. The statistics for 2001–04 are from the authors' compilation of data obtained in connection with a public expenditure review, 2005, in preparation for the World Bank (Ahmed and Mudahar 2006 forthcoming).

share of both development and current budgets than noncrop institutes, although the crop share has declined a little since 1976. Fisheries research comes next, with about 9 percent of the total research budget. It reflects a slightly smaller share of the agricultural development budget in 2001–04 than in 1976–81, and a modest increase in the current budget share. Forestry commands 6 percent of total agricultural R&D spending, with a modestly increasing share of the development budget but a declining share of the current budget. Livestock research accounts for the smallest share of the agricultural research budget, although this share has increased markedly since 1976 in both the development and current budgets.

By the very nature of agricultural R&D there are long lags between investment and reaping the returns on that investment, and therefore some stability is needed in the flow of funds to research. Unfortunately, in the case of Bangladesh the revenue flows to agricultural research are not only relatively small but also highly unstable (Table 6.10). The yearly fluctuations in agricultural research expenditure vary from –49.88 to 73.36 percent, and they are significantly larger than fluctuations in other fiscal variables, such as ADP, current expenditures, and project aid. Nominal expenditures in agricultural research fell in 6 of the 21 years examined; other fiscal factors declined in only 2 or 3 of the 21 years.[6]

Table 6.10 Bangladesh: Range of annual fluctuation in selected fiscal variables, 1978–99

Fiscal variable	Range of fluctuation (percent)	Number of years with negative fluctuation
Development budget (ADP)	−2.41 to 33.2	2
Current budget	6.11 to 23.93	0
Total project aid	−5.30 to 35.19	3
Development budget for agriculture	−18.21 to 30.63	2
Agricultural research budget	−49.88 to 73.36	6

Sources: Calculated from data in unpublished Government of Bangladesh budget documents and information collected from BARC.

Human Resources for Agricultural Research

Innovation processes are critically reliant on access to appropriately trained and creative scientists and technicians. There are at least four dimensions to the human resource requirements of agricultural research: staff strength, balanced composition, training, and incentives.

Number of Scientists with Required Disciplinary Knowledge

Research managers, senior scientists, and junior research scientists constitute the largest group of research staff in national research institutes. Table 6.2 gives a 2001 snapshot of the scientific staff strength in various agricultural research institutes. It shows that 2,185 research managers and scientists were employed in the main agricultural research organizations of Bangladesh. About 12 percent held Ph.D.s, 75 percent M.Sc.s, and 13 percent B.Sc.s. Generally, the most senior scientists are engaged in research management; these constitute about 9 percent of the scientists employed.

Typically, an agricultural research institute is headed by a director or director general. Under the head, there are chief scientific officers (CSOs), principal scientific officers (PSOs), senior scientific officers (SSOs), and scientific officers (SOs). In addition, there are technicians to support the scientists in specific scientific operations. The head and CSOs jointly constitute the group of research managers. The PSOs, SSOs, and SOs conduct research. The PSO is the leader, the SSOs carry out the research, and the SOs provide support to the senior investigators. Based on international practices and local realities, a report on human resource development in agricultural research recommended a ratio of 1:2:4 among the positions of PSO, SSO, and SO as optimal for the agricultural research system in Bangladesh (Hasanuzzaman 2000).

However, because of a large-scale migration of scientists to jobs abroad, primarily during the years 1995 to 2000, not only the absolute levels but also the optimal mix of senior and junior scientists has been adversely affected. The extent of this attrition for the period 1995–2000 is shown in Table 6.2. The loss of scientists from the Bangladesh Agricultural Research Institute (BARI), the Bangladesh Rice Research Institute (BRRI), BARC, and the Forestry Research Institute (FRI) has been serious; about a quarter to half of the scientists working in these institutes have left their jobs, mostly to pursue opportunities abroad. Because the better-qualified and skilled scientists are more likely to get jobs abroad than the ones with lesser qualifications, these departures imply a loss not only in number but also in quality. Research managers feel that the migration of scientists has created a vacuum of crisis proportions in agricultural research, and it warrants a commensurate effort to minimize the adverse impact of this brain drain.

Unfortunately, it is difficult to remedy a brain drain, especially in an era of global integration. To minimize the negative effects, efforts to develop capacity will have to be expanded, and incentives will have to be enhanced so that at least some scientists find sufficient reason to stay home.

Motivation and Incentives

Knowledge, skill, and experience are necessary but not sufficient to guarantee a productive outcome from research. The dedication and motivation of scientists are also important, and these elements are especially sensitive to the incentive structures in research institutions. Yet it is virtually impossible to offer an incentives structure to a particular branch of the government (for example, agricultural re-search) that is fundamentally different from that in other branches of government. Nevertheless, small improvements are possible, and a combination of some of these may be sufficient to better motivate agricultural scientists.

The salary structure of scientists ranges from about $113 to $345 per month, depending on rank. This structure cannot be changed in isolation from the gov-ernment system as a whole. Some fringe benefits, such as special allowances, could be increased, but only with great difficulty. Therefore, the scope of any special change in salary and benefits exclusively for scientists remains extremely slim. Improvements in promotion procedures and special recognition, together with enhancement of the social image of scientists, could conceivably improve motiva-tion among scientists.

Currently, even scientists with advanced degrees from Western universities are typically employed in the same position for 8 to 12 years before promotion. This peculiar situation has developed because of the small number of approved senior positions in most research institutes. The number of approved positions was deter-mined when the various institutes were first established, and changing it is difficult within Bangladesh's public-service rules and tradition. However, with the increasing autonomy of research institutes, granting promotion based on experience and performance, regardless of the number of approved positions, may become possible.

Social image is important in cultivating a sense of pride among scientists, particularly in societies like that of Bangladesh, whose government officers are classified into explicit classes. Not too long ago, graduates in agricultural science were held in much lower esteem than graduates in medicine or engineering. Although these attitudes and practices persist, they are undesirable and sustain an artificial and demeaning culture in public service.

Impact of Agricultural Research

Recently an opportunity opened up for a review of public expenditures in Bangladesh for a multilateral donor. In the course of this assignment, a strong case for increasing resources for agricultural research was presented. The policymakers and top professional advisers responded by contending that the success in rice production resulted from irrigation development and fertilizer policy, and the complementary inputs for high-yielding varieties (HYV) of rice. They apparently did not understand the contribution of research in the development of HYV. Increased use of fertilizers and irrigation were tried in the 1960s with little success; production increased only in the 1980s and 1990s, when modern HYVs became part of the package of complementary inputs. When this contrast was pointed out to policymakers, they seemed to be lost for a moment; strong disagreement turned to skepticism. The dialogue ended with a vague agreement to revisit this issue.

This episode is indicative of the challenge in measuring research benefits and communicating the results to policymakers. Empirical studies on returns from research are numerous. Estimated rates of return vary widely but are generally high (see Alston et al. 2000 for an excellent analytical review). It is the measurement of benefits that is the source of most confusion. The concept of total factor productivity (TFP) is useful for measuring aggregate research benefits (see Solow 1957 and Griliches 1963). The fact that real costs of complementary inputs are netted out from gross revenue in the measurement of TFP makes the residual a suitable measure of technology's contribution, particularly when the effect of any plausible economies of scale is accounted for. Nevertheless, the approach is not free of controversies (see Fagerberg 1994 and Felipe 1999).

The contribution of research to growth in rice production in Bangladesh can be measured through the estimates of TFP. Rice production represents half of agriculture, and rice research has received the highest priority. About 45 modern varieties have been released that cover 70 percent of the country's rice area. Rice yield

Table 6.11 Bangladesh: Annual growth rates in rice revenue, input costs, and total factor productivity (TFP), 1975–76 to 1997–98

	1975–76 to 1986–87	1987–88 to 1997–98	1975–76 to 1997–98
Based on current prices			
Output	10.71	3.72	7.22
Input	9.52	2.86	6.19
TFP	1.19	0.86	1.03
Based on constant prices			
Output	2.91	4.02	3.51
Input	2.12	2.65	2.41
TFP	0.79	1.37	1.10

Source: Ahmed 2001.
Note: Constant prices are for 1981–82.

has doubled, contributing to the doubling of rice production during the past two decades (Shahabuddin and Rahman 1998).

Estimates of the average rate of growth in output, input, and TFP are presented in Table 6.11. (For details on the method of calculation, see Ahmed 2001.) Values for individual years vary widely because of floods, droughts, and other natural factors, so averages over a number of years are shown—for 1975–76 to 1986–87, for 1987–88 to 1997–98, and for the entire period 1975–76 to 1997–98. Two sets of measures are provided, based on nominal and real (1981–82) prices.

In spite of the comparatively small investments in agricultural research documented above, the technological progress in agriculture, as measured by total factor productivity growth in rice, has been solid. The growth rate in TFP in rice production was slightly higher than 1 percent per annum in the period 1975–76 through 1997–98. Comparing growth rates in TFP estimated using nominal and real prices, it appears that over the entire period, the difference between the two narrows, but in the first and second decades, using different prices can influence the perspective on TFP growth. Prices do matter, mostly in the shorter rather than the longer run, in the measurement of TFP.

How does this growth in TFP compare with similar agricultural products in India? Evenson, Pray, and Rosegrant (1999), who estimated the TFP for crops in eastern India (West Bengal, Orissa, and Behar), found that the annual growth rate in crop TFP was 0.75 percent during the period 1956–87. The Bangladesh estimate considers only rice, while the Indian estimate includes rice and other crops, and so the two estimates are not strictly comparable. However, since rice is the largest crop in eastern India as well as in Bangladesh, such a comparison is still useful.

In the rice economy of Bangladesh, the real price of rice declined over the period 1975–76 to 1997–98; the decline was sharper in the second decade than in the first (Ahmed 2001). But the growth in production of rice, in the face of this declining real price, has been spectacularly sustained. This growth has been possible because of the sustained improvement in TFP. Rice prices in Bangladesh have come very close to world prices. Therefore, for further increases in production, productivity will play a more strategic role than prices.

Rice research has indeed paid off in Bangladesh. The increase of 1 percent annually in TFP in rice production implies an annual contribution of about 170,000 metric tons of rice, valued at about $42.5 million (equivalent to Tk. 1.913 billion at the official exchange rate). Annual public expenditure on rice development, using total expenditures of the BRRI and 50 percent of total expenditures on agricultural extension services, averaged Tk. 118.9 million from 1990 through 1997. Based on these figures, a crude estimate of the benefit–cost ratio of rice research is 16:1, an extremely high rate of return.

Concluding Observations

Bangladesh has a rich history of agricultural research. But building on this historical foundation has been slow, as the resources available for research have remained very limited. Only about 4 percent of total public developmental expenditure in agriculture, which is equivalent to about 0.25 percent of agricultural GDP, is allocated to agricultural research. Because of the legacy of strategic research institutions, the achievements of agricultural research have indeed been remarkable. Total factor productivity in rice, a major crop example, has grown, enabling rice production to double even though the real price of rice has fallen sharply and the area under rice has declined slightly. About 70 percent of rice area is currently planted with high-yielding varieties.

The forces of globalization have brought a number of new challenges to agricultural research in Bangladesh. The first is the ability of agricultural research to contribute to the low-cost supply of agricultural products in intensely competitive world markets. Unfettered competition in world markets offers a comparative advantage to countries with superior research skills and institutions to support their agricultural sectors, not least because nonagricultural sectors can rely on imported technology with greater ease than agriculture can. For example, imported biotechnologies often require some adaptation, and local testing and screening, at least, before release to farmers.

The second challenge facing agricultural R&D in Bangladesh is to meet the needs of agricultural diversification. Mobilizing the resources required for research on livestock, fisheries, forestry, and high-value crops, particularly research focusing on quality improvement, must occur faster. Because the proportion of scientists with advanced degrees in noncrop branches of agricultural research is very low, developing the personnel to address these areas of research must become a high priority (Hasanuzzaman 2000).

The third challenge relates to opportunities presented by scientific developments in biotechnology. As the human-health and environmental concerns over biotechnology are adequately addressed, this relatively new branch of agricultural research is destined to cause a sea change in agricultural markets around the globe. Bangladesh has taken some initial steps to develop research capabilities in biotechnology (BARC 2001). Initiatives under the Ministry of Science and Technology include the organization of a biotechnology research institute in Bangladesh.

The systemic problem of inadequate and unstable allocation of public resources for agricultural research has been a common theme in national research evaluation documents (BANSDOC 1997). Discussions with policymakers suggest that resource availability is not perceived as a problem; resource utilization is considered the critical constraint. Scientists, on the other hand, complain about meager and uncertain resource flows, as well as the slow disbursement of funds, as the real constraints. The basic problem is rooted in institutional deficiencies.

The financing mechanism for agricultural research has to be extricated from the current budgetary process, perhaps by establishing some sort of autonomous foundation or trust fund to be administered by a body like BARC. The fund will depend primarily on public resources; therefore budgetary allocations to agricultural research will have to be included in the annual budget. Such a funding mechanism will enable scientists to pursue research activities according to a long-term research plan, avoiding the vicissitudes of annual budgetary allocations and cumbersome financial approvals required by current mechanisms.

The problems of sustaining human resource development in agriculture in general, and the situation arising from outmigration of scientists in particular, call for thoughtful evaluation and corrective measures. It is extremely difficult to stop migration by regulation. While internal improvements in incentives may reduce the outflow, it is doubtful that they can stop it. Therefore, a strong program for training and education of scientists should be undertaken, so that the vacuum can be filled quickly, with the least possible damaging effects on research activities.

Historically, agricultural research institutions have witnessed moments of enormous frustration followed by bold measures of institutional strengthening. Perhaps the current deteriorating situation in agricultural research will herald another resurgence. This time around, perhaps the resurgence will be sustained enough to render the long-run future of agricultural R&D less uncertain.

Notes

1. The subsectoral shares in agricultural GDP for 1972–75 show that the crop subsector accounted for 70 percent, fisheries 11 percent, livestock 10 percent, and forestry 9 percent. Over the past 20 years, the share of the crop subsector fell from 78 percent to 52 percent, while the share of noncrop subsectors increased from 30 percent to 43 percent by 2003/4.

2. Bangladesh has been a signatory to the Trade Related Aspects of Intellectual Property (TRIPs) agreement since January 1995, and to the World Intellectual Property Organization (WIPO) Convention since May 1985, but has yet to join the Patent Cooperation Treaty administered by that organization. The Bangladesh Patent Office operates out of the Ministry of Industries.

3. Pardey, Kang, and Elliott (1989) provided evidence on the political-economy aspects of agricultural R&D using the same sets of ratios as a basis for comparison among countries. In addition to conventional agricultural research-intensity ratios, they developed measures of a public agricultural-expenditure ratio (government expenditure on agriculture relative to AgGDP) and a relative research-expenditure ratio (public agricultural-research expenditure relative to government expenditure on agriculture).

4. In addition to food marketing, there are significant elements of input marketing and service provision in other subsectors; therefore, the share of all types of marketing in the agricultural sector could be as high as 40 to 45 percent (see World Bank, Bangladesh Country Operations Division 1996).

5. Expenditures by BARC, BARI, BRRI, BJRI, BINA, BSRI, BLRI, BFRI, BTRI, BFORI, and SRDI were included as research expenditures. Information on both development and current expenditures was collected from these institutes to supplement statistics in budget documents.

6. We attempted to use statistical regression methods to estimate the extent of the influence of various fiscal variables on the instability of research expenditures. The results were statistically poor, but the variability in project aid for research was found to be a significant cause of variability in research expenditures.

References

Ahmed, R. 2001. *Retrospects and prospects of the rice economy of Bangladesh.* Dhaka: University Press.

———. 2002. Public expenditure and rural development in Bangladesh. Unpublished report submitted to the Asian Development Bank under T.A. No. 3649.

Ahmed, R., and M. Mudahar. 2006. *Government and rural prosperity: The Bangaldesh transformation.* Washington, D.C.: World Bank, Rural Development Department, South Asia region (forthcoming).

Ahmed, R., S. Haggblade, and T. E. Chowdhury, eds. 2000. *Out of the shadow of famine: Evolving food market and food policy in Bangladesh.* Baltimore: Johns Hopkins University Press.

Alim, A., and J. L. Sen. 1969. *Half a century of rice research in east Pakistan.* Dhaka: Banglabazar Press.

Alston, J. M., G. W. Norton, and P. G. Pardey. 1998. *Science under scarcity: Principles and practice for agricultural research evaluation and priority setting.* Wallingford, U.K.: CAB International.

Alston, J. M., C. Chan-Kang, M. C. Marra, P. G. Pardey, and T. J. Wyatt. 2000. *A meta-analysis of rates of return to agricultural R&D: Ex pede Herculem.* Research Report No. 113. Washington, D.C.: International Food Policy Research Institute.

BANSDOC (Bangladesh National Scientific and Technical Documentation Center). 1997. *Survey of research and development (R&D) activities in Bangladesh.* Dhaka.

BARC (Bangladesh Agricultural Research Council). 2001. *Annual report 2000.* Dhaka: BARC.

BBS (Bangladesh Bureau of Statistics). 1977, 1979, 1993. *Labor force surveys.* Dhaka: BBS.

———. 1996. *Agricultural census.* Dhaka: BBS.

BBS (Bangladesh Bureau of Statistics), Planning Commission. Various years, 1975–76 to 1999–2000. *Annual development programmes.* Dhaka: BBS.

Evenson, R. E., Pray, C. E., and M. W. Rosegrant. 1999. *Agricultural research and productivity growth in India.* Research Report No. 109. Washington, D.C.: International Food Policy Research Institute.

Fagerberg, J. 1994. Technology and international differences in growth rates. *Journal of Economic Literature* 132: 1147–1175.

FAO (Food and Agriculture Organization of the United Nations). 2005. FAOSTAT database. http://faostat.fao.org. Accessed July 28, 2005.

Felipe, J. 1999. Total factor productivity growth in East Asia: A critical survey. *Journal of Development Studies* 35 (4): 1–41.

Griliches, Z. 1963. The sources of measured productivity growth: Agriculture, 1940–1960. *Journal of Political Economy* 71 (4): 331–346.

Hasanuzzaman, S. M. 2000. *Report on human resource development for agricultural research.* Dhaka: Bangladesh Agricultural Research Council.

Pardey, P. G., and N. M. Beintema. 2001. *Slow magic: Agricultural R&D a century after Mendel.* IFPRI Food Policy Report. Washington, D.C.: International Food Policy Research Institute.

Pardey, P. G., M. S. Kang, and H. Elliott. 1989. Structure of public support for national agricultural research systems: A political economy perspective. *Agricultural Economics* 3 (4): 261–278.

Pray, C. E. 1979. The economics of agricultural research in Bangladesh. *Bangladesh Journal of Agricultural Economics.* December: 1–34.

———. 1980. The economics of agricultural research in British Punjab and Pakistani Punjab, 1905–1975. *Journal of Economic History* 40 (1): 174–176.

———. 1987. *Agricultural research and technology by the private sector in Bangladesh.* Newark, N.J.: Department of Agricultural Economics and Marketing, Rutgers University.

Sen, B., and M. Mujeiri. 2000. Dynamics of poverty in Bangladesh. Bangladesh Institute of Development Studies, Dhaka. Mimeo.

Shahabuddin, Q., and R. I. Rahman. 1998. *Agricultural growth and stagnation in Bangladesh.* Dhaka: Center for Integrated Rural Development for Asia and Pacific.

Solow, R. M. 1957. Technical change and the aggregate production function. *Review of Economics and Statistics* 39 (3): 312–320.

United Nations. 1974. *The world food problem: Proposals for national and international action.* Provisional agenda from the United Nations World Food Conference, November 5–16. Rome: United Nations.

World Bank. 1981. *Agricultural research: Sector policy paper.* Washington, D.C.: World Bank.

———. 2001. *World development indicators 2001.* Washington, D.C. CD-ROM.

———. 2005. *World development indicators.* http://devdata.worldbank.org/dataonline. Accessed July 10, 2005.

World Bank, Bangladesh Country Operations Division. 1996. *Public expenditure review.* Dhaka.

Chapter 7

India: The Funding and Organization of Agricultural R&D—Evolution and Emerging Policy Issues

Suresh Pal and Derek Byerlee

Introduction

India has one of the largest and most complex agricultural research systems in the world, with more than a century of organized application of science to agriculture. A proactive policy by the government toward agricultural research and education (R&E),[1] coupled with support from a number of bilateral and multilateral donors, has produced an institutionally diverse research system that has achieved many successes, most notably the Green Revolution in the 1960s and 1970s. The country is not only self-sufficient in food but also commands a strong position in world markets for some commodities. Many studies have empirically shown the impressive performance of the system, with annual rates of return to investment in research ranging from 35 to 155 percent (Evenson, Pray, and Rosegrant 1999). Notwithstanding these achievements, the system must now address a more complex and expanding research agenda of sustaining natural resources, enhancing product quality, and ensuring food safety, in addition to increasing household food and nutritional security and reducing poverty. These new challenges require a rematching of needs with resources, and a reorientation of R&E policy.

Redirection of R&E policy and strategy must be in tune with national and international developments. The increasing role of markets, growing participation of the private sector in research, rapid advances in science, and strengthening of intellectual property rights have a significant bearing on the organization and management of agricultural research. The Indian system has also reached a stage where it must address "second-generation problems" relating to organizational rigidities, inefficiencies, and difficulties in sustaining funding. These issues are particularly important in an era of a liberalizing economy, India's entry into the World Trade Organization (WTO), and a tightening of the public purse.

Against this background, this chapter reviews the funding and organization of agricultural R&E in India. After presenting the macroeconomic and sectoral policy context for agricultural development in India, the chapter reviews the historical evolution of R&E policies and institutions and summarizes the current situation. Next it summarizes sources of and trends in public funding and human resources and the allocation of funds to providers of research services. It concludes with a discussion of the emerging policy issues for agricultural R&E in India.

The Context

The Macroeconomic Environment

Following independence, India pursued a socialistic development path, emphasizing heavy industry, import substitution, high levels of protection of domestic industry, public-sector regulation, and public investment. Allocation of capital and foreign exchange was controlled through a highly bureaucratic system of licenses and permits, leading to what was termed the "license Raj" (Das 2001). Although this strategy created a massive industrial base and infrastructure in the public sector, it could generate only a modest economic growth rate (around 3.5 percent per annum) in the first three decades after independence.

By 1991, a mounting balance-of-payment deficit forced the government to implement drastic reforms throughout the economy. These reforms liberalized imports by dismantling the quota system and cutting tariffs, reducing the fiscal deficit, deregulating most industries, and openly soliciting private investment (including foreign direct investment). The reforms were further reinforced by India's commitments as a founding member of the WTO. A second phase of reform covering the financial sector, public-sector organizations, intellectual property rights, and labor regulations has recently been initiated. As a result of the reforms, economic growth accelerated to over 6 percent annually in the 1990s, the economy became more export-oriented, and poverty declined significantly.

Economic reform was not targeted toward agriculture, and in fact liberalization of the agricultural sector has lagged behind that of most other sectors. However, agricultural exports increased significantly, and there was greater participation by the private sector in agricultural input industries like the seed industry. Also, the rate of private capital formation in agriculture accelerated because of improved terms of trade. Investment in infrastructure, R&E interventions in food-grain markets designed to enhance national food security, and various public programs for conservation of natural resources and poverty reduction continued to be high priorities for government support. Subsidies on agricultural inputs, especially water, electricity, fertilizer, and food marketing and distribution, continued at high levels, reaching 7 percent of agricultural gross domestic product (AgGDP) (Gulati and Sharma 1995). However, it is expected that the policy of market-led development will be extended to the agricultural sector, adding urgency to the need to clearly define the role of the state, enhance the efficiency of state interventions, and promote partnerships with the private sector.

Agricultural Development: Issues and Policies

Indian agriculture is highly diversified in terms of both production environments and activities. Smallholder farmers (those of less than 2 hectares) constitute about 80 percent of total farm holdings and occupy 40 percent of the agricultural land area. Despite a rapid increase in livestock production, the crop sector still contributes three-quarters of the total value of agricultural output. Agricultural growth registered a sharp increase in the late 1960s and 1970s as a result of the widespread adoption of the new seed- and fertilizer-based Green Revolution technology for rice and wheat in irrigated areas (Table 7.1). This growth spread to rainfed areas from the 1980s onward, with the adoption of hybrid strains of maize, sorghum, pearl millet, and cotton, although the effects were less widespread, and many areas with harsh growing conditions continue to experience low and unstable production. Average crop yields have increased by an average of 1.6 percent annually over the past three decades as a result of a marked increase in irrigated area and the use of modern inputs (especially seed and fertilizer). Yield growth and increased cropping intensity resulted in impressive growth in agricultural production despite little change in cultivated area. Since 1980, these trends have been echoed in the livestock sector, which has grown even faster, at 5 percent annually, mainly because of rapid growth in milk, poultry, and fish production.

Studies have shown that irrigation, land reform, infrastructural development, and technical change were the main sources of agricultural growth (Desai 1997; Fan, Hazell, and Thorat 1999). Estimates of total factor productivity (TFP) growth for Indian agriculture since the Green Revolution average 1.5–2.0 percent annually, in line with growth in industrialized countries (Murgai 2001; Pingali and Heisey 2001). In addition, the contribution of TFP to output growth has become more important in recent years. Much of the growth in TFP has been attributed to investment in agricultural research that provided high payoffs (Mruthyunjaya and Ranjitha 1998; Evenson, Pray, and Rosegrant 1999).

Table 7.1 India: Trends in agricultural input use and yields, 1961–2004

Indicator	1961	1971	1981	1991	2002
Average size of holding (hectares)	2.69	2.30	1.84	1.57	1.41[a]
Net cropped area (million hectares)	133.2	140.3	140.0	143.0	141.1[b]
Gross cropped area (million hectares)	152.8	165.8	172.6	185.7	187.9[b]
Gross irrigated area as percentage of gross cropped area	18.3	23.0	28.8	33.6	40.0[b]
Fertilizer nutrient use (kilograms per hectare)	1.9	13.1	31.8	67.4	89.8
Food grain production (million tons)	82.0	108.4	129.6	176.4	212.0
Milk production (million tons)	20.0	22.0	31.6	53.9	88.1
Fish production (million tons)	1.2	1.8	2.4	3.8	6.4
Egg production (billions)	2.8	6.2	10.1	21.1	40.4
Percentage of total value of production					
Crops	82.4	84.4	81.4	74.7	71.2
Livestock	17.6	15.6	18.6	25.3	28.8
Percentage of agriculture in					
Total export value	44.3	36.8	35.5	22.5	12.4
Total import value	36.4	37.0	18.3	11.3	6.2
Crop yields (tons per cultivated/sown/harvested hectare)					
Rice	1.01	1.11	1.29	1.74	2.00
Wheat	0.85	1.32	1.71	2.33	2.70
Coarse cereals	0.71	0.85	1.03	0.91	1.14

Sources: Reserve Bank of India 2000; Ministry of Finance, *Economic survey,* various years.
Note: Crop yields are three-year averages—that is, 1961 refers to 1961–63, and so on.
[a]Figure is from 1995 census.
[b]Figure is for 2001.

Overall, India's agricultural achievements are impressive, with increased per capita food production and accumulating food stocks. Despite this success, India still faces many challenges in increasing agricultural productivity. First, to reduce poverty and malnutrition, which are most prevalent in rural areas, India needs not only to improve the availability of food (through higher production and better distribution) but also to generate income and employment opportunities for the poor to provide them with access to food. Second, because accelerated economic growth and rapid urbanization are driving demand for high-value commodities, particularly livestock and horticultural products, future agricultural growth needs to be much more diversified. Third, sustainable management and use of natural resources is a growing challenge, with depletion of groundwater, agrochemical pollution, and land degradation by waterlogging, salinity, soil erosion, and deterioration of soil fertility.

Fourth, public investment in agriculture in real terms has shown a persistent decline, while subsidies for agriculture have increased over time despite the new economic policies. The decline in public investment has serious implications for agricultural growth and poverty reduction (Roy 2001). Fan, Hazell, and Thorat (1999) found that investment in agricultural research provides a high marginal return relative to other investments in terms of both growth and poverty reduction, and this return may now be higher in rainfed areas. Careful targeting of public investment—incorporating subsectoral and regional priorities and efficient use of existing infrastructure, particularly irrigation—is essential for achieving the 4 percent growth per annum contemplated in the current national agricultural policy. However, high levels of subsidies compete with funds available for needed public investment, including investment in agricultural research.

The current national agricultural policy anticipates that market forces will guide future agricultural growth through domestic market reforms, an increasing role for the private sector, and removal of price distortions. The policy of interventions in food-grain markets to stabilize prices will continue, but efforts will be made to make these interventions more effective and efficient by improving management of the Food Corporation of India and by targeting public distribution of food grains to the poor. These reforms, coupled with a focus on value-added and commercialization, and improved product quality and comparative advantage, are essential for successful transition to a knowledge-based and competitive agricultural sector. The role of the agricultural research system will be central in these processes.

Historical and Institutional Development of the Indian Research System

Historical Evolution

The first organized attempt to promote agricultural development, including R&E, in India began in the last quarter of the 19th century with the establishment of the Department of Revenue, Agriculture, and Commerce in the imperial and provincial governments, together with a bacteriological laboratory and five veterinary colleges. Around 1905, the Imperial (now Indian) Agricultural Research Institute (IARI) was established, along with six agricultural colleges.[2] A milestone in the history of Indian agricultural R&E system was the establishment of the Imperial (now Indian) Council of Agricultural Research (ICAR), in 1929, as a semi-autonomous body to promote, guide, and coordinate agricultural research nationally. Between 1921 and 1958, a number of central commodity committees were formed to develop commercial crops: cotton, lac (a hardened resin secreted by lac insects on the leaves of various trees), jute, sugarcane, coconut, tobacco, oilseeds, areca nut (from a palm of the genus *Areca*), spices, and cashews. These committees—also semi-autonomous and financed by government grants and revenues from a levy on the output of each commodity—set up research stations for each commercial crop. Initially, the commodity committees served the interests of the imperial government by providing revenue and ensuring raw materials for industry; later they focused on national development objectives, including research. Participation in the commodity committees was eventually broadened to include producers and representatives of trade and industry.

An important institutional innovation in the post-independence period was the establishment of the All India Coordinated Research Projects (AICRPs), initiated in 1957 under ICAR to promote multidisciplinary and multi-institutional research. The success of the first project for maize led to numerous AICRPs covering all major commodities. The concept also spread to noncommodity research.

In 1965, ICAR was mandated to coordinate, direct, and promote agricultural research in India by overseeing all the research stations previously controlled by commodity committees and various government departments. Subsequently, the Department of Agricultural Research and Education (DARE) was created in the central Ministry of Agriculture to facilitate linkages between ICAR and the central and state governments and with foreign research organizations.

On the recommendation of two joint Indian–American review teams (in 1955 and 1960), state agricultural universities (SAUs) were established, following the land-grant pattern of the United States. The first SAU was opened at Pantnagar in the state of Uttar Pradesh in 1960. The SAUs were autonomous, funded by the government of the respective states; they integrated education with research and (to some extent) frontline extension, although mainstream extension remained the responsibility of the state departments of agriculture.

A number of international agencies played important roles in the development of the public agricultural R&E system in India. Notable among these were the Rockefeller Foundation, which provided support to AICRPs (Lele and Goldsmith 1989), and the U.S. Agency for International Development, which played an active role in the establishment of the SAUs and the training of staff through partnerships with U.S. land-grant universities. The World Bank has provided considerable resources to agricultural research since 1980. The initial phase of this support emphasized the development of research infrastructure and human resources, while recent support has focused on strategic research areas, priority research themes, and institutional reforms.

The Current Structure of the Public Research System
Currently, the public agricultural R&E system consists of ICAR and its various institutes, and the SAUs and their various campuses and regional institutes. At the center, ICAR funds and manages a vast network of research institutes, including

national institutes for basic and strategic research and postgraduate education;[3] central research institutes for commodity-specific research; national bureaus for conservation and exchange of germplasm and soil-survey work; and national research centers (NRCs) for applied, commodity-specific strategic research in "mission mode."[4]

In addition, ICAR manages a large number of AICRPs (as mentioned above), which draw scientists from both ICAR institutions and the SAUs. Most AICRPs centers are located on SAU campuses under the administrative control of the respective SAUs. However, for the most important AICRPs (those for rice, wheat, maize, cattle, oilseeds, water, cropping systems, and biological control of pests), ICAR has established special project directorates with their own research infrastructure, under ICAR administrative control, that consist of teams of multidisciplinary scientists.

In 2000, ICAR had 5 national institutes (including an academy for agricultural research management), 42 central research institutes, 4 national bureaus, 10 project directorates, 28 NRCs, and 82 AICRPs (ICAR 2001). In addition, ICAR established 261 *krishi vigyan kendras* (agricultural science centers, or KVKs) at the district level that are responsible for the transfer of new technologies and for training farmers. Some of these KVKs are managed by SAUs and nongovernmental organizations (NGOs). In addition, there are 8 training centers that train the educators in areas such as livestock, horticulture, fisheries, and home science.

There are now 31 SAUs in India with faculties that include agriculture, veterinary science, engineering, and home science. Depending on the nature of the state's agriculture, SAUs may also have faculties of horticulture, fisheries, and forestry, and some SAUs focus exclusively on animal sciences. In addition, there is 1 central agricultural university under ICAR to cater for the needs of small states in northeastern India. SAUs also have zonal research stations to address research problems for each agroclimatic zone.

In addition to the traditional national agricultural research system (NARS)—that is, the ICAR/SAU system—there are nonagricultural universities and organizations that support or conduct agricultural research either directly or indirectly. For example, the departments of biotechnology (DBT), science and technology (DST), and scientific and industrial research (DSIR) under the Ministry of Science and Technology support and conduct agricultural research at their institutes and sometimes fund research in the ICAR/SAU system. Similarly, a number of nonagricultural universities have faculties of agriculture.

Private-Sector Development

Initially, a few private companies dealing with agricultural inputs (pesticides, fertilizers, and machinery, for example) invested modestly in product development, although there was little effort to establish in-house research capacity. The situation changed in the 1980s with the growing availability of trained scientists, rapid expansion of markets for agricultural inputs and processed foods, and liberalized policies to support private-sector development. The private sector now supplies half of all certified seed, half of all fertilizer, and most of the pesticide and farm machinery. Private investment in research currently focuses on hybrid seed, biotechnology, pesticides, fertilizer, machinery, animal health, poultry, and food processing.

The government has provided strong incentives in the form of tax exemptions on research expenditures and venture capital, and liberal policies on import of research equipment to encourage participation of the private sector in research. The most significant development has occurred in the seed sector after the implementation of a new seed policy in 1988, which allowed the importation of seed materials, as well as majority ownership of seed companies by foreign companies (from 1991). A number of foreign seed companies entered the market, and several local seed companies have established considerable research capacity (Pray, Ramaswami, and Kelley 2001). Some local companies collaborate with overseas companies for access to proprietary tools and technologies. Private hybrids now account for a significant share of the market for sorghum, maize, and cotton (Singh, Pal, and Morris 1995; Pray, Ramaswami, and Kelley 2001), and companies with some foreign ownership account for about one-third of this market (Pray and Basant 2001). Developments in biotechnology have further strengthened these trends.

With implications for innovation that are not yet clear, the Indian government recently approved the Protection of Plant Varieties and Farmers Rights Act (2001) to provide intellectual property protection to plant breeders. At the same time, the act emphasizes farmers' rights to save, exchange, and sell unbranded seed of a protected variety. India has also amended the Patent Act (1970) to make it compatible with WTO agreements. A third set of amendments enshrined in the Patents (Amendment) Act (2005) grants process and product patents in all fields of technology. These are likely to stimulate research in the biotechnology and plant and animal health sectors.

Participation of private nonprofit organizations in agricultural research has also increased. There are now a few private foundations, as well as NGOs, actively engaged in agricultural research. In particular, the M. S. Swaminathan Research Foundation and Mahyco Research Foundation have developed considerable research capacity with a national presence and are working in close collaboration with the ICAR/SAU system. In addition, many small, regional, and local NGOs are engaged in agricultural research, such as those managing some ICAR-sponsored KVKs.

Contemporary Developments

The ICAR/SAU system has reached a stage where it needs to consolidate past gains through modernization of research infrastructure, development of human capital, innovations in research management, and stronger linkages with clients. The system is responding to these challenges, albeit to varying degrees and with varying speed (Mruthyunjaya and Ranjitha 1998). Several of these challenges will be addressed in the concluding section of this chapter. Here we note two recent developments: ecoregional research initiatives for research planning, and responses to new science.

Ecoregional Research Initiatives

Although the Green Revolution technologies were rapidly adopted in large areas, further gains in irrigated areas, as well as in rainfed areas that have enjoyed fewer benefits, require more location-specific research to adapt technologies to local and seasonal conditions. The system has been constrained in responding to this challenge because of the limitations of the structure underpinning national or regional ICAR institutes and SAUs due to their strong commodity and disciplinary orientation. Accordingly, an ecoregional approach to planning and organizing agricultural research was introduced in 1978 to better target research efforts, integrate research across disciplines, and locate appropriate sites for research programs. Under the National Agricultural Research Project (NARP), implemented with World Bank funding, the entire country was divided into 126 agroclimatic zones, each consisting of several districts. In each of the zones, a research station was established under a specific SAU to carry out applied and adaptive research relevant to the zone (Ghosh 1991). An advisory committee with a wide representation of farmers, NGOs, and the state department of agriculture was created to link scientists more closely with farmers and other stakeholders, and research programs were developed through a bottom-up participatory approach. These zonal research stations also provided technical support to the KVKs and state extension departments.

The ecoregional approach was further developed under the National Agricultural Technology Project (NATP), again implemented with financial support from the World Bank. Under NATP, the country is divided into 5 ecoregions (arid, coastal, hill and mountain, irrigated, and rainfed), which are further delineated into 14 production systems. Research programs for each of the production systems are identified in a participatory mode and implemented using a multi-institutional and multidisciplinary systems approach. These research programs are intended to complement the AICRPs and the zonal research stations by promoting a systems approach to planning and implementing research.

Biotechnology

Over the past decade or so, revolutionary advances in biotechnology have transformed the way agricultural research is organized and funded. To meet this challenge, the Department of Biotechnology (DBT) was created in 1986 under the Ministry of Science and Technology to support research and human resources and infrastructure development in biotechnology related to agriculture, health care, the environment, and industry. DBT has established 6 autonomous institutions for biotechnology research. It also funds biotechnology research in other institutions, including ICAR institutes and SAUs, through special projects and grants, and through its competitive grants program. In addition, ICAR has developed capacity in biotechnology research in several of its research institutes and has created new entities exclusively for biotechnology research. These initiatives have allowed India to develop considerable capacity in this area of science, although much of it is outside the ICAR/SAU system.[5] At least 10 research institutes have capacity in genetic engineering.

The private sector is also responding to developments in biotechnology, with up to 45 companies active in agricultural biotechnology research (broadly defined) for a market that was estimated to be worth US$75 million in 1997 (Qaim 2001). Both foreign and domestic companies are included, although all of the domestic companies with significant biotechnology programs have developed joint ventures with global companies. At least 3 foreign companies have major biotechnology research facilities in India, 1 with a team of 34 scientists (Pray and Basant 2001).

Given that several genetically modified products are now moving into field testing and commercial release, the government is currently focusing on establishing a framework to regulate biotechnology research and the testing and release of genetically modified organisms (GMOs). The Review Committee on Genetic Manipulation (RCGM) under DBT (comprising members from various scientific organizations) is responsible for monitoring biotechnology research, safety, and the import and export of GMOs. The Genetic Engineering Approval Committee of the Ministry of Environment and Forestry assesses GMOs for environmental safety and approves them for wide-scale testing and commercial release. India has allowed field experiments of GMOs, and commercial cultivation of transgenic cotton was approved in 2002.

Funding of Research

The amount of research funding and the mechanisms for fund allocation are powerful instruments of research policy in India as elsewhere. Most funds for agricultural research in India are allocated through block grants, but funding through competitive grants is now gaining acceptance, especially for operating and equipment costs.

Methods for Allocating Public Funding

Most public funding to agricultural R&E in India takes the form of block grants to ICAR and the SAUs, with allocations determined by five-year plans. At the beginning of each plan, the Planning Commission constitutes a working group to agree on broad agricultural R&E priorities and to assess financial requirements for their implementation. Recommendations of the working group are discussed in several consultations between DARE and the Planning Commission. Based on the outcome of these deliberations, DARE develops its five-year plan, and plan outlays are communicated by the Planning Commission on approval by the Ministry of Finance. Next, five-year plans are developed for each ICAR institute. Depending upon the level of proposed outlays, these plans are evaluated by committees composed of directors of the institutes, senior research managers from ICAR, and representatives of the Planning Commission, Ministry of Finance, and other departments. The approved outlays are the basis for each institute's funding during the plan period, and funds received are demarcated as "plan funds." The ongoing activities of the previous plan are financed under "nonplan funding," which primarily pays salaries and other fixed costs.

A similar procedure is followed for state funding, except that state allocations are first determined by the Planning Commission as part of total plan allocations to states. Both plan and nonplan expenditures on R&E are then approved by the respective state governments.

This process implies that resource-allocation decisions are made through informed opinion and collective wisdom regarding research priorities that address developmental objectives. Institutions are directly involved in the allocation decisions, and other stakeholders are widely consulted. Historical trends also play an important role, especially for nonplan funding.

Use of formal economic methods for allocating agricultural research funds is a recent phenomenon in India. These methods are being tested under NATP for research programs at the ecoregional level. Another innovative method for resource allocation is followed in the AICRPs, which ICAR and SAU fund at the ratio of 75 to 25 percent, respectively. The locations of AICRP centers are decided based on priority ecoregions, and funds are allocated accordingly.

In general, resource allocation appears to have been relatively efficient. Jain and Byerlee (1999) computed a congruency index of 0.88 between value of production and resource allocation in 20 production environments for wheat. The main discrepancy has been the strong tendency for research intensity to be higher in smaller production environments. There is good evidence that resources have shifted with changing production conditions. In the case of wheat, this implies an increase in resources allocated for breeding for late planting and a decrease in resources for rainfed areas, in accordance with increased cropping intensity and irrigation, respectively.

Competitive Funding

Competitive funding is gaining popularity in India. It is regarded as a powerful mechanism to direct funds to high-priority areas, improve quality and accountability, and promote wider participation of research providers and innovative partnerships. There are at least five different competitive funds operating at the national and state levels to support agriculture research. Unlike those of other developing countries, where these funds have been established mostly with donor support, several of the Indian funds were initiated with domestic resources and may therefore be more sustainable (Carney, Gill, and Pal 2000). Although these funds are increasing, they still account for only about 3 percent of public research funding.

ICAR's Ad Hoc Research Scheme, financed by the agricultural cess on selected commercial crops, is the oldest competitive fund, supporting research in emerging areas and research to fill critical technology gaps. NATP's Competitive Grant Program (CGP) and the Competitive Agricultural Research Program (CARP) of the Uttar Pradesh Council of Agricultural Research (UPCAR) are more recent and are donor-supported.[6] The competitive funds of DST and DBT support upstream research in all fields of science, including agriculture. All these funds have similar operational modalities: short-term research projects selected through peer review and provision of funds for operating costs but not for salaries and infrastructure (Table 7.2).

Although these funds are operating quite successfully and are in high demand, a number of issues need to be addressed. Because research priorities are not well defined in the request for proposals, the number of proposals is large, and the success rate is low. (CGP addresses this problem to some extent.) Most operate at the national level, and there is no systematic mechanism to ensure that regional priorities are addressed. This problem, coupled with weak capacity to develop competitive proposals in institutions located in less-developed regions, leads to a low success rate in those regions. More effort is needed to train scientists in weaker institutions in developing research proposals. The experience of CGP has also shown that prompt evaluation is important in attracting quality proposals. Finally, because research projects under competitive grants are time-bound, timely release of funds and efficient administrative procedures are critical.

Table 7.2 India: Important competitive funds for agricultural research

Details	Ad hoc Agricultural Produce Cess Fund; ICAR research scheme	ICAR National Agricultural Technology Project (NATP) Competitive Grant Program	Department of Science and Technology (DST)	Department of Biotechnology (DBT)	Competitive Agricultural Research Program (CARP) of the Uttar Pradesh Council of Agricultural Research (UPCAR)
Institutional base	ICAR headquarters	ICAR headquarters	DST headquarters	DBT headquarters	UPCAR
Size of fund	US$5.8 million (1999–2000)	US$21.1 million over five years (1998–99 to 2002–03)	US$10.5 million annually	US$9.5 million annually	US$2.5 million over five years (1998–99 to 2002–03)
Source of finance	Cess collected by the Government of India under the Agricultural Cess Act of 1940 and 1966 (amendment)	NATP funds of the World Bank	DST budget	DBT budget	World Bank funds
Purpose	To fill critical gaps in scientific fields and address research problems for agriculture and allied sectors through short-term, results-oriented ad hoc research	To support agroecosystem research under NATP with enhanced basic and strategic research; product, process, and market development with greater partnership between public and private sectors	To promote research in frontline science and engineering areas, develop research capacity, and encourage young scientists	To support R&D in biotechnology to achieve excellence and develop new products, processes, patents, and applied technology	To draw on the comparative advantage of research capacity outside state agricultural universities, including the private sector, for synergies and cost-effectiveness through collaboration
Eligibility	All public, recognized private, and nongovernmental organizations capable of undertaking research	All public, private (foundations and companies), and nongovernmental research organizations, and international research centers collaborating with national programs on a cost-sharing basis	Recognized public, private, and nongovernmental organizations capable of undertaking research	Recognized public, private, and nongovernmental organizations capable of undertaking research	Recognized public, private, and non-governmental organizations capable of undertaking research and located in the state of Uttar Pradesh
Components of project grant	Operating expenses, equipment costs, contract staff salaries, and minor civil works in exceptional cases	Operating expenses, equipment costs, contract staff salaries, and minor civil works in exceptional cases	Operating expenses, equipment costs, and contract staff salaries	Operating expenses, equipment costs, and contract staff salaries	Primarily operating expenses; equipment, training, and consultancy costs for basic and strategic research only

Source: Pal 1999.

Overview of Sources of Funding and Fund Flows

Figure 7.1 provides a schematic representation of the sources and flows of funds in the Indian NARS around 2000. Though agriculture is a state responsibility, the central government funded a block grant of US$300.9 million in 2000 through ICAR, which also manages grants and loans from multilateral donors, and collaborative research programs funded by bilateral donors and international organizations. The World Bank is the primary source of such funds. ICAR managed a loan of US$180 million from the World Bank under NATP for strengthening research and extension for the period 1998–2003. A small loan was also provided for human resources development in SAUs in four states (less than US$10 million for 1995–2001).

In addition, ICAR manages the Agricultural Produce Cess Fund, levied at 0.5 percent (ad valorem) on specified export commodities and accounting for about 2 percent of the total ICAR budget in 2000.[7] Finally, with implementation of a new policy on self-generated income (ICAR 1997), ICAR earns some resources through consultancies, contract research and services, sale of seed and other planting material, and royalties on research products through partnerships with the private sector. However, progress has been modest: ICAR generated just 3 percent of its total budget in 2000 through these means.

Overall, the central government provides 52 percent of public funding for agricultural R&E in India, almost all of which passes through ICAR.[8] A significant proportion of the ICAR funds (30 percent) is made available for extramural funding (Figure 7.1), and a large proportion of this (87 percent) is directed to the SAUs. Nonagricultural public research institutions and private (profit and nonprofit) research organizations obtain 7 percent and 6 percent, respectively, of ICAR's extramural funding through competitive research programs and support to KVKs.

In terms of funding mechanisms, about 30 percent of the extramural funding from ICAR is disbursed through the AICRPs in the form of block grants, 12 percent through competitive funding, 34 percent through donor-funded projects, 17 percent through grants to KVKs, and 7 percent as development grants to SAUs.[9]

Annual block grants from the state governments to the SAUs totaling US$277 million in 2000 are the second major source of funding. Virtually all of these funds are used intramurally by the SAUs. State funds are not used by ICAR institutes, with the exception of a small competitive fund in Uttar Pradesh that is open to all research organizations in the state, including ICAR institutes.

The remaining significant source of research funds is private firms. Nearly all of this funding is used for intramural research, which accounts for about 11 percent of the total. Private funding of research in public organizations is negligible. The most often cited example was a research contract between ICAR and the Mahyco

Figure 7.1   India: Funding channels for agricultural R&E, 2000

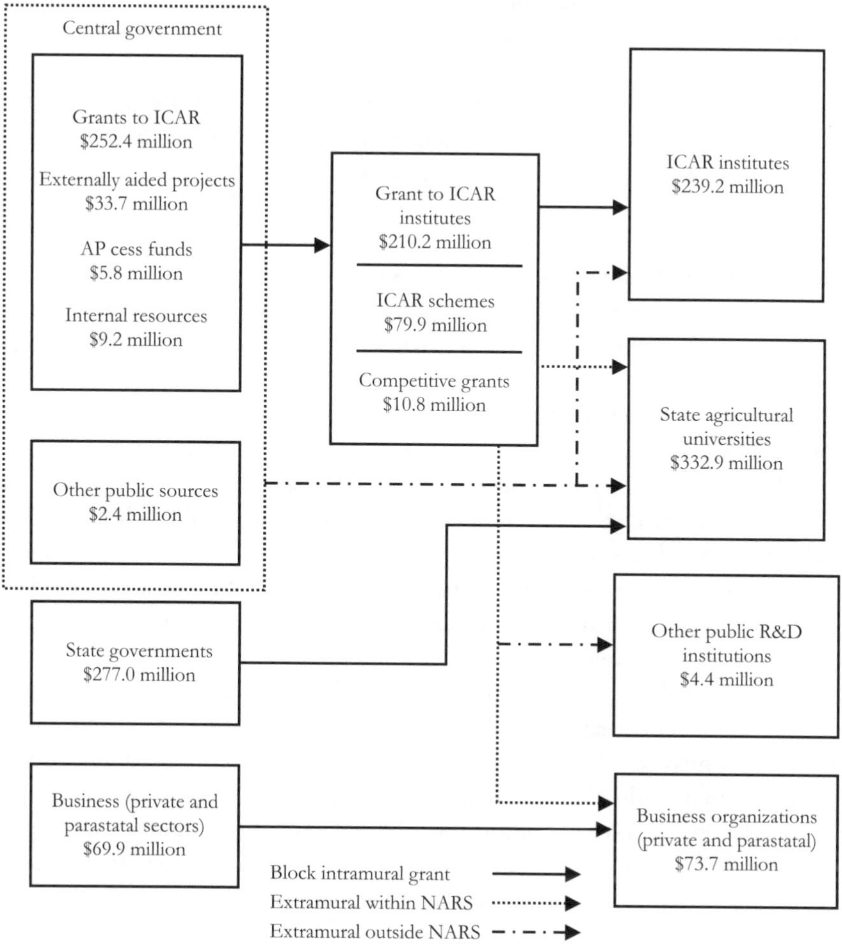

Central government

Grants to ICAR
$252.4 million

Externally aided projects
$33.7 million

AP cess funds
$5.8 million

Internal resources
$9.2 million

Other public sources
$2.4 million

Grant to ICAR
institutes
$210.2 million

ICAR schemes
$79.9 million

Competitive grants
$10.8 million

ICAR institutes
$239.2 million

State agricultural
universities
$332.9 million

State governments
$277.0 million

Other public R&D
institutions
$4.4 million

Business (private and
parastatal sectors)
$69.9 million

Business organizations
(private and parastatal)
$73.7 million

Block intramural grant
Extramural within NARS
Extramural outside NARS

Source: Compiled by authors from various sources.
Notes: Data are in nominal U.S. dollars. State funding data are revised estimates. ICAR funding
was apportioned using budget estimates. Private R&D investment data were available for 1997
(DBT 1999), and were extrapolated for 2000 using the growth rate reported in Table 7.5. Extrap-
olated expenditure on seed research reported in Table 7.5 was also included in this figure, as
DST data do not cover private seed research.

Research Foundation for hybrid rice development in 1995. Such linkages could increase in the future because of concerted efforts by ICAR, but they are unlikely to make a significant contribution to total agricultural research efforts in the country for many years.

In terms of spending (the right side of Figure 7.1), ICAR institutes together accounted for 37 percent of the national expenditure on agricultural R&E and SAUs for 51 percent. The remaining 12 percent was spent by other public and private organizations.

Trends in Overall Public Funding for Research

India has consistently committed substantial government funds to research in all fields of science, including agriculture. Figure 7.2 shows the trends in public funding, in real terms, for agricultural R&E in India. Total funding increased in real terms, from $284 million 1999 PPP or international dollars in 1961 to $875 million in 1981. This figure rose to $2.893 billion in 2000 international dollars—a 10-fold increase over the past four decades (Figure 7.2).[10] In nominal terms at the prevailing exchange rate, public funding to agricultural R&E reached US$578 million in 2000. Increases are observed for both central and state funding. Funding from the states grew rapidly during the 1960s, during which time a large number of SAUs were established. Central funding outpaced state funding thereafter until their shares roughly equalized in the 1980s and the 1990s.

Using simplifying assumptions,[11] nearly three-quarters of this total R&E expenditure goes to research (net of education), and research expenditure in absolute terms amounted to $1.898 billion 1999 international dollars in 2000. Overall public research funding grew at 3.16 percent in the 1970s and 7.03 percent in the 1980s, slowing to 4.61 percent in the 1990s. These trends show a continuing, strong political commitment to research despite a pluralistic political system, changes in governments, and shifts in public-investment priorities.

Intensity of Research Funding

Another way to assess funding is to compute various intensity ratios, such as expenditure per agricultural worker, expenditure per unit of agricultural land, and share of agricultural GDP (AgGDP) (Table 7.3). All the intensity ratios registered impressive growth over time despite significant growth in population, land area, and AgGDP. Agricultural research expenditure as a percentage of AgGDP increased significantly during the 1960s and 1980s but remained around 0.3 percent during the 1990s (Figure 7.3).[12] This slowdown is worrying given that the developing-country public-research average is 0.62 percent and the global average is 1.04 per-

Figure 7.2   India: Trends in real public agricultural R&E funding, 1961–2000

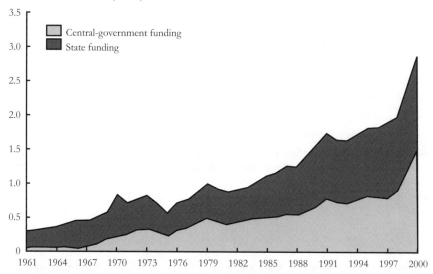

1999 international dollars (billion)

Central-government funding
State funding

Sources: Developed by the authors from expenditure data obtained from the Comptroller and
Auditor General of India, various years; the Reserve Bank of India, various years; and the Ministry
of Finance, *Finance accounts,* various years. See also Appendix Table 7A.1.
Notes: "Central-government funding" includes funding directed to ICAR institutes and research
structures, along with other central-government activities related to agricultural R&D; "state
funding" refers to funding of state-government undertakings, which mainly consist of research
undertaken by the state agricultural universities (SAUs).

cent (Pardey and Beintema 2001). Part of the difference can be attributed to the
relative importance of agriculture and economies of scale and scope in agricultural
research (Alston, Pardey, and Roseboom 1998), but there appears to be a clear case
of underinvestment in India: China, a country of comparable size and level of
development, spent 0.43 percent of AgGDP on research in 1995. Even comparing
agricultural research with general science and technology research in India, ICAR
received only about 10 percent of total central-government research funds in 1997
(although state funding is more important for agriculture than for other fields).

Funding by States

Table 7.4 gives real growth and intensity of agricultural research funding at the state
level. The growth in real funding was highly uneven among states during the 1970s.

Table 7.3 India: Intensity of public agricultural R&E funding, 1961–99

Indicator	1961–63	1971–73	1981–83	1991–93	1997–99
R&E expenditure					
Constant local currency units (billion 1999 rupees)	2.697	6.576	7.892	14.335	17.885
Total expenditure (million 1999 international dollars)	312	760	912	1,657	2,068
Per capita expenditure (1999 international dollars)	0.71	1.39	1.34	1.97	2.14
Expenditure per agricultural worker (1999 international dollars)	2.38	6.04	6.17	8.94	9.76
Expenditure per hectare of net cropped area (1999 international dollars)	2.29	5.47	6.50	11.75	14.52
Expenditure as percentage of AgGDP	0.20	0.35	0.36	0.44	0.42
Research expenditure (net of education and extension)					
Constant local currency units (billion 1999 rupees)	1.511	4.054	5.057	9.069	11.404
Research expenditure (million 1999 international dollars)	175	469	589	1,049	1,318
Research expenditure as percentage of AgGDP	0.11	0.22	0.23	0.28	0.31

Sources: Developed by the authors from expenditure data obtained from the Comptroller and Auditor General of India, various years; the Reserve Bank of India, various years; and the Ministry of Finance, *Finance accounts,* various years; plus other data obtained from the Government of India and from the Reserve Bank of India 2000.

Note: Figures are three-year averages. See Table 7A.1 for details of international dollars.

Figure 7.3   India: Trends in level and intensity of public agricultural-research funding in India, 1961–2000

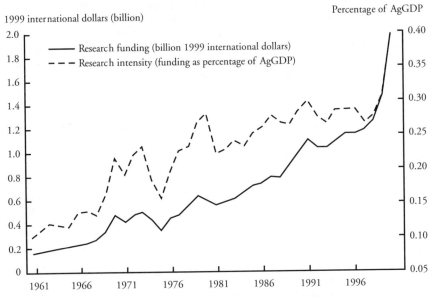

Sources: Developed by the authors from expenditure data obtained from the Comptroller and Auditor General of India, various years; the Reserve Bank of India, various years; and the Ministry of Finance, *Finance accounts,* various years.

Table 7.4 India: Growth and intensity of agricultural R&E funding by state governments, 1972–99

State	Annual growth rate in real funding (percent)			Funding per hectare (1999 international dollars)		Funding per agricultural worker (1999 international dollars)		Funding as percentage of AgGDP		Percentage of total funding by all states
	1972–81	1982–91	1992–99	1981–83	1995–97[a]	1981–83[b]	1991–93[b]	1981–83	1997–99	1997–99
Andhra Pradesh	11.40	6.47	5.23	3.03	9.02	2.11	3.48	0.16	0.28	8.08
Assam	-0.07	9.51	-0.03	7.36	11.06	NA	10.13	0.28	0.33	2.84
Bihar	18.52	8.55	5.10	3.00	8.32	1.42	1.86	0.13	0.25	4.96
Gujarat	0.61	9.71	4.78	3.24	9.85	4.72	8.33	0.19	0.41	7.52
Haryana	28.56	5.16	8.18	8.16	22.69	13.17	16.66	0.28	0.44	6.23
Himachal Pradesh	-0.09	12.76	10.21	17.42	65.64	NA	18.46	0.62	1.52	3.31
Jammu and Kashmir	-0.08	10.97	12.79	8.48	34.12	5.66	NA	NA	NA	2.25
Karnataka	12.91	7.54	3.03	2.61	6.02	3.04	4.48	0.19	0.28	5.74
Kerala	25.40	5.23	1.85	11.57	28.08	8.97	17.13	0.31	0.41	5.65
Madhya Pradesh	-0.08	13.29	1.09	0.60	2.10	0.74	2.16	0.07	0.14	3.42
Maharashtra	0.74	7.06	2.43	4.86	9.82	5.89	7.75	0.39	0.43	14.21
Orissa	7.75	6.50	-0.02	1.65	3.22	1.55	3.02	0.10	0.21	1.78
Punjab	3.43	10.28	2.41	8.40	17.92	12.33	19.28	0.24	0.30	6.48
Rajasthan	3.63	10.95	3.58	1.11	3.22	2.34	4.11	0.12	0.18	4.13
Tamil Nadu	3.80	13.00	7.44	4.18	18.52	2.07	5.24	0.21	0.59	9.34
Uttar Pradesh	-0.06	5.74	2.06	3.31	5.21	2.37	3.00	0.13	0.16	8.03
West Bengal	12.13	2.35	4.73	5.34	7.57	3.48	3.07	0.17	0.17	4.89
Average for all states	1.34	8.23	3.82	3.45	7.86	3.27	4.99	0.19	0.24	100[c]

Sources: Developed by the authors from expenditure data obtained from the Comptroller and Auditor General of India, various years; the Reserve Bank of India, various years; and the Ministry of Finance, *Finance accounts*, various years; plus other data obtained from the Government of India and from the Reserve Bank of India 2000.

Notes: Funding intensities and shares represent annual averages for the respective periods. See Table 7A.1 for details of international dollars.

[a]Computed using triennium average of NCA, ending in 1997.

[b]Computed using census data for agricultural workers for 1981 and 1991, respectively.

[c]Excludes small share representing expenditure for small states.

These differences narrowed in the 1980s, with steady growth in all states. Total state funding increased from 1.3 percent per annum in the 1970s to 8.2 percent in the 1980s, slowing to 3.8 percent in the 1990s. The intensity of state funding has increased in all states except West Bengal since the 1980s. However, wide variation persists between states with comparatively high ratios, over 0.4 percent of AgGDP (Himachal Pradesh, Tamil Nadu, Haryana, Maharashtra, Gujarat, and Kerala) and states with very low ratios, under 0.2 percent (Madhya Pradesh, Rajasthan, Uttar Pradesh, and West Bengal).

A host of factors may explain variations in the intensity of agricultural research. (Rose-Ackerman and Evenson 1985; Judd, Boyce, and Evenson 1986; Alston, Pardey, and Roseboom 1998). Pal and Singh (1997) applied a political-economy model to analyze the determinants of the level of state funding to agricultural research in India using cross-sectional and time-series data for the period 1982–94. Although the results were mixed, and unmeasured state-specific attributes were important, per capita state funding was found to be strongly related to per capita AgGDP, indicating that states with higher income levels spend comparatively more on agricultural research. Rural literacy and the share of agriculture in government expenditure also had a positive and significant effect on research intensity. Other factors, such as sources of growth in agriculture (for example, expansion of agricultural land and irrigated area), crop diversification, and terms of trade, were insignificant. It seems that the availability of public resources and the importance assigned to agriculture have important consequences for the amount of public funding directed toward agricultural research.[13]

Donor Funding

The U.S. Agency for International Development (USAID) has been a significant funder of agricultural research. USAID supported SAU development from the early 1960s until 1977. Its support peaked in the 1980s, when a major agricultural research project was under way (Alex 1997). In total, USAID invested some US$108 million (in 1999 prices) in Indian agricultural research until about 1990, when support was terminated.

Beginning in 1980, the World Bank became a significant supporter of agricultural research at the state and zonal levels, and from 1997 at the national level. The World Bank has also supported human-resource development in the SAUs since 1995, and a number of state projects have financed agricultural research, especially in Rajasthan and Uttar Pradesh. In total, the World Bank has provided US$538 million (in 1999 prices) to agricultural research since 1975 (Appendix Table 7A.2).[14]

One important implication of these results is that in low-income countries like India, donor support to agricultural research can help increase intensity levels.

However, long-run funding sustainability depends on India's giving higher priority to agricultural research investment over nondevelopment expenditures, many of which are subsidies. This is particularly true when the rates of returns to agricultural research are found to be high.

Private Research Funding

The recent rapid growth in private research spending in India has outpaced the capacity to track its intensity, orientation, and impact. Based on broad estimates for each subsector (seed, pesticide, machinery, livestock, and food processing), total private or business funding for agricultural research (including funding by state-owned enterprises) in India doubled from an estimated US$24 million in 1985 dollars to US$51 million in 1995 (Table 7.5),[15] or from $119 million to $253 million in 1999 international dollars. Private research funding has grown at 7.5 percent, compared with 5.1 percent in the public sector over the same period, and accounted for 11 percent of total funding of agricultural research in 2000 (Figure 7.1).

Table 7.5 shows that the largest investment has occurred in pesticides and food processing, followed by seed, fertilizer, and machinery. The most rapid increases in private growth have occurred in food processing, seeds, veterinary products, and sugar. More recently, there has also been strong investment in biotechnology, animal health, and the poultry sector. This has been accompanied by significant growth in research expenditure by multinational companies.

Table 7.5   India: Agricultural research expenditures by private firms and state-owned enterprises, 1984–95

Industry	Research expenditure (million 1995 U.S. dollars) 1985	Research expenditure (million 1995 U.S. dollars) 1995	Research expenditure (million 1999 international dollars)[a] 1985	Research expenditure (million 1999 international dollars)[a] 1995	Annual growth rate (percent)[a] 1985–95	Share in state enterprises (percent) 1995
Seed	1.33	4.93	6.62	24.55	13.1	0
Machinery	3.70	6.48	18.43	32.27	5.61	13
Fertilizers	6.80	6.65	33.87	33.12	−0.22	67
Pesticides	9.00	17.02	44.82	84.76	6.37	15
Veterinary	0.90	2.72	4.48	13.54	11.06	5
Sugar	0.90	2.49	4.48	12.40	10.17	1
Food processing	1.34	10.47	6.67	52.14	20.56	1
Total	23.97	50.75	119.38	252.78	7.50	16

Source: Pray and Basant 2001.

Note: See Table 7A.1 for details of international dollars.

[a]Calculated by authors.

Providers of Research: Human Resources and Patterns of Expenditures

Human Resources for R&E

Although precise and consistent estimates of scientific staff in the ICAR/SAU system over time are not available, the number of scientists working in the ICAR/SAU system during the late 1980s was estimated to be 4,189 at ICAR and 14,851 at the SAUs, totaling 19,040 (ICAR unpublished management records). The number of scientists remained steady at ICAR during the 1990s (4,092 in 1998) but decreased significantly at the SAUs (17,678 in 1992); it has likely fallen further since that time through attrition.

Adjusting the number of scientists by share of research expenditure relative to extension and education (for ICAR) and share of time spent on research (for SAUs), the number of full-time equivalent (fte) scientists in the late 1990s was 2,999 within ICAR and 8,132 within the SAUs. This amounts to a total of 11,131 fte researchers nationally, in line with staffing levels in the United States (Table 7.6). This is a substantial increase from the estimated 5,666 fte researchers in the ICAR/SAU system in 1975, and 8,389 in 1985 (Pardey and Roseboom 1989).

The educational qualifications of Indian researchers are also impressive: about two-thirds of researchers hold Ph.D. degrees, and the balance hold M.Sc. degrees. The proportion of female researchers is very low, however—7.5 percent within ICAR and 2.1 percent in the SAUs.

Scientific staff are supported by a large number of technical and administrative staff. The ratio of scientists to administrative staff is especially high in the universities, at 1:2.5. ICAR and the SAUs (to a lesser extent) are attempting to balance these numbers by reducing administrative staff.

Resource Expenditure Patterns

In terms of research expenditures, in 2000, 37 percent was spent by ICAR institutes, 51 percent by SAUs, and the remaining 12 percent by private and other public organizations. By comparison, ICAR provided about half the funding, resulting in a net flow of funds from ICAR to SAUs, largely through the AICRPs. A more disaggregated analysis of expenditure patterns by providers of R&E is difficult, as India has no ready means of tracking the allocation of overall expenditures below the institute level. However, a number of proxies are used in this section to gain insights into the overall allocation of expenditures.

Strategic versus Applied Research

Funding allocation can be examined by R&E type (strategic, applied, and adaptive research, and extension and education) by reviewing the mandates of research

Table 7.6   India: Composition of research staff and allocation of R&E expenditure within
            ICAR and SAUs

Indicator	Indian Council of Agricultural Research (ICAR) 1996–98	State agricultural universities (SAUs) 1992
Number of researchers	4,092	17,678
Number of full-time equivalent researchers	2,999	8,132
Education levels of researchers (percent)		
Ph.D.	68.8	62.6
M.Sc.	31.2	35.7
Female researchers (percent)	7.5	2.1
Ratio of scientific to technical and administrative staff	1:1	1:2.5
Allocation of expenditure[a] (percent)		
Research	73.3	45.0
Education	5.2	33.0
Extension	6.1	5.0
Other (administration, publications, recruitment, and so on)	15.4	17.0

Sources: ICAR data compiled by authors from ICAR records; SAU data from Rao and Muralidhar 1994.

Note: For ICAR, full-time-equivalent researchers are calculated based on the share of total expenditures on research; for SAU, full-time-equivalent researchers are based on the share of time devoted to research.

[a]ICAR expenditure also includes externally aided projects.

providers.[16] On this basis, basic and strategic research (conducted mainly within ICAR institutes) accounted for 21 percent of total agricultural R&E expenditure, and applied and adaptive research (conducted by ICAR institutes, SAUs, and AICRPs) accounted for 53 percent. Of the balance, 20 percent was spent on education and human resources development (mostly by SAUs), and 6 percent was allocated to frontline extension-related research in ICAR institutes and SAUs, including KVKs (meaning assessment, transfer, and refinement of new technologies).

While these expenditures seem reasonably well distributed, weakening of the basic and strategic research in the system remains a cause for concern. In addition, research capacity in the SAUs is slowly eroding: retiring faculty are not being replaced because of inadequate funding from the states.

Favored versus Less-Favored Regions

The irrigated ecoregion received high priority during the Green Revolution, primarily because of its high growth potential. This focus resulted in a quantum leap in crop yields, but it neglected rainfed and marginal lands. This disparity was corrected in the Seventh Plan (1985–90), which gave high priority to research for rainfed agriculture.

Figure 7.4   India: Allocation of research expenditures by environment, 1996–98

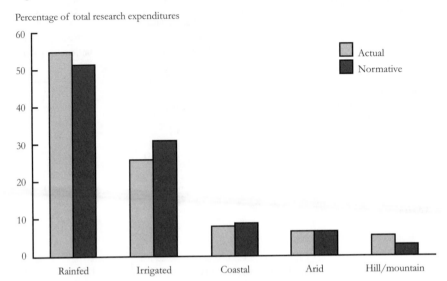

Percentage of total research expenditures

Source: Computed by authors.

To see whether past imbalances have been corrected, we compared actual research expenditure in different ecoregions with the normative allocation using the congruence rule (value of production), modified by criteria for sustainability (area under degraded lands) and equity (number of illiterate females).[17] The estimates in Figure 7.4 show no indication of underinvestment in less-favored ecoregions. Contrary to general belief, less-favored environments received slightly more resources than those justified by the efficiency criterion, even after the inclusion of natural resources and equity concerns that favored allocation to rainfed areas. These very broad observations are supported by an analysis of resource allocation for wheat by Byerlee and Morris (1993), who used the number of field experiments as a proxy for investment by agroclimatic zone. They found that despite the predominance of irrigated wheat and its high research payoffs, there was no evidence of underinvestment in marginal environments. This conclusion was further reinforced by a detailed study by Traxler and Byerlee (2001), which showed that rainfed and hill environments accounted for 30 percent of resource allocation to wheat-breeding research, although these environments only produced 12 percent of all India's wheat. More revealing is the estimate that these research programs for rainfed and marginal areas produced only 1.3 percent of the benefits generated from wheat research in India during the post–Green Revolution period, 1976–93.

Allocation by Subsectors and Commodities

Data on research expenditure by subsector and commodity are available only for ICAR, but they include research expenditure on AICRPs in SAUs.[18] Together these represent 67 percent of total research expenditures in the ICAR/SAU system. Within ICAR, crop research received the highest proportion, followed by animal sciences and natural resource management (Figure 7.5). Recall that the normative allocation pattern based on value of production (see footnote 12) indicates that crop research should receive 51 percent of resources, followed by animal science (including fisheries) at 28 percent and horticultural crops at 21 percent.[19] Both livestock and horticulture are high-growth subsectors that might justify slightly more resources than indicated by value of production, although this argument might be counterbalanced by the fact that livestock research is known to be less location-specific, with higher spillovers.

Figure 7.5   India: Subsectoral allocation of research resources within ICAR, 1996–98

Percentage of total research expenditures

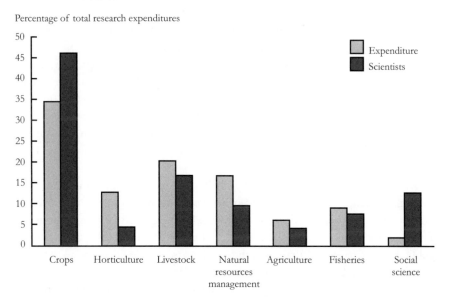

Source: Computed by authors.

Accountability and Research Impact

A number of monitoring and evaluation mechanisms have been instituted at the national, system, institute, and project levels to ensure the relevance of research and accountability in the use of public funds. At the national level, the Planning Commission and various government committees monitor progress and achievements during the preparation of annual and five-year plans. At the regional level, eight committees, made up of representatives from ICAR, the SAUs, and government departments, assess the status of agricultural research in the regions (covering several states) and make recommendations on research priorities. At the institute level, management and research advisory committees oversee administrative and financial matters, advise on research programs, and monitor progress. In each ICAR institute, a staff research council that includes external expert reviewers evaluates research projects.

An external review team undertakes a more substantive external review of each ICAR institute and SAU every five years. The review process covers organizational, management, scientific, and other matters relating to effectiveness, efficiency, and the relevance of the institute. In addition, for SAUs, a committee determines the norms for accreditation and financial assistance from ICAR and periodically assesses performance against the norms.

Through these mechanisms, accountability for the use of public funds is kept high. However, questions are often raised (especially in recent years) about the effectiveness and impact of the research system, despite its success in leading technological innovation in the agricultural sector. Many studies have examined the impact of agricultural research in India by estimating internal rates of return to investments (Table 7.7). Most have analyzed returns to crop research, individually or for the entire subsector. Although there is considerable variation, the average return was about 70 percent, with a median value in excess of 50 percent. Interestingly, there is no evidence that the rate of return has declined since the Green Revolution. The studies have also shown that returns to public research investments have been higher than those for public extension or private research (Evenson, Pray, and Rosegrant 1999).

These results provide a convincing case for enhancing public funding to agricultural research. This point has been made repeatedly by research leaders to build the case for higher budget allocations, particularly during five-year plan preparation. These efforts have achieved some success, as demonstrated by the steady rise in public funding to agricultural research over the past two decades despite the fiscal restraint adopted by the government during the 1990s.

It should be noted that high aggregate rates of return may be hiding considerable inefficiencies in the Indian public research system. Traxler and Byerlee (2001),

Table 7.7   India: Internal rates of return to research investment (percent)

Measure	Aggregate analysis	Analysis for individual crops	All
Mean	75.4	69.9	71.8
Median	58.5	53.0	57.5
Minimum	46.0	6.0	6.0
Maximum	218.2	174.0	218.2
Number of studies	10	18	28

Sources: Based on information in Alston et al. 2000 and Evenson, Pray, and Rosegrant 1999.
Note: Mode could not be calculated because no value is repeated in the observations.

analyzing rates of return to 20 wheat breeding programs across 50 research stations, found that although the aggregate rate of return to wheat improvement research in India from 1978 to 1991 was estimated to be 55 percent, eight programs had negative rates of return when spillins were taken into account. Research output was concentrated in the two strongest programs, which generated 75 percent of all benefits even though they claimed just 22 percent of research resources. Clearly there is considerable scope for increasing the overall return on research investment by redirecting money from unproductive research programs.

Emerging Policy Issues

Agricultural research policy must respond to a changing agricultural, scientific, and economic environment. In the industrialized countries, agricultural research reforms originated from the declining importance of agriculture in the economy and the rapid increases in private research investments. These reforms included separating research funding from research execution, encouraging competitive allocation of funds, improving the accountability of research institutions, and shifting near-market research to the private sector (Alston, Pardey, and Smith 1999). The new paradigm underscores pluralistic institutional structures, new sources and mechanisms for research funding, organization and management reform of public institutions, and management of intellectual property (Byerlee 1998).[20] These same reforms are generally proceeding more slowly in developing countries, where there is a large proportion of small-scale farmers and the public sector still dominates the research system (Byerlee 1998). Thus the focus of research policy should remain on improving efficiency of the public research system and encouraging participation of the private sector where possible.

Balancing Multiple Research Objectives

The Indian NARS must balance multiple objectives, from food security to emerging demands to serve a more market-oriented economy to meeting the needs of more sophisticated consumers and preserving the environment. Striking this balance has major implications for organizing research, setting research priorities, and managing intellectual property.

The public sector is under increasing pressure to provide public-good technologies that address market failures and various social and environmental objectives. This demand puts further pressure on scarce research resources, and hence public research investment in India needs to redress its large shortfall against the global average investment of 1 percent of agricultural GDP. Further, public research institutions must work closely with key stakeholders to define priorities that employ formal research prioritization approaches to address multiple objectives. This is extremely important with such a large system, where objectives conflict and clients have difficulty articulating their research needs. A starting point would be careful tracking of current resource allocations, making necessary adjustments as priorities change.

Center versus State Roles

The distinction between the roles of the center (including ICAR institutes and research structures, along with other central government activities related to agricultural R&D) and the state government undertakings (mainly via the SAUs) in agricultural research has become blurred. In practice, SAUs should have primary responsibility for applied and adaptive research to meet local demands, and ICAR should take the lead in overarching strategic and applied research, in which states tend to underinvest because of spillovers. However, SAUs are generally starved for operating funds and largely dependent on ICAR. A shortage of SAU funding has had adverse effects on human resources development, research infrastructure, and linkages with farmers. There is an urgent need to make policymakers at the state level aware of the payoffs to investing in research. At the same time, the central government might develop a funding formula to support the economically weaker states and provide incentives to the stronger states to increase their funding (for example, through matching grants).

A key role of central research is to generate spillovers to enhance efficiency in state research programs. In some areas, especially crop breeding, spillovers are pervasive. The AICRPs provide a mechanism for facilitating such spillovers. For example, Traxler and Byerlee (2001) found that spillovers from IARI's wheat research program accounted for a large share of the benefits from wheat breeding research in India following the Green Revolution.

Toward a More Pluralistic System

The modern concept of a NARS emphasizes a pluralistic system of research that recognizes the comparative advantages of different providers and the complementarity that can be achieved by forging close linkages among different actors. The leadership of ICAR has noted these requirements and taken a number of initiatives to promote such linkages (Mruthyunjaya, Pal, and Bawa 2000). But effective implementation needs greater awareness further down the line. In particular, the growing role of private research and the implications for public institutions are not widely appreciated. Where the private sector can efficiently provide near-market research services with scope for appropriation of benefits, the public sector should play a complementary rather than a dominant role. Private research is stimulated by strategic research support from the public sector, and there are many areas where public–private linkages can enhance the effectiveness of both sectors. Enabling institutional mechanisms, especially intellectual property rights (IPR) protection and capacity within the public sector to manage partnerships, can help develop and sustain these linkages (Hall et al. 2002).

Sustainability of Research Funding

The Indian public NARS has been relatively successful in increasing government funding for R&E. However, the current funding situation is not sustainable, for a number of reasons. First, because funding has not kept pace with the continuing expansion of the number of R&E institutions, the share of salary and overhead expenditures has gradually increased at the expense of operating expenditures (Pal and Singh 1997). In ICAR, the ratio of salary to operational expenses has increased to 70:30, compared with a target of 60:40, and the situation is even more serious for the SAUs. Second, although competitive funding has increased, it still accounts for only a minor share of total funding. Because competitive funding has the potential to enhance the accountability, quality, and efficiency of the system despite somewhat higher overheads and time costs, a higher share of funds should gradually be shifted to competitive funding. Of course, regular block grants must continue to support research infrastructure and strengthen basic and strategic research.

Finally, new resource-generation opportunities could be tapped, including payments for services by farmers growing high-value crops (commercial livestock and fruit crops), income generation through commercialization of technology and services, and contract research with the private sector. ICAR has set a goal of deriving 25 percent of its budget from these sources by 2020. Achieving this goal will require the development of capacities in IPR and business skills in public research organizations. ICAR has already developed such a policy, and the government has offered matching grants for self-generated income as an incentive.

Challenges of Modern Science

Although India has developed relatively good capacity in new areas of science, especially biotechnology, these new undertakings have raised a number of challenges:

the development of research capacity, biosafety and IPR regulations, and management of public dialogue on controversial issues.

Establishment of biotechnology capacity is relatively capital- and human-
resource-intensive. Although it is expected that the private sector will be active in
biotechnology in India, the public sector will have to play a dominant role, especially for noncommercial agriculture. Therefore, mechanisms to access proprietary
technologies by using resources in the public sector (such as germplasm) as bargaining chips and segmentation of markets deserve special attention. Also, given
the number of public and private institutions involved, there is much potential for
forging public–private linkages to enhance productivity. These include sharing of
costs and benefits, joint ventures, and management and ownership of intellectual
property.

Advances in biotechnology have also blurred the differences between general
sciences and the agricultural sciences, requiring close linkages with general science
and technology providers. These are the more necessary when the major responsibility for promotion of biotechnology in India rests with DBT in the Ministry of
Science and Technology.

Given the current debate on biotechnology in India and elsewhere, effective
biosafety regulations must be in place that are credible, cost-effective, and properly
coordinated. Biosafety is the single biggest constraint to application of transgenic
technology in India, which still has only just released its first product for commercial use (*Bacillus thuringiensis* cotton), despite many years of research and many
products in the pipeline. A consideration often neglected is the provision of information about these new technologies to farmers (Tripp and Pal 2001). Since much
of this information is a public good, public institutions will have to take responsibility for providing information to farmers and educating consumers.

Organization and Management Reforms in the Public Sector

The public sector in India is generally overly centralized and bureaucratic, creating
high transaction costs at all levels. Despite a certain level of autonomy, the research
system is no exception. Although ICAR recognizes these problems and has initiated a
number of organizational and management reforms, important gaps and implementation problems still exist. First, institutional rigidities imposed by commodity
and disciplinary boundaries restrict the flow of information between hierarchies
and organizations in a large system such as India's. The decision to review the functioning of the AICRPs—originally established to forge interdisciplinary and inter-
institutional research—was an important step toward addressing these rigidities
(ICAR 1999).[21] But much remains to be done to decentralize and devolve power
before transaction costs can be reduced to acceptable levels for efficient research
management.

Second, the lack of movement of research staff within the system or among ICAR, the SAUs, and other agencies (with the problem being particularly acute for SAU scientists) inhibits the overall quality of researchers. Scientific linkages with institutions and individuals outside India are deteriorating. In the 1960s and 1970s, a significant proportion of scientists were educated abroad, and Indian scientists were generally well integrated with regional and international networks. This situation has deteriorated significantly, with scientists often working in the institution from which they received their Ph.D., professionally isolated from developments internationally and even elsewhere in India. This trend must be arrested. One possibility is to earmark greater shares of foreign grants and loans for human-resource development and to support participation by researchers in international scientific networks and other initiatives. Advances in information and communication technologies also have the potential to foster linkages and improve access to international literature and scientific databases.[22] At the same time, performance-based evaluation linked with incentives and rewards is long overdue.

Third, research institutions require improved accountability through the institutionalization of objective and transparent evaluation mechanisms for research planning, monitoring, and impact assessment. The proliferation of research programs has meant that many programs serving small states and agroecological zones are inefficient. Much of the inefficiency found in the Traxler and Byerlee (2001) study results from research programs serving small ecologically and politically defined markets, so that even if they are productive in terms of the technologies produced, they are used only in a small area. Resource allocation needs to be linked to research planning based on bottom-up approaches involving relevant stakeholders and feedback from monitoring processes and impact assessment. Implementation of such processes has been attempted several times, with varying degrees of success. Effectiveness depends on harmonization across the planning, monitoring, and evaluation phases, the decisionmaking process for funding, and performance-evaluation procedures at all levels.

Although successive ICAR review panels have raised these concerns and recommended changes, past attempts at reform failed because of a lack of financial flexibility and autonomy. A package of reforms aimed at enhancing autonomy, improving decentralization and devolution of power, and improving financial management through project-based budgeting is required. Both ICAR and the SAUs should commit to such reforms. Support from high level policymakers at both central- and state-government levels is needed if this far-reaching reform agenda is to succeed.

Technology Transfer

It is generally agreed that payoffs to agricultural research could be much higher with a stronger research-extension interface. The weaknesses of the current system can be attributed to a number of factors. First, because adaptive research and technology transfer is considered to be less challenging, few scientists are attracted to it. Second, scientists working in technology assessment and transfer are disadvantaged because performance-evaluation criteria tend to emphasize the number of publications. Third, most scientists lack the skills to assess farmers' research needs and design appropriate technologies; they also lack operating expenses for on-farm research. In addition, supply-driven extension approaches focused on the public sector in India are long overdue for a drastic overhaul. Strategies of improving accountability to clients through various incentive schemes in the research system and piloting more pluralistic, demand-driven extension systems are now receiving priority as a means of speeding technology transfer.

Conclusions

The Indian agricultural research system has a long and distinguished history that evolved from a decentralized, imperial system into a highly centralized one created to respond to the food crisis in the 1960s. With the goal of increased food production as the driving force, the system grew rapidly, through both central and state fiscal appropriations. The impacts of this investment were impressive: India became self-sufficient in food, and numerous studies documented high payoffs.

In the 1990s, new challenges arose, forcing changes in the organization and funding of research in India. Food security is now only one of several goals of the research system. Globalization and rapid developments in science, privatization and liberalization of the economy, and challenges of sustainable resource management and diversification are now placing new demands on the system.

Clearly a strong central research system is still required, but the role of this system must evolve to focus on upstream and strategic research to generate spillovers at the national level. Other actors will play an increasing role in the system, especially the SAUs, general science research institutes, and the private sector. The articulation of actors in this more diverse and decentralized NARS is evolving. Inevitably there will be tensions that must be resolved, such as the effort to organize research along agroecological lines to enhance efficiency, while at the same time attempting to attract funding at the local level within the context of politically defined administrative boundaries.

Even with a rapidly expanding private sector in agricultural research, the public sector will continue to play a dominant role for many years to come. However, the efficiency and effectiveness of the public sector will depend on critical policy changes and institutional and management reforms to drastically improve its performance. These reforms must center on autonomy, decentralization, financial flexibility, and accountability. The proposed reforms are not new, but their implementation must be streamlined at two levels. First, policymakers must acknowledge the need for reform to keep pace with global changes. Second, the public research system requires an internal paradigm shift that links funding to research outcomes by improving the relevance of research through participatory approaches and instituting a performance-based incentive and reward system. Finally, there is a need for much greater awareness of the development, protection, commercialization, and application of intellectual property and technologies in enhancing research impact and access to modern scientific tools.

Some important lessons can be learned from the Indian NARS. First, political commitment through sustainability of public funding is essential. The Indian system has ably demonstrated this over the long term, despite the transition at independence and successive governments of different political ideologies thereafter. However, as the system expands and becomes more complex, a number of organizational and management problems emerge. The system has also shown that these problems could be addressed with appropriate management leadership and a willingness to learn from the past, as well as from contemporary institutional developments in research systems around the world.

Appendix Table 7A.1   India: Public funding for agricultural R&E, 1961–2003

| | Research and education | | | | Research only[a] |
| | | | | | |
Year	Current prices (million rupees)	1999 prices (million rupees)	Current prices (million international dollars)	1999 prices (million U.S. dollars)	Current prices (million rupees)
1961	126.00	2,407.70	294.12	58.36	70.62
1962	142.41	2,609.42	318.76	63.24	80.30
1963	158.47	2,690.23	328.63	65.20	88.23
1964	184.83	2,888.84	352.89	70.02	101.49
1965	223.26	3,234.07	395.06	78.38	122.21
1966	266.93	3,411.62	416.75	82.69	143.03
1967	306.47	3,606.50	440.56	87.41	170.42
1968	358.98	4,126.40	504.07	100.01	205.59
1969	431.34	4,797.28	586.02	116.27	256.58
1970	645.13	7,062.50	862.73	171.17	373.70
1971	555.62	5,775.11	705.47	139.97	337.00
1972	637.08	5,971.45	729.45	144.73	396.45
1973	747.77	5,945.06	726.23	144.09	463.21
1974	768.34	5,234.53	639.43	126.87	476.03
1975	709.37	4,908.89	599.65	118.98	445.54

(continued)

Appendix Table 7A.1 (continued)

	Research and education				Research only[a]
Year	Current prices (million rupees)	1999 prices (million rupees)	Current prices (million international dollars)	1999 prices (million U.S. dollars)	Current prices (million rupees)
1976	885.17	5,780.83	706.17	140.11	561.56
1977	1,005.67	6,220.76	759.91	150.77	641.84
1978	1,219.98	7,360.76	899.16	178.40	786.91
1979	1,414.06	7,368.06	900.06	178.58	914.98
1980	1,523.43	7,118.74	869.60	172.54	984.02
1981	1,623.60	6,880.60	840.51	166.76	1,030.91
1982	1,875.57	7,378.55	901.34	178.83	1,199.65
1983	2,075.41	7,498.60	916.00	181.74	1,343.55
1984	2,432.76	8,182.28	999.52	198.31	1,568.98
1985	2,830.89	8,882.41	1,085.04	215.28	1,811.15
1986	3,197.21	9,395.41	1,147.71	227.72	2,026.08
1987	3,645.81	9,810.18	1,198.38	237.77	2,309.46
1988	3,944.67	9,801.41	1,197.31	237.56	2,488.02
1989	4,825.58	11,066.57	1,351.85	268.22	3,026.72
1990	5,825.75	12,085.63	1,476.34	292.92	3,666.70
1991	7,137.03	13,008.52	1,589.07	315.29	4,520.13
1992	7,717.98	12,924.15	1,578.77	313.24	4,887.72
1993	8,329.44	12,740.20	1,556.30	308.78	5,258.00
1994	9,599.61	13,386.57	1,635.25	324.45	6,080.95
1995	11,063.24	14,157.44	1,729.42	343.13	7,018.51
1996	12,149.85	14,498.55	1,771.09	351.40	7,679.70
1997	13,663.07	15,307.66	1,869.93	371.01	8,526.88
1998	15,156.88	15,739.85	1,922.72	381.49	9,632.26
1999	19,925.17	19,925.17	2,433.99	482.92	12,908.57
2000	23,820.93	22,950.87	2,803.60	556.26	15,819.11
2001	25,853.60	23,981.61	2,929.51	581.24	16,823.44
2002	25,204.49	22,597.76	2,760.46	547.70	16,425.02
2003	26,799.77	23,176.48	2,831.16	561.73	17,296.82

Sources: Data in current local currency compiled by author from Ministry of Finance, *Finance accounts*, various years; Reserve Bank of India, various years; and other data.

Notes: Data are actual expenditures. International dollars are obtained by currency conversion using purchasing power parity (PPP) indexes in conjunction with rupee-denominated expenditures. PPP indexes are the purchasing power of currencies by comparing prices among a broader range of goods and services than conventional exchange rates.

[a] See footnote 11 for details on constructing research only series.

Appendix Table 7A.2 India: Annual international lending for agricultural R&E, 1963–2002

Period	USAID (million U.S. dollars)	World Bank (million U.S. dollars)	Total (million U.S. dollars)	Total (million 1999 international dollars)
1963–65	3.24	—	3.24	6.15
1966–77	2.84	—	2.84	7.10
1978–85	4.94	17.15	22.09	57.76
1986–91	4.12	27.46	31.59	106.13
1992–97	—	7.78	7.78	36.51
1998–2002	—	37.94	37.94	192.94

Sources: USAID data from Alex 1997; World Bank data calculated from unpublished World Bank files.

Note: A dash indicates either negligible or no expenditure. Data may not tally exactly with those in Figure 7.1, because these are averages. See Table 7A.1 for details of international dollars.

Notes

The authors thank ICAR for allowing one of the authors to collaborate on this study and Raka Saxena for her excellent research assistance during preparation of this chapter.

1. In India, agricultural research and education are carried out mainly in the same institutions, and for the most part they are treated together in this chapter. Agricultural research also includes some frontline extension, consistent with the mandate of the national agricultural research system. Further, in this chapter, agricultural research includes research on crops, livestock, fruits, plantation crops, fisheries, and agroforestry, but not forestry, for which there is a separate research system.

2. One college established in Faisalabad is now in Pakistan, and the others are at Pune and Nagpur (Maharshtra), Kanpur (Uttar Pradesh), Sabor (Bihar), and Coimbatore (Tamil Nadu).

3. Four national institutes are recognized as "deemed university," meaning that they offer regular postgraduate degree courses in their respective fields of specialization in addition to conducting research.

4. "Mission-mode" research is multidisciplinary research directed toward the development of technologies or components of national importance. NRCs are smaller than other institutes and organized into multidisciplinary teams.

5. Only 8 of the 18 public institutes identified by Qaim (2001) as having significant capacity in biotechnology are part of the traditional NARS (6 within ICAR and 2 within the SAUs).

6. The CGP has developed a systematic and rigorous procedure for evaluating proposals, based on objective criteria like research relevance, researcher competence, scientific quality, probability of research success, and equity concerns, such as development of marginal areas, poverty alleviation, and gender impact.

7. India's financial year begins in April and ends in March. Data are reported on a year's-end basis; hence 2000, for example, refers to 1999–2000.

8. The other central-government funding is through the Ministry of Science and Technology (DBT and DST).

9. Estimates of funding transfers through competitive grants, KVKs, and externally aided projects are available in ICAR's budget records. AICRP funds were apportioned based on the ratio of centers located in SAUs and within ICAR institutes (70:30) (ICAR n.d.).

10. Pal and Singh (1997) compiled the research funding series in India for 1961 through 1995 from various government publications. These data series were used with minor refinement and updates for subsequent years from the same sources (Comptroller and Auditor General of India, various years; Ministry of Finance, various years; Reserve Bank of India, various years; and Reserve Bank of India 2000). The nominal expenditure data were first converted to constant 1999 local currency (Indian rupees) using the implicit GDP deflator. These data were then converted to 1999 international dollars using a purchasing power parity (PPP) conversion factor of 8.65.

11. Separating research expenditure from total research and educational expenditure is difficult, particularly for SAUs. Using survey estimates for one year for SAUs (Rao and Muralidhar 1994) and information available in ICAR budget documents, the share of "research" expenditure (net of education and frontline extension) was calculated as 80 percent for ICAR and 50 percent for SAUs (see Table 7.7). In the absence of time-series data on these shares, constant shares were used to estimate a time series on "research" expenditures.

12. Our estimates are considerably lower than estimates reported by the IFPRI–ISNAR ASTI initiative for earlier periods because the latter series included expenditures for agencies deemed to be outside the agricultural research system for the purposes of this study. See http://www.asti.cgiar.org.

13. A similar conclusion was drawn in another study analyzing the determinants and impact of public investment in Indian agriculture (Roy 2001).

14. These are conservative figures for World Bank and USAID assistance. Since we assumed that most donor aid is spent in foreign currency, the data were also deflated with the U.S. GDP deflator, in addition to being converted to international dollars.

15. The Pray and Basant (2001) private-sector data include spending by nonprofit producer organizations, whereas Pardey and Beintema (2001) included research done by these entities as part of public research. Distinguishing research from product promotion and extension expenditures is a major difficulty when constructing private-sector research data.

16. For institutions with multiple R&E categories, such as the SAUs and the national institutes of ICAR, total expenditure was first apportioned using the respective shares of R&E categories (see note 12). Research expenditure was then apportioned into basic, applied, and adaptive research based on the mandate of the institution.

17. These estimates are taken from a research prioritization exercise undertaken by the senior author for NATP. Since ecoregions do not correspond with state boundaries, total state research expenditure was apportioned to different ecoregions within the state based on their shares of crop area for crop research, net sown area for noncommodity research, livestock population for animal science research, and state-level production for fisheries research.

18. The number of scientists working on AICRPs is 3,862 (ICAR 1999), and most of them are in SAUs (ICAR n.d.).

19. These normative, commodity-based allocations also include research expenditures on natural resource management, social science, and agricultural engineering, which are common to all commodities.

20. See several papers on the evolution of national agricultural research systems in a special 1998 issue of *World Development* (26/6).

21. The committee recommended that AICRPs for crops or resources with applicability in different agroclimatic zones should be continued, and others should be phased out or converted to networks. It also suggested streamlining the AICRPs' priority-assessment and review processes.

22. As noted earlier, some efforts in this direction were made under AHRD and NATP, but these need to be streamlined and upscaled.

References

Alex, G. 1997. *USAID and agricultural research: Review of USAID support for agricultural research, 1952–1996.* Washington, D.C.: World Bank Agricultural Research and Extension Unit.

Alston, J. M., P. G. Pardey, and J. Roseboom.1998. Financing agricultural research: International investment patterns and policy perspectives. *World Development* 26 (6): 1057–1071.

Alston, J. M., P. G. Pardey, and V. H. Smith, eds. 1999. *Paying for agricultural productivity.* Baltimore: Johns Hopkins University Press.

Alston, J. M, C. Chan-Kang, M. C. Marra, P. G. Pardey, and T. J. Wyatt. 2000. *A meta analysis of rates of return to agricultural R&D: Ex pede Herculem.* Research Report 113. Washington, D.C.: International Food Policy Research Institute.

Byerlee, D. 1998. The search for a new paradigm for the development of national agricultural research systems. *World Development* 26 (6): 1049–1055.

Byerlee, D., and M. Morris. 1993. Have we underinvested in research for marginal environments? The example of wheat breeding in developing countries. *Food Policy* 18: 381–393.

Carney, C., G. J. Gill, and S. Pal. 2000. *Improving competitive agricultural research funding in India.* Policy Brief 12. New Delhi: National Centre for Agricultural Economics and Policy Research.

Comptroller and Auditor General of India. Various years. *Combined finance and revenue accounts of the Union and State Governments.* New Delhi: Comptroller and Auditor General of India.

Das, G. 2001. *India unbound.* New York: Alfred Knopf.

Desai, B. M. 1997. *Agricultural development paradigm for the Ninth Plan under New Economic Environment.* New Delhi: Oxford & IBH Publishing.

Evenson, R. E., C. Pray, and M. W. Rosegrant. 1999. *Agricultural research and productivity growth in India.* IFPRI Research Report No. 109. Washington, D.C.: International Food Policy Research Institute.

Fan, S., P. Hazell, and S. Thorat. 1999. *Linkages between government spending, growth, and poverty in rural India.* IFPRI Research Report No. 110. Washington, D.C.: International Food Policy Research Institute.

Ghosh, S. P. 1991. *Agroclimatic zone specific research: Indian perspective under NARP.* New Delhi: Indian Council of Agricultural Research.

Gulati, A., and A. Sharma. 1995. Subsidy syndrome in Indian agriculture. *Economic and Political Weekly* 30 (39): A93–102.

Hall, A., R. Sulaiman, N. Clark, M. V. K. Sivamohan, and B. Yoganand. 2002. Public–private sector interaction in the Indian agricultural research system: An innovation systems perspective on institutional reform. In *Agricultural research policy in an era of privatisation,* ed. D. Byerlee and R. G. Echeverria. Wallingford, UK: CAB International.

ICAR (Indian Council of Agricultural Research). N.d. *ICAR Vision 2020.* New Delhi: ICAR.

————. 1997. *Training, consultancy, contract research and contract service in ICAR system.* New Delhi: ICAR.

————.1999. *Report of ICAR review committee on all India coordinated research projects.* New Delhi: ICAR.

————.2001. *Annual report 2000/2001.* New Delhi: ICAR.

Jain, K. B. L., and D. Byerlee. 1999. Investment efficiency at the national level: Wheat improvement research in India. In *The global wheat improvement system: Prospects for enhancing efficiency in the presence of spillovers,* ed. M. K. Maredia and D. Byerlee. Research Report No 5. Mexico City: International Maize and Wheat Improvement Center.

Judd, M. A., K. A. Boyce, and R. E. Evenson. 1986. Investing in agricultural supply: The determinants of agricultural research and extension investment. *Economic Development and Cultural Change* 35 (1): 77–113.

Lele, U., and A. A. Goldsmith. 1989. Development of national agricultural research capacity: India's experience with the Rockefeller Foundation and its significance for Africa. *Economic Development and Cultural Change* 37: 305–343.

Ministry of Finance. Various years. *Economic survey.* New Delhi: Ministry of Finance.

————. Various years. *Finance account.* New Delhi: Ministry of Finance.

Mruthyunjaya, and P. Ranjitha. 1998. The Indian agricultural research system: Structure, current policy issues, and future orientation. *World Development* 26 (6): 1089–1101.

Mruthyunjaya, S. Pal, and A. K. Bawa. 2000. *ICAR-industry interface in agricultural research: Workshop proceedings.* New Delhi: National Centre for Agricultural Economics and Policy Research.

Murgai, R. 2001. The Green Revolution and the productivity paradox: Evidence from the Indian Punjab. *Agricultural Economics* 25: 199–200.

Pal, S. 1999. *Competitive agricultural technology funds in India.* NCAP/ODI Report. http://www.oneworld.org/odi. Accessed March 2002.

Pal, S., and A. Singh. 1997. *Agricultural research and extension in India: Institutional structure and investments.* Policy Paper 7. New Delhi: National Centre for Agricultural Economics and Policy Research.

Pardey, P. G., and N. M. Beintema. 2001. *Slow magic: Agricultural research a century after Mendel.* Food Policy Report. Washington, D.C.: International Food Policy Research Institute.

Pardey, P. G., and J. Roseboom. 1989. *ISNAR agricultural research indicator series.* Cambridge, UK: Cambridge University Press.

Pingali, P. L., and P. W. Heisey. 2001. Cereal-crop productivity in developing countries: Past trends and future prospects. In *Agricultural science policy: Changing global agendas,* ed. J. M. Alston, P. G. Pardey, and M. J. Taylor. Baltimore: Johns Hopkins University Press.

Pray, C. E., and R. Basant. 2001. India. In *Private investment in agricultural research and international technology transfer in Asia,* ed. C. E. Pray and K. Fuglie. AER–805. Washington, D.C.: Economics Research Service, U.S. Department of Agriculture. http://www.ers.usda.gov/publications/aer805. Accessed March 2002.

Pray, C. E., B. Ramaswami, and T. Kelley. 2001. The impact of economic reforms on research by the Indian seed industry. *Food Policy* 26: 587–598.

Qaim, M. 2001. The situation of agricultural biotechnology in India. Center for Development Research (ZEF), University of Bonn. Draft.

Rao, D. R., and U. Muralidhar. 1994. *A study on agricultural universities information system.* Hyderabad: National Academy of Agricultural Research Management.

Reserve Bank of India. Various years. *State finances: A Study of budgets.* Mumbai: Reserve Bank of India.

————. 2000. *Handbook of statistics on the Indian economy.* Mumbai: Reserve Bank of India.

Rose-Ackerman, S., and R. E. Evenson. 1985. The political economy of agricultural research and extension: Grants, votes and reapportionment. *American Journal of Agricultural Economics* 67: 1–14.

Roy, B. C. 2001. Investment and productivity in Indian agriculture. Unpublished Ph.D. thesis, Indian Agricultural Research Institute, New Delhi.

Singh, R. P., S. Pal, and M. Morris. 1995. *Maize research, development and seed production in India: Contributions of the public and private sectors.* Economics Working Paper 95–3. Mexico City: International Maize and Wheat Center.

Traxler, G., and D. Byerlee. 2001. Linking technical change to research effort: An examination of aggregation and spillover effects. *Agricultural Economics* 24: 235–246.

Tripp, R., and S. Pal. 2001. The private delivery of public crop varieties: Rice in Andhra Pradesh. *World Development* 29 (1): 103–117.

Chapter 8

South Africa: Coping with Structural Changes

Frikkie Liebenberg and Johann Kirsten

Introduction

Analyzing the evolution of agricultural research and development policy in South Africa is a fascinating but difficult task, primarily because of the large number of structural, institutional, and political changes that took place during the 20th century. This chapter tracks the history of South Africa's agricultural research and development system against this background, highlighting changes over the past 20 years. Such changes have enabled better documentation of public spending on R&D and assessments of changes in the methods by which those funds are disbursed.

Public-sector financing remains the dominant source of funding, but, as in so many countries, public funding has come under severe pressure in recent years. In recent years, contributions by producer organizations and international donors to the funding of agricultural research have increased, and universities play a much greater role as research providers. Declining core government funding and changes in leadership and management styles have driven large numbers of the most highly qualified researchers out of South Africa's primary research provider—the Agricultural Research Council (ARC). The prospect of the demise of the agricultural research system led to an initiative to coordinate the funding and provision of agricultural research in South Africa through a National Agricultural Research Forum (NARF).[1]

This chapter presents South Africa's agricultural research and development policy within this historical framework. In the next section we provide a brief overview of the agricultural sector and a review of policy changes with a view to highlighting the increased flexibility in input substitution, to which the research system has likely contributed. Thereafter we provide an overview of the overall science and technology policy and a detailed account of agricultural R&D policy focusing on the institutional structure, priority setting, sources of support, and agricultural R&D providers. We conclude by discussing major lessons learned and summarizing the debate on a more sustainable national agricultural research system for the future.

Overview of South African Agriculture

Macroeconomic Environment

South Africa is a lower-middle-income country where approximately half the population lives in poverty.[2] According to the results of the 1996 census, the South African population is estimated at 40.584 million, with population growth of about 2 percent per annum—down from 2.5 percent per annum during the 1980s. The census results indicate that total employment in the economy is 9.1 million, of which about 1.8 million are informal job opportunities.[3] About 34 percent of the economically active population of 27.8 million people are unemployed and seeking work.[4] The rural unemployment rate for South Africa is 44.2 percent (the urban unemployment rate is 28.7 percent). The Development Bank of Southern Africa (DBSA 2000) estimates that 57 percent of the South African population live in poverty; May (2000) estimates that 30 percent of the urban population are poor, but poverty rates are highest, at about 70 percent, outside urban areas. Many rural people in South Africa live under conditions of deprivation as harsh as those in poorer African countries.

With the fall of the apartheid regime, the government undertook a commitment to reduce rural poverty and adopted programs of land reform and improved service delivery in rural areas. Program results, although commendable in some respects, have been insufficient, slow, and costly relative to expectations and the scale of the task. In the meantime, rural areas face new challenges as the crisis of HIV/AIDS reduces resources flowing to households and severely increases the pressures on families and communities.

Overview of the Agricultural Sector and Changing Productivity

Primary agriculture, which consists of farm-based production, accounted for 3.4 percent of the GDP of South Africa in 2004 (Table 8.1). Gross value of agricultural production is estimated at 66 billion rand[5] in 2001–02—an increase of 30.9 percent over 2000–01. Animal products made up 35.3 percent of this figure, field crops 41.0 percent, and horticulture 23.7 percent (Table 8.2). The most important

Table 8.1 South Africa: Indicators of structural change in the economy, 1970–2004

Indicator	1970	1975	1980	1985	1990	1995	2000	2004
Value-added as percentage of gross domestic product at basic prices								
Agriculture	7.2	7.7	6.2	5.2	4.6	3.9	3.2	3.4
Industry	35.7	38.9	45.4	39.6	36.1	31.3	28.8	24.7
Manufacturing	22.8	22.7	21.6	21.8	23.6	21.2	18.5	20.0
Construction	4.1	5.1	3.2	3.5	3.3	3.2	3.0	2.4
Mining of mineral resources	8.8	11.1	20.6	14.2	9.2	7.0	7.3	7.1
Services (tertiary sector)	54.7	51.2	45.4	51.2	55.3	61.3	65.2	64.9
Per capita income (rand at current prices)	548	1,034	2,114	3,822	7,861	13,656	20,596	28,823
Exports of goods and services as percentage of GDP at market prices	21.8	27.7	35.4	31.5	24.7	23.0	27.9	26.6
Goods (percent)	18.6	23.8	32.3	28.5	21.7	19.9	24.1	22.7
Services (percent)	3.2	3.9	3.0	3.0	3.0	3.1	3.8	3.9
Imports of goods and services as a share of GDP at market prices (percent)	25.3	30.2	27.3	22.6	18.8	22.1	24.9	27.1
Goods (percent)	20.8	25.3	23.3	18.7	15.4	18.1	20.5	22.7
Services (percent)	4.5	4.8	4.1	3.9	3.3	4.0	4.4	4.4
Employment (thousands)[a]								
Agriculture			1,306	1,181	1,224	810	964	NA
Industry			2,760	2,681	2,785	2,217	2,111	NA
Mining			836	744	841	542	384	NA
Manufacturing			1,464	1,380	1,417	1,120	1,207	NA
Construction			460	557	527	555	520	NA
Services			2,722	2,723	3,642	3,791	3,190	NA

Sources: SARB n.d.; labor statistics are from NDA 2005.

Notes: NA indicates data not available. For employment data, 1980 data exclude the former independent states and homelands of Transkei, Bophutatswana, and Venda; 1985 and 1991 data also exclude Ciskei; 1996 data include the former Transkei, Bophutastwana, Venda, and Ciskei (TBVC) states. Employment data for 1995 and 1999 apply to the age group 15 to 65.

[a] 1991 data used for 1990, 1996 for 1995, and 1999 for 2000.

Table 8.2   South Africa: Trends in agricultural output and yields, 1970–2000

Indicator	1970	1975	1980	1985	1990	1995	2000
Average size of holding (hectares)	987.6	1,102.0	1,338.9	1,307.7	1,427.4	1,349.1	1,794.3
Gross cropped area (thousand hectares)		10,212	10,625		12,900		
Gross irrigated area as percentage of gross cropped area		10.9	7.8		10.5		
Food grain production (thousand tons)[a]	11,000	10,010	17,696	10,899	11,469	13,693	13,844
Milk production (million liters)	1,276	1,376.5	1,471	1,731	1,993	2,149	1,926
Egg production (thousand tons)	107	166	162	195	262	339	361
Meat Production (thousand tons)							
Red meat	9,755	6,756	7,395	8,058	9,763	5,408	4,803
White meat	121	294	364	474	587	708	796
Pork	81	87	89	107	131	127	121
Poultry[b]	40	207	275	367	456	582	675
Total fruit (thousand tons)	2,319	2,667	2,947	3,081	3,860	4,041	4,777
Vegetables (thousand tons)	1,728	2,028	2,418	2,786	3,207	3,575	3,748
Sugar (thousand tons)	330	341	384	411	375	404	429
Percentage of total gross value of agricultural production							
Field crops	46.7	41.7	48.5	40.2	34.7	36.5	30.8
Horticulture	17.3	17.5	14.4	18.8	21.9	23.3	26.4
Animal production	36.1	40.7	37.1	41.1	43.4	40.2	42.7
Percentage of agriculture							
In total exports	30.3	31.4	10.3	6.5	8.7	7.9	8.8
In total imports	5.2	4.6	2.6	5.7	5.0	6.9	6.1
Crop yields (tons per hectare)							
Maize	1.8	1.5	3.3	1.8	2.3	2.7	2.7
Wheat	0.7	1.0	0.9	0.9	1.1	1.5	2.4
Grain sorghum	1.5	1.5	2.5	1.3	1.8	3.1	3.1
Sunflower seed	0.7	0.9	1.6	0.9	1.0	1.3	1.4
Groundnuts	0.7	0.5	0.7	0.4	0.8	1.1	1.4

Sources: NDA 2003 and SSA 1985.

[a]Food grain production equals the sum of maize, wheat, grain sorghum, sunflower seed, and soybean.

[b]Poultry is estimated as the difference between total white meat production and pork production.

earners of foreign exchange in the agricultural sector are sugar, wine, citrus, and deciduous and subtropical fruits. The agrofood complex, which consists of primary production plus the input and agroprocessing sectors, accounts for around 14 percent of GDP. In 2000 the agrofood complex exported about R16 billion worth of primary and processed food products, nearly 9 percent of South Africa's total exports (Table 8.2).

There are about 60,938 large commercial farmers, who are predominantly but not exclusively white. Commercial farms employed about 1 million workers in 1999, which is 8.1 percent of total formal-sector employment (NDA 2003). Many of these workers live on commercial farms, and their children are educated in farm schools. Thus commercial farms provide livelihoods, housing, and education for the nearly 6 million family members of these 1 million employees.

Furthermore, an estimated 1.3 million households, primarily located in the communal areas of the former homelands, largely produce to meet part of their family's overall needs. Finally, almost all the productive and social activities of rural towns and service centers are dependent on primary agriculture and related activities, which include the increasingly popular and economically significant agrotourism and game farming. Taking all of these activities into account, more than half the provinces, and about 40 percent of the country's total population, are primarily dependent on agriculture and its related industries.

A Review of Policy Changes in South African Agriculture

Deregulation and liberalization were distinctive features of the agricultural sector of South Africa during the 1980s.[6] The deregulation process was characterized by changes within the existing institutional structure, through a process of scaling back state intervention. Despite these changes, the main actors in the sector remained the same. This situation changed with the election of the Government of National Unity in 1994, although in agriculture, at least, some direct policy changes were stalled until 1996 (until after the withdrawal of the National Party from the Government of National Unity). The most important policy initiatives taken subsequently included land reform, institutional restructuring in the public sector, the promulgation of new legislation (including the Marketing of Agricultural Products Act and the Water Act), and trade and labor market policy reform. These reforms were intended to correct the injustices of past policy (principally through land reform), to direct the agricultural sector toward a less capital-intensive growth path, and to enhance the sector's international competitiveness.

One of the main features of South African agricultural policy in the 1990s was institutional restructuring. The public-sector agencies supporting the agricultural sector were subjected to the same processes of "provincialization" that came about with the adoption of the Interim Constitution. In the case of agriculture, the former "own affairs" (whites-only) and "general affairs" departments were amalgamated to form the core of the new National Department of Agriculture. Functions and staff were redeployed from the former homeland departments of agriculture to new national and provincial departments, and the relationship between the national and provincial departments of agriculture and farmer lobby groups was modified.[7]

Agricultural institutions in the public sector were also reoriented in line with new policy directions. The most radical of these changes occurred in agricultural marketing policy. The promulgation of the Marketing of Agricultural Products Act, No. 47 of 1996, represented a radical departure from the marketing regime to which farmers had been accustomed since the 1930s (Groenewald 2000). Though far-reaching, the deregulation of the 1980s and early 1990s was piecemeal and uncoordinated, and was accomplished within the framework of the old Marketing Act so that policy changes could be reversed easily. The new act changed the way agricultural marketing policy would be managed.

The new South African government also embarked on a process of trade policy reform to reverse decades of "inward industrialization" strategies. The distinguishing characteristic of these reforms was a willingness to expose national businesses to tariffs that were often below the lower bounds negotiated in the Uruguay Round of the General Agreement on Tariffs and Trade (GATT). Whereas agricultural trade had been managed through quantitative controls, the Marrakech Agreement called for the tariffication of all agricultural goods and a phased reduction in the tariffs. South Africa also participated in the renegotiation of the Southern African Customs Union treaty, agreed to the new Southern African Development Community (SADC) trade protocol, and negotiated a free trade agreement with the European Union. In all these cases, the country agreed, in principle, to liberalize agricultural trade further. Finally, the country gained membership in the Cairns Group,[8] thus signaling its intention to unilaterally liberalize its trade regardless of progress made by developed countries in withdrawing farm support programs.

Effects of policy changes. These policy changes created a number of pressures on farm profits. The analysis of total factor productivity (TFP) in South African agriculture presented below clearly shows that farmers adapted to these changes by decreasing their level of input use, by increasing output from a constant level of input use, or by a combination of these approaches. Whatever the case, productivity has increased. In South Africa, real gross annual capital formation—which was fairly stagnant in the 1980s—has increased at a higher rate since 1990 (Table 8.3). Thus, since the beginning of the 1990s, farmers have reacted positively to political changes,

Table 8.3   South Africa: Growth in employment and capital formation, 1947–96

Period	Change in number of farm employees (percent per year)	Real gross capital formation (percent per year)
1947–96	0.16	2.01
1947–80	1.16	2.65
1980–96	−1.86	0.68
1990–96	−4.22	7.79

Source: Thirtle and van Zyl 1994.

greater access to international markets, and positive real interest rates. The TFP ratio provides a more comprehensive measure of productivity growth in agriculture. The TFP for commercial agriculture in South Africa to 2000 is shown in Figure 8.1, from which it is evident that input use increased slightly faster than the growth in agricultural output from the late 1940s to late 1960s, and so TFP declined. Thereafter, the pace at which aggregate output grew exceeded the growth in aggregate input use (which actually began to decline around 1986–87) and so

Figure 8.1   South Africa: Total factor productivity growth for commercial agriculture, 1947–2000

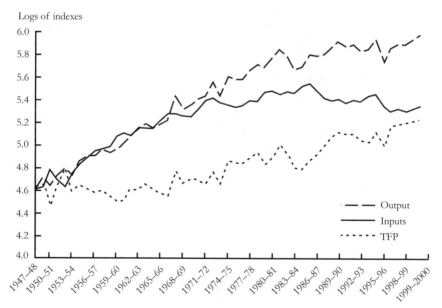

Source: Thirtle 2001.

TFP rose. Thirtle (2001) described these trends and some ancillary developments in more detail:

- The domestic terms of trade for intermediate and capital goods for commercial farmers were negative throughout the period 1960–96, and hence the input prices they paid rose faster than the output prices they received throughout that period.

- The rate at which the domestic terms of trade turned against commercial farmers worsened during the first phase of deregulation (from roughly 1984); they improved subsequently but were still far higher than between 1960 and 1980.

- The terms of trade measure the rate of change in the prices of intermediate and capital goods relative to the rate of change in output prices only. TFP measures the relative rate of growth in the value of inputs (including land and labor) and outputs. The data show that TFP growth slowed during the first phase of deregulation, between 1985 and 1994, and increased again thereafter.

- From 1980 through 1990, when inflation rates in South Africa peaked and TFP growth was weakest, net farm income growth was negative (that is, commercial farmers' profit margins grew thinner every year). However, by 1990 TFP growth had recovered sufficiently to cause a positive annual growth in net farm income through 1996.

These TFP results reflect the extent to which farmers have reacted to the cost–price squeeze, and it is clear that one of the principal solutions was to change not only the volume of inputs used but also the input mix. Thus farmers' ability to adopt new modes of production depends critically on their ability to substitute inputs in reaction to relative price changes. Some years ago, research showed that farmers' ability to substitute inputs was severely constrained by state intervention in the sector but that this situation had improved as a result of the first stages of deregulation during the 1980s (van Zyl and Groenewald 1988; Sartorius von Bach and van Zyl 1991). Overall, there is some evidence of improved flexibility in input substitution in South African agriculture.

Overall R&D Policy and Funding Trends
Like the rest of its economy, the South African science and technology institutions (SETIs) have experienced momentous policy changes since the early 1990s. Prior

to 1994, SETIs were funded under a policy of "framework autonomy," introduced in 1988. Reduced to its essentials, framework autonomy entailed the following elements:

- The determination of so-called maximum average expenditure per full-time equivalent (fte) staff member (divided into three categories), which was monitored by the Science Council

- The provision of baseline funding, that is, "costs of . . . basic infrastructure (expertise and other capacity) necessary for the realization of the aims of the institution" (DNE 1988, p. 43) based on expenditure for those essential activities in 1986–87, annually adjusted in line with appropriate inflation indexes and the available money

- The provision of discretionary financing of, for instance, the agency function, meaning funding of research in the higher-education sector, the operation of national facilities, and so on

In summary, the system of framework autonomy was designed to restrict government control to the *overall* framework within which the science councils operated, while restricting parliamentary funding to supporting the essential research infrastructure. Within this framework, science councils were given the management flexibility to generate additional income from contracts, and, thus, within limits, to shape their own research agendas.

Each SETI received its budget from its overseeing department (the National Department of Agriculture, for ARC) according to the baseline funding formula. Based on its own internal processes and priorities, the management of SETI allocated its own resources. Science policy was drafted by the Chief Directorate of Science Planning under the Department of National Education (DNE), after which comments from major stakeholders were invited, processed, and submitted to the Science Advisory Council (SAC) for amendment and approval.

Although subject to ARC guidance, the different research institutes were left with significant freedom in setting their own research agendas, in collaboration with industry and peer-review committees. By 1994 these processes still reflected those in existence under the former Department of Agriculture.

In 1994, the Department of Arts, Culture, Science, and Technology (DACST) was established from the relevant elements of the DNE. The creation of DACST introduced a period of rapid changes in science and technology policy in South Africa. Two prominent initiatives taken by DACST since its inception were the

Table 8.4   South Africa: Allocation of the science budget, 1996–97 and 1999–2000

Science Council	1996–97 (million rand)	1999–2000 (million rand)	Nominal change (percentage)
Agricultural Research Council (ARC)	319.10	279.24	–12
Human Sciences Research Council (HSRC)	87.63	64.42	–26
National Research Foundation (NRF)	138.12	162.00	17
Medical Research Council (MRC)	57.91	79.57	37
Council for Mineral Technology	82.77	81.77	–1
Council for Geosciences	63.56	63.79	0
Council of Scientific and Industrial Research (CSIR)	274.36	310.65	13
South African Bureau of Standards (SABS)	45.93	73.72	61
Total	1,069.37	1,115.16	4

Source: DACST 2001.

formulation of a white paper on science and technology (completed in 1996) and the establishment for the National Advisory Council on Innovation (NACI) (legislation approved in 1997). The new policy places a strong emphasis on innovation, and hence on the direction of research resource allocation.

The science and technology branch of DACST took over the administration of an annual budget allocated under the "science vote" of approximately R1.4 billion.[9] Following the white paper, the principle of baseline funding according to a base formula was replaced, and SETIs now receive their core funding through a parliamentary grant allocated on a competitive basis.

Other sources of funding available to SETIs are the innovation fund and the National Research Foundation (NRF), established in 1998 from the former Foundation for Research and Development. The purpose of the innovation fund is to encourage and enable long-term extensive innovation projects in the higher-education sector, SETIs, civil society, and the private sector. The NRF is mandated to ensure the support of research and the building of research capacity within the higher-education sector and other research institutions. For both undertakings, funds are allocated on a competitive basis. It is envisioned that the innovation fund will grow to about 20 percent of the annual budget, forming a strong mechanism to reallocate resources within the national system of innovation (NSI).

Table 8.4 provides an indication of the government funds earmarked for the different science councils for 1996–97 and 1999–2000. It shows a shift away from agricultural and human sciences toward the Medical Research Council (MRC) and the Council for Scientific and Industrial Research (CSIR).

In 1999–2000 the science budget also included R78.3 million for national facilities, such as the National Laser Centre, and a further R146 million for other programs, such as the innovation fund (R75 million) and special investigations

(R33 million). The growth in the innovation fund was paid for from the institutional funding of the science councils, with dire consequences for its sustained capacity development. The priority-setting criteria are not favorable to primary agricultural research: they focus, for example, on third-generation biotechnology.

Financing and Provision of Agricultural R&D

We provide a brief history of the agricultural research system in South Africa to put the system's current policy and structural changes in perspective.

Institutional Structure

Prior to 1990.[10] Following the establishment of the Union of South Africa in 1910, public interventions in agriculture were the responsibility of a central Department of Agriculture. The department also held responsibility for education and training in agriculture. In 1958, the Department of Agriculture was split into two to form the Department of Agricultural Economics and Marketing and the Department of Agricultural Technical Services. The latter focused on production issues and provided services such as agricultural research, education, extension, and regulatory services. In 1962, the Department of Agricultural Technical Services was reorganized as two directorates: the Directorate of Agricultural Research and the Directorate of Agricultural Field Services. The Directorate of Agricultural Research was given responsibility for 10 research centers and directorates that later became institutes. There were also 7 regionally based adaptive research and extension institutes, called agricultural development institutes (ADIs), each with centers for delivering extension services.

Further institutional changes took place in 1970, the most significant of which was the transfer of administrative responsibilities for the faculties of agriculture and veterinary sciences to the Ministry of Education. The Department of Agricultural Technical Services continued to finance research at the universities and supported a substantial, though declining, number of research positions at the various faculties of agriculture.

In rationalizing the public service, the two departments of agriculture were amalgamated in 1980 to form the Department of Agriculture and Fisheries, which was renamed the Department of Agriculture and Water Supply in 1982. Following the establishment of the tricameral legislature,[11] the department was again divided in 1984 to form the Department for Agricultural Development, largely incorporating the branches of the old Department of Agricultural Technical Services, dealing with "own affairs," and the Department of Agriculture, for "general affairs."

All funding for research came through the Department of Agricultural Development, which was initially responsible for 11 research institutes, and later 12. The overall direction of research was mostly determined centrally but was guided by regional development plans. This approach resulted in problems with administration and overall coordination. Links with nationally based institutes, focused on strategic or basic research, and the ADIs also became problematic. The agricultural research system of South Africa at this stage followed a mostly bureaucratic and top-down approach to technology development and transfer.

In a 1984 report by the Committee of Inquiry into Agricultural Service Provision, eight alternative models for the delivery of agricultural research were proposed. The preferred option was the creation of a national agricultural development council. The apartheid dispensation and the various independent homeland governments created problems for its full implementation. ARC (the Agricultural Research Council) was established as a first step toward such a system.

1990 to 1994. Most of the agricultural research activities under the Department of Agricultural Development were transferred to ARC beginning in April 1992, following the passing of the Agricultural Research Act of 1990. This process was completed only in 1995. Thus, by the end of this period, ARC had yet to develop an identity as an organization. The lack of consolidation left ARC incapable of facing the changes in South Africa's constitution and in its own governance structure following the democratic elections of 1994.

More important than the reorganization itself, a business-like management style was introduced into ARC institutes. ARC embarked upon a more aggressive cost-recovery program by introducing a user pays principle. This change introduced a stronger client orientation. Targets were set to rapidly increase external funding, with the goal of recovering 30 percent of total expenditures from the commercial agricultural sector (Roseboom et al. 1995). This shift happened much more rapidly than planned as a result of successive cuts in the parliamentary grant to the ARC.

Following the new constitutional dispensation in 1994, nine provinces were created from the former four, and agriculture became the joint responsibility of the national and provincial governments. The previous agricultural development institutes (ADIs) formed the basis of the nine provincial departments of agriculture (PDAs), although the Grootfontein Agricultural Development Institute became the responsibility of the National Department of Agriculture (NDA), where it still resides, because of issues relating to its location.

Funding of agricultural R&D now came from two streams: ARC received its funding through the National Department of Agriculture, and the PDAs were allocated a portion of the former national agricultural budget according to a formula. The provincial legislature was not compelled to honor this formula, however.

The current situation. The present structure of the South African national agricultural research system (NARS) consists of agricultural research institutes operating under the ARC, departmental research entities, faculties of agriculture and veterinary sciences, institutes operating under the Department of Environmental Affairs, the Council of Scientific and Industrial Research (CSIR), and some semipublic research agencies supported by industry (see Appendix Table 8A.1). ARC is the principal national agricultural research entity. It oversees 13 agricultural research institutes with a network of experimental farms and modern equipment throughout the country, and, with the exception of sugarcane, supports all the major agricultural commodities in South Africa.

Two groups were created to coordinate and integrate these efforts: MINMEC, an interministerial committee headed by the national minister of agriculture and comprising the members of the provincial executives of agriculture, and the Interdepartmental Technical Committee on Agriculture (ITCA), comprising department heads. ITCA had several subsidiary technical and advisory committees. Most of these were disbanded for lack of effectiveness, except for those dealing with natural-resource management and veterinary services. In early 2003 the Agricultural Economics Working Group was reintroduced by ITCA.

Funding for the PDAs and, as such, for provincial agricultural research began to deviate from the 1995 formula guidelines. Provincial R&D capacity dwindled and in some cases ceased. High costs and poor restructuring plans led to the disappearance of agricultural research in some provinces, such as the Eastern Cape. A reasonable degree of research competence exists in only two provinces—the Western Cape (Elsenburg) and Kwazulu-Natal (Cedara)—but these programs remain severely underfunded in some aspects. Most of the provinces had to rely on donor funding and the operations of NGOs and producer or commodity organizations. ARC has provided increasing support to the provinces.

The management of ARC has changed substantially since the new science and technology policy was introduced in 1997. Following various reviews of the agricultural research system and strong criticism of the way ARC was managed, the governance structures were changed, and a number of research institutes were merged. One of the important criticisms was that ARC research dealt mainly with capital-intensive farming operations, thereby benefiting commercial farmers rather than farmers from previously disadvantaged communities. The reviews and recommendations required a shift in research focus and service provision by the ARC while its parliamentary grant dwindled in line with the perceived new direction in the science system. Changes in leadership, among other factors, left ARC increasingly isolated and its stakeholders uninformed of the consequences of these changes. It is possible that ARC's council, being relatively inexperienced, did not foresee and clearly communicate the consequences of the changes satisfactorily. To become an active and integrated member of the country's agricultural research system, the ARC was under pressure to improve its performance and ensure the relevance of its research.

This process involved interactions with a number of stakeholders during 1999. In a series of meetings with PDAs and representative bodies in organized agriculture, stakeholders were asked to critique ARC's performance as an agricultural service provider. Insights gained from this exercise enabled ARC to initiate strategic workshops on its research agenda and on the funding of agricultural research. A system was also introduced whereby research on the problems and needs of resource-poor farmers was detached from the overall parliamentary grant and managed under a separate program for sustainable rural livelihoods. In addition, commercialization of research outputs was given greater emphasis.

Setting Priorities

Oversight of the national system of innovation is the responsibility of the National Advisory Council on Innovation (NACI), which was established to advise DACST on the direction of scientific research. This entity, together with the requirements of the new Public Finance and Management Act (PFMA), plays a major role in influencing research priorities. Under this new act, and in line with the existing medium-term expenditure plan, public entities like ARC are expected to submit three-year budget requests directly linked to strategic plans.

Within ARC, the national institutes previously relied primarily on peer reviews and institute-level priority setting under a regime of (mostly) state-funded research, with the relative share of government funding for each institute remaining fairly stable. The change to the national system of innovation, followed by the subsequent cuts in core funding, mandated a change in the relative share of core funding among institutes. The introduction of corporate programs in 1999 was seen as both a means to drive greater integration in research activities between institutes within a systems-research framework, and a framework to introduce interinstitute priority-setting mechanisms. However, the significant differences in the ability of industries and other clients to pay for research and the severity of the cuts in core funding have led to current core funding ratios that reflect the ability to pay rather than any serious national priority considerations.

Research priorities are also determined by DACST's recently completed national research and development strategy. This department has also been split into two separate departments, with the Department of Science Technology now being responsible for the science vote (DST 2002). This national strategy identifies research needs in all sectors of the economy, including agriculture and agribusiness. These priorities influence the allocation of the different competitive funds, such as the innovation fund, the Technology and Human Development Research for Industry Program (THRIP), and the funding programs of the National Research Foundation. Most universities doing agricultural research, as well as NGOs, submit applications to these funds.

Previously, funding for agricultural research in the provinces followed the priorities of the provinces' agricultural development programs. The establishment of the provincial departments of agriculture, and the associated restructuring initiatives, has led to a breakdown in this practice. ARC is now assisting provinces to redevelop their research capacity. There is very little coordination among the various players in setting research priorities in agriculture. Universities, ARC, and the PDAs rarely collaborate in research and often compete for research funds. The new NARF (described earlier) may improve this situation, but it has yet to secure funding for its initiatives in this regard (NDA 2001).

Sources of Funding for Agricultural R&D

The funds allocated to agricultural research in South Africa come from four sources. At the central-government level, the science budget is allocated by DST and various national government departments. Other national revenue sources include commodity trusts and levies from producer organizations and research funding from private-sector enterprises.[12] The increasing prominence of these enterprises in terms of research funding and the use of research services distinguishes South Africa's NARS from those of other African countries.

In addition to the structural changes in the agricultural R&D system, competitive bidding with other science councils for parliamentary grants (PGs) was introduced in 1997–98. Furthermore, it was decided that all external research contracts would be based on full cost recovery. This principle was not readily accepted by the various commodity organizations that fund research. As a compromise, a 50:50 cost-sharing arrangement was negotiated between the relevant institutes and commodity organizations.

Other major funders of agricultural research over the past five years have been various commodity trusts, which were established following market deregulation that involved the abolition of all marketing boards. The assets of these boards were transferred to trusts such as the Maize Trust, the Wool Trust, and the Red Meat Trust, and the returns from these assets are used to fund the activities of producer organizations and to fund agricultural research and the activities of the producer

Table 8.5   South Africa: Annual contribution by commodity organizations to agricultural research, 1999–2001

Source	Contribution (thousand rand)		
	1999	2000	2001
Trust contributions			
Animal	3,578.09	3,468.82	7,222.26
Crops	13,060.67	18,732.63	21,338.85
Horticulture	5,280.91	4,200.00	3,684.21
Subtotal	21,919.67	26,401.45	32,245.32
Levy income			
Crops	11,194.27	11,491.69	12,337.12
Horticulture	19,156.31	25,665.74	27,521.31
Subtotal	30,350.58	37,157.43	39,858.43
Total contributions from commodity organizations			
Animal	3,578.09	3,468.82	7,222.26
Crops	24,254.95	30,224.32	33,675.97
Horticulture	24,437.22	29,865.74	31,205.52
Total	52,270.25	63,558.88	72,103.75

Source: Information provided by various trusts and commodity organizations (personal communications).

organizations. Table 8.5 provides an indication of the extent of research funding provided by commodity trusts and by statutory and voluntary levies managed by certain producer organizations since 1999.

Figure 8.2 shows the flow of funds within the South African NARS for 1999–2000. At the central-government level, the parliamentary grant from the science vote totaled R295.5 million, consisting of R292.9 million allocated to ARC and the balance allocated by the CSIR to its Division of Food, Biological, and Chemical Technologies (DFBCT). The various national departments allocated a further R68.1 million to agricultural research through performance and service contracts and competitive-bidding funds: the latter were mainly allocated through the THRIP programs and the innovation fund administered by the NRF, as well as the lead programs of DACST. An amount of R29.2 million is generated internally by ARC from its own resources.

Other public sources include R4.5 million allocated to agricultural research by the Water Research Commission. This represents 9.1 percent of the total research budget of the Water Research Commission, which receives its funding from a levy paid by all water use authorities. Funding from commodity and producer organizations supports research commissioned by the commodity trusts (R26.4 million) and levy income (R39.2 million for nonsugar commodities, R48.8 million for sugar). Funding from private enterprises comes mainly from input suppliers and

Figure 8.2   South Africa: Funding channels for agricultural R&D, 1999–2000

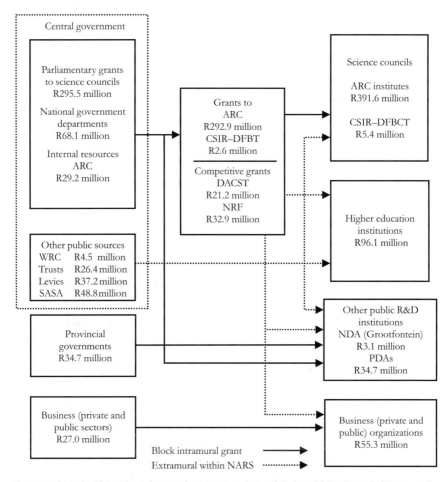

Sources: Compiled by authors from various sources, but mainly from Liebenberg, Beintema, and Kirsten 2004.

Notes: Data are nominal South African rand. Values may not tally exactly with those reported in other tables and figures because estimates of researcher expenditures were used elsewhere, and ARC corporate expenditures are included here.

WRC = Water Research Commission; SASA = South African Sugar Association.

agroprocessors, who outsource some research on a contract basis but also do in-house research. Monies allocated from these sources amounted to R27.0 million in 1999–2000.

ARC and the higher-education institutions dominate expenditure by research performers. Total expenditure in 1999–2000 is estimated at R586.2 million, of which R139.4 million came from nongovernment income sources. The total donor contribution to South African research is difficult to estimate but is assumed to be relatively small.

Agricultural research at the different faculties of agriculture is also funded from a range of sources. Commodity organizations and private companies gener-ally support the major and longer-term projects; funds are also supplied to success-ful bidders under the innovation fund and the NRF. In addition, donor agencies have also recently provided some support for university research and postgraduate teaching initiatives.

Agricultural R&D Patterns

ARC is by far the largest provider of agricultural research in South Africa, employ-ing 59.8 percent of the country's agricultural researchers in 1999 and account-ing for 57.9 percent of total agricultural research expenditure—slightly more than ARC's 54 percent of total share at the time of its establishment (Roseboom et al. 1995). Universities have also shown strong growth in market share since 1992 (Table 8.6).

The situation appears to have changed significantly since 2000. The number of research staff at ARC dropped from 751 in 1992 to 682 (non-fte) in 2000 and 525 in April 2003. The biggest change in terms of qualifications was among Ph.D.- and M.Sc.-qualified researchers. Ph.D. numbers fell from 206 in 1997 to 179 in 2000. Of greater concern, ARC records at the end of April 2003 reflected only 144 staff with Ph.D.s employed at all the institutes (only 87 of whom were researchers), a decline of 35. The corresponding decline for research staff holding M.Sc. degrees is 41. By inference, 76 key research staff have left ARC since 2000, adding to the decline of the previous few years. This rapid decline is disturbing and could signal the demise of the agricultural research system in South Africa.

Ratios of support staff to scientists dropped from as high as 10.7:1 in 1992 to 3.9:1 in 2001. The ratio of technicians to researchers in ARC institutes fell from 1.7:1 in 1992 to 0.8:1 in 2001, indicating that research support is dwindling and that the remaining researchers and technicians must now spend more of their time on mundane duties. This trend has severe implications for ARC's capacity to maintain performance levels, which in turn will strongly affect the ability of South Africa's agricultural sector to support regional and local rural development initiatives.

Table 8.6 South Africa: Composition of agricultural research expenditures and total number of researchers, 1999

	Spending			Percentage		Number of
	Million	Million 1999	Researchers			
Type of agency	1999 rand	international dollars	(fte)	Spending	Researchers	agencies in sample
Government agencies						
Agricultural Research Council (ARC)	429.3	234.9	634.3	57.9	59.8	14
Other	123.4	67.5	168.4	16.7	15.9	12
Nonprofit institutions	56.1	30.7	56.0	7.6	5.3	3
Higher-education agencies	106.9	58.5	158.0	14.4	14.9	12
Business enterprises	25.2	13.8	44.5	3.4	4.2	9
Total	740.8	405.3	1,061.1	100	100	50

Sources: Recalculated from Liebenberg, Beintema, and Kirsten 2004. Deflators and PPP conversion from World Bank 2003.
Note: Expenditures for nine government agencies, two nonprofit institutions, and the higher-education agencies are estimates based on average expenditures per researcher for ARC; expenditures for three business enterprises are estimates based on average expenditures per researcher for the six business enterprises for which data were available. The 634 fte researchers listed include research technicians with degree qualifications. Rand converted to international dollars using purchasing power parity (PPP) indexes, which reflect the purchasing power of currencies by comparing prices across a broader range of goods and services than conventional exchange rates.

Figure 8.3   South Africa: The history of the parliamentary grant to the Agricultural Research Council, 1992–2002

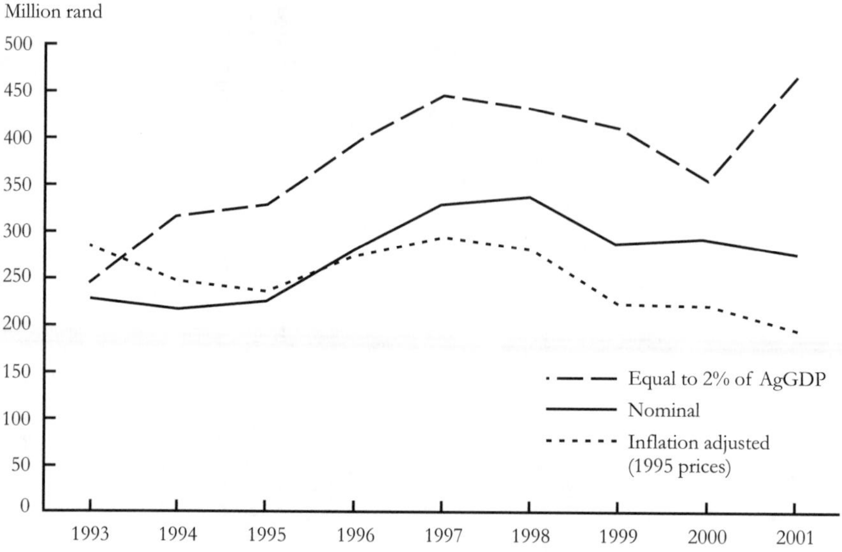

Million rand

Sources: Compiled by authors from NDA 2003; and ARC *Annual report,* 1993–2002.

The budgetary pressures resulting from the drop in the parliamentary grant could be the main reason behind the reductions in these ratios.

ARC funding provided by the government through the parliamentary grant system dropped from a peak of R337 million in 1997–98 to R262 million in 2001–02. The history of the parliamentary grant to ARC is well illustrated by the trend in Figure 8.3. The extent of the decline in funding is emphasized by the rapidly declining real value of the grant. By 2001–02, ARC received only 55 percent, in real terms, of the parliamentary grant it received in 1992. As a consequence, external income had to increase significantly to maintain overall spending at an estimated R450 million for 2001–02. Also shown in Figure 8.3 is ARC's level of baseline funding had it been maintained at 2 percent of AgGDP. Under the new Agricultural Sector Strategy (NDA 2001), it is envisioned that this target should be in the range of 3 percent.

Table 8.7 shows sources of ARC funding from 1998 to 2000, and relative shares for each year. External income for ARC came from commodity and producer organizations and donor funding. Income from commodity organizations contributed between 11.1 and 12.9 percent of ARC expenditure in the period 1998–2000. As shown in Figure 8.2, commodity organizations, as a whole, fund a total of 19.7

Table 8.7   South Africa: Agricultural Research Council funding sources, 1998–2000

| | Total funding | | | | | | | | |
| | Million rand | | | Million international dollars | | | Funding share | | |
Source	1998	1999	2000	1998	1999	2000	1998	1999	2000
Government	304.5	282.9	265.0	166.6	154.8	145.0	66.6	63.8	62.0
Bilateral donors	0.2	2.3	3.6	0.1	1.3	2.0	0.1	0.5	0.8
Multilateral donors	2.5	0.9	0.8	1.3	0.5	0.4	0.5	0.2	0.2
Producers and marketing boards	52.9	57.4	47.4	28.9	31.4	25.9	11.6	12.9	11.1
Public and private enterprises	50.3	62.5	60.9	27.5	34.2	33.3	11.0	14.1	14.2
Own income	32.1	29.2	44.2	17.5	16.0	24.2	7.0	6.6	10.3
Other	14.7	8.3	5.8	8.0	4.5	3.2	3.2	1.9	1.4
Total	457.2	443.5	427.7	249.9	242.7	234.0	100	100	100

Sources: Recalculated from Liebenberg, Beintema, and Kirsten 2004. Deflators and currency conversion from World Bank 2003.

Note: See Table 8.6 for details of international dollars.

percent (R112.4 million) of total R&D expenditure in South African agriculture. A few statutory levies were introduced by producer organizations as a way to raise funding for agricultural research, among other things. Voluntary levies are also used by some commodity groups, but income from these sources is highly unstable. Donor funding to ARC is growing, but access to it is severely limited by policy constraints. However, it seems that more donor funding has been flowing to universities for basic and applied agricultural research. Private funding to ARC is estimated at 14.2 percent of total ARC funding, and intramural research in many agricultural input firms has been growing because of the high returns on intellectual property rights (IPR) and patents in this industry. In addition, many private companies have awarded research contracts to universities. ARC's "own income" from royalties and IPR increased over the three years shown, from almost 7 percent to 10.3 percent.

Despite the growth in external funding, the government (through the parliamentary grant and a range of contracts) remains the largest single source of funding (around 62 percent) for ARC. However, the dual accountability of ARC institute directors to public and private funders is becoming a serious issue in resource-allocation decisions.

Institutional Accountability Mechanisms

Science Councils report both to the line ministry and to the Minister of Arts, Culture, Science, and Technology on their annual performance. For PDAs, the line of reporting is under the various provincial legislatures, with coordination through

ITCA. Universities report to DNE, coordinated by a committee of the heads of the agriculture faculties. Given the strong degree of autonomy of the various research service providers, no single authority has control over the activities of all the country's research providers. This situation reinforced the need for establishing the NARF, which was recommended as early as 1996 but only eventuated in 2002. Although recognized and funded by the NDA, the NARF is still battling to become fully operational.

The promulgation of the Public Finance and Management Act in 1999 (Act 1 of 1999) has led to a legal requirement on public entities (parastatals) to report to Parliament on their service delivery according to a set of formal, predetermined objectives and performance indicators. DACST has taken the lead in harmonizing the diverse basis of reporting from the various science councils to authorities such as NACI and Parliament.

Using a "balanced scorecard" technique, a set of 25 indicator areas has been identified in the areas of finance, stakeholder satisfaction, internal business organization, and internal learning and growth. To include the performance of delivery on equity legislation, a fifth reporting category was identified and included: human resources and transformation. Each science council developed its own set of indicators for measuring and reporting on performance under each of these categories (where applicable). Steps are being implemented to develop greater uniformity in the measures used by the various science councils to facilitate intercouncil comparisons and reduce the administrative burden of reporting.

In 1995, ARC established a small impact-assessment unit, the Group for Development Impact Analysis, to introduce social sciences research into ARC's activities. Being small, the unit was located centrally and provides services to institutes throughout the country. One of the unit's first initiatives was to contract a series of aggregate rate-of-return studies (Table 8.8). Results show that on average, the social rate of return on the investment in agricultural research has been positive and fairly high. A number of cost–benefit impact-assessment case studies have also been done.

Further, the unit actively participated in project feasibility studies and the training of researchers and research managers in project-level monitoring and evaluation techniques. A further area of activity since 1998 involved support to corporate management in policy advice and planning. Although, to date, formal mechanisms for priority setting have been restricted to the institute level, there is a growing need to expand them to the corporate level within ARC. Stakeholders requested this change in March 2001. In the seven years since its establishment, the demand for the unit's services and appreciation of the importance of the information it generates have grown exponentially, although trends in public funding to ARC have

Table 8.8 South Africa: Rate-of-return studies on the impact of agricultural research by level of aggregation

Level	Commodity	Method	Period	Rate of return (percent)	References
National	Research and development	Two-stage decomposition	1947–91	60–65	Thirtle and van Zyl 1994
	Extension			28–35	
	Research and development	Profit function	1947–92	44	Arnade et al. 1996; Khatri et al. 1995
	–Short-term			58–113	Arnade et al. 1996; Khatri et al. 1995
	–Long-term			Very low	Arnade et al. 1996; Khatri et al. 1995
	Extension				
Agricultural subsectors	Field crops	Profit function	1947–92	30	Thirtle et al. 1998
	Horticulture		1947–92	100	Thirtle et al. 1998
	Livestock		1947–92	5	Thirtle et al. 1998
Enterprises	Animal health	Production function	1947–82	>36	Thirtle et al. 1998
	Animal production	Supply response	1947–94	11–16	Thirtle et al. 1998
	Bananas	Supply, area, and yield	1953–95	50	Thirtle et al. 1998
	Deciduous fruit	Supply response	1965–94	78	Thirtle et al. 1998
	Groundnuts	Yield changes	1968–95	50	Thirtle et al. 1998
	Maize	Error-correction model	1950–95	29–39	Thirtle et al. 1998
	Sorghum	Error-correction model	1950–95	50–63	Thirtle et al. 1998
	Sweet potatoes	Supply response	1952–94	21	Thirtle et al. 1998
	Tobacco	Supply, price lags	1965–95	50–53	Thirtle et al. 1998
	Wheat	Error-correction model	1950–95	26–34	Thirtle et al. 1998
	Wine grapes	Error-correction model	1987–96	40–60	Townsend and van Zyl 1998
Research programs	Dairy, beef, mutton, and pork performance, and progeny testing schemes	Economic surplus	1970–96	2–54	Mokoena, Townsend, and Kirsten 1999
	Cover-crop management	Yield and residual	1987–96	44	Thirtle et al. 1998
	Lachenalia research and development[a]	Economic surplus	1965–2015	7–12	Marasas et al. 1998
	Proteaceae research and development[a]	Economic surplus	1974–2005	8–12	Wessels et al. 1998
	Russian wheat aphid integrated-control program[a]	Economic surplus	1980–2005	22–28	Marasas 1999

Source: Compiled by authors.

[a]Preliminary results of these studies were published as reports by the Agricultural Research Council and the Southern African Centre for Cooperation in Agricultural and Natural Resources Research and Training.

stymied efforts to expand the unit by placing personnel in the institutes. Unit-facilitated policy workshops disseminating the information developed have succeeded in building understanding among key NARS stakeholders regarding the future direction of agricultural research. In line with the exodus of researchers from the ARC, the staffing of the unit has fallen from 11 in 2000 to 2 in April 2003.

The Provision of Agricultural R&D Services

The dominance of ARC in South African agricultural research is evident through an overview of its various research providers (Table 8.9).

Government and local agencies. The national government has introduced a number of programs to direct resources toward priority initiatives, responding to pressure to fulfill its growth and development strategy and to deal with the difficulties experienced by provincial research agencies in adapting to their new mandate. These changes have directly affected ARC's priorities and activities. ARC was continuously urged to adjust its operations in line with the seven presidential imperative programs (PIPs), one of which focuses on rural development. Government departments were clustered around these PIPs according to their potential ability to deliver on the initiatives from their existing budgets. Meetings between the minister of agriculture and the provincial ministers (MINMEC) have also identified five-year priorities for agriculture that closely relate to the PIPs. Since November 2001, the new sector strategy for agriculture has formed the basis for policy and service-provision alignment (NDA 2001). Producer and commodity organizations often enter partnerships with public-sector R&D service providers such as ARC. The greatest successes have come when ARC has taken the lead in project management, and the universities, provincial departments, producer organizations, and farmers have each contributed financially or in kind.

Universities. Faculties of agriculture at the larger universities are in a much better position to maintain capacity under the current circumstances. Core funding for universities is provided by the National Department of Education (NDE) and primarily underwrites salaries and overhead. Direct research costs are usually funded through research contracts with producer organizations, private companies, and some international donors. In addition, researchers at universities compete for research funds such as the innovation fund and annual grant funding for researchers from the NRF. The large variety of funding sources makes it difficult to develop a clear picture of spending on agricultural R&D by universities. There is growing concern that universities are venturing into applied research, thereby usurping potential

Table 8.9 South Africa: Agricultural research expenditure by institutional category, 1992–2000

Institution	1992	1993	1994	1995	1996	1997	1998	1999	2000
Million 1999 rand									
Government agencies									
Agricultural Research Council (ARC)	422.9	414.2	404.4	480.3	494.1	483.4	519.5	452.9	429.3
Other	126.9	135.0	126.5	138.3	133.5	129.5	130.2	116.3	123.4
Subtotal	549.8	549.1	530.9	618.6	627.6	612.9	649.7	569.3	552.6
Nonprofit institutions	60.6	55.0	49.3	51.6	53.1	50.9	54.2	56.7	56.1
Higher-education agencies	72.8	78.9	77.0	85.8	82.8	80.2	101.4	101.7	106.9
Business enterprises	27.2	27.1	27.6	28.7	27.7	26.0	26.6	21.3	25.2
Public total	683.2	683.1	657.2	755.9	763.5	744.0	805.3	727.7	715.6
Total	710.4	710.1	684.8	784.6	791.2	770.0	831.9	749.0	740.8
Million 1999 international dollars									
Government agencies									
Agricultural Research Council (ARC)	231.4	226.6	221.2	262.8	270.3	264.5	284.2	247.8	234.9
Other	69.4	73.8	69.2	75.7	73.0	70.8	71.3	63.7	67.5
Subtotal	300.8	300.4	290.5	338.5	343.4	335.3	355.5	311.5	302.3
Nonprofit institutions	33.2	30.1	27.0	28.2	29.1	27.9	29.7	31.0	30.7
Higher-education agencies	39.9	43.2	42.1	46.9	45.3	43.9	55.5	55.6	58.5
Business enterprises	14.9	14.8	15.1	15.7	15.1	14.2	14.6	11.6	13.8
Public total	373.8	373.7	359.5	413.6	417.7	407.0	440.6	398.1	391.5
Total	388.7	388.5	374.6	429.3	432.9	421.3	455.2	409.8	405.3

Sources: Recalculated from Liebenberg, Beintema, and Kirsten 2004. Deflators and currency conversion from World Bank 2003.

Notes: Expenditures for nine government agencies, two nonprofit institutions, and the higher-education institutions are estimates based on average expenditures per researcher for ARC; expenditures for three business enterprises are estimates based on average expenditures per researcher for the six business enterprises for which data were available. The 634 FTE researchers listed include research technicians with degree qualifications. See Table 8.6 for details of international dollars.

projects from ARC. This shift is partly a result of commodity organizations either perceiving that ARC's capacity is declining or being attracted by lower rates charged by universities.

International agencies. The CGIAR system has provided useful support and information since 1994. There has been little direct involvement in South African agricultural research, however, apart from a few donor-driven projects. Involvement is increasing, and the establishment of a regional office for the International Water Management Institute (IWMI) in Pretoria is an example of this growing trend. IWMI works in close collaboration with ARC, the government, and universities on issues related to the rehabilitation of irrigation schemes, the development of an irrigation policy, and the development of irrigation scheme management.

Regional R&D organizations, such as the Southern African Centre for Co-operation in Agricultural and Natural Resources Research and Training (SACCAR), are becoming more important. SACCAR, under the auspices of the SADC, used to allocate certain research initiatives to specific SADC member states. Following the restructuring of SADC, SACCAR now takes greater direct responsibility for research. Member states no longer have the sole responsibility to fund and manage these initiatives, with only the review and consultation of the SACCAR council and its subsidiary technical committees. ARC used to represent South Africa's R&D interests at SACCAR. Whereas universities still have representation, NDA has now taken over this responsibility, for all foreign representation and liaison of agricultural R&D.

The World Bank–funded Special Program on African Agricultural Research (SPAAR) has also been changed to a more permanent initiative with the creation of the Forum on Agricultural Research in Africa (FARA) in Addis Ababa in April 2001. The intention is to provide a forum for harmonizing agricultural R&D in Africa through the initiatives of the three regional agricultural research organizations in Sub-Saharan Africa: SACCAR, the Association for Strengthening Agricultural Research in East and Central Africa (ASARECA), and the Western and Central African Council for Agricultural Research and Development (CORAF). This arrangement allows Africa to take greater ownership of its R&D. The Mbeki government is also taking the lead in implementing the New Partnership for Africa's Development (NEPAD), which has a strong focus on agricultural development.

Lessons Learned and Future Challenges

The changes that began in the early 1970s led to an increasingly fragmented agricultural research system, and efforts to integrate the system's components and improve overall efficiency are incomplete. In the process of reforming the national agricultural research system in South Africa, several lessons have been learned.

It is important to maintain continuity in NARS leadership and for those leaders to have direct communication with institutional leaders. Commitment to goals, and the initiatives implemented to achieve them, is imperative, as is the capacity to monitor and adjust to changes. Ad hoc, uncoordinated responses to change within such a complex system as South Africa's NARS is, perhaps, the most important cause of fragmentation and duplication of effort.

Stakeholders must have access to appropriate information and analyses when making decisions, and their roles and responsibilities must be clearly established and understood. Memoranda of understanding or contracts can be used to communicate and clarify this information. Throughout, the focus should be on the coordination, content, and evaluation of programs.

A crucial factor is the policy environment that supports mobilizing funds, developing and maintaining the human-resource capacities of the system, and facilitating communication. This is one of the most neglected areas from the viewpoint of agricultural R&D policy in South Africa. These issues are emphasized only periodically; consistent effort by a critical mass of policy researchers is needed, as is an effective, world-class agricultural science fraternity to encourage greater numbers of students to train in the agricultural sciences. A substantial scholarship program for students is urgently needed to redress the substantial loss of qualified scientists from South Africa.

The increased role of private organizations and commodity trusts in funding the ARC illustrates the general experience of public research entities that increasingly rely on nonpublic sources of funding. Commodity trusts have shown a strong willingness and ability to increase their contributions. However, the amount of funding from these sources fluctuates markedly depending on industry market conditions. In South Africa it is also susceptible to the vagaries of sectoral politics and the failure of public entities to allow private funders of public research to secure intellectual property rights on research output. If public-research service providers fail to reach mutually acceptable positions with private funders on intellectual property rights issues (and, relatedly, the allocation of research resources), they may well be unable to ensure a stable flow of adequate funding and retain competent staff.

The establishment of the NARF in 2002 marked the beginning of a new phase in South Africa's agricultural R&D. The NARF could be critical in securing not only the future of agricultural research in South Africa but also the sustained international competitiveness and prosperity of agriculture in South and southern Africa. Unfortunately, since its establishment, the NARF has failed to become operative as a policy advisory body or to formulate appropriate policy responses to the issues listed here. ARC's experience over the past 10 years could be invaluable in the planning and implementation of a much more effective NARS into the future.

Appendix Table 8A.1 South Africa: Structure of the agricultural research system, 2000

Institutional category	Supervising agency	Executing agency	Research focus	Number of staffed research sites	Number of researchers in 2000 (1993 figures in parentheses)
Government	Agricultural Research Council (ARC)	Grain Crops Institute (GCI)	Groundnuts, sunflower, sorghum, soybeans, maize, dry beans, lupines, and cowpeas	1	37 (84)
		Small Grains Institute (SGI)	Wheat, oats, barley	5	27 (29)
		Institute for Industrial Crops (IIC)	Cotton, tobacco, hemp, flax	1	17 (25)
		Vegetable and Ornamental Plant Institute (VOPI)	Vegetables and ornamental plants	1	21 (55)
		Institute for Tropical and Subtropical Crops (ITSC)	Tropical and subtropical fruits	9	37 (41)
		Infruitech-Nietvoorbij	Pome and stone fruit, viticulture, and enology; breeding, physiology, horticulture; biotechnology; postharvest technology	4	139 (82)
		Rangeland and Forage Institute (RFI)	Grassland and forage	1	32 (40)
		Animal Improvement Institute (AII)	Animal production and improvement	1	43 (52)
		Animal Nutrition and Products Institute (ANPI)	Animal nutrition; farming systems; animal products; food security; small, medium, and micro-enterprise development	2	32 (66)
		Onderstepoort Veterinary Institute (OVI)	Animal health	1	61 (78)
		Plant Protection Research Institute (PPRI)	Plant protection	8	103 (105)
		Institute for Agricultural Engineering (IAE)	Agricultural engineering, wine technology	2	20 (23)[a]
		Institute for Soil, Climate, and Water (ICSW)	Soil science, climatology, hydrology, water	1	76 (62)
		Development Impact Assessment Unit	Socioeconomic studies	1	8 (–)
		Biometrics Unit	Biometrics	1	12 (30)
Government	National Department of Agriculture	Grootfontein Agricultural Development Institute	Production and resource utilization technology	1	7 (23)
	Free State Department of Agriculture	Glen	Crops, livestock, pastures, natural resources; production technology	4	13 (26)
	Northwest Department of Agriculture	Potchefstroom	Crops, livestock natural resources; production technology	5	23 (41)

Category	Institution	Unit	Field	Researchers	Staff
	Kwazulu-Natal Department of Agriculture	Cedara	Crops, livestock, natural resources	6	44 (18)
	Mpumalang Department of Agriculture	Nelspruit	Animal science, crops science, natural resources	3	12 (–)
	Western Cape Department of Agriculture	Elsenburg	Animal science, crops science, natural resources	7	59 (31)
	Northern Cape Department of Agriculture	Upington	Animal and crop production and resource utilization	2	6 (–)
	Council for Scientific and Industrial Research (CSIR)	Bio/Chemtek	Food; biological and chemical technologies	2	15 (–)
Academic	University of Stellenbosch	Faculty of Agriculture and Forestry Sciences	Agriculture and forestry	1	94 (95)
	University of Pretoria	Faculty of Natural and Agricultural Sciences	Agriculture and natural sciences	1	108 (59)
		Faculty of Veterinary Science	Animal health	1	114 (77)
	University of Natal	Faculty of Science and Agriculture	Agriculture and natural sciences	1	31 (72)
	University of the Free State	Natural and Agricultural Sciences	Agricultural and natural sciences	1	54 (52)
	University of the North	Faculty of Sciences, Health, and Agriculture	Agriculture and natural sciences	1	(14)[b]
	University of Fort Hare	Faculty of Agriculture	Agriculture	11	(37)[b]
		Agricultural and Rural Development Institute	Agriculture and rural development		
	University of North West	Faculty of Agriculture	Agriculture		
	University of Zululand	School of Agriculture	Agriculture		
	University of Venda	School of Agriculture	Agriculture		32
Semipublic	South African Sugar Association (SASA)	SASA experiment station	Sugar	1	31 (33)
Private	Capespan	Capespan Technology Development	Deciduous fruit postharvest research	1	17
	Intervet	Malelane Research Unit	Veterinary products	1	4
	Hortech	Hortech	Horticulture, entomology, pathology	1	9
	Kynoch	Kynoch Agronomy Research	Fertilizer, agronomy	1	4
	GrainSA	Grain SA R&D unit	Socioeconomics, farming systems	1	5
	Dow Agri	Dow Agrosciences	Crop pest and disease control	1	3
	Sugar Milling Research Institute		Sugar processing	1	18
	Epol	Technical Department	Animal feed	1	1

Source: Compiled by authors from Liebenberg, Beintema, and Kirsten 2004.

Note: Staffing numbers here do not refer to full-time equivalents and should thus not be compared with those of ARC, where researchers spend almost 100 percent of their time on research. The institutions included here indicated in the 2001 ASTI survey that they were engaged in agricultural research. A dash within parentheses indicates that agencies did not exist in 1993.

[a] 1995 estimate.

[b] No response to 2000 survey.

Notes

1. On May 23, 2002, the first steering committee of NARF was elected by the stakeholders. The committee has developed a number of project proposals on NARS policy issues.

2. Given a poverty line of R352 monthly household expenditure per adult equivalent (May 2000).

3. People not formally employed, which typically includes those engaged in subsistence activities enterprises, casual labor, street traders, and hawking.

4. The DBSA (2000, p. 193) used the following definition for unemployment: persons 15 years of age and older who, during the reference week, were not in paid work or self-employment, were available for paid work or self-employment, took specific steps during the four weeks preceding the interview to find paid work or self-employment, or had the desire to work and would be available to take up a suitable job were one offered.

5. In June 2002 the South African rand was trading at R10.05 to the U.S. dollar, and the World Bank purchasing parity exchange rate was R2.2 to the U.S. dollar.

6. This section draws largely from a paper by van Zyl, Vink, and Kirsten (2001) prepared for the *Journal for International Development*. See Vink 2000 for a review of recent South African literature on the process and results of deregulation in agriculture since the early 1980s.

7. Until the 1990s, the policy of the Department of Agriculture was to negotiate with only one representative body of farmers—the South African Agricultural Union (SAAU), now known as Agriculture South Africa (Agri-SA).

8. A group of countries, including Australia, New Zealand, South Africa, Brazil, and Argentina, that support the principle of free trade in agricultural commodities.

9. This refers to the amount authorized annually by the national government for all the science and technology initiatives it funds.

10. For more details, see Roseboom et al. 1995.

11. Following the 1983 referendum, a three-chamber parliament was established, but all government affairs were still classified according to race, with "own" affairs and "general" affairs departments.

12. Levies can be voluntary or statutory, the latter having been introduced under the Agricultural Marketing Act. The rate varies from commodity to commodity, but the National Agricultural Marketing Council prescribes that it should not exceed 5 percent of the guideline price.

References

Arnade, C., Y. Khatri, D. Schimmelpfennig, C. Thirtle, and J. van Zyl. 1996. Short and long run returns to agricultural R&D in South Africa, or Will the real rate of return please stand up? In *Global agricultural science policy for the twenty-first century: Conference proceedings vol. 2 (contributed papers)*. Melbourne, Australia.

DACST (Department of Arts, Culture, Science, and Technology). 2001. *The science vote.* http://www.dacst.gov.za. Accessed November 26, 2001.

DBSA (Development Bank of Southern Africa). 2000. *Development report: Building developmental local government.* Halfway House: Development Bank of Southern Africa.

DNE (Department of National Education). 1988. *A System of Framework Autonomy for Science Councils.* Pretoria: DNE.

DST (Department of Science and Technology). 2002. *South Africa's National Research and Development Strategy.* Pretoria: DST.

Groenewald, J. A. 2000. The Agricultural Marketing Act: A postmortem. *South African Journal of Economics* 68 (3): 364–402.

Khatri, W. E., D. Schimmelpfennig, C. Thirtle, and J. van Zyl. 1996. Refining returns to research and development in South African commercial agriculture. *Agrekon* 35 (4): 283–290.

Liebenberg, F., N. M. Beintema, and J. F. Kirsten. 2004. *South Africa: Agricultural science and technology indicators country brief no. 14.* Washington, D.C., and The Hague: International Food Policy Research Institute, International Service for National Agricultural Research, and Agricultural Research Council.

Marasas, C. N., P. Anandajayasekeram, J. G. Niederwieser, M. Coetzee, D. Martella, B. J. Pieterse, and C. J. van Rooyen. 1998. The future of wildflower research and development in South Africa: The Lachenalia case study. *Agrekon* 37(4): 23–60.

May, J. 2000. *Poverty and inequality in South Africa: Meeting the challenge.* Cape Town: David Phillip.

Mokoena, M. R., R. F. Townsend, and J. F. Kirsten. 1999. Cattle improvement schemes in South Africa: Measuring the returns to research investment. *Agrekon* 38 (1): 78–89.

NDA (National Department of Agriculture). 2001. *The strategic plan for South African agriculture.* Pretoria: NDA.

———. 2003. *Abstract of agricultural statistics, 2003.* Pretoria: Directorate of Agricultural Statistics.

———. 2005. *Abstract of agricultural statistics, 2005.* Pretoria: Directorate of Agricultural Statistics.

Roseboom, J., P. G. Pardey, H. J Sartorius von Bach, and J. van Zyl. 1995. *Statistical brief on the National Agricultural Research System of South Africa.* ISNAR Indicator Series Project. Statistical Brief No. 23. The Hague: International Service for National Agricultural Research.

SARB (South African Reserve Bank). N.d. Historical data. www.resbank.co.za. Accessed December 2002.

Sartorius von Bach, H. J., and J van Zyl. 1991. Have recent structural changes caused agriculture to become less rigid? *Development Southern Africa* 8 (3): 399–404.

SSA (Statistics South Africa). 1985. *Agricultural census, 1985.* Pretoria: SSA.

Thirtle, C. 2001. TFP index for South African agriculture. Unpublished data and monograph. Department of Agricultural Economics, University of Pretoria.

Thirtle, C., and J van Zyl. 1994. Explaining total factor productivity growth and returns to research and extension in South African commercial agriculture, 1947–91. *South African Journal of Agricultural Extension* 23: 21–27.

Thirtle, C., R. F. Townsend, J. Amadi, A. Lusigi, and J. van Zyl. 1998. The rate of return on expenditures of the South African Agricultural Research Council (ARC). *Agrekon* 37 (4): 621–631.

Townsend, R. F., and J. van Zyl. 1998. Estimation of the rate of return to wine grape research and technology development expenditures in South Africa. *Agrekon* 37 (2): 189–210.

Van Zyl, J., and J. A. Groenewald. 1988. Flexibility in inputs substitution: A case study of South African agriculture. *Development Southern Africa* 5 (1): 2–13.

Van Zyl, J., N. Vink, and J.F. Kirsten. 2001. South African Agriculture Transition: The 1990s. *Journal of International Development* 13 (September): 725–739.

Vink, N. 2000. Agricultural policy research in South Africa: Challenges for the future. *Agrekon* 39 (4): 432–470.

Wessels, J., P. Anandajayasekeram, C. J. van Rooyen, C. N. Marasas, G. Littlejohn, and C. Coetzee. 1998. Does research and development pay? The case for Proteaceae. *Agrekon* 37 (4): 610–620.

World Bank. 2003. *World development indicators 2003.* Washington, D.C. CD-ROM.

Chapter 9

Zambia: A Quiet Crisis in African Research and Development

Howard Elliott and Paul T. Perrault

Introduction

The evolution of agricultural research and development policy in Zambia is emblematic of the quiet crisis in African agricultural research. Zambia, a medium-sized country that has avoided internal conflict, has, until recently, been spared from natural disasters. It has also enjoyed periods of relative economic well-being and institutional growth based on its copper industry. Zambia has a number of distinct agricultural regions that generally have good (but not always effective) access to water resources and promising agricultural potential. This potential has not been realized because of post-independence national policies that involved a suite of state interventions, which became unsustainable with falling copper revenues. In the past decade, Zambia has largely adhered to structural adjustment measures; however, as a consequence, its agricultural R&D institutions have lost significant key resources and subsequently credibility, when the research agenda failed to evolve quickly enough to respond to, much less lead, the changes in the economy.

Economy and Agriculture

Zambia is a landlocked republic in central Africa, with an area of 752,620 square kilometers and a population of 10.3 million in 2001. It is marginally self-sufficient in food, with irregular maize surpluses, and suffers from internal food-distribution problems because of poor road infrastructure and marketing facilities.

Formerly part of the Federation of Rhodesia and Nyasaland and known as Northern Rhodesia, Zambia gained independence peacefully from the United

Kingdom in 1964. At that time, Zambia's copper-based economy made it one of Africa's most prosperous countries. It developed a high level of urbanization early on, as well as a dualistic system of agriculture, with large-scale commercial farmers serving the urban demand, and a large population of subsistence farmers (smallholders).

From independence until 1991, the government under Kenneth Kaunda was pervasively involved in all aspects of agriculture through direct production, parastatal organizations, credit, and subsidies, in an effort to share the benefits of independence. Policies focused on cereals to make the country self-sufficient in food staples, with maize as the principal commodity (Jansen 1977). The role of the government in encouraging the adoption of hybrid maize through its research, seed policy, and subsidized input distribution became unsustainable with the decline of copper revenues (Howard 1994). From 1991 to 2001 a new government, under Frederick Chiluba, followed policies of structural adjustment and liberalization, with some commitment and success in the first half of the decade (Howard and Mungoma 1996; Jayne et al. 1999).

The Agricultural Sector: Agroecology and Research Infrastructure
Zambia's climate is dry, with large regions considered semiarid. There are three broad agroecological regions. Region I is a narrow band, lying mostly in the southern areas of the southern and western provinces, comprising the Zambezi and Luangwa valleys. It is a sparsely populated region, with low and unevenly distributed rainfall (less than 800 millimeters per year). The area has livestock enterprises despite endemic trypanosomiasis and other animal diseases. It is, however, a region where irrigated agriculture is possible all year round. Region II is a well-watered zone of high potential (800–1,000 millimeters of rainfall per year) running east to west and constituting a central belt through the country. Its crops include maize, cotton, sugarcane, oilseeds, food legumes, vegetables, and tree crops. Region III, in the north of the country, has adequate rainfall (above 1,000 millimeters annually), but productivity is limited by soil acidity and low fertility. As farmers have moved away from input-intensive maize following structural adjustment, Region III has been expanding production of roots and tubers. Figure 9.1 shows the agroecological regions of Zambia superimposed with the distribution of research infrastructure and research mandates.

Zambia had an extensive research infrastructure, which was later reduced through structural adjustment. The existing network of research stations still covers the major production areas of the country. Consequently, proposals for strengthening the research system do not require the creation of major new stations.

Figure 9.1   Zambia: Agroecological regions—Research stations and major programs

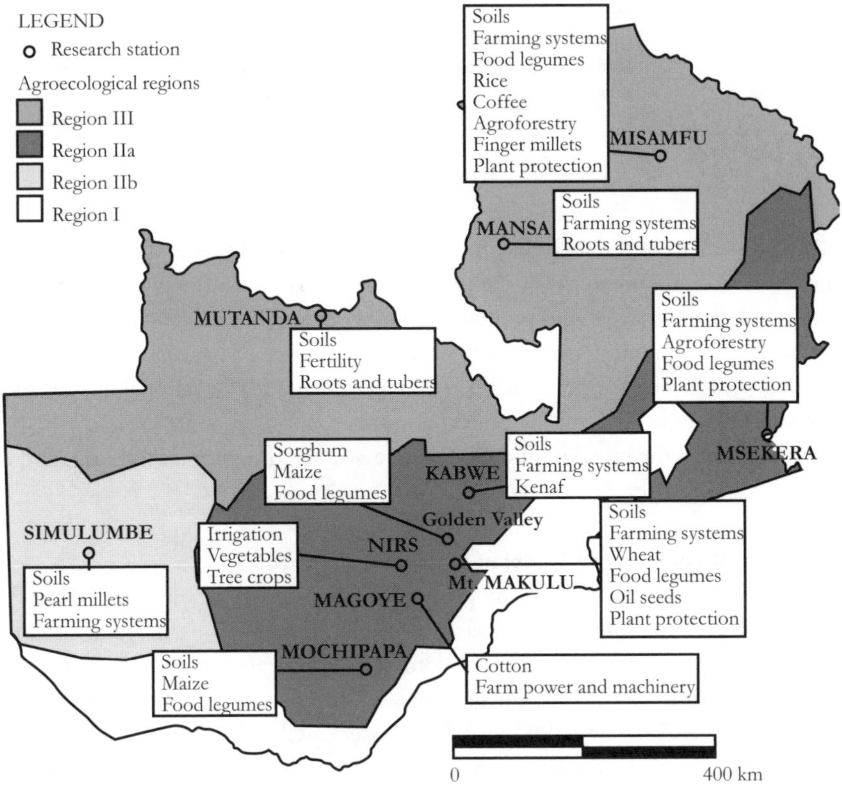

LEGEND

o   Research station

Agroecological regions

Region III

Region IIa

Region IIb

Region I

Soils
Farming systems
Food legumes
Rice
Coffee
Agroforestry
Finger millets
Plant protection

MISAMFU

MANSA

Soils
Farming systems
Roots and tubers

MUTANDA

Soils
Fertility
Roots and tubers

Soils
Farming systems
Agroforestry
Food legumes
Plant protection

MSEKERA

Sorghum
Maize
Food legumes

KABWE

Soils
Farming systems
Kenaf

Golden Valley

Soils
Farming systems
Wheat
Food legumes
Oil seeds
Plant protection

SIMULUMBE

Irrigation
Vegetables
Tree crops

NIRS

Soils
Pearl millets
Farming systems

MAGOYE

Mt. MAKULU

MOCHIPAPA

Soils
Maize
Food legumes

Cotton
Farm power and machinery

0   400 km

Source: SCRB 2001.

The Dualistic Agricultural Sector

Zambia's farming population of some 605,000 households has recently been classified into four categories: small-scale, emergent, medium-scale, and large-scale farmers (MAFF 2001b). Table 9.1 shows the numbers in each farm class and the production focus of each.

About 75 percent of farm households cultivate an average of 2 hectares or less, using very few modern inputs and producing primarily for subsistence purposes. At the other extreme are approximately 25,000 medium-scale (subsistence and commercial) farmers and 740 large-scale commercial farmers, who are responsible for all of the marketed wheat and flue-cured tobacco, about 30 percent of the maize,

Table 9.1   Zambia: Classification of agriculture, 1999

Characteristics	Small-scale	Emergent	Medium-scale	Large-scale
Number of farms	459,000	119,200	25,230	740
Size (hectares)	0.5–10	10–20	20–60	More than 60
Crops grown	Food crops	Food and cash crops	Food and cash crops	Cash crops
Production focus	Subsistence	Commercial and subsistence	Commercial and subsistence	Commercial

Source: MAFF 2001b.

50 to 60 percent of the soybeans, most of the commercial beef and dairy production, and around 60 percent of the poultry output. Between the two extremes are the "emergent farmers," who produce significantly for the market using appreciable quantities of modern inputs and cultivate an average of 10 to 20 hectares. The development of smallholder agriculture properly linked to the national market and global economy is a key policy objective. Various approaches are currently being tried, including the creation of commodity associations, contract farming, and a cottage seed industry.

Structural Change in the Zambian Economy, 1975–2000

During the 1980s, the World Bank proposed a program of liberalization, diversification, and privatization that was overshadowed by currency (and price) stabilization concerns and characterized by lack of domestic support for structural adjustment. An accumulation of arrears by the government led to a suspension of World Bank lending between 1987 and 1991. In 1991, Frederick Chiluba's Movement for Multiparty Democracy (MMD) came to power on a platform of reform and accepted a number of structural adjustment measures.

The new government observed many of its fiscal and monetary obligations under adjustment lending between 1991 and 1994, with positive results on inflation and the budget. The adjustment away from the high-income copper economy was reflected in the decline in the government's share of the economy. The government had enjoyed a relatively high rate of tax collections (18.4 percent of GDP), to which foreign grants added another 8.3 percent of GDP for a high government share of 27 percent. The dependence on external funds became one of Zambia's problems (World Bank 2001).

In 1994, the attention of the World Bank—a major external source of funding for the country—shifted to poverty alleviation, with emphasis on privatization and sectoral investment programs. In the early 1990s, the country experienced very high rates of inflation because of fiscal and quasi-fiscal deficits caused by the losses of parastatal industries covered by the government.[1] Monetization of these deficits exacerbated the problem of inflation that affected the poor disproportionately because of their relative lack of access to credit and inputs. Thus poverty reduction required a direct attack on the two deficits.

Spending on agriculture was also negatively affected by budget policy. In addition to setting general restrictions, the budgetary process had a bias against any ministry or sector according to the share of investment in the sector. Ministries such as transport, agriculture, tourism, energy, and water experienced a systematic reduction in investments, determined ad hoc by shortfalls in budget allocations, which were worsened by reallocations to noneconomic sectors (World Bank 2001, pp. 44–47).

There followed a privatization of parastatal firms and a divestiture of underutilized public properties and productive facilities to intermediate public–private trusts. The rapid inflation of this period eroded the real value of salaries in the public service, including those of scientists in public research institutions. Inflation still hovers around 20 percent annually (which, although high, is far below rates in excess of 100 percent in the early to mid-1990s).

The large change in the structure of the economy over the period 1979–99 is shown in Table 9.2. Declines in the percentage of both industry and government consumption in GDP indicate how dependent the economy had been on copper revenues. The recent rise in the share of agriculture demonstrates a recovery of agricultural production and some movement into new crops. The food production index for the period 1997–2000 fluctuated around the base level of 1989–91, but agricultural productivity fell significantly. The recent rise in agriculture's share in GDP therefore appears more pronounced because of the relative decline of industry (Table 9.2).

The population of Zambia is still growing at a rate of 2.2–2.4 percent annually, despite the high prevalence of HIV/AIDS. Largely because of the copper industry, Zambia was already 40 percent urbanized in 1980. This proportion has stayed relatively constant, with recent figures showing it rising to 44.5 percent in 2000 (World Bank 2002). Zambia is also experiencing an unusual phenomenon of urban-to-rural migration, possibly related to the economic situation and the impact of HIV/AIDS.

Development of Agricultural Policy and the Impact of Structural Adjustment on Agriculture

The roots of current government policy for the agricultural sector are found in the Ministry of Finance's "Agricultural Sector Letter of Development Policy" (MFNP 1995). This letter was an integral part of its request to the World Bank for the Agricultural Sector Investment Program (ASIP) funded by the International

Table 9.2 Zambia: Structural change in the economy, 1975–2000

Indicators	1975	1985	1990	1995	1996	1997	1998	1999	2000
Percentage of GDP									
Agriculture	14.3	14.6	20.6	18.4	17.6	18.7	21.2	24.1	27.3
Industry	43.6	44.8	49.1	35.9	34.8	34.2	29.1	25.3	24.0
Manufacturing	6.8	9.9	14.0	11.3	13.4	13.2	13.0	12.0	49.0
Services	42.1	40.6	30.3	45.7	47.7	47.1	49.7	50.9	49.0
Government consumption	26.8	23.9	19.0	12.5	11.4	10.9	11.2	9.7	10.6
Per capita income (constant 1995 U.S. dollars)	680	512	479	386	401	405	388	389	392
Agricultural production and productivity									
Food production index (1989–91 = 100)	83.1	82.0	93.9	94.5	113.6	107.1	93.4	105.9	103.2
Agricultural value-added per worker (constant 1995 U.S. dollars)	210	190	199	231	225	210	208	219	NA
Rate of inflation (GDP deflator)	–14.2	41.1	106.0	37.3	23.6	26.0	19.5	20.5	18.1
International trade									
Imports as percentage of GDP	56.3	37.2	36.6	39.8	38.9	35.3	39.2	41.5	45.8
Exports as percentage of GDP	36.6	36.4	35.9	36.1	31.3	30.1	26.7	22.6	30.6
Ores and metals as a share of exports	97.5			86.5					
Population									
Total population (million)	4.8	6.7	7.8	9.0	9.2	9.4	9.7	9.9	10.1
Urban population (percentage of total)	34.8	39.8	42.0	43.0	43.3	43.6	43.9	44.2	44.5

Source: World Bank 2002.

Note: NA indicates data are not available.

Development Association. In that letter, the government committed itself to actions to liberalize the economy and restrict the role of the state.

Four other documents implicitly followed policies affecting agriculture and agricultural research. These include "Formulation of a National Seed and Research Policy" (MAFF 1998), the draft National Agricultural Policy (MAFF 2000a), and various drafts of the Poverty Reduction Strategy Paper (MFNP 2002). Finally, proposals from 15 working groups preparing the ASIP successor program were synthesized in an agricultural commercialization program (ACP) (December 2001) that was scheduled for World Bank appraisal early in 2003.

In its 1995 letter on development policy, the Ministry of Finance agreed to the following specific policy thrusts:

1. Liberalize agricultural markets by relying on market-based prices for all crops, privatizing agricultural parastatals, and removing trade restrictions

2. Increase the role of the private sector by privatizing companies, seeking cost recovery, or privatizing services outright

3. Diversify agricultural production by shifting from maize to groundnuts, soybeans, tobacco, cotton, horticulture, and floriculture

4. Improve services to smallholders through research, extension, credit, and land tenure

5. Improve the economic status of women through access to credit, extension, land tenure, and other services

6. Make better use of available natural resources by accelerating land registration, increasing investment in infrastructure, and permitting land subdivision to create a market in land

7. Ensure food security by creating a food reserve for transitory insecurity and a financial mechanism to finance imports

8. Broaden rural finance by ensuring pluralism in provision of financial services through incentives to private-sector services

The Zambian government made some progress in implementing these commitments, with a few lacunae that had implications for agricultural research and development.

The Ministry of Agriculture, Food, and Fisheries (MAFF) began preparing a full national agricultural policy (NAP) in early 2000. Insofar as they were discussed, the draft objectives for soil and crop research were a mix of general and specific topics covering appropriate technology and varieties, conservation farming, a focus on smallholders, and the participation of the private sector. In the livestock sub-sector, the primary objective was disease prevention and control through provision of services by the private sector. In fisheries, attention was expected to shift to aquaculture and production of fingerlings because capture fisheries were at their limit. The draft policy also mentioned instituting emergency-preparedness measures to mitigate the effects of drought, and programs for the prevention and control of crop pests and livestock diseases of national importance.

On the institutional side, the stated objectives were to develop an efficient private-sector marketing system, facilitate the development of farmer groups, and implement a seed policy to create a dynamic seed industry offering a reliable quantity and quality of seed. The intricacies of public–private sector collaboration are exemplified by the Zamseed case, discussed in the next section.

The donor group reaction to the draft National Agricultural Policy (MAFF 2001a) can be summarized as follows:[2] From among all the activities mentioned, the two priorities should be to link small-scale farmers to agro-industry and to reduce dependence on external inputs through better management practices, such as conservation farming. On principle, the government should stick to its core functions of regulation, facilitation, coordination, and monitoring so as not to crowd out the private sector. Moreover, concern with smallholders should not lead to neglect of large-scale farmers, who can make opportunities for smallholders through market creation, outsourcing, contract farming, and technical knowledge. Finally, certain types of support from donors and government could be made conditional on the adoption of environmentally friendly practices, such as conservation farming (Agricultural Consultative Forum 2001).

These market-oriented views have found strong expression in the poverty reduction strategy paper (PRSP):

Zambia recognizes that future growth potential will be based on increased market competitiveness and that the liberalization process embarked on earlier is virtually irreversible if market players have to respond to the emerging structure and requirements of the global economy. In this regard, agricultural producers, processors, and merchandisers will be enabled to rapidly reposition themselves in the face of increasing competition, changing customer preferences, and new distribution channel designs. Both agricultural producers and agribusiness players will be encouraged to produce competitively and reach out to emerging markets more proactively.

In this regard, one of the priorities will be to complete the policy reform agenda set at the beginning of the 1990s, and to ensure that institutions in the agricultural sector attain a capacity level that makes them responsive to their clients. To provide policy clarity that appears to have been lacking in the last few years and avoid confusion regarding some aspects of the sector, government will issue within a year after the adoption of the PRSP clear policies and guidelines regarding agricultural inputs and output markets, mainly fertilizer and maize, as these appear to be areas where policy inconsistencies have been observed. (MFNP 2002, p. 56).

The principal interventions in the three years of Poverty Reduction Strategy Programme implementation focus on improvements in the following areas: the finance and investment climate; the marketing, trade, and agribusiness climate; land and infrastructure development; technology development and dissemination (TDD); and a targeted support system for food security (MFNP 2002). For the fourth intervention, the emphasis shifted to packaging and dissemination and away from technology development and research itself.

Several of the donors that were strong supporters of public-sector research in previous eras—for example, Sweden, the United States, the Netherlands, and Japan—have shifted their support in recent years to various projects linked to private-sector development, or channeled funding to agricultural projects managed through semipublic trusts. The draft "Formulation of a National Seed Policy" (MAFF 1998) provided a useful recognition of the role of public research in supporting the development of a domestic industry. More of this debate would have been a useful addition to the Agricultural Commercialization Programme and PSRP. As it stands, these documents have not adequately dealt with the importance of public research, the commitment of the government, and the role it should play in current debates on biosafety, the genetic modification of crops, and disaster preparedness—all issues that arose during the drought of 2002.

Implementation of the Structural Adjustment Policy, 1991–2001

At the macro level, budgeting under structural adjustment had a bias against the agricultural sector. There were also intrasectoral difficulties. The University of Zambia identified three major weaknesses in the implementation of structural adjustment in the agricultural sector (INESOR 1999). These weaknesses, reiterated in the PSRP (MFNP 2002), are the rapid pace of policy reforms without transitional

Table 9.3   Zambia: Actual and projected average research expenditure shares, 1996–2000

Research focus	Average actual allocation in 1996–99 (percent)		Average projected allocation in 2000 (percent)	
	Government of Zambia	Donor	Government of Zambia	Donor
Headquarters	66.9	0.0	33.3	10.7
Soils and crops research	5.3	10.7	11.6	9.6
Seed control and certification	0.5	6.0	0.9	1.1
Policy and planning	3.5	8.4	4.3	4.7
Animal production and health	5.4	16.8	8.7	19.5
Agricultural training	4.3	0.0	7.0	8.2
Farm power and mechanization	1.3	4.2	2.1	3.2
Irrigation and land use	2.2	20.0	3.5	5.3
Marketing and trade	1.7	16.9	7.2	16.1
Agricultural extension	5.5	0.0	14.6	15.1
Fisheries research	0.4	6.5	1.0	1.1
Fisheries extension	1.2	0.0	3.1	2.3
National agricultural information services	1.8	10.3	2.7	3.2
Total	100	100	100	100

Source: World Bank 2001.

mitigation measures, inadequate resource allocation for agricultural services, and unclear and inconsistent policy statements from politicians.

First, no provision was made to help marginal farmers adjust to the new market conditions: they were left to their own devices to bear the brunt of the policy shift, with resulting hardship and impoverishment. Second, public services such as research and extension were starved for resources to provide marginal farmers with technologies deemed more in line with new product prices and relative prices of factors of production. Support to field operations was neglected or left to donors, as can be seen from Table 9.3 (World Bank 2001).

Third, government officials have given unclear and often contradictory signals to the private sector and other stakeholders on the long-term policy direction of the agricultural sector. In 2001, the government again became involved in the distribution of inputs through the Program against Malnutrition. The Food Pack Program provided free fertilizer and planting materials to the poor for a cereal, a legume, and a root crop. However, in an election year, it both crowded out the private sector and gave mixed signals on future policy.

The Impact of Adjustment: Recent Evolution in Production
Researchers at the Food Security Research Project (a joint project of MAFF and Michigan State University) have used census and postharvest survey data to iden-

tify trends in production and provide a quantitative look at the impact of the post-1991 agricultural reforms (Zulu et al. 2000). They qualify the view that Zambian agriculture is in a decline. Their analysis shows change but no decline during the 1990s. They find, for example, that the national value of smallholder crop production shows no clearly discernible rise or fall during the mid- to late 1990s. Substantial reductions in areas under maize (22 percent), soybeans (60 percent), and sunflowers (70 percent) have been accompanied by equally impressive increases in areas under cotton (65 percent), groundnuts (76 percent), cassava (65 percent), and sweet potatoes (54 percent). Diversification, therefore, is taking place. This massive adjustment took place despite a series of extreme events: a countrywide drought in 1992, a partial drought in 1995, El Niño in 1998, and floods in 2001. The reform has not been harmful. The value of crop production has remained basically constant despite a reduction in government subsidies to agriculture.

The Food Security Research Project also identified some distributional effects of the reforms. There is increased differentiation between farmers who have been able to adjust and those who have not. Access to land is a significant factor in the way farmers adapt: in 1997–98, the value of the crop output per capita produced by the top 25 percent of farmers, ranked by land quartile, was 8 to 10 times higher than the value of crop output per capita produced by the bottom 25 percent. The top 20 percent of farming households produce about 60 percent of the value of crop output. Others note that smallholders have reduced their purchased inputs for maize and returned to subsistence cultivation or turned to substitute crops, thereby increasing the burden on women (Copestake 1997, pp. 17, 49). During this period of transition, the research system has been facing its own crisis and unable to take the lead in making needed changes.

The Evolution of Agricultural Research in Zambia

The History of the Research System
Agricultural research in Zambia began in 1922 and has evolved in scale, scope, and focus since then. Key events (points of growth, reorganizations, and changes in focus) are summarized in Table 9.4. The system began with a concern to serve European commercial farmers producing for the mining-sector labor force and a relatively urbanized population. It functioned essentially with expatriate staff. The first Zambian-national scientist was appointed only in 1967. During the 1970s and 1980s, the system, principally represented by the Soils and Crops Research Branch (SCRB) of the Ministry of Agriculture, Food and Fisheries, expanded with the aid of significant donor support and built an impressive record of achievements

Table 9.4   Zambia: Evolution of the research system, 1922–2002

Date	Event	Focus and impact
1922	Creation of experimental gardens	Cash crops, cotton, tobacco
1928	Establishment of veterinary research facility at Mazabuka	Livestock disease
1930	Creation of forestry research department	Exotic hardwoods, pine
1937	First evaluation of local varieties	Evaluation of local varieties
1940s	Expansion of research network and creation of Lusaka research station at Chalimbana	Crops research, entomology, pathology, pest and disease research, wheat research
1951	Creation of Central Fisheries Research Institute with network of stations	Capture fisheries in rivers and lakes; fish farming
1953	Soils and Crops Research Branch separated from other ministerial departments; creation of Mount Makulu Central Research Station	Focus on commercial crops grown by European farmers; intensive maize promoted to smallholders
1959	Livestock research transferred from veterinary branch to research branch	Animal production
1960	Expansion of research station network	Broader geographical coverage of research
1963	Initiation of forest products research and development	Processing and use of wood
1960s–1970s	Research branches organized by discipline	Component research of input-intensive production systems
1978	Creation of Central Veterinary Research Institute and transfer of research to Balmoral	Veterinary research; vaccine production
1980s	Reorganization of research: creation of nine commodity research teams, seven specialist research teams, and nine adaptive-research planning teams	On-station component research; farming systems research; and on-farm trials using a multi-disciplinary approach
1994	Reorganization of research: abolition of agricultural research planning teams; livestock research separated from Soils and Crops Research Branch; creation of farming systems and social sciences unit	Fiscal retrenchment; loss of multidisciplinary approach of agricultural research planning teams
1995	Creation of Agricultural Sector Investment Program	Implementation of structural adjustment, with focus on poverty reduction, privatization, and liberalization
1997	Creation of National Science and Technology Council; proposed transfer of Soils and Crops Research Branch to Ministry of Science, Technology, and Vocational Education	Governance change: coordination of science and technology institutes and proposed autonomous agricultural research institute under National Science and Technology Council (not implemented)
2001	Preparation of Agricultural Sector Investment Successor Program	Working groups prepare component strategies for formulation committee
2002	Agricultural Commercialization Program published and submitted to World Bank	Preappraisal agrees on creation of autonomous institute but recommends no direct institutional support
2002	Poverty Reduction Strategy Paper (2002–2004) published	Limited details on research role

Source: Compiled by authors.

in new varieties and farming-systems research. It was retrenched as the support of donors declined.

As a result of this expansion, both staff qualification ratios and expenditure per researcher were relatively high for African countries similar to Zambia. In 1991, the agricultural research intensity ratio (measuring agricultural research spending relative to the value of agricultural GDP) was above that of Malawi, Kenya, and Zimbabwe. However the gradual withdrawal of donor assistance in recent years occurred without compensatory support from the government. Together with changes in demand for research that occurred in tandem with the increasing liberalization of the economy, this lack of financial support has led to structural imbalances that the system has yet to address.

The Erosion of Research Capacity in Zambia

We have described the erosion of the current research capacity in Zambia as the "quiet crisis." It is quiet because it takes place against a positive chorus of achievements in liberalization and privatization while ignoring the simultaneous serious and perhaps permanent loss of institutional and human capacity.

A recent survey by ISNAR and IFPRI (ASTI 2001) reports on the institutional infrastructure for agricultural and related research (Table 9.5). These data report full-time equivalent positions, not least because growth in the formal establishment of positions does not reflect the true research capacity. Many positions remain unfilled after staff departures, largely because of formal and informal hiring constraints; other staff nominally on indefinite leave are effectively departed, but their positions are not listed as vacant. The SCRB reported formal vacancies of around 25 percent in August 2002; a head count by the authors determined that even fewer staff were physically present. Other parts of the agricultural research and education sectors are also suffering. The 20 percent decline in research capacity in the university and related institutes reflects the growing teaching load, the unfilled vacancies, and the increase in consulting activities by faculty staff. The observed growth in private-sector involvement in research (for example by the cotton company Dunavant and the private seed companies) partially fills a vacuum created by the weakening of public research.

Both the institutional complexity of the agricultural knowledge system and the formal establishment numbers have grown over the past decade. However, the system's principal institution, SCRB, has weakened considerably. The loss of many of its senior staff has also led to a loss of institutional memory, understanding, and accumulated wisdom. As in many other African countries over the past few decades, the Zambian research system is in danger of losing its accumulated stock of scientific knowledge as scientists leave research and even the country itself

Table 9.5   Zambia: Full-time equivalents in agricultural and related research, 1991–2000

Institute	Status	1991	1995	1996	1997	1998	1999	2000
Soils and Crops Research Branch (SCRB)	GD	91.0	139.0	147.0	156.0	162.0	167.0	168.0
Forestry Research Branch	GD	11.0	6.0	9.0	9.0	8.0	8.0	8.0
Central Fisheries Research Institute	GD	6.0	6.0	6.1	6.1	6.0	6.3	6.3
MSTVE institutes[a]	IN	27.3	22.9	21.9	20.9	19.7	19.9	18.9
Maize Research Institute	PS	3.0	3.0	3.0	4.0	3.0	3.0	3.0
Zamseed	PS	0.0	0.3	0.3	0.3	0.6	2.3	3.0
Dunavant Cotton Zambia	PS	0.0	4.0	4.0	4.0	4.0	4.0	4.0
Golden Valley Agricultural Research Trust	TR	0.0	1.0	5.0	5.0	7.0	7.0	9.0
Cotton Development Trust	TR	0.0	0.0	0.0	0.0	0.0	0.0	2.0
University of Zambia faculties[b]	UZ	27.2	32.0	31.2	30.4	28.7	23.5	23.5
Total		165.5	214.2	227.5	235.7	239.0	241.0	245.7

Source: Compiled by authors.

Notes: GD indicates government department; IN, institutes under the Ministry of Science, Technology, and Vocational Education (MSTVE); PS, private-sector companies; TR, public trusts; and UZ, schools and faculties of the University of Zambia. Full-time equivalents (fte's) are based on staff head counts and adjusted by respondents according to four criteria: (1) whether the staff member was engaged for a full year; (2) whether the appointment was full-time; (3) whether the person was on secondment or special leave for any period; and (4) the percentage of total time devoted to research.

[a]MSTVE institutes include the Livestock Production Research Center, the Water Resources Research Institute, and the Food Technology Institute of the National Institute for Scientific Research.

[b]University of Zambia schools and departments include the School of Agricultural Sciences, the School of Veterinary Medicine, Department of Agricultural Economics, and the Institute of Economic and Social Research.

(Pardey and Beintema 2001). Moreover, the fragmentation of responsibility for research has made it more difficult to establish a strong and unified voice to advocate for the sector as each research and development body pursues its particular interest.

The ASTI series provides a long-term view of the evolution of the system. Information from the recent 2001 survey was linked to data from an earlier survey described by Roseboom and Pardey (1995) to indicate trends in the number of scientists and the amount of total expenditures and expenditure per scientist over the period 1971–2000 (Figure 9.2). The decline in real expenditures per researcher during the 1980s and 1990s results from a combination of declining real investments and the growth of staff emerging from training. In recent years, the system suffered attrition from staff departures and morbidity. Staff have left SCRB, in particular, for other sectors and nonresearch occupations with acceptable conditions of service; HIV/AIDS has also taken its toll, although no official figures are available to demonstrate it.

The incoming government (as of January 2002) published the 2002–04 PRSP and based its request to the World Bank on the Agricultural Commercialization Plan.

Figure 9.2   Zambia: Trends in researchers, expenditures, and expenditure per researcher, 1971–2000

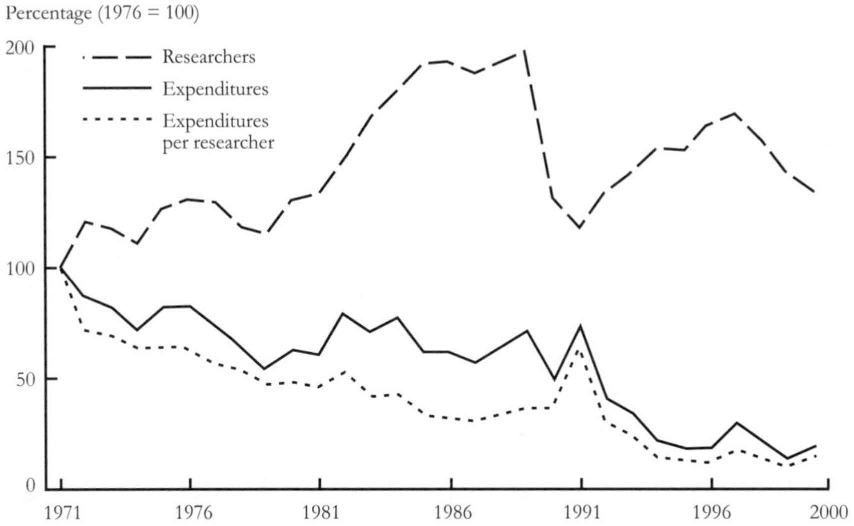

Percentage (1976 = 100)

Source: Special compilation of Agricultural Science and Technology Indicators (ASTI) data by Beintema (2002)

Unfortunately, the policy statements and details of support planned for agricultural research in both of these documents were weak, and unclear research policy will only lead to further erosion of the system.

SCRB: The Bellwether of the System

SCRB still employs the largest number of scientists in the country. The loss in its scientific resources observed in 2001 was not accompanied by a similar reduction in other staff categories with less mobility; the result was an imbalance in the staff mix, as shown in Table 9.6. Within the scientific category, a de facto hiring freeze has led to an increasing number of vacancies in the agricultural research officer category.

SCRB has too large a support staff for the number of scientists, and the latter are not optimally deployed to meet future demands for research. Spending limited financial resources on staff overheads while neglecting field sites is exacerbating the degradation of the physical infrastructure of the still-active stations.

Funding for the SCRB, part of the Ministry of Agriculture, Food and Fisheries, has also suffered in recent years. As the largest component of the country's research

Table 9.6   Zambia: SCRB staffing levels, 2001

Location	Professional	Technicians	Administration	General	Total
Mount Makulu (headquarters and program)	36	41	14	110	201
Golden Valley (SCRB staff)	3	6	NA	21	30
Kabwe	4	11	5	11	31
Magoye	0	4	1	12	17
Mansa	5	13	3	20	41
Misamfu	17	21	4	31	73
Mochipapa	8	18	6	38	70
Mongu (Simulumbe)	3	16	2	18	39
Msekera	8	29	2	29	68
Mufulira	1	11	1	19	32
Mutanda	6	9	2	18	35
Nanga	7	24	6	60	97
Total	98	203	46	387	734

Source: Compiled by authors from data collected in the various stations.
Note: NA indicates data are not available.

system, SCRB reflects the state of the system as a whole. Table 9.7 is a compilation of SCRB funding by source and use over the last decade of adjustment.

The staff and funding patterns in Tables 9.6 and 9.7, combined with insights gained through field visits by the authors, point to several key problems. First, funding for research over the past decade experienced substantial year-to-year fluctuations, gaps between approved budgets and disbursements, and a decline in the real value of expenditures over time. Second, the decline in both resources and staff has not occurred in a strategic or purposeful way that reorganizes priorities, retains the best staff, and improves conditions of service and operating resources for those remaining. Third, at any given time, the operational support of SCRB has been heavily dependent on project-based support from a few key donors. When a donor closes its project, the affected research unit suffers significantly. With the advent of the Agricultural Sector Investment Program, the World Bank/IDA program took over a sustaining role previously played by the Swedish International Development Cooperation Agency (Sida). Closure of the ASIP program in December 2001, without a successor program in place, would have been paralyzing without the 2 million kwacha in bridging funds from the interim PRSP. Continued and direct support under the Agricultural Commercialization Programme is in question.[3]

Although the bilateral donors have shifted their support away from purely public institutions, they are not necessarily abandoning the rural sector or even research in particular. They have continued to support activities of the semiprivate sector, NGOs, and agricultural development trusts. The tendency of bilateral donors to

Table 9.7   Zambia: Evolution of support to the SCRB, million kwacha (preliminary data)

Source of support	1992 Capital	1992 Operations	1998 Capital	1998 Operations	1999 Capital	1999 Operations
Government of Zambia			1,149.0	2,656.0	1,700.0	2,299.0
Bilateral agencies	297.1	NA	219.4	289.1	943.8	1,345.8
Multilateral agencies	0	0	448.1	566.4	489.2	856.0
Producer organizations	0	0	0	0	0	0
Private enterprises	0	0	0	0	0	0
Research partners	6.2	0	390	120.5	0	75.3
Own income						
Total	303.3		2,206.5	3,632.0	3,133.0	4,576.1

Sources: Compiled by authors from SCRB 1999, 2000.

Note: NA indicates data are not available.

eschew sectoral approaches and funding for government agencies owes much to their concern about the high levels of expenditure in MAFF's headquarters rather than out in the field. Shifting from institutional to project-based modes of support exacerbates the dependence of operational research on soft funding. This stance by the donors highlights how important it is for researchers and policymakers not only to reassert the nature of public-sector research as a core function of government but also to create governance structures for research that will restore the confidence of donors.

The decline in commitment to research by the government may also reflect the lack of political pressure by farmers and other stakeholders in favor of research. Farmers may perceive their long-term individual benefits from research to be low compared with the immediate benefits of a school, dispensary, or rural feeder road. The benefits of public-good research in Zambia must be identified and publicized so that it can command attention and resources.

Other stakeholders of research (NGOs and development projects) have not been strong supporters of research. In some cases they have been vocal in criticizing the system for its lack of presence in the field or its lack of responsiveness when called upon. Though not always acknowledging their debt, NGOs and development projects have derived real benefit from the system in the form of advice, training, and access to planting materials. Both of the research trusts (explained below) and the university have grown by drawing human resources from the research and development system. The NGOs either hire staff away from the system or access human resources at partial cost to their programs by topping up the salaries of field staff in extension. Moreover, many former SCRB scientists have become either regular staff or frequent consultants to donor offices.

The Soils and Crops Research Working Group for the ASIP successor program has made proposals for a decentralized, autonomous Zambia Agricultural Research Institute in line with government policies for reduction of poverty, public–private sector partnerships, decentralization, and participation by farmers' organizations. The proposals also satisfy donor needs for operational autonomy and accountability. Sustained commitment by the government is critical to develop and maintain the base on which the private sector can build. The level of funding requested is within the capability of the government and its donors.

Key Policy Issues

This section deals with macro-level and sectoral policy issues. Macro policy issues concern the need for a government commitment to maintain a research capacity to lead and support the goals laid out in the Agricultural Commercialization Programme (MAFF 2001b) and Poverty Reduction Strategy Paper (MFNP 2002) within the constraints of fiscal discipline. Sectoral policy issues concern the institutional and programmatic changes needed within the R&D sector to generate political and client support for research.

Fiscal Capacity and Commitment to Agricultural Research

Zambian fiscal policies and budgetary practices have been biased against agriculture (World Bank 2001). Despite the obvious importance of agriculture in employment and the agriculturally based share of manufacturing, the share of agriculture in public expenditures has been low, fluctuating between 2.5 and 10 percent but averaging only 4 percent between 1994 and 2000. This low priority cannot be explained away by the need for fiscal prudence alone, because expenditures were small relative to the quasi-deficits of state-owned enterprises. Within the agricultural budget, the share of research has been equally modest, at only 5.3 percent (World Bank 2001).

However, structural adjustment and correction of the quasi-fiscal deficits will not restore research funding to previous levels. Since all sectors have experienced reductions from previous peaks, it is necessary to establish agriculture's priority in terms of efficiency, equity, and implementability. To demonstrate efficiency, research must show that it will make the greatest impact relative to the counterfactual scenario—what would happen if the government did not spend the money to undertake this activity. To demonstrate equity, it must show that the research will help the poor, and—since poverty is widespread—that expenditure on research is a better way to help the poor (especially the rural poor) than other forms of expenditure. Finally, to demonstrate implementability, it must show that research is able to do what it promises (World Bank 2001).

Coordination and Control in the NARS

There are two aspects to the coordination of agricultural research in Zambia: the first is coordination of the components of the broader R&D system, and the second is coordination within the public research organization itself. Over the past decade, Zambia's national agricultural research system has grown in complexity but not in full-time equivalent (fte) scientist numbers or in research capacity. Meanwhile, there are more research partners: the university, the semipublic research trusts, the seed industry, and technology service providers such as extension and NGOs. Pluralism is generally a positive thing. However, the increase in the number of part-time research providers with primary mandates for education or development at the expense of the main research body, SCRB, weakens the research system. Three examples highlight the need for better coordination and guidance of the system.

In 1991, gray leaf spot of maize appeared in the country, probably via seed imported from other countries of the region.[4] The arrival of the fungus had grave consequences for national maize production because Zambian hybrids were found to be highly susceptible to it. Not only did some time elapse before the impact of this unregulated and untested technology importation was brought to the attention of research, but SCRB had few resources to respond to the threat. A strengthened Seed Control and Certification Institute (SCCI) with better control measures could have prevented the problem, and better coordination between SCRB and Zamseed (a joint public–private seed company described in more detail below) could have brought it under control much sooner.

The second example involves incentives and recognition for research contributions. Seeds and varieties provided freely by SCRB are marketed by some technology service providers without recognition of their SCRB origins. The absence of a mechanism for SCRB to earn revenue by charging royalties or a price for its basic seed, as well as the failure to give public credit to SCRB through brand recognition, deprives SCRB of needed political and financial support. MAFF is responsible for setting policies that create incentives for both research and development projects under its purview.

Finally, SCRB is hampered in its efforts to involve farmers in its technology-development efforts by the practice of some NGOs that pay sitting fees, missed-lunch allowances, and other allowances to attract farmers to their technology-diffusion sessions. Because this practice is not uniform among donor projects, some donors who do not pay such allowances also complain about their inability to compete with those that do. These three examples highlight the need to coordinate efforts among those involved in technology generation and transfer activities within the agricultural sector.

There are also coordination problems within the official ministerial structures. Governance and management of public R&D efforts have been fragmented among the ministries concerned with agriculture, education, and science and technology. Within MAFF, research functions are divided among several departments and located at different levels within departments. In 1997, the government of Zambia passed a Science Policy Act that created the National Science and Technology Council (NSTC). This legislation provided for the transfer of agricultural research from MAFF to the Ministry of Science, Technology, and Vocational Education. However, this decision was opposed within MAFF and by researchers and has never been implemented.

The official functions of the NSTC are to promote science, regulate research, advise the government on science policy, and mobilize resources. NSTC also claims an implicit fifth mandate, to "coordinate science activities" (including agricultural research). The debate over its mandate remains open. Would NSTC do a better job coordinating agricultural research with other scientific endeavors? Has MAFF failed to create the necessary synergies between research and development activities within its own sector? Would NSTC be able to do this?

The lack of integration of livestock research with soils and crops research can also be seen as a coordination problem within the ministry, with consequences for research agendas. Uncomfortable in a crops-dominated institute, livestock researchers requested to be separated from SCRB. When they became a unit in the Animal Production and Health Branch, they found that research took second place to operational activities. This isolation of research units in separate "silos" also describes the situation of the Livestock Pest Research Center, which falls outside MAFF under the National Institute for Science and Industrial Research Center (Ministry of Science and Technology). Likewise, aquaculture research stands apart from agricultural research under the Fisheries Research Branch of MAFF.

The Working Group on Soils and Crops Research argued for closer integration of soils, crop, livestock, and aquaculture research in its submission to the ACP team. Its argument depends on the complementarities of these research activities at the farm level, and on the cost of maintaining a meaningful research infrastructure in the different ecological areas. Unfortunately, the Agricultural Commercialization Plan did not address the structural issues, notably the complementarity of crops livestock and fisheries at the farm and local levels, the necessary relationship to MAFF to achieve synergies, and the degree to which the autonomy of research branches may serve both operational and donor-financing goals.

Public–Private Sector Collaboration: The Seed Industry

As illustrated by the gray leaf spot problem, the development of a vibrant and responsive seed sector involves a proper regulatory framework, cooperation between the public and private sectors, and close relations with the informal as well as formal seed multiplication projects. The seed industry could be seen as both a scientific partner and a source of financial support for agricultural research. Relations between research and Zamseed, the public–private joint venture mentioned above, provide several insights into the potentials and the pitfalls.

The Zambian seed industry has undergone a number of transformations since the liberalization of 1991, which have been aimed at converting it from a publicly controlled sector into a mixed public and private sector, comprising a formal and an informal subsector. The formal sector includes the public research entities (SCRB and the Golden Valley Agricultural Research Trust, known as GART) and the commercial seed companies. The commercial seed companies can be broken down further into a domestic component (Zamseed and MRI Seed) and a foreign component (Pannar and SeedCo, which have parent companies in South Africa and Zimbabwe, respectively).[5] The informal seed sector involves systems of production, distribution, and marketing involving NGOs operating at the community level, small companies, and importers. The Seed Control and Certification Institute (SCCI) is expected to provide quality control to the industry.

Zamseed is struggling to maintain its strategic role as the primary supplier of seed to smallholders, even in a period of liberalization. Zamseed was created as a private company in 1980 with support from Sida; 40 percent of its shares are owned by the Government of the Republic of Zambia and the rest by its Swedish partners Svalölof Weibull AB and Swedfund International AB.[6] Since that time, the partners have increased their shares to a majority interest. During the 1980s, Sida provided major support to SCRB, notably to the programs for cereals, roots, and tubers and for pasture breeding, while the Swedish seed company had a contract to provide technical assistance to both Zamseed and the research system. Thus there were very close connections between research, Zamseed, and their common donor. Research was relatively well funded during this period. Sida helped develop the facilities at Golden Valley through financial assistance and breeders attached to SCRB. When Sweden withdrew its support to SCRB, it was hoped that the newly created GART would assume the breeding functions of SCRB and would be supported by commercial agriculture. This development has not occurred. One result of this hiatus in attention to breeding was the gray leaf spot incident discussed above.

The seed industry offers the potential for only partial cost recovery by an SCRB breeding program. Even for a strategic crop like maize, a donor subsidized the major development costs, while the small size of the domestic market was artificially enhanced by price policies that encouraged hybrid maize. Until the liberalization policy, the market for hybrid maize was significant and growing.

In that favorable context, SCRB and Zamseed negotiated a royalty agreement in return for exclusive rights to SCRB varieties. However, the final agreement came only in 1993, just when the market was being liberalized and the demand for hybrids fell dramatically. Although demand for open-pollinated varieties (OPVs) increased, these offered a much lower potential for cost recovery, as farmers, to reduce their own costs, did not renew their seed stock annually. Moreover, SCRB varieties (OPV, seedlings, and cuttings) faced the increasing competition that accompanied market liberalization. Finally, Zamseed suffered both increased competition and poor repayment of deliveries to NGOs and government programs. As a result, Zamseed did not pay royalties, and their nonpayment became the subject of strained relations with SCRB.

The informal seed sector also compounds the problems of creating a dynamic and reliable commercial seed sector. Both researchers and the Seed Control and Certification Institute point to large-scale, uncontrolled, and unmarked imports of seeds. These present potential disease risks as well as disruption of domestic policy. Until a code of conduct—with enforceable intellectual property rights and associated use-rights contracts—is adopted for the informal sector, the private sector will make little contribution to funding research through the purchase of planting materials.

The Trusts: Public–Private Partnerships

With the active support of bilateral donors, the Zambian government has overseen the formation of several autonomous trusts with greater and lesser research mandates.[7] The three most relevant and recent trusts for agricultural research are GART (created in 1997), the Cotton Development Trust (created in 1999), and the Livestock Development Trust (created in 2002).

Rationales for the creation of trusts vary. They may permit a much higher level of commercialization within undertakings traditionally managed by the public sector; allow the government to transfer physical assets and human resources into more cost-effective arrangements; provide an alternative development funding option for donors; create strong linkages between the public and private sector; and provide a politically acceptable method of introducing commercialization and privatization (MAFF 2000b).

The government creates a trust by devolving publicly owned assets to a mixed public- and private-sector board. The trusts have generally benefited from significant reinvestment by donors to prepare them for their mission. Because of their autonomous status and their relative financial independence, the trusts have been able to pay salaries to their staff comparable to those of locally recruited experts of

UN organizations. However, their immediate advantage is clearly that they are an alternative funding option for donors who want to support agriculture but do not want to put money in a government department.

Golden Valley Agricultural Research Trust (GART). GART has a broad mandate to support agriculture and has been successful at exploiting opportunities for projects. Early concerns were that it would not serve resource-poor farmers and would focus on its commercial farm base. In fact, it has hosted donor-funded projects focusing on smallholders: a project of the Zambian National Farmers' Union focusing on conservation farming, and a second to develop a model agroforestry-based farm. On the other hand, GART is sometimes criticized domestically for failing to take over the breeding of key crops demanded by the emerging informal seed sector and commercial farmers. Without saying what is cause and what is effect, we observe that there has been negligible private-sector financial support for GART.

Golden Valley supports some of its overheads by the commercial production of maize and soybeans. Under the best of circumstances, GART could generate a profit to be invested in research, but this alone will not be sufficient to fund research even on the scale expected by its broad mandate. GART receives compensation for hosting donor projects and recognition for its managerial flexibility and entrepreneurship. It has served as a good vehicle for keeping donor funds in the agricultural sector as they are withdrawn from government departments. It may have a future role as a flexible vehicle for facilitating and maintaining donor support to the research system through contract research, including subcontracting projects to SCRB, which normally should be the intellectual leader of the system.

Cotton Development Trust (CDT). CDT is a more typical example of a single-commodity research institute with potential for strong industry support. However, the government has yet to pass legislation mandating a cess on ginning or marketing. Legislation is moving slowly through the bureaucratic and political processes. In the meantime, the industry has made symbolic contributions to CDT and formally supports a cess of some type.

A few key issues must be resolved before CDT will be on a sound footing. Key members of the industry believe that the government cannot devolve all responsibility for cotton research onto the industry. First, there remains long-term, public-good research that requires continued public support. Second, the structure of the industry does not create the proper incentives necessary for it to assume collective responsibility for research. The cotton industry is characterized by a few major companies that are willing to invest in outgrower capacity and maintenance of brand-name quality, along with a number of smaller firms with short-term perspectives.

The two groups have quite different market behavior and willingness to invest in R&D.[8]

For example, Dunavant Zambia Ltd. carries out research locally, draws on support from its affiliate in South Africa, and runs a strong outgrower scheme with a database of 120,000 farmers. However, its predecessor, Lonrho, found that new entrants to the liberalized cotton market did not provide extension or carry out research but then purchased the output of Lonrho farmers at a premium. As a result of this effective piracy, Lonrho suffered a low rate of loan recovery and did not capture sufficient cotton to run its ginneries at capacity. With falling world prices, it could not recover its development costs. In response, Lonrho first cut its extension staff and then sold the company.

Dunavant is reviving the outgrower program. To solve the extension and credit problem, Dunavant will provide inputs and credit to some 55,000 to 75,000 farmers through a network of distributors, who are themselves cotton farmers, responsible for a group of 40 farmers cultivating an average of 1.5 hectares each. These distributors provide their farmers with inputs and technical support on behalf of the company. Depending on each distributor's loan-recovery rate, the level of credit in the subsequent year will be increased.

Dunavant is in principle favorable to a public–private partnership. It is willing to contract with CDT for research services, training for its agents, and seed multiplication. However, it argues that the public sector has a responsibility to commit to long-term research. Moreover, the industry and government must come to grips with the excess ginning capacity that encourages piracy. It must design and legislate an effective and efficient levy on exports and domestic sales that goes into a research fund for the maintenance of research capacity.

Livestock Development Trust (LDT). The creation of the LDT was assisted by the Netherlands, which has continued to support it during an establishment period. In the long run, LDT hopes to support itself through its commercial activities, special services (especially training), and public-good research contracted by various donors. The promoters of the trust also hope to generate funds for public-good research from their operating profits through a conglomerate of former public properties (not all revenue-earning).

The experience from the cases of Zamseed and the trusts leads to several conclusions. First, their autonomy of operation and attractive conditions of service genuinely encourage initiative; however, these are not sufficient conditions for sustainability. Second, the structure of the parent industry clearly affects its willingness to fund research. For example, GART, which has a broad mandate and no single client, is consequently open to donor projects of various types; CDT's survival will be dependent on the industry's final agreement to accept a cess. Third, trusts may require continued public support. Even a single-commodity institute may claim public support on the basis of the public part of its agenda or for its attention to the needs of smallholders. Fourth, concerns by the trust with the commercial success of its operation will lead some stakeholders to reproach them for weakness in capacity or lack of attention to research. Finally, the current donor attention to the trusts and relatively high salaries paid by the trusts, while motivating, cannot be generalized to the whole research system. The trusts will thrive to the degree that they remain focused, responsive to clients (industry or donor), and agile in meeting commercial needs. However, they run the risk of thereby failing to meet the needs of poor farmers in most of the country, outside the most accessible places, and to deal with public-good issues, such as environmentally sustainable farming practices.

Demand-Responsive Research following Structural Adjustment

Until the structural-adjustment years of the 1990s, SCRB and its partners responded well to prevailing policies and market conditions. Highly subsidized maize and input prices induced the development of a high-input agriculture that was seen as a vehicle for the transformation of smallholder agriculture and the appropriate response to feed the urban industrial centers, especially when the investments to bring the smallholder into the market economy were not made (roads, access to land, and market infrastructure in the countryside). Research institutions (such as SCRB and the University of Zambia) could have voiced their concern about this development strategy had the environment been conducive to such policy debate, and providing they had the capacity for policy analysis. This situation illustrates the need for the research establishment to have access to a strong policy-analysis capacity to contribute to the national debate on development issues, particularly as they affect the research agenda. Given the difficulty of maintaining in-house social-science capacity, most agricultural research institutes would be better off establishing good partnerships or contracting the necessary policy work in their respective domains to specialized institutes of the University of Zambia.

Research will have to shape its agenda and develop new forms of collaboration to respond to the changing development environment (see Chapter 1, this volume). While GART and CDT are well placed to meet the needs of particular farmers (large commercial farmers and cotton farmers, respectively) the SCRB will be expected to attend to long-term public-good issues focusing on the needs of resource-poor farmers, developing appropriate responses for sustainable production, maintaining the genetic resources bank, and conducting some long-term strategic research. Proper collaborative modes need to be developed between research partners so that the derived demand for SCRB is properly expressed and supported financially.

Addressing the needs of poor smallholders is potentially a core function for the public research system. They represent a much less attractive target group for private research. Smallholders have more limited means to purchase inputs, they operate in a variety of environments with smaller application domains for research results, and they generally have more limited market opportunities. Research on behalf of such farmers will be not only riskier but also costlier.

Strengthening the role of farmer organizations to articulate demands for research and to channel donor funding is an expressed goal of the PRSP and ACP. Research will also have to develop new partnerships with other technology service providers operating at the field level so that technologies are appropriate and well supported, and costs are recovered when possible.

Finally, SCRB should also be positioning itself to play a pivotal role in issues of public policy where agriculture is central. Such issues include biosafety and the importation of genetically modified food; preparing for extreme natural events such as floods, droughts, and climate-induced changes; and addressing the links between agriculture and HIV/AIDS, including gender implications.

The above considerations were the basis for the recommendation of the ASIP working group to continue support for public research focusing essentially on the smallholder and operating in a decentralized mode in each of the principal agro-ecological zones of the country, in close collaboration with farmers and technology service providers.

Lessons Become Proposals for System Reform and Sustainability

The foregoing discussion has traced the evolution of a relatively small research system with an important role to play in enhancing productivity of the Zambian economy and lifting large numbers of the rural poor out of poverty. The country's research and development system has faced change before. Following independence, the system shifted from one serving primarily white commercial farmers to one serving the wider community, and, thanks to a solid performance by its farming systems research program, it offered a better understanding of smallholder agriculture and appropriate practices and planting materials. Aided by donors and technical assistance, agricultural research became strong and responded to the needs of the time, which were largely defined by an inappropriate agricultural policy.

It adapted less well to the changes that occurred in the 1990s, mainly because the changes in development policy were more fundamental, and the necessary supporting institutional changes were not anticipated and acted on. The research system became reactive rather than proactive in the changing environment. It is imperative that the research system develop the policy-analysis capacity to allow institutions to understand how their environment is changing, voice their concerns on societal choices, and make necessary adjustments.

Over the past decade, the number and diversity of institutions engaged in agricultural research, development, and education have grown, and they will continue to grow. Public–private partnerships in research will emerge in areas where cost recovery is easiest, as with cotton. Private agencies in technology transfer will add their flexibility of operation to find new modes to serve the resource-poor farmer, given donor and government support. With proper links to regional and international research, the latter is expected to play a more significant role as national research draws more heavily on experiences in similar agroecological environments abroad in its own efforts to borrow, copy, and adapt. This change in the institutional landscape should be beneficial if proper coordination mechanisms are set up to limit rent-seeking behaviors over attribution of benefits or improper service practices.

A public research organization refocused on societal objectives of poverty reduction and environmental sustainability will not be cheaper than the present system. It will require a decentralized structure that operates in innovative ways, close to its stakeholders, associating farmers, and technology service providers in all aspects of technology development, and which trains and advises staff on the proposed technologies. Although some of these services may be provided for a fee, thus reducing the burden of research on the national treasury, the most important aspects of this decentralization may be that research will become more demand-driven and focused on the needs of the resource-poor farmer, and that it increases the visibility of research and extension in the minds of farmers, thereby contributing to building a national consensus to support public research through general tax revenues and the like.

The Working Group on Soils and Crops Research built these considerations into its proposal for support under the Agricultural Commercialization Programme. The proposal calls for the creation of a demand-responsive and decentralized system for technology generation based on an autonomous Zambian Agricultural Research Institute (ZARI). ZARI would cover the main agroecological zones through a network of eight or nine zonal agricultural research stations (ZARSs). Each station would have a critical minimum number of staff capable of three functions: participating in national commodity and global thematic research, undertaking research related to farming systems to understand and help farmers of the zone, and actively developing linkages and outreach activities to NGOs, community-based organizations, extension, and farmer organizations.

The demand for research will come through enhanced scientific partnerships, closer links with clients, and a demonstrated capacity to address emerging issues proactively. However, ensuring sustainable capacity requires upfront commitment from the government, expressed through clear policy statements, prioritization of research, rapid action on governance issues affecting donors, and adequate resources to ensure the retention and productivity of scientists.

Notes

1. Quasi-fiscal deficits are those deficits accumulated by public institutions for which the state is the ultimate guarantor. In practice, conventional measures of the fiscal deficit exclude the activities of public financial institutions. As a result, fiscal policies may be applied inappropriately when these institutions run large losses.

2. This summary is drawn from a note prepared by H. Elliott on the donor response as reported in ACF 2001.

3. In 2002, SCRB received a bridging grant from the PRSP interim program. It expected to receive additional funding from the agricultural commercialization program, the successor program to ASIP, but this was not included in the appraisal report. Instead SCRB was invited to seek support through the demand-driven mechanisms to be put in place by the ACP, namely through the district councils, which may be a long way in the future.

4. Personal communication from A. Bola Nath, director of production and research at Zamseed 2001.

5. The Maize Research Institute Limited (MRI Seed) is the first and only totally private seed company in Zambia. It claims to breed and sell the highest-yielding maize seed varieties in sub-Saharan Africa. Pannar is a company founded in 1958 in South Africa. It initiated its maize breeding programs in 1960 and a few years later was the first company in South Africa to register a maize hybrid for the local market. SeedCo is a Zimbabwean company which has operated in various forms since its creation in 1940. It initially depended on government research for its new breeding material, but in 1973 it began its own research. A seed cooperative company was formed in 1983, and the cooperative was transformed into a public company in 1986 through a public offer which allowed it to expand its research activities. It is now involved in developing and marketing seed products for maize, wheat, soybean, barley, sorghum, and groundnuts. It derives 85 percent of its income from the sale of hybrid maize seed.

6. Svalölof Weibull AB is a Swedish company owned by the Swedish Farmers' Supply and Crop Marketing Association and by BASF Plant Science Holding. It is one of the leading plant breeding companies in Europe. It focuses on small grain cereals and oilseeds, although it has also done considerable research on forage crops, potatoes, and vegetables. Swedfund International AB was part of Swedfund AB until it was given its own identity in 2002. Swedfund was formed in 1979 to offer Swedish companies venture capital and know-how for investing in emerging markets. It is fully owned by the Swedish government.

7. Roseboom et al. (1995) and Benyon et al. (1998, Chapter 6) describe various commodity-trust arrangements in Zimbabwe.

8. Alston and Pardey (1996) describe the effects that industry structure has on the incidence of the costs and benefits from research, which influence the incentives for industry to pay directly for agricultural R&D.

References

Agricultural Consultative Forum. 2001. Consolidated comments on the draft national agricultural policy paper. ACF Secretariat, Lusaka. Mimeo.

Alston, J. M., and P. G. Pardey. 1996. *Making science pay: The economics of agricultural R&D policy.* Washington, D.C.: American Enterprise Institute Press.

ASTI (Agricultural Science and Technology Indicators). 2001. Zambia survey, conducted by M. S. Mwala, H. Elliott, and P. T. Perrault. Unpublished data files. International Food Policy Research Institute, Washington, D.C., and International Service for National Agricultural Research, The Hague.

Beintema, N. M. 2002. Special compilation using Agricultural Science and Technology Indicators (ASTI) data. International Food Policy Research Institute, Washington, D.C.

Benyon, J., with S. Akroyd, A. Duncan, and S. Jones. 1998. *Financing the future: Options for agricultural research and extension in Sub-Saharan Africa.* Oxford: Oxford Policy Management.

Copestake, J. G. 1997. *Encouraging sustainable smallholder agriculture in Zambia.* Bath: Center for Development Studies.

Howard, J. A. 1994. The economic impact of improved maize varieties in Zambia. Ph.D. thesis, Michigan State University.

Howard, J. A., and C. Mungoma. 1996. *Zambia's stop and go revolution: The impact of policies and organizations on the development and spread of maize technology.* MSU International Development Working Paper No. 61. East Lansing: Department of Agricultural Economics, Michigan State University.

INESOR (Institute of Economic and Social Research). 1999. *Zambia agricultural sector performance analysis 1997–1998.* Prepared for the Ministry of Agriculture, Food and Fisheries. Lusaka: INESOR.

Jansen, D. 1977. *Agricultural policy and performance in Zambia: History, prospects, and proposals for change.* Berkeley: Institute of International Studies, University of California, Berkeley.

Jayne, T., M. Mukumba. M. Chisvo, D. Tschirley, B. Zulu, M. Weber, R. Johansson, P. Santos, and D. Soroko. 1999. *Successes and challenges of food market reform: Experiences from Kenya, Mozambique, Zambia, and Zimbabwe.* MSU International Development Working

Paper No. 72. East Lansing: Department of Agricultural Economics, Michigan State University.

MAFF (Ministry of Agriculture, Food and Fisheries). 1998. Formulation of a national seed and research policy. Lusaka: Ministry of Agriculture, Food and Fisheries. Mimeo.

———. 2000a. National agricultural policy. MAFF, Lusaka. Mimeo.

———. 2000b. *Livestock Development Trust: Strategic establishment plan.* Lusaka: MAFF.

———. 2001a. Draft national agricultural policy. MAFF, Lusaka. Mimeo.

———. 2001b. Agricultural Commercialization Programme 2002–2005. MAFF, Lusaka. Mimeo.

MFNP (Ministry of Finance and National Planning). 1995. Agricultural sector letter of development policy. MNFP, Lusaka. Mimeo.

———. 2002. Poverty reduction strategy paper (2002–2004). MNFP, Lusaka. Mimeo.

Pardey, P. G., and N. M. Beintema. 2001. *Slow magic: Agricultural R&D a century after Mendel.* IFPRI Food Policy Report. Washington, D.C.: International Food Policy Research Institute.

Roseboom, J., and P. G. Pardey. 1995. *Statistical brief on the national agricultural research system of Zambia.* The Hague: International Service for National Agricultural Research.

Roseboom, J., P. G. Pardey, N. M. Beintema, and G. D. Mudimu. 1995. *Statistical brief on the national agricultural research system of Zimbabwe.* The Hague: International Service for National Agricultural Research.

SCRB (Soils and Crops Research Branch). 1999. *Workplan and budget for the year 2000.* Chilanga: Mount Makulu Research Station, SCRB.

———. 2000. *Workplan and budget for the year 2001.* Chilanga: Mount Makulu Research station, SCRB.

———. 2001. Agro-ecological regions: Research stations and major programmes in Zambia. Map prepared for ISNAR. Soil Survey Unit, SCRB, Lusaka.

World Bank. 2001. Zambia: Public expenditure review. Report No. 22543-ZA. World Bank, Washington, D.C. Mimeo.

———. 2002. *World development indicators 2002.* CD-ROM. Washington, D.C.

Zulu B., J. J. Nijhoff, T. S. Jayne, and A. Negassa. 2000. *Is the glass half-empty or half-full? An analysis of agricultural production trends in Zambia.* Working Paper No. 3. Lusaka: Food Security Research Project. Lusaka.

Chapter 10

Brazil: Maintaining the Momentum

Nienke M. Beintema, Philip G. Pardey, and Flavio Avila

Introduction

After a period of slow or no growth during the late 1970s and 1980s, public agricultural research investments in Latin America rebounded during the early 1990s.[1] These regional trends were heavily influenced by developments in Brazil, which accounted for close to half of the region's total agricultural research expenditures (Beintema and Pardey 2001). Consequently, developments in Brazilian agricultural R&D are of great significance to the rest of the region and to the developing world more generally.[2] But agricultural research investment has grown much more rapidly in Brazil than in many other Latin American countries, reaching intensity ratios close to those found in the developed world.

Central to agricultural R&D in Brazil is the Brazilian Agricultural Research Corporation (Embrapa), created in 1972. In addition, Brazil has a large number of state government agencies, numerous faculties and schools of agriculture, and some nonprofit agencies conducting agricultural research. Brazil has an active and growing private sector—involving for-profit enterprises and various multinational companies—providing technologies and technical services concerned mainly with farm inputs; most of these technologies, however, appear to represent spillins to Brazil from research done elsewhere.

Macroeconomic Context

As in many of its neighboring countries, Brazil's economy grew briskly during the 1970s and 1980s, but this growth was followed by a series of economic crises, including bouts of hyperinflation, shrinking levels of output, and increasing rates of unemployment. After strong efforts by the government to stabilize the Brazilian economy—including a number of significant currency devaluations—inflation rates declined, and the economy strengthened during the mid-1990s, though it fell into crisis again during the late 1990s and appears to have recovered only slightly since then. Agriculture's share of total GDP fell from 12.3 percent in 1970 to 5.8 percent in 2002 (Table 10.1). In 2002, 15.6 percent of the labor force worked in the agricultural sector (FAO 2005).

Traditionally, the Brazilian government has pursued import-substituting industrialization policies, despite the country's abundance of natural resources and comparative advantages in agricultural and wood products. Following the trade-liberalizing policy reforms introduced in the early 1990s, production and productivity in crop and livestock products have increased substantially (EIU 1998). Brazil is a significant exporter of several agricultural products. However, the share of agricultural goods in total merchandise exports decreased from 71 percent in 1970 to only 23 percent in 2000. The main agricultural export commodities were sugarcane, coffee, and soybeans, which accounted for 17, 14, and 9 percent of total agricultural export revenues, respectively. Brazil is the largest coffee producer in the world and the second-largest producer of soybeans (following the United States) and sugarcane (following India). Soybean production has increased substantially in recent years, replacing production of other food crops such as beans and rice (EIU 1998 and IBGE 1999).

Historical Developments and Current Structure of Agricultural Research

Historical Developments

Formalized agricultural research began in Brazil in the mid-1800s with the establishment and operation of two imperial research institutes, one in Rio de Janeiro and one in Bahia.[3] In 1887, the federal government established the Imperial Agronomic Station of Campinas.[4] This station was transferred to the state government of São Paulo only a few years later and renamed the Agronomic Institute of Campinas (IAC), which still exists today. Following a period of deterioration of existing agricultural research facilities (with the exception of IAC) at the end of the 19th century, a number of agricultural research institutes and experiment stations were established and coordinated by the government. Mostly located in the richer states, these focused on export crops like cotton and sugarcane. The world economic crisis of the 1930s, collapsing coffee prices, and the subsequent shifting emphasis of the Brazilian economy from agriculture to industry led to several rounds of reorganization of the Federal Ministry of Agriculture and the Secretariat of Agriculture of the

Table 10.1 Brazil: Overview of agricultural indicators, 1970–2002

Indicator	1970	1980	1990	2000	2002
Agricultural sector as a percentage of					
Total GDP	12.3	11.0	8.1	7.3	5.8
Total labor force	47.2	36.7	23.3	16.7	15.6
Agricultural imports					
Total (million 2000 U.S. dollars)	1,055.3	4,575.3	2,767.3	4,279.0	3,115.4
As a percentage of total merchandise imports	10.4	9.9	10.1	7.3	6.5
Agricultural exports					
Total (million 2000 U.S. dollars)	6,951.3	17,260.2	10,687.5	12,761.3	16,089.1
As a percentage of total merchandise exports	71.1	46.3	27.9	23.2	27.7
Agricultural area (million hectares)	195.4	224.3	241.6	261.4	263.6
Permanent pasture (million hectares)	154.1	171.4	184.2	196.2	197.0
Arable and permanent crops (million hectares)	41.3	52.9	57.4	65.2	66.6
Main crops					
Coffee					
Total production (million metric tons)	0.8	1.1	1.5	1.9	2.6
Area under production (million hectares)	2.4	2.4	2.9	2.3	2.4
Average yield (metric tons per hectare)	0.3	0.4	0.5	0.8	1.1
Total value of exports (million 2000 U.S. dollars)	3,354.5	4,603.8	1,349.1	1,559.6	1,150.0
Sugarcane					
Total production (million metric tons)	79.8	148.7	262.7	327.7	363.7
Area under production (million hectares)	1.7	2.6	4.3	4.8	5.1
Average yield (metric tons per hectare)	46.2	57.0	61.5	67.6	71.3
Total value of exports (million 2000 U.S. dollars)	452.3	2,385.8	639.7	1,199.4	2,013.9
Soybeans					
Total production (million metric tons)	1.5	15.2	19.9	32.7	42.1
Area under production (million hectares)	1.3	8.8	11.5	13.6	16.4
Average yield (metric tons per hectare)	1.1	1.7	1.7	2.4	2.6
Total value of exports (million 2000 U.S. dollars)	96.7	729.5	1,109.7	2,187.9	2,916.6
Oranges					
Total production (million metric tons)	3.1	10.9	17.5	21.3	18.5
Area under production (million hectares)	0.2	0.6	0.9	0.9	0.8
Average yield (metric tons per hectare)	15.3	18.9	19.1	24.9	22.4
Total value of exports (million 2000 U.S. dollars)[a]	64.9	654.7	1,813.2	1,049.9	844.2
Maize					
Total production (million metric tons)	12.2	20.4	21.3	31.9	35.9
Area under production (million hectares)	9.9	11.5	11.4	11.6	11.8
Average yield (metric tons per hectare)	1.4	1.8	1.9	2.7	3.1
Total value of exports (million 2000 U.S. dollars)	287.8	2.1	0.2	9.4	257.4

Sources: World Bank 2005 and FAO 2005.

[a] Includes oranges and orange juice.

state of São Paulo, and to declining support for agricultural research. A military government was formed in 1964, leading to a further round of reorganization of federal agricultural research in subsequent years.

In 1973, following an evaluation of the federal agricultural research system by a special committee appointed by the minister of agriculture, Embrapa was created as a public corporation, a status that gave it more freedom in its financial and human-resource policies. During its early years, Embrapa focused on applied research, which was undertaken in national commodity and regional centers throughout the country. During the 1970s and early 1980s, funding for Embrapa increased markedly, and the agency achieved significant research results. But, beginning in the mid-1980s, the government suffered a series of financial crises, which resulted in severe budget cuts for most public agencies. During the 1990s, Embrapa underwent two major reorganizations under new boards of directors. The changes involved, among other things, refocusing the agency's research priorities toward the perceived needs of Embrapa's clients and end users, decentralizing some administrative management aspects, and strengthening collaborations at the national and international levels.

During the 1960s, agricultural research by state governments was insignificant except in São Paulo, Rio Grande do Sul, and Pernambuco. In São Paulo, four additional state agricultural research agencies were established during the 1960s, bringing the state's total to six and forming the largest state agricultural-research system in Brazil.[5] During the 1970s and continuing into the 1980s, Embrapa stimulated the creation of state corporations for agricultural research based on its own (semi-public) model, which allowed greater flexibility in management practices. As a result of the aforementioned financial crises, state support for agricultural research declined after the mid-1980s. Most states suffered from financial crises and poorly managed public institutions, and the return to democracy in 1986 politicized many of the state governments in ways that negatively affected agricultural research agencies, especially in the northeast—the poorest region of the country (Alves 1992). As a result, over the ensuing years, a number of state agricultural research agencies were closed or merged with state extension agencies.

The first agricultural school to have a significant research program was the Luis de Queiroz Higher School of Agriculture, which was located in the state of São Paulo and began operating in 1901. In 1960, Brazil had 12 higher schools of agriculture and 8 veterinary schools, but none undertook much research. This situation changed in 1963, when an intensive collaboration began among four Brazilian and four U.S. universities, financially supported by the U.S. Agency for International Development (USAID).

Current Structure of Public Agricultural R&D

The organization of agricultural R&D in Brazil is complex, partly because of the size of the system and the number of agencies involved and partly because of the involvement of both the federal and state governments.[6] Embrapa, which continues to be the central agency, falls under the administration of the Ministry of Agriculture and Food Supply. Although Embrapa was created as a corporation, largely unencumbered by the customary government regulations, its semi-autonomous status has eroded over time, and funding from general government revenues continues to predominate. Embrapa conducts applied research and currently consists of 15 central units, 2 service units, and 37 research centers located throughout the country.[7] Two other federal agencies involved in agricultural R&D are the Executive Commission for Cocoa (CEPLAC), which oversees the Research Center for Cacao (CEPEC), and the Brazilian Institute for the Environment and Renewable Natural Resources (IBAMA). The latter focuses its research on fisheries, forestry, natural resources, and the environment.

Currently, state government agricultural research agencies operate in 16 of the 26 states. Six states in the northern region (Pará, Amazonas, Acre, Rondônia, Roraima, and Amapá) as well as Piauí in the northeastern region, have no local institutes, foundations, or private firms engaged in agricultural research. In Ceará and Maranhão, the state agencies were closed in 1998–99. In the state of Tocantins, agricultural research is conducted at the Faculty of Agronomy of the University of Tocantins. All 16 states have a single state government research agency, with the exception of São Paulo, which has 6, each with a distinct mandate. São Paulo's agricultural R&D agencies are being reorganized, and plans also exist to make the São Paulo Agency for Agribusiness Technology (APTA), which coordinates the state's agricultural research, an autonomous agency with some degree of independence from the state government, again to create flexible management practices and attract private funding. As of 2003, the future of the state agricultural research agencies was unclear. Only a few state agencies have sufficient resources for effective research, and several agencies that were amalgamated with their respective state agricultural-extension services now appear to focus on extension more than research. Further, state governments are becoming less willing to fund the state institutes because they feel that agricultural research is primarily the federal government's responsibility, through Embrapa. In an effort to overcome the state agencies' financial and operational difficulties, Embrapa is assisting the state agencies in developing new institutional arrangements.

Brazil has a substantial number of universities, with over 100 faculties or schools of agricultural sciences that conduct research. Most of these are federal and state universities; only a few of the private universities offer training and research in the agricultural sciences (Alves 1992).

We identified five Brazilian nonprofit institutions engaged in agricultural research in the late 1990s. The Cooperative for Sugarcane, Sugar, and Alcohol Producers of the State of São Paulo (COPERSUCAR) is a cooperative of 36 sugar mills located in São Paulo, including a technical center that conducts sugarcane breeding, postharvest research, and technology transfer activities. The Fund for Citrus Plant Protection (FUNDECITRUS) is financed by a tax on citrus production; it monitors citrus health and funds citrus research projects conducted by various Brazilian agencies. It also conducts its own research at its Citrus Research Center (created in 1994) in collaboration with various national and international agricultural organizations (FUNDECITRUS 2001). The Rio Grande Rice Research Institute (IRGA) primarily conducts rice research but also undertakes some research on maize, sorghum, and soybeans. Two other nonprofit institutions conducting agricultural research are the Foundation Center for Wheat Experimentation and Research (FUNDACEP) and the Central Agricultural Cooperative for Technology Development and Economics (COODETEC), which are linked to and financed by producer organizations in Rio Grande do Sul and Paraná, respectively. Both these agencies conduct research on corn, wheat, and soybeans; COODETEC also conducts cotton research.

Brazilian Public Agricultural Research Investments

In 1996, public agricultural research investments totaled $1.3 billion (in 1999 international prices)[8] in a 57-agency sample, employing a total of 4,620 full-time equivalent (fte) agricultural researchers (Table 10.2). The 28-agency sample for higher-education institutions developed by Beintema, Avila, and Pardey (2001) included most of the important agricultural research agencies, but we suspect we missed about one-third of the total fte agricultural researchers working in Brazil's higher-education sector. Scaling up our estimated national totals to account for missing higher-education data brings the total fte agricultural researchers to 4,895 and total spending to $1.4 billion.[9]

In contrast to the situation in some other Latin American countries, such as Mexico, Costa Rica, and Honduras, government agencies in Brazil accounted for the majority of the agricultural research investments and researcher numbers (Beintema and Pardey 2001). In 1996, $1.1 billion of the $1.4 billion total public agricultural R&D spending (adjusted for missing higher-education agencies) was spent by government agencies; Embrapa accounted for 58 percent of the total public agricultural spending, the state agencies for 20 percent.[10]

Table 10.2 Brazil: Composition of public agricultural research expenditures and researchers, 1996

| Type of institution | Spending | | | | Researchers | | | Number of agencies in sample |
| | Million 1999 reais | Million 1999 international dollars | Share of total (percent) | | Full-time equivalents | Share of total (percent) | | |
			Actual	Adjusted[a]		Actual	Adjusted[a]	
Federal government agencies								
Embrapa	671.0	828.4	61.9	58.4	2,092.0	45.3	42.7	1
CEPEC	20.2	24.9	1.9	1.8	89.0	1.9	1.8	1
State government agencies	231.9	286.3	21.4	20.2	1,762.4	38.1	36.0	22
Nonprofit institutions	31.2	38.5	2.9	2.7	117.0	2.5	2.4	5
Higher-education agencies[a]	129.9	160.3	12.0	16.9	559.2	12.1	17.1	28
Total								
Actual	1,084.2	1,338.5	100		4,619.6	100		57
Adjusted[a]	1,148.2	1,417.5		100	4,895.0		100	

Source: Beintema, Avila, and Pardey 2001.

Notes: See Beintema, Avila, and Pardey 2001 for specific information on agency samples. Embrapa data for 1995 were used as a basis for the calculation to compensate for the spike in Embrapa's 1996 expenditures.

[a] We estimated that our sample included about two-thirds of the fte research staff employed at higher-education agencies; hence we estimated expenditures for these agencies based on average expenditures per researcher for government agencies and nonprofit agencies. These estimates are reflected in the adjusted shares and totals.

The breakdown of fte researchers differs from the institutional structure of agricultural R&D expenditures. In 1996, Embrapa accounted for 43 percent of total fte public agricultural research staff and 58 percent of total spending, while state agencies had 36 percent of the fte researchers and 20 percent of the expenditures. These data reflect Embrapa's generally stronger financial situation compared with the state agencies and the 1996 spike in Embrapa funding resulting from atypical retirement benefits paid out that year.

Trends in Public Investments

Expenditures. Agricultural research spending for a sample of 45 agencies grew substantially in the late 1970s, at an average rate of 9.9 percent per year. Total R&D investments declined slightly during the early 1980s but grew again during the late 1980s and 1990s, at rates of 4.6 and 2.8 percent per year, respectively—well below the rates of the late 1970s (Table 10.3). Embrapa's total expenditures grew faster than those of the state agencies between 1976 and 1996 (4.1 versus 3.1 percent, respectively), peaking in 1996. After adjusting for inflation, Empraba's total spending in 2000 was 13 percent lower than in 1996. Also, spending by the state agencies declined during the 1996–98 period: total spending for a 19-agency sample contracted by 8 percent. No quantitative information on total expenditures was available for the years following 1998, but they appear to have continued to decline.

Researchers. Between 1976 and 1996, the total number of fte researchers employed by the 45 public agricultural R&D agencies in the sample reported here grew at an average rate of 2.3 percent per year (Table 10.4). The institutional distribution of agricultural researchers has changed comparatively little in Brazil since the mid-1970s. By contrast, in other countries in the region (such as Colombia and a number of Central American countries), the higher-education sector and other (often nongovernment) agencies now employ a significantly larger share of total agricultural researchers.[11]

While the institutional distribution of agricultural researchers remained fairly constant, educational levels of researchers have changed substantially since the mid-1970s. In 1996, more than half of the fte researchers in Brazil were trained to the M.Sc. level, and close to one-third held doctoral degrees. These shares are higher than those in other Latin American countries in the same year. For six countries in a ten-country Latin American sample, fewer than 40 percent of the researchers held postgraduate degrees in 1996 (Beintema and Pardey 2001). The 1996 picture for Brazil is very different from two decades earlier, when only a quarter of the researchers (in a 39-agency sample) had postgraduate training (Figure 10.1). Embrapa has invested heavily in research staff training and received considerable

Table 10.3 Brazil: Trends in public agricultural research expenditures, 1976–2000

| Period | Government agencies | | | Nonprofit institutions | Higher-education agencies[a] | Total |
	Embrapa	CEPEC	State			
Agencies in sample	1	1	22	4	17	45
Expenditures in constant local currencies (million 1999 reais)						
1976–80	284.3	16.1	158.3	4.2	50.8	513.7
1981–85	382.3	20.4	189.1	6.8	67.7	666.2
1986–90	403.7	21.1	240.4	5.8	65.1	736.1
1991–95	516.1	21.6	257.8	5.8	80.5	881.8
1996	671.0	20.2	231.9	8.2	86.9	1,018.2
1998	566.9	NA	213.6[b]	NA	NA	NA
2000	582.5	NA	NA	NA	NA	NA
Expenditures in constant international dollars (million 1999 international dollars)						
1976–80	351.0	19.9	195.5	5.2	62.7	634.2
1981–85	471.9	25.2	233.4	8.4	83.6	822.5
1986–90	498.3	26.0	296.8	7.2	80.4	908.7
1991–95	637.1	26.6	318.3	7.2	99.4	1,088.6
1996	828.4	24.9	286.3	10.1	107.3	1,257.1
1998	699.9	NA	263.6[b]	NA	NA	NA
2000	719.2	NA	NA	NA	NA	NA
Annual growth rate (percent)[c]						
1976–81	12.6	17.8	4.7	12.9	8.8	9.9
1981–86	−2.9	−5.1	4.1	0.9	−1.2	−0.7
1986–91	8.1	4.6	−1.1	−6.0	3.6	4.6
1991–96	4.8	−3.0	−0.9	12.3	2.0	2.8
1976–96	4.1	1.8	3.1	2.2	3.0	3.6

Source: Beintema, Avila, and Pardey 2001.

Notes: See Beintema, Avila, and Pardey 2001 for specific information on agency samples. Data from 1976 to 1995 are presented as five-year averages. NA indicates data are not available.

[a] Higher-education agency expenditures were estimated using average expenditures per researcher for government agencies and nonprofit institutions.

[b] Data for 6 of the 22 state agencies (accounting for 13 percent of total fte research expenditures at state agencies in 1996) were estimated using the trend from 1996 to 1998 for the 16 agencies for which data were available.

[c] Least-squares growth rates.

support from the Inter-American Development Bank (IDB) and the World Bank for upgrading staff qualifications. Largely because of these extensive investments in human capital development, the total share of Embrapa researchers trained to the postgraduate level increased from 17 percent in 1976, lower than the Brazilian sample average that year, to 93 percent in 1999.[12] However, Embrapa will need to continue investing heavily in human capital to maintain the quality of its research

Table 10.4 Brazil: Trends in numbers of public agricultural researchers, 1976–2001

Trend/ period	Government agencies			Nonprofit institutions	Higher-education agencies	Total
	Embrapa	CEPEC	State[a]			
Agencies in sample	1	1	22	4	17	45
Researchers (fte's)						
1976–80	1,395.2	111.6	1,296.2	38.2	276.1	3,117.2
1981–85	1,610.4	115.2	1,641.5	50.0	315.5	3,732.6
1986–90	1,963.4	135.6	1,785.3	52.2	349.6	4,286.1
1991–95	2,111.8	115.6	1,824.9	48.6	364.2	4,465.1
1996	2,092.0	89.0	1,762.4	57.0	374.3	4,374.6
1998	2,063.0	NA	1,547.5[b]	NA	NA	NA
2001	NA	NA	NA	NA	NA	NA
Annual growth rate (percent)[b]						
1976–81	4.2	4.8	4.5	4.0	3.2	4.3
1981–86	1.6	–0.3	3.0	3.3	1.6	2.2
1986–91	4.5	1.1	0.2	–1.6	1.2	2.2
1991–96	0.4	–6.9	0.5	1.9	1.5	0.3
1976–96	2.8	0.1	2.1	1.5	1.8	2.3

Source: Beintema, Avila, and Pardey 2001.
Notes: See Beintema, Avila, and Pardey 2001 for specific information on agency samples. Data from 1976 to 1995 are presented as five-year averages. NA indicates data are not available.
[a] Data for 6 of the 22 state agencies (accounting for 13 percent of total fte research expenditures at state agencies in 1996) were estimated using the trend from 1996 to 1998 for the 16 agencies for which data were available.
[b] Least-squares growth rates.

staff, because more than one-third of the 1998 research staff (750 researchers) will retire before 2008 (Embrapa 1999a).

Spending per scientist. Because the growth rate of real research spending was higher than the corresponding rate of growth for the total number of fte researchers, spending per scientist increased by about 50 percent between 1976 and 1996 (Figure 10.2). In general, the trends in spending per scientist showed the same erratic nature as trends in total spending, with two spikes in the early 1980s and 1990s.

Average expenditures per researcher in Brazil were considerably higher than in other Latin American countries (with the exception of Chile). In 1996, spending per scientist in Brazil was $290,000—more than three times the average in Central America, for example (Beintema and Pardey 2001).[13]

Within Brazil there were substantial differences among the various institutional categories. Embrapa's spending per scientist, at $396,000 in 1996, was more than

Figure 10.1 Brazil: Postgraduate share of total research staff, by institutional category, 1976–96

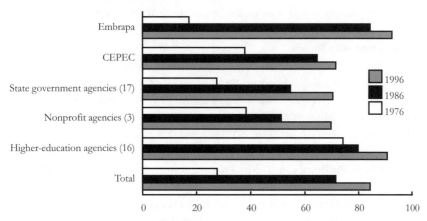

Source: Beintema, Avila, and Pardey 2001 (Figure 5a).
Note: Figures in parentheses indicate the number of agencies in each category.

Figure 10.2 Brazil: Agricultural research expenditures, researchers, and expenditures per researcher, 1976–96

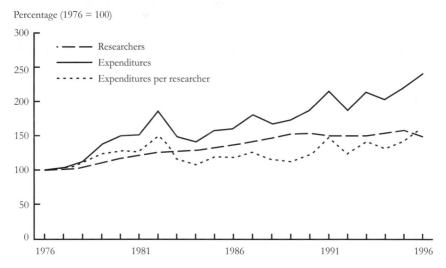

Source: Beintema, Avila, and Pardey 2001.
Note: We used the data in Table 10.3, along with other information, to scale up the estimates for the 17 higher-education agencies for which time-series data were available; we adjusted for the fact that many of the significant faculties engaged in agricultural R&D originated only in the 1980s and early 1990s.

twice the comparable figure for the state government agencies, at $162,000. More recent data for Embrapa and the state agencies show that expenditures per researcher declined with the decline in total expenditures between 1996 and 1998.[14]

Research-Intensity Ratios

Total public spending as a percentage of agricultural output (AgGDP) helps place a country's agricultural R&D spending in an internationally comparable context and normalizes for changes in the size of a country's agricultural sector over time. According to our adjusted estimates, the public-sector intensity ratio more than doubled from 0.8 percent in 1976 to 1.7 percent in 1996. The growth in intensity has been uneven, however, with significant spikes in 1982 and 1991–93 (Figure 10.3). Notably, Brazil's agricultural research intensity in 1996 was considerably higher than those in other countries in the region. The Brazilian ratio is moving closer to the lower end of the range observed for developed countries and is comparable to that of such countries as Ireland, Italy, Portugal, and Spain (Pardey and Beintema 2001).

Since 1996, the intensity ratio has no doubt declined, given the drop in spending by Embrapa and the state agencies, which, combined, account for the preponderance of public agricultural R&D expenditures in Brazil. If expenditures by other public agencies (such as CEPEC, the nonprofit institutions, and the higher-

Figure 10.3 Brazil: Public agricultural R&D spending relative to AgGDP, 1976–96

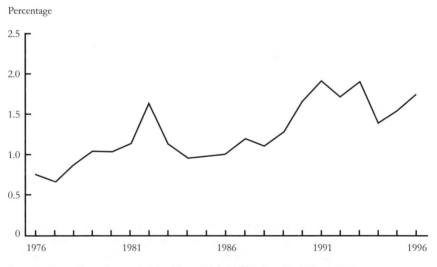

Sources: Expenditure data underlying Figure 10.2; AgGDP from World Bank 2000.

Figure 10.4 Brazil: Spending per capita and per economically active member of agricultural population, 1971–96

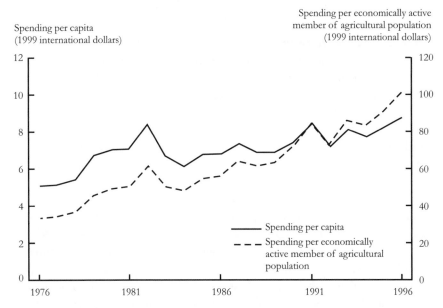

Sources: Expenditure data from Table 10.3; population and economically active member of agricultural population from FAO 2005.

education institutions for which we do not have data) remained unchanged after 1996, Brazil's 1998 intensity ratio would have declined to 1.5; however, it was likely lower in reality because, given Brazil's generally poor economic performance in recent years, spending by most public agencies probably contracted.

These trends for agricultural R&D spending per capita and per economically active member of the agricultural population paralleled those for research spending as a percentage of agricultural GDP (Figure 10.4). Agricultural R&D spending per capita (adjusted for expenditures deemed missing from our sample) increased from $4.7 per capita in 1976 to $7.8 in 1996 (at 1999 international prices). Spending per economically active member of the agricultural population increased more than spending per capita, an unsurprising result given the declining proportion of farmers in the total population. Agricultural R&D spending per capita of economically active agricultural population was $101 in 1996, compared with only $33 in 1976 (at 1999 international prices). By comparison, in 1996 Colombia spent $4.2 per capita and $45 per capita of economically active agricultural population on agricultural R&D, well below the corresponding Brazilian figures (Beintema, Romano, and Pardey 2000).

Private-Sector Involvement

Brazil has an active and growing private sector, providing technologies and technical services mainly concerned with farm inputs (including agrichemicals, animal feeds and breeding services, fertilizers, seeds, veterinary medicines, and machinery) and food processing. There is little specific information available on the local research underpinning these technologies, but the qualitative responses to our surveys, combined with other sources, imply that many of the technologies represent spillins to Brazil from research done elsewhere. Some of the national seed companies conduct some research in Brazil, much of which involves local testing and screening of improved germplasm developed elsewhere. Since the mid-1990s, a considerable number of these national seed companies (especially those marketing corn and soybeans) have been taken over by multinational corporations.

The 11 firms from which we received survey responses employed an estimated total of 88 fte scientists and spent $28 million (Table 10.5). We identified 27 additional firms[15] that probably provide input technologies or technical services to production agriculture or are involved in postharvest (mainly food-processing) activities, but a sizable share of the relevant technologies is developed outside Brazil.[16] We estimate that the 11 private companies in our sample accounted for about half

Table 10.5 Brazil: Private agricultural research spending and researchers, 1996

	Expenditures		
Type of agency	Million 1999 reais	Million 1999 international dollars	Researchers (fte's)
Private enterprises (11-agency sample)			
National	17.8	22.0	70.5
Multinational	4.9	6.0	17.0
Subtotal	22.7	28.0	87.5
Adjusted subtotal[a]	45.4	56.0	175.0
Adjusted subtotal for public agencies	1,193.5	1,473.5	4,895.0
Adjusted subtotal for private enterprises as a percentage of total[b]	3.8	3.8	3.5

Sources: Table 10.1 and Beintema, Avila, and Pardey 2001.

[a]Adjusted based on the estimation that our sample included only about half the fte research staff employed in private enterprises.

[b]Includes public and private agricultural R&D, adjusted for omitted higher-education agencies and private enterprises.

the total agricultural R&D spending and fte researchers working in the private sector in 1996.

After adjusting for these omitted private agencies, we estimate that in 1996 agricultural R&D spending by private firms totaled $56 million, which was 4 percent of the $1.5 billion of total (public and private) spending that year. This figure is considerably higher than the corresponding shares in most other Latin American countries for which we have data (Beintema and Pardey 2001) but less than one-tenth of the average share of 52 percent for developed countries in 1995 (Pardey and Beintema 2001).

Funding for Agricultural Research

Despite the development of some new funding sources and mechanisms, agricultural research in Brazil remains heavily reliant on government sources. Between the mid-1970s and the mid-1990s, funding for agricultural R&D generally increased. Since then, financial support to Embrapa and the state agencies has contracted significantly. Spurred by these declines, Embrapa examined options for a new mechanism to finance the agricultural research conducted by federal and state government agencies. The main proposal under consideration was the creation of a voluntary tax for research and promotion, to be sanctioned by statute and based on the "check-off" (levy) programs used in other countries, such as the United States and Canada. This program, dubbed the voluntary tax for technology development (AGROMAIS), had as one of its objectives to increase the role of the private sector in financing agricultural technology development (Portugal et al. 1999). However, the proposal failed to obtain government backing.

In part, this initiative targeted to agricultural R&D funding was overtaken by a much broader-ranging policy initiative to develop a Brazilian innovation law. The law, which received congressional approval in December 2004, came into force in mid-2005, but, as of early 2006, awaits regulation intended to provide the legal framework to improve the country's capacity to generate and commercialize technology. The law deals directly with incentives to foster cooperative links between public scientific and technological institutions (STIs) and the private sector. It gives STIs more flexibility to negotiate technology licensing agreements and to strike deals with private enterprises for use of public labs. Public researchers will be free to work for other STIs for the time it takes to conclude joint projects, while continuing to receive their regular salaries, and can also request special leave without pay if they opt to become involved with a start-up company to further develop their technologies (Páscoa 2005).

Funding Support at Government Agencies

Embrapa. In nominal terms, direct funding for Embrapa (detailed below) increased from 1986 to 1996, with some marked fluctuations, but total funding has declined in more recent years. In 2000, Embrapa's direct funding was $583 million (in 1999 international dollars), 20 percent lower than the 1996 comparable total (Table 10.6). This decline occurred in all four funding categories but was higher for nongovernment than for government funding. In 2000, 94 percent of Embrapa funding came from government sources, highlighting the agency's continuing dependence on the government.

In addition to Embrapa's line-item funding in the national budget, its direct funding includes grants and contracts with other federal agencies and other institutions, plus license income and revenues from sales of produce, seeds, and so on. Embrapa also receives so-called indirect funds that include donations and payments for publications and events by third parties (as well as scholarship support to researchers not formally employed at Embrapa, such as undergraduate and graduate students or temporary staff). The amount of indirect funding coming to Embrapa increased during the 1990s, but the share remains small overall (3 to 4 percent of total funding).

Over the years, Embrapa has had three loans from the IDB and four from the World Bank.[17] With the exception of the last World Bank loan, these funds have been used to improve Embrapa's infrastructure and train its research staff. The fourth World Bank loan was approved in 1996, and, in a marked departure from previous practice, 60 percent of the total was earmarked for operational expenses disbursed through a competitive funding arrangement (see next section). In 2004, the Brazilian government completed negotiations on a new loan to Embrapa Agrofuturo, which was financed by the IDB and became operational in early 2006.

State government agencies. The state government agencies in our sample depend primarily on contributions from their respective state governments. In 1996, 81 percent of total funding for a sample of 11 agencies came from government—mostly state—contributions, with only a small share of funds provided by the federal government through Embrapa (Beintema, Avila, and Pardey 2001). During the early 1990s, total funding for state agencies declined, and the decline appears to have continued in recent years. As mentioned, two state agencies have closed, and others have been merged with state extension agencies; a few others are bankrupt but lack sufficient funding to reconcile their debt. State government contributions are declining and often are sufficient to cover only salaries and basic operational costs like electricity.

Table 10.6 Brazil: Embrapa's funding sources, 1986, 1991–96, and 2000

Funding source	Total funding (million 1999 reais)				Total funding (million 1999 international dollars)				Percentage of direct funding			
	1986	1991–95	1996	2000	1986	1991–95	1996	2000	1986	1991–95	1996	2000
Direct funding												
Government	340.7	529.3	591.3	547.6	420.6	653.4	730.0	676.1	78.3	88.1	81.2	94.0
Donor contributions	34.6	26.4	56.6	6.0	42.7	32.6	69.8	7.4	7.9	4.4	7.8	1.0
Research contracts	3.9	2.7	17.3	—	4.8	3.3	21.3	—	0.9	0.4	2.4	—
Sales	56.1	42.5	62.9	28.9	69.3	52.4	77.7	35.7	12.9	7.1	8.6	5.0
Subtotal	435.3	600.9	728.0	582.5	537.4	741.8	898.8	719.2	100	100	100	100
Indirect funding	—	—	18.6	NA	—	—	23.0	NA				
Total	435.3	600.9	746.6	NA	537.4	741.8	921.7	NA				

Source: Beintema, Avila, and Pardey 2001.

Notes: See Beintema, Avila, and Pardey 2001 for specific information on agency samples. A dash indicates nonexistent; NA indicates not available.

Table 10.7 Brazil: IAC's funding sources, 1995–98

Funding source	Total funding (million 1999 reais)				Total funding (million 1999 international dollars)				Percentage of total funding			
	1995	1996	1997	1998	1995	1996	1997	1998	1995	1996	1997	1998
Direct funding												
State budget	21.9	25.0	26.7	21.8	27.0	30.8	32.9	26.9	80.4	72.0	78.0	80.0
State fund	1.1	1.3	0.6	0.8	1.3	1.6	0.8	1.0	4.0	3.7	1.8	2.9
Subtotal	23.0	26.3	27.3	22.6	28.3	32.4	33.7	27.9	84.4	75.7	79.8	82.9
Other funding												
FUNDAG	1.2	1.6	2.4	0.9	1.5	2.0	3.0	1.1	4.5	4.6	7.1	3.4
FINEP	1.0	0.3	1.1	0.5	1.2	0.4	1.4	0.6	3.5	1.0	3.2	1.8
FAPESP	2.0	6.3	3.3	1.8	2.5	7.8	4.1	2.2	7.4	18.3	9.6	6.5
FUNDEPAG	0.0	0.0	0.0	0.3	0.0	0.0	0.0	0.4	0.1	0.0	0.1	1.1
Embrapa	0.0	0.1	0.0	0.0	0.0	0.2	0.1	0.0	0.0	0.4	0.1	0.1
PRONAF	—	—	—	0.6	—	—	—	0.8	—	—	—	2.4
FUNCAFE	—	—	—	0.5	—	—	—	0.6	—	—	—	1.8
Subtotal	4.2	8.4	6.9	4.6	5.2	10.4	8.5	5.7	15.6	24.3	20.2	17.1
Total	27.2	34.7	34.2	27.2	33.6	42.8	42.2	33.6	100	100	100	100

Source: Beintema, Avila, and Pardey 2001.

Notes: FAPESP (São Paulo Research Support Foundation) is a state foundation; FUNCAFE (Fund for Protection of the Coffee Economy), PRONAF (National Program for Strengthening Family Agriculture), and FINEP (Financing Agency for Studies and Projects) are federal funding programs. FUNDAG (Foundation for Agricultural Research Support) and FUNDEPAG (Foundation for Agricultural Development and Research) are private foundations. A dash indicates not applicable.

In recent years, state agencies have become increasingly reliant on funding from nongovernment sources. For example, between 1995 and 1998, IAC received an average of 80 percent of its funding from the state government (77 percent directly and 3 percent by way of a special fund). The remaining 20 percent came from various public and private foundations (Table 10.7). These funds were used mainly for operational costs but also covered some expenses made for capital improvement and salaries paid to additional research staff (often hired as consultants).

Competitive Funding Mechanisms

In many developing countries, competitive funding mechanisms have been introduced as one of a number of new instruments for disbursing research resources.[18] This has been the case for a number of Latin American countries where diminishing public support for agricultural research, beginning in the 1980s, led to various institutional and policy reforms in the funding of research. Competitive funding mechanisms have gained favor among some policymakers, donors, and even researchers. They are seen as a means of redirecting research priorities, increasing the role of the private and academic sectors in the performance of research, and, perhaps, forging new links among government, academic, and private research agencies. The use of competitive funding has advantages and disadvantages over block grants. Competitive funding mechanisms involve relatively high transaction costs (such as writing and screening proposals) and rent-seeking costs (such as lobbying for support), but could lower the social costs arising from the misallocation of funds. Further, the use of competitive funds tends to increase flexibility, but it often forces a short-term, applied research orientation at the expense of more basic, longer-term research (Echeverría, Trigo, and Byerlee 1996; Echeverría 1998; Alston and Pardey 1999).

Competitive funding mechanisms have existed in Brazil for some time. Since its inception, Embrapa has disbursed resources to finance projects through a competitive national program open to Embrapa's research centers and all other national public research agencies, including state agencies and universities. This program funds 500 to 600 projects each year. About 95 percent of the funded projects are conducted by Embrapa scientists, although state and higher-education agencies had a larger presence in the program during the 1970s and 1980s. The new IDB loan, which became operational in early 2006, will continue the competitive fund scheme under much the same rules established as part of an earlier World Bank loan (see below), but only Embrapa scientists will be eligible. This change was mandated by the fact that only half the amount proposed ($60 million, not the $120 million sought) was approved.

Agricultural Technology Development Project (PRODETAB). A World Bank loan of US$60 million was approved in 1996 to support the Agricultural Technology Development Project (PRODETAB) over five years. The funds were matched by an additional US$60 million from the Brazilian government, Embrapa, and various other public and private agricultural R&D agencies. PRODETAB has three components. The largest share supports a competitive funding program (60 percent); 37 percent is earmarked for institutional development and training activities at Embrapa and state government agencies (particularly in the historically weak north and northeast regions), plus the development of international research linkages; and 3 percent supports the administration, monitoring, and evaluation of PRODETAB itself (Reifschneider and Lele 1998).

The primary objective of PRODETAB is to integrate and diversify the national agricultural R&D system through collaborative research and technology transfer, thereby promoting private-sector participation. Five priority areas were established: biotechnology, natural resource management, small-farm development, agribusiness, and strategic research on high-priority issues not already undertaken by Embrapa's programs (Lele 1998; Lele and Anderson 1999).[19]

By the end of 2000, 4 calls for proposals had been made—1 in 1997, 2 in 1998, and 1 in 1999—resulting in 392 proposal submissions, of which 46 were approved (12 percent). The total approved funding from the four submission rounds was $21.8 million in 1999 international prices (Embrapa 1999b).

PRODETAB represents a new approach to disbursing Embrapa's research funds, and funds in Brazil more generally, but block funding still predominates. Annual disbursals from the World Bank component of PRODETAB averaged $12 million over the five years of the project, just 2 percent of Embrapa's annual budget and around 1 percent of Brazil's total agricultural R&D expenditures. The PRODETAB funds made available to Embrapa during the period 1997–99 represented only 1 percent of the agency's total funding for that period.

Conclusion

At 1.5 billion (1999 international dollars) in 1996, Brazil accounts for about half the total agricultural R&D investments made in Latin America and the Caribbean (Pardey and Beintema 2001) and employs the third largest number of agricultural scientists (about 5,000 ftes). Agricultural R&D in Brazil is organizationally complex, encompassing numerous federal and state government agencies, higher-education institutions, nonprofit institutions, and private enterprises. Nonetheless, the public sector is still the predominant agricultural R&D provider in Brazil; by our estimates, government agencies accounted for 79 percent of the country's agricultural R&D expenditures in 1996. An increasing amount of agricultural technology appears to be provided by the private sector, but comparatively few of these technologies are the result of private research conducted in Brazil.

Among the government agencies, Embrapa dominates, accounting for 72 percent of government agricultural R&D spending. Spending per scientist for the state agencies is about half the comparable Embrapa figure. Both Embrapa and the state government agencies still rely on government sources of support. In 1996, government sources provided about 80 percent of the funds disbursed to Embrapa and the state research agencies. Funding for Brazilian agricultural R&D tends to rise and fall with the general state of the economy. Although funding has increased overall since the mid-1970s, the economic downturns of the early 1980s and the late 1990s saw a commensurate cutback in funding for agricultural R&D.

The intensity of investment in agricultural R&D in Brazil is comparable to that of developed countries, albeit at the lower end of the range. In 1996, Brazil invested $1.70 for every $100 of agricultural output, more than double the 1976 figure and well above the intensity of investment of most other Latin American countries. How agricultural R&D in Brazil fares in the future will depend on continuing government commitment, in the form of policies to encourage the international flows of technologies and technical know-how, sustained support for building and maintaining the country's scientific expertise, fostering economic conditions and protection for intellectual property rights that encourage private participation in R&D, and, perhaps most critically, continuing to fund the basic and strategic science that underpins the private roles in technology generation and transfer.

Abbreviations and Acronyms

AGROMAIS	Taxa voluntária de desenvolvimento tecnológico (Voluntary tax for technology development)
APTA	Agência Paulista de Tecnologia dos Agronegócios (São Paulo Agency for Agribusiness Technology)
CEPEC	Centro de Pesquisa do Cacau (Research Center for Cacao)
CEPLAC	Comissão Executiva do Plano da Lavoura Cacaueira (Executive Commission for Cocoa)
COODETEC	Cooperativa Central Agropecuária de Desenvolvimento Tecnológico e Econômico Ltda (Central Agricultural Cooperative for Technology Development and Economics)

COPERSUCAR	Cooperative dos Produtores de Cana, Açúcar e Alcool do Estado de São Paulo Ltda (Cooperative for Sugarcane, Sugar, and Alcohol Producers of the State of São Paulo)
EMBRAPA	Empresa Brasileira de Pesquisa Agropecuária (Brazilian Agricultural Research Corporation)
FUNDACEP	Fundação Centro de Experimentação e Pesquisa Fecotrigo (Foundation Center for Wheat Experimentation and Research)
FUNDECITRUS	Fundo de Defesa da Citricultura (Fund for Citrus Plant Protection)
IAC	Agronomic Institute of Campinas
IBAMA	Instituto Brasileiro do Meio Ambiente e dos Recursos Naturais Renováveis (Brazilian Institute for the Environment and Renewable Natural Resources)
IRGA	Instituto Rio-Grandense do Arroz (Rio Grande Rice Research Institute)
ISNAR	International Service for National Agricultural Research
PROCENSUL	Projeto Fortalecimento da Pesquisa e Difusão de Tecnologia na Região Centro-Sul (Project for Strengthening Research and Technology Transfer in the Center-South Region)
PRODETAB	Projeto de Apoio ao Desenvolvimento de Tecnologia Agropecuária para o Brasil (Agricultural Technology Development Project)
PROMOAGRO	Programa de Madoernização Tecnológica da Agropecuária da Região Centro-Sul do Brazil (Program for Modernization of Agricultural Technology in the Center-South Region of Brazil)

Notes

This chapter is adapted from *Agricultural R&D in Brazil: Policy, Investments, and Institutional Profile*, a report prepared by the authors as part of the Agricultural Science and Technology Indicators (ASTI) initiative.

　　1. Public agricultural R&D agencies include government agencies, higher-education institutions, and nonprofit institutions. For additional information and other definitions used in this chapter, see the ASTI website at http://www.asti.cgiar.org.

　　2. Brazil has the third-largest total public agricultural R&D investment among less-developed countries, after China and India. Together, these three countries accounted for 44 percent of total

agricultural research investments in the developing world in the mid-1990s (Pardey and Beintema 2001).

3. Five imperial research institutes were established in total, but only these two became operational.

4. IAC was an exception in the developing world, as most (if not all) of the other research centers created around that time were established by colonial powers.

5. This state government has had a long history of involvement in agricultural R&D. It created the Biology Institute (still in operation) in 1927.

6. See Beintema, Avila, and Pardey 2001 (Appendix B) for an institutional summary of Brazilian agricultural research agencies.

7. There are 13 ecoregional, 15 commodity, and 9 thematic centers.

8. The financial data in this chapter were converted to 1999 international dollars by first deflating funds compiled in current local-currency units, using a Brazilian GDP deflator with the base year 1993, and then converting to U.S. dollars using a 1999 purchasing power parity (PPP) index from World Bank 2000.

9. Compiling expenditure data for higher-education institutions proved difficult. The minimal data obtained often indicated direct expenditures—such as the operational costs or project funds received from external sources—rather than a comprehensive accounting of all costs, including salaries, rent, and utilities, appropriately prorated to reflect the shares of faculty time spent on research. To redress these problems, an estimate of total expenditures for the higher-education sector was calculated using the average expenditures per researcher for government agencies and nonprofit institutions, scaled by the number of fte researchers employed by the higher-education agencies in our sample.

10. Data for 1996 are not representative of Embrapa's spending pattern at that time because of the extraordinary costs of an early-retirement scheme made available to Embrapa staff that year. Regardless, these one-off costs ($25 million reais) represent only 1 percent of Embrapa's share of total Brazilian expenditures in 1996.

11. Recall that we have less than complete coverage of higher-education institutions, though this lacuna is unlikely to affect information on the institutional distribution of Brazilian agricultural researchers.

12. In 1998, a total of 2,077 Embrapa researchers had completed M.Sc. or Ph.D. studies (Embrapa 1999a), but in recent years the number of Embrapa researchers receiving postgraduate training has decreased. These trends reflect the high proportion of Embrapa researchers who have earned postgraduate degrees while employed and of new hires already holding higher degrees.

13. This average includes four of the six Central American countries: Costa Rica, Guatemala, Honduras, and Panama.

14. This decline in spending per scientist was for Embrapa as a whole. Spending per scientist varied considerably among the various Embrapa centers. In general, centers with comparatively high 1996 spending ratios experienced larger declines than those with lower initial ratios, so that spending-per-scientist ratios became more uniform across Embrapa centers.

15. See Beintema, Avila, and Pardey 2001 (Appendix B).

16. Roseboom (1999) supports our own impressions that comparatively little private food-processing and agricultural-machinery research takes place in Brazil and that much of the agrochemical research conducted by multinational companies is done elsewhere.

17. The three IDB loans were parts 1 and 2 of the Project for Strengthening Research and Technology Transfer in the Center-South Region (PROCENSUL), at US$66.4 and $67.8 million,

and the Program for Modernization of Agricultural Technology in the Center-South Region of Brazil (PROMOAGRO), at US$77.8 million. The four World Bank loans are known as the Agricultural Research Projects 1, 2, and 3, at US$40, 60 and 42 million, respectively, and PRODETAB at US$60 million.

18. For more discussion on alternative funding options, see Echeverría 1998 and Alston and Pardey 1999.

19. Beintema, Avila, and Pardey (2001) give a more detailed description of the PRODETAB competitive fund.

References

Alston, J. M., and P. G. Pardey. 1999. The economies of agricultural R&D policies. Chapter 2 in *Paying for agricultural productivity,* ed. J. M. Alston, P. G. Pardey, and V. H. Smith. Baltimore: Johns Hopkins University Press.

Alves, R. E. A. 1992. Getting beyond the "national institute model" for agricultural research in Latin America: Case study one, agricultural research in Brazil. World Bank, Washington, D.C. Mimeo.

Beintema, N. M., and P. G. Pardey. 2001. Recent developments in the conduct of Latin American agricultural research. Paper prepared for the International Conference on Agricultural Science and Technology, Beijing, November 7–9.

Beintema, N. M., A. F. D. Avila, and P. G. Pardey. 2001. *Agricultural R&D in Brazil: Policy, investments, and institutional profile.* Washington, D.C.: International Food Policy Research Institute, Embrapa, and FONTAGRO.

Beintema, N. M., L. Romano, and P. G. Pardey. 2000. *Agricultural R&D in Colombia: Policy, investments, and institutional profile.* Washington, D.C.: International Food Policy Research Institute and FONTAGRO.

Echeverría, R. G. 1998. *Will competitive funding improve the performance of agricultural research?* Discussion Paper No. 98-26. The Hague: International Service for National Agricultural Research.

Echeverría, R. G., E. J. Trigo, and D. Byerlee. 1996. *Institutional change and effective financing of agricultural research in Latin America.* Technical Paper No. 330. Washington, D.C.: World Bank.

EIU (The Economist Intelligence Unit). 1998. *Country profile 1998–99: Brazil.* London: EIU.

Embrapa (Empresa Brasileira de Pesquisa Agropecuária). 1999a. *Annual report 1998.* Brasilia: Embrapa.

————. 1999b. PRODETAB data tables. Embrapa, Brasilia. Computer diskette.

FAO (Food and Agriculture Organization of the United Nations). 2005. FAOSTAT database. http://faostat.fao.org/default.htm. Accessed September 2005.

FUNDECITRUS (Fundo de Defesa da Citricultura). 2001. FUNDECITRUS: Fund for citrus plant protection. http://www.fundecitrus.com.br/indiceus.html. Accessed May 17, 2001.

IBGE (Instituto Brasileiro de Geografia e Estatística). 1999. *Brasil en números / Brazil in figures.* Rio de Janeiro: IBGE.

Lele, U. 1998. Building regional cooperation from the bottom up and top down: The case of Southern Cone countries. In *Guidelines for designing new organization and funding ways for agricultural and agroindustrial innovation systems in the Southern Cone,* ed. IICA (Instituto Interamericano de Cooperación para la Agricultura). Montevideo: IICA.

Lele, U., and J. R. Anderson. 1999. Brazil agricultural technology development project aide-memoire. World Bank, Washington, D.C. Mimeo.

Pardey, P. G., and N. M. Beintema. 2001. *Slow magic: Agricultural R&D a century after Mendel.* IFPRI Food Policy Report. Washington, D.C.: International Food Policy Research Institute.

Páscoa, M. B. A. 2005. In search of an innovative environment: The new Brazilian innovation law. http://www.wipo.int/sme/en/documents/brazil_innovation.htm. Accessed August 8, 2005.

Portugal, A. D., F. J. B. Reifschneider, E. Contini, and A. B. de Oliveira. 1999. *Taxa Voluntária de Desenvolvimento Tecnológico (AGROMAIS): Um mecanismo inovador de financiamento para a pesquisa, desenvolvimento e promoção do agronegócio.* Brasilia: Instituto Teotônio Vilela.

Reifschneider, F. J. B., and U. Lele. 1998. Making competitive grants programs of the national agricultural research systems work: Learning from the Brazilian experience. Paper prepared for the workshop on PRODETAB and Embrapa Planning, Evaluation and Management Systems, Brasilia, May 24.

Roseboom, J. 1999. *Sources of technological innovation in Brazilian agriculture.* ISNAR Discussion Paper No. 99-12. The Hague: International Service for National Agricultural Research.

World Bank. 2000. *World development indicators 2000.* Washington, D.C. CD-ROM.

———. *World development indicators 2005.* Washington, D.C. CD-ROM.

Chapter 11

Colombia: A Public–Private Partnership

Nienke M. Beintema, Luis Romano, and Philip G. Pardey

Introduction

Despite efforts in many Latin American countries to diminish the government role in the funding and performing of agricultural research and development (R&D), general government revenues are still the predominant source of support for agricultural research, as in many less-developed countries (Pardey and Beintema 2001). Colombia is an exception, evidenced by the presence of 12 nonprofit organizations, which together accounted for about a quarter of the country's agricultural research investments in 2000. Many of these organizations are linked to producer organizations and are funded largely through export or production taxes or voluntary contributions.[1] In addition, public agricultural research in Colombia underwent a major reform in 1993 with the creation of the Colombian Corporation for Agricultural Research (CORPOICA).[2] The main objective of its creation was to give the agency more flexibility in its organization compared with its predecessor, the Colombian Agricultural Institute (ICA), in addition to stimulating private-sector involvement and investment. Nonetheless, CORPOICA remained heavily dependent on government contributions. In recent years, the agency's funding situation has deteriorated, but this trend is common to all agricultural R&D agencies in Colombia as a consequence of the country's ongoing economic and social crises.

Macroeconomic Context

Since the beginning of the 1990s, Colombia has grappled with a number of serious social and economic issues that have influenced the economic situation generally, and the performance and funding of the agricultural research system specifically. Because of internal political conflict, an increasing share of budget resources has been diverted to deal with guerrilla activity, eroding the share available for other national goals. In addition, Colombia's economy is stagnant, if not near recession. In 2001 the fiscal deficit was close to 3.3 percent of total GNP, while the internal and external debt ratio to total GNP was 46 percent (*El Espectador* 2002; *El Tiempo* 2002). Understandably, the government budget allocation to science and technology (S&T), including agricultural research, has diminished over the years.

During the 1990s, Colombia also faced the difficult task of becoming competitive in international markets while adjusting to reductions in tariff protections that were first put in place during World War II. The agricultural sector underwent a restructuring that saw the cultivated area of annual crops (such as cotton, wheat, sorghum, and soybeans) decline by 800,000 hectares, and a 200,000-hectare increase in the area under permanent pasture and perennial crops (such as oil palm, banana, and sugarcane). Between 1970 and 2000, the value of agricultural imports— adjusted for inflation— increased by more than $1 billion, while the total value of agricultural exports declined slightly (Table 11.1). The decline is partly attributable to a currency overvaluation and a precipitous drop in international prices for commodities that are especially important to Colombia (Machado 2000). The coffee sector was particularly hard hit. The total export value of coffee, which accounted for 60 percent of the total value of agricultural exports in 1990, declined by one-third over the subsequent decade. Colombia's coffee production dropped by 25 percent over the same period. In contrast, the total production and export value of other major crops increased. For example, the production and export value of bananas increased by 13 percent; plantains increased by 22 percent.

Colombia's recent agricultural problems reflect not only its institutional, social, and political problems but also substantial policy changes and other economic shifts. The rapid reduction in import tariffs for many crops reduced their profitability for Colombian producers, and the pace of change did not allow adjustment processes to take effect. Credit costs also increased as the subsidy on interest rates for agricultural producers was removed. These domestic policy reforms, in conjunction with widespread use of older farm technologies and limited access to timely market information, compounded the effects of declining world agricultural prices to precipitate the agricultural sector's recent problems.

Historical Developments and Current Structure of Agricultural Research

Historical Developments

Institutional agricultural research in Colombia began in 1879, with the establishment of a livestock acclimatization farm as part of the Institute of Agriculture at the

Table 11.1 Colombia: Overview of agricultural indicators, 1970–2002

Indicator	1970	1980	1990	2000	2002
Agricultural sector as a percentage of					
Total GDP	25.7	19.9	16.7	14.0	13.6
Total labor force	45.1	40.5	26.6	20.4	19.3
Agricultural imports					
Total (million 2000 U.S. dollars)	288.9	989.8	448.2	1,314.1	1,542.3
As a percentage of total merchandise imports	10.7	11.5	6.6	11.4	12.6
Agricultural exports					
Total (million 2000 U.S. dollars)	2,134.1	5,638.4	2,909.2	2,914.9	2,620.9
As a percentage of total merchandise exports	81.2	77.2	35.4	22.2	22.9
Agricultural area (million hectares)	43.0	45.3	45.1	45.5	45.9
Permanent pasture (million hectares)	38.0	40.1	40.1	40.9	42.1
Arable and permanent crops (million hectares)	5.0	5.2	5.0	4.5	3.9
Main crops					
Coffee					
Total production (million metric tons)	0.5	0.7	0.8	0.6	0.7
Area harvested (million hectares)	0.8	1.1	1.0	0.9	0.8
Total value of exports (million 2000 U.S. dollars)	1,666.9	4,371.9	1,725.3	1,069.4	751.6
Sugarcane					
Total production (million metric tons)	12.7	26.1	27.8	33.5	35.8
Area harvested (million hectares)	0.2	0.3	0.3	0.4	0.4
Total value of exports (million 2000 U.S. dollars)	50.1	305.0	172.3	194.1	202.7
Rice					
Total production (million metric tons)	0.8	1.8	2.1	2.3	2.3
Area harvested (million hectares)	0.2	0.4	0.5	0.5	0.5
Total value of exports (million 2000 U.S. dollars)	2.2	30.9	23.3	0.03	0.2
Bananas and plantains					
Total production (million metric tons)	2.4	3.3	3.8	4.2	4.3
Area harvested (million hectares)	0.2	0.4	0.4	0.4	0.4
Total value of exports (million 2000 U.S. dollars)	64.6	174.3	387.8	480.6	423.7
Potatoes					
Total production (million metric tons)	0.9	1.7	2.5	2.8	2.8
Area harvested (million hectares)	0.1	0.1	0.2	0.2	0.2
Total value of exports (million 2000 U.S. dollars)	0.1	0.2	3.0	14.1	7.4

Sources: World Bank 2005 and FAO 2005.

Botanical Gardens in Bogotá. In 1925, crop research was initiated with the creation of the first experiment station under the Ministry of Agriculture and Commerce; this was followed by the establishment of additional experiment stations over the next two decades. The government invited the Rockefeller Foundation to establish a cooperative program to improve Colombian food-crop production along the same lines as a successful program established by the foundation in Mexico. The Colombian program began in 1950 with the creation of the Office of Special Research (OIE). It initially focused on wheat and maize breeding, but the scope of its research soon expanded to include a large range of other crops as well as livestock. In 1955, with the impetus of the Rockefeller Foundation program, a Division of Agricultural Research (DIA) was created under the Ministry of Agriculture and became responsible for all the ministry's experiment stations. OIE continued to exist and support Colombian public agricultural research; it also continued to finance fellowships for Colombian scientists to undertake postgraduate training abroad.[3]

Hindering the successes of the agricultural research program was a higher-education system that lacked financial and physical resources, and hence could not meet the demand for well-trained scientists (World Bank 1983; Weersma-Haworth 1984). In an effort to integrate agricultural research, extension, and education—and with the assistance of the Rockefeller, Ford, and Kellogg foundations—the Colombian government established the Colombian Agricultural Institute (ICA) in 1962. ICA inherited DIA's network of experiment stations and was given semi-autonomous status. ICA was reorganized in 1968 and 1976, and the change ultimately resulted in a more complex and decentralized structure. The orientation and relevance of ICA's research and extension activities were increasingly criticized in the late 1970s, particularly for the lack of coordination and communication between ICA researchers and farmers. ICA also experienced serious funding problems during this period because financial contributions from the government were substantially curtailed, and legal restrictions made it difficult—if not impossible—for ICA to secure other sources of funding, especially from the private sector.

In the mid-1980s ICA was further reorganized, resulting in two separate sub-directorates—one for research and technology, and one for services. Despite the reorganization and initial funding from the World Bank and other international donors, ICA maintained a broad range of activities with insufficient funds to support them. In 1990, ICA was again reorganized, and its research mandate was broadened to include biotechnology and natural-resources research. In an effort to give greater coherence to ICA's multiple functions and to improve its efficiency, in 1993 the agency was separated into two institutes. ICA maintained responsibility for plant and animal health and quarantine, input regulation, and public research coordination and supervision. The research and technology transfer activities were relocated to a newly created institution, CORPOICA. CORPOICA was established as a joint venture between the Colombian government and various producer associations, universities, and regional institutions. The goal was to create an institute with greater flexibility in its organization, planning, and staff-recruitment policies, ultimately providing opportunities for collaboration with the private sector (CORPOICA n.d.).

Research activities conducted by producer associations have been, and still are, an important component of Colombian agricultural R&D. The first producer association to initiate research was the National Federation of Coffee Producers (FEDECAFE, created in 1928), which in turn established a National Coffee Research Center (CENICAFE) in 1938 to study the main problems of coffee production in Colombia. Cotton producers created the Institute for Cotton Development (IFA) in 1948, primarily to assess the performance of various cotton varieties introduced from the United States and elsewhere. In 1968, IFA was closed, and ICA assumed the more basic aspects of cotton research, while applied research (such as the testing of new varieties) became the responsibility of the National Federation of Cotton Producers (FEDERALGODON). The National Federation of Rice Producers (FEDEARROZ) was established in 1948 but initially focused most of its activities on extension. It began to undertake signficant research in 1968, in a joint program with ICA and the International Center for Tropical Agriculture (CIAT). ICA and CIAT jointly developed new rice varieties that were field-tested by FEDEARROZ.

In the 1950s and 1960s, additional producer associations were created for cacao (FEDECACAO, 1962), oil palm (FEDEPALMA, 1962), and cereals (FENALCE, 1963), but it took several decades before these associations initiated programs of research. The Colombian Enterprise for Veterinary Products (VECOL) was established in 1974 to conduct research on and produce vaccines for foot-and-mouth disease. In 1977 the country's sugar mills created the Colombian Sugarcane Research Center (CENICAÑA), which assumed responsibility for all sugarcane research previously conducted by ICA. The Association of Flower Exporters (ASOCOFLORES, established in 1976) formed a technical division in 1987. Other, more recent research initiatives by producer groups are the Grape Research Center (CENIUVA, established in 1989), FEDEPAPA, which began research on potatoes in 1991, and the Colombian Research Center for Aquaculture (CENIACUA, established in 1993).

Current Structure of Public Agricultural R&D

The main agricultural research agency in Colombia continues to be CORPOICA, which accounts for about half of the country's total agricultural R&D resources. CORPOICA, established in 1993, is a nonprofit private corporation, although it still has some of the traits of a public agency. The agency is contracted by the Ministry of Agriculture and Rural Development (MADR) to provide public goods and services, but, as a private organization, it can set its own administrative policies (regarding, for example, management, staff recruitment, and salary structure). CORPOICA also has more freedom to obtain additional funding from the private sector through research contracts than did its forerunner ICA, but to date these types of funds account for only a small portion of its budget.

The producer associations mentioned above are heavily engaged in crop research. In some instances the research activities of these associations have replaced those previously undertaken by ICA; in other cases they complement current research. Consequently, some producer associations have joint research projects with CORPOICA. The research activities of these associations are organized in various ways. Some producer associations have created separate research centers (such as FEDECAFE's CENICAFE, ASOCAÑA's CENICAÑA, and FEDEPALMA's CENIPALMA), but others have created technical departments within the respective associations, or else they outsource most of the research to CORPOICA, universities, and other agencies (for example, FEDEARROZ, FEDEPAPA, and FENALCE).

The four most important producer organizations in the Colombian context are CENICAFE, FEDEARROZ, CENICAÑA, and CENIPALMA. CENICAFE—the largest and oldest research center among the producer associations—is mainly involved in developing new coffee varieties, but it does conduct some research intended to solve production problems. It is also active in the transfer of technologies and the production and sale of coffee seeds. FEDEARROZ is currently the second largest producer association in terms of research personnel. It is constituted not as a "CENI" (research center) but rather as a research division within the producer association. Its activities involve the development of new varieties, facilitated by a joint research program with CORPOICA and CIAT. CENICAÑA does research in areas such as genetic improvement, agronomy, entomology, soil, postharvest technologies, and socioeconomics. In contrast to most other producer organizations, CENIPALMA has continued to expand its research activities in recent years and is now among the largest producer organizations in terms of research staff. Its research activities are applied in nature, focusing on soil-fertility improvement and integrated pest and disease management.

A recent development is the planning and creation of "virtual centers." These involve networks of researchers engaged in existing research, thereby eliminating the need to create additional physical infrastructure. The first virtual center was created in 1999 by FEDEPAPA together with CORPOICA, ICA, the Colombian Institute for Science and Technology Development (COLCIENCIAS), the academic sector, and various producers and distributors.[4] Three more virtual centers (for cereal, irrigation, and cut flowers) are under development.

Several other government agencies conduct agricultural research in areas other than crops and livestock. These include the National Institute for Fisheries and Aquaculture (INPA, also under MADR), which conducts research on fisheries and water, and five relatively small agencies under the Ministry of Environment engaged in environmental, biological, and marine sciences research. Public and private universities also conduct some agricultural research—the main one being the National University of Colombia—but most universities concentrate on providing higher-education services, and so their combined contribution to Colombian agricultural R&D is quite small.

Colombian Science and Technology Policy

Colombia's science and technology (S&T) policy during the second half of the 20th century falls into three distinct phases. From 1957 to 1974, Colombia pursued an import-substitution strategy that was common throughout the region at the time (UNCSTD, UNTAD, and COLCIENCIAS 1997). This economic strategy also involved a national S&T policy geared toward achieving self-sufficiency in food. A principal concern of the government was to control technological transfer processes and the foreign investment that typically accompanies it. For its part, ICA sought to develop improved local varieties as substitutes for imported rice, soybeans, sorghum, cotton, and wheat.

From 1974 to 1989, Colombia's economy slowly opened up, and this change was reflected in the national S&T policy. Facing increased international competition, local industrial firms (including the farm-input supply sector) began restructuring themselves. Agricultural producers followed suit beginning in the early 1990s, with substantial acreage shifted out of annual crops and into perennial crops and livestock. At the same time, COLCIENCIAS received a loan from the Inter-American Development Bank (IDB) to modernize existing R&D systems, thereby reinforcing its role as promoter of technological development to the other official agencies and the industrial sector. ICA continued to be the main research provider for the agricultural sector, supported by an injection of loan monies from the World Bank in 1983 to improve the institute's infrastructure, programs, and equipment, and to provide funds for training ICA researchers (UNSCTD, UNTAD, and COLCIENCIAS 1997).

From 1990 to 2001, further economic liberalization called for changes in Colombia's S&T strategy to respond to increased external competition. In 1990, a new S&T law was approved that included support for a national system of science and technology (NSST). NSST is an "open system," meaning that it includes all S&T programs, strategies, and activities, both public and private (DNP COLCIENCIAS 2000). The NSST includes programs for each of the 11 productive sectors, including 1 for the agricultural sector called the Agricultural Science and Technology Program. This program is managed by a council that formulates national strategies and programs for agricultural technological development. The council consists of representatives of the government (including MADR), universities, farmer and researcher groups, and the private sector. The council also makes decisions on the distribution of government funds to agricultural S&T, channeled through COLCIENCIAS, but these funds are relatively small compared with the government funds disbursed directly to MADR; hence the role of the council in setting national agricultural research policies is—in reality—limited.

The same law also provided incentives for public and private associations to develop joint S&T activities, facilitating collaboration between government and private institutions—something that was prohibited prior to 1990. For the agricultural sector, this change resulted in the aforementioned transfer of ICA's research activities to the newly created CORPOICA.

Financing Agricultural Research

Colombia has diverse sources of funding for agricultural research, but government contributions continue to dominate. They are distributed in a variety of ways, including block grants to various institutions, special programs, cofinancing, external loans and donations, and competitive funds awarded through COLCIENCIAS and the National Program for the Transfer of Agricultural Technology (PRONATTA).[5] The private sector is increasing its participation through direct funding and through levies. However, as already mentioned, the national economic crisis in recent years has led to a reduction in the government contributions and levies made available to agricultural research. Funds from external sources and international cooperative activities have also contracted in recent years (Acosta and Gómez 1998).

In 1989, the National System for Agricultural Technology Transfer (SINTAP) was established, with the intention of reducing the dominance of scientists in determining agricultural research and extension priorities. The objective was to develop a more participatory system by fostering the decisionmaking role of government departments and municipalities, as well as the private sector, and to give added emphasis to the problems facing smallholder farmers (World Bank 1995, 1999). As a part of this decentralization effort, the government and the World Bank agreed to establish PRONATTA, which consisted of two components. The first aimed to improve the management capacity of institutions at the municipal and regional levels; the second aimed to strengthen public and private institutions through the competitive allocation of public funds for agricultural research and extension. Only projects directed toward smallholder farmers in poor rural areas were eligible for these funds.

PRONATTA ran from 1995 until the end of 2002. From 1995 to 2001, PRONATTA's budget totaled US$56.4 million, the majority of which was earmarked for technology development (the remaining 5 percent, or US$2.8 million, was allocated to training activities). These figures include the World Bank loan disbursed via PRONATTA; counterpart funding from MADR, which included a 50 percent contribution toward technology development activities; and a 15 percent contribution to training activities (Berdegue and Escobar 1999). Despite PRONATTA's objective of stimulating private-sector involvement in agricultural R&D, the share of disbursed funds for research executed by the private sector totaled only 2 percent for the period 1995–99 (Estrada, Holmann, and Posada 2002). Of the total approved projects during this period, 44 percent were from CORPOICA (PRONATTA 2000); however, in the 1998 call for proposals, CORPOICA's share of the total successful submissions dropped to around 35 percent. Notable was the high proportion of projects approved from nongoverment natural-resource organizations and farmer groups: their combined share accounted for around 30 percent (D. Byerlee, pers. comm., 2000).

Funding of Government-Performed Research

Not surprisingly (and consistent with the situation in the developing world in general), publicly performed agricultural research in Colombia remains heavily reliant on shrinking government sources of support. In addition, CORPOICA receives a smaller share of the government agricultural research budget because, in recent years, nonprofit institutions and international organizations like CIAT (headquartered in Cali) and the International Maize and Wheat Improvement Center (CIMMYT) have taken a share of the pie.[6] Disbursement methods have also changed recently, moving away from a virtually exclusive reliance on open-ended block-funding arrangements toward more time-bound research contracts.

In 2000, CORPOICA's funding totaled $81 million (1999 international dollars);[7] three-quarters of these funds came from the government through MADR (Table 11.2). While about 80 percent of these "direct" government funds came in the form of line-item payments from the national budget, the remaining funds came in the form of contracts for specified projects. The share of project funding has increased in recent years, causing financial difficulties for CORPOICA because project funds do not allow recovery of overhead costs or the salaries of permanent staff (only for contract labor). CORPOICA also received government contributions through COLCIENCIAS and PRONATTA's competitive grant schemes, but their combined share of total funding declined considerably in 2000, as there was no call for proposals that year. Contributions to CORPOICA from producer organizations have remained relatively small (2 percent of the agency's total funds) despite the goal of increasing private-sector involvement that precipitated CORPOICA's creation. But this situation is not surprising, given that the main focus of the producer organizations is short-term, highly targeted adaptive research, whereas

Table 11.2 Colombia: CORPOICA's funding sources, 1998–2000

Source	Million 1999 pesos			Million 1999 international dollars			Percentage of total		
	1998	1999	2000	1998	1999	2000	1998	1999	2000
MADR									
Budget	31,371.0	31,738.0	33,179.0	49.2	49.8	52.1	62.8	57.7	64.2
Research contracts	6,762.3	7,100.0	6,682.8	10.6	11.1	10.5	13.5	12.9	12.9
Subtotal	38,133.3	38,838.0	39,861.7	59.8	60.9	62.6	76.3	70.6	77.1
Other government sources									
COLCIENCIAS	878.8	329.0	1.8	1.4	0.5	0.0	1.8	0.6	0.0
PRONATTA	115.9	3,796.0	42.4	0.2	6.0	0.1	0.2	6.9	0.1
Other	987.9	1,079.0	351.3	1.6	1.7	0.6	2.0	2.0	0.7
Subtotal	1,982.6	5,204.0	395.5	3.1	8.2	0.6	4.0	9.5	0.8
Other funding sources									
Funds from producer organizations	1,447.0	787.0	1,709.5	2.3	1.2	2.7	2.9	1.4	3.3
Other (CENA)	1,935.3	4,234.0	4,789.9	3.0	6.6	7.5	3.9	7.7	9.3
Subtotal	3,382.3	5,021.0	6,499.4	5.3	7.8	10.2	6.8	9.1	12.6
Sales	6,494.5	5,912.0	4,924.5	10.2	9.3	7.7	13.0	10.8	9.5
Total	49,992.7	54,975.0	51,681.1	78.5	86.3	81.1	100	100	100

Sources: Data are from CORPOICA, personal communication, 2001; deflators and PPP value are from World Bank 2001 and IMF 2001.

CORPOICA undertakes more strategic or basic research. CORPOICA's funding sources have varied substantially over the years, with the share of government contributions declining steadily (from 100 percent) since the agency's first year of operation in 1994 (Beintema, Romano, and Pardey 2000).

Research Financed by Producer Organizations

As mentioned above, agricultural R&D in Colombia differs from that in other Latin American countries in that producer associations conduct a significant amount of research. Table 11.3 gives an overview of these organizations, their operations, and their funding. Most finance their research activities through a mandatory cess or tax (*parafiscal* or *cuota de fomento* in Spanish) that is imposed on the farm sales of crops like rice, cereals, and cocoa, or on export crops such as coffee and flowers. A few associations, such as ASOCANA and FEDEPAPA, do not impose commodity taxes but instead receive voluntary contributions from their members.[8] There are large variations in the shares of cess revenues assigned to research activities: for the four organizations for which relevant data were available, amounts ranged from less than 0.1 percent for ASOCOFLORES to 70 percent for FEDEPALMA. The balance of these funds are used for a variety of purposes, including technology extension, market development, and commodity promotion.[9] The division between in-house research activities and those outsourced also differed considerably among eight producer organizations for which data were available. ASOCOFLORES and FENALCE outsourced all of their research, whereas ASOCANA, FEDERACAFE, and FEDEPALMA spent most of their research funds on in-house R&D.

In addition to collecting tax revenues and voluntary contributions from producers, some producer associations fund research through research contracts, and in some cases they reinvest the profits earned from product sales (CENICAFE, for example, receives part of FEDECAFE's sales revenue from coffee). On average, these sources accounted for about 10 percent of total funding for the producer organizations. Some organizations (including CENICAFE, CENICAÑA, CENIPALMA, and FEDEPAPA) also receive contributions from the government, but these tend to be small: in 1996, the share of funds from government sources ranged from a negligible 0.003 percent of CENICAFE's revenues to 10 percent of FEDEPAPA's (Beintema, Romano, and Pardey 2000). Compounding the declines from economic crisis, some cess revenues for crops have contracted considerably as a result of waning production (as with coffee and cereals) or falling prices (as with oil palm). Many producer organizations are now reluctant to invest further in research, perhaps in response to a lack of perceived payoffs to past investments or the delays in realizing these payoffs in the face of a more immediate crisis.

Table 11.3 Colombia: Producer organizations

Producer organization	Name of research unit	Start year	Type	Size of contribution (percent)
				Details of producer contribution
ASOCOFLORES	Virtual research center	1974	Voluntary contributions	Varies with product
ACUANAL	CENIACUA	1993	Voluntary quota	NA
FEDECAFE	CENICAFE	1934	Levy on export value of coffee	Negotiated annually based on export price
ASOCANA	CENICAÑA	1997	Voluntary contributions	0.55
FEDEPALMA	CENIPALMA	1994	Levy on value of crude palm oil	1
FENEPANELA	NA	NA	Levy on production value of raw sugar	0.5
Cooperativa Agricultores	CENIUVA	1987	Voluntary quota	NA
FEDEARROZ	—	1952	Levy on production value of rice	0.5
FEDECACAO	—	1983	Levy on production value	3
FEDEPAPA	CEVIPAPA	2000	Voluntary contributions	1 percent of sales value
FEDERALGODON	—	NA	Levy on production value	0.5 percent on fiber: 1 percent on seed
FENALCE	—	1984	Levy on production value	0.75 percent of domestic sales value

Sources: Personal communications with producer organizations and other professionals; Estrada, Holmann, and Posada 2002.
Notes: A dash (—) indicates not applicable; NA indicates data not available.

Colombian Public Agricultural Research Investments

In 1996, about 1,000 full-time equivalent (fte) researchers worked in the 30 Colombian public agricultural R&D agencies for which Beintema, Romano and Pardey (2000) compiled data, spending $167 million on agricultural research (Table 11.4). More than half these expenditures were made by CORPOICA, and nonprofit institutions accounted for about a quarter of the total. CENICAFE accounted for more than half of the nonprofit institutions' spending, with FEDEARROZ, the second largest nonprofit institution, accounting for one-fifth of the total. The other government and higher-education agencies each accounted for about 9 percent of the national total spending.[10] The number of higher-education agencies in the sample was low, so, in reality, the higher-education share should be slightly—though not substantially—higher.

Percentage for research	Other activities	Research contracted out	
		Percentage	Agencies
<0.1	Administration and operational costs	100	CIAT, Centro de Investigaciones y Asesorías Agroindustriales (CIA), universities
70	Technical assistance, training, laboratory services	<10	INPA
NA	Technology transfer	<10	CIAT
0.75	Technology transfer, laboratory services	<10	Universidad del Valle
60–70	Dissemination, economic and statistical information, commercialization	<5	CIAT
60	Training, promotion	NA	CORPOICA
NA	Technical assistance, training	NA	NA
NA	Administration, commercialization	>10	FLAR
13.6	Technology transfer, commercialization	80	CORPOICA
Determined by board of directors	Promotional activities	100	CORPOICA, ICA, FEDEPAPA
75	Technology transfer	90	CORPOICA
10	Technology transfer	100	CORPOICA

Table 11.4 Colombia: Composition of public agricultural research expenditures and total researchers, 1996

	Spending			Share (percent of total)		Number of agencies in sample
Type of agency	Million 1999 pesos	Million 1999 international dollars	Researchers (fte)	Spending	Researchers	
Federal government agencies						
CORPOICA	61,005.9	95.7	519.0	57.4	51.5	1
Other	9,666.1	15.2	143.2	9.1	14.2	6
Nonprofit institutions	26,232.3	41.2	229.6	24.7	22.8	11
Higher-education agencies[a]	9,341.4	14.7	116.1	8.8	11.5	12
Total	106,245.7	166.7	1,007.9	100	100	30

Source: Calculated by authors from Beintema, Romano, and Pardey (2000).

[a]Expenditures for the higher-education agencies are estimates based on average expenditures per researcher for government agencies.

Trends in Public Investments

Expenditures. Following a decade of decline in the 1970s, total agricultural research expenditures in Colombia grew considerably in the 1980s and early 1990s (Table 11.5 and Figure 11.1). These totals are strongly influenced by the trends for CORPOICA and its predecessor ICA (hereafter referred to as ICA/CORPOICA), especially in earlier years, when the great majority of agricultural R&D was conducted by ICA. ICA/CORPOICA's total expenditures grew sevenfold over the past four decades, exhibiting a notably erratic year-to-year pattern of real spending that was particularly volatile in the late 1980s and early 1990s. Following the 1994 transfer of ICA's research and technology-transfer activities to CORPOICA, the financial situation stabilized somewhat, but in more recent years it has once again contracted to levels well below those recorded in the mid-1980s. Although the other government-agency share of total research spending is comparatively small, total spending in this category remained fairly stable in constant prices prior to 1990. Following the creation of the new institutes under the Ministry of the Environment, total spending by other government agencies grew considerably during the 1990s, at an average annual rate of 91 percent, albeit from an extremely small base. Total spending by nonprofit institutions increased fourfold, from $11 million in the early 1960s to $41 million in 1996.

More recent data on research expenditures were available for CORPOICA and six nonprofit institutions only (Table 11.5).[11] In 2000, CORPOICA's total spending was $92 million, 4 percent less, in inflation-adjusted terms, than in 1996. Total real spending for the nonprofit institutions also declined by 4 percent over the same period.

Researchers. From 1971 to 1996, total numbers of fte research staff grew by 3 percent per year on average (Table 11.6). ICA/CORPOICA accounted for a large share of the total agricultural research staff, and again the overall growth rate is heavily influenced by this agency rate of growth, especially in the earlier decades. ICA's total number of researchers fluctuated substantially from year to year, and this pattern persisted in CORPOICA. In 1996, CORPOICA's fte research staff totaled 519, dropping to 485 in 1997, and increasing again to 524 in 1998. During the first seven months of 1999, many research positions were terminated because of budget constraints, and by July 1999 the total number of fte researchers had dropped to 421. This decline has continued. As of the end of 2001, CORPOICA employed only 393 researchers.

One of the motivations behind CORPOICA's creation was to gain the flexibility to compete for qualified staff with other, often private-sector, agencies by offering more attractive salaries and other benefits, but budget limitations have

Table 11.5 Colombia: Trends in public agricultural research expenditures, 1961–2000

Trend/period	Government agencies		Nonprofit institutions	Higher-education agencies[b]	Total
	ICA/ CORPOICA	Other[a]			
Agencies in sample	1	6	12	7	26
Expenditures in constant local currencies (billion 1999 pesos)					
1961–65	8.3	—	6.8	NA	NA
1966–70	19.1	0.2	7.2	NA	NA
1971–75	58.9	0.4	11.0	1.5	71.8
1976–80	41.8	0.4	12.9	2.2	57.2
1981–85	64.0	0.5	19.1	4.2	87.8
1986–90	82.8	0.5	27.5	7.1	117.9
1991–95	46.7	2.4	23.5	7.1	79.8
1996	61.0	9.7	26.2	9.3	106.2
2000	58.8	NA	25.1[c]	NA	NA
Expenditures in constant international dollars (million 1999 international dollars)					
1961–65	13.0	—	10.7	NA	NA
1966–70	30.0	0.4	11.3	NA	NA
1971–75	92.4	0.6	17.3	2.4	112.7
1976–80	65.5	0.6	20.3	3.4	89.8
1981–85	100.5	0.7	30.0	6.6	137.8
1986–90	129.9	0.8	43.1	11.2	185.1
1991–95	73.3	3.8	36.9	11.2	125.2
1996	95.7	15.2	41.2	14.7	166.7
2000	92.3	NA	39.5[c]	NA	NA
Annual growth rate (percent)[d]					
1961–71	20.5	—	3.5	NA	NA
1971–81	–5.0	–2.1	4.8	5.6	–2.8
1981–91	3.1	3.9	4.9	11.8	4.0
1991–96	6.5	91.0	4.1	6.6	8.0
1961–96[e]	6.2	9.0	5.2	9.0	2.3

Source: Calculated by authors from Beintema, Romano, and Pardey 2000.

Notes: Data presented are five-year averages. For additional notes, see Beintema, Romano, and Pardey 2000 (Table 4).
A dash indicates zero; NA indicates not available.

[a]Research at the government agencies (excluding ICA) was initiated in 1968.

[b]Expenditures for the higher-education agencies are estimates based on average expenditures per researcher for government agencies.

[c]Data for 6 of the 12 nonprofit institutions (accounting for 20 percent of total fte research expenditures in 1996) were estimated using the trend from 1996 to 2000 for the 6 agencies for which data were available.

[d]Least-squares growth rates.

[e]1971–96 for higher-education subtotal and total.

Figure 11.1 Colombia: Long-term composition of agricultural research expenditures, 1971–96

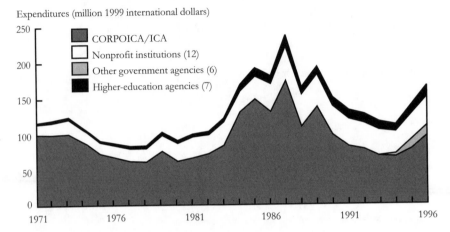

Expenditures (million 1999 international dollars)

Source: Calculated by authors from Beintema, Romano, and Pardey 2000.
Note: Figures in parentheses indicate the number of agencies in each category.

seen CORPOICA's salary levels fall well below those of the universities and private sector. Writing in 1996, Hertford noted that a large number of senior CORPOICA staff were due for retirement in subsequent years: in 1995, 60 percent of the research staff (75 percent of whom held Ph.D.s) was over 40 years old (Hertford 1996). CORPOICA (like other Colombian institutes) has insufficient resources to support junior staff in obtaining postgraduate degrees, either locally or abroad, so the quality of staff will deteriorate over time.[12]

The research shares of the nonprofit institutions increased substantially over time. In 1971, only three producer associations had research programs; these accounted for 9 percent of the total fte research staff that year. The fte share increased to 17 percent in 1985 and to 24 percent in 1996 because of staff increases by the three largest producer associations (CENICAFE, CENICANA, and FEDEARROZ) and the initiation of research by other nonprofit institutions. Despite declining spending since 1996, total researcher numbers have increased slightly in recent years, a change attributable entirely to the substantial increase in the number of researchers employed by CENIPALMA. Total research staff for the other five nonprofit institutions remained constant or decreased slightly.

Spending per scientist. In 1996, average spending per Colombian scientist was $171,000, consistent with the average level for Latin America as a whole (Beintema

Table 11.6 Colombia: Trends in public agricultural research, 1961–2000

Period	Government agencies ICA/ CORPOICA	Other[a]	Nonprofit institutions	Higher-education agencies[b]	Total
Agencies in sample	1	6	12	7	26
Number of researchers (fte's per year)					
1961–65	169.7	—	22.0	NA	NA
1966–70	310.3	3.0	28.3	NA	NA
1971–75	463.2	3.0	60.1	12.3	538.5
1976–80	357.7	3.0	64.3	18.6	443.6
1981–85	400.8	3.0	87.6	25.4	516.9
1986–90	537.4	4.1	153.2	46.3	740.9
1991–95	468.6	39.6	220.5	70.5	799.2
1996	519.0	143.2	229.6	92.3	984.1
2000	419.0	NA	253.8[c]	NA	NA
Annual growth rate (percent)[d]					
1961–71	11.6	—	7.4	NA	NA
1971–81	–3.0	0.0	3.0	7.9	–1.9
1981–91	3.8	11.3	12.1	12.3	6.1
1991–96	4.8	62.7	0.4	8.5	6.7
1961–96[e]	2.9	10.1	7.9	9.3	2.8

Source: Calculated by authors from Beintema, Romano, and Pardey 2000.
Notes: Data presented are five-year averages. For additional notes, see Beintema, Romano, and Pardey 2000 (Table 4). A dash indicates zero; NA indicates data not available.
[a] Research at the government agencies (excluding ICA) was initiated in 1968.
[b] Expenditures for the higher-education agencies are estimates based on average expenditures per researcher for government agencies.
[c] Data for 6 of the 12 nonprofit institutions (accounting for 19 percent of total fte researchers in 1996) were estimated using the trend from 1996 to 2000 for the 6 agencies for which data were available.
[d] Least-squares growth rates.
[e] 1971–96 for higher-education subtotal and total.

and Pardey 2001). The overall trend is less reassuring. Since 1971, the growth in the number of fte researchers has outpaced the growth in real research spending, so that spending per scientist in Colombia declined by about one-third from 1971 to 1996 (Figure 11.2). In general, spending per scientist followed the same erratic trends as those for total spending, spiking in the early 1980s and 1990s.

Research Intensity Ratios

Total public spending as a percentage of agricultural output (AgGDP) is a commonly used measure for comparing agricultural R&D spending among countries

Figure 11.2 Colombia: Agricultural research expenditures, researchers, and expenditures per researcher, 1971–96

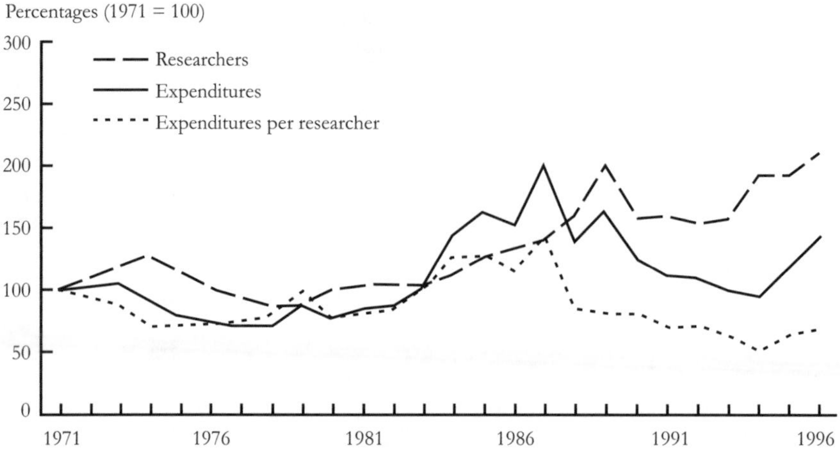

Percentages (1971 = 100)

Source: Tables 11.5 and 11.6.
Notes: We used the data in Tables 11.5 and 11.6, along with other information, to scale up the estimates for the six higher-education agencies for which time-series data were available.

and tracking the intensity of R&D investment within a country over time. Colombia's agricultural R&D intensity ratio declined from 0.45 percent in 1971 to 0.22 percent in 1977 and 1978 (Figure 11.3). The ratio increased between the late 1970s and late 1980s but since then has fluctuated considerably from year to year. These trends mirror—albeit less dramatically—the erratic trend in total spending rather than fluctuations in the value of agricultural output. In 1996, the intensity ratio was only 0.53 percent, comparable with levels of the late 1980s, but it nonetheless represented a recovery from the drop in the early 1990s; the increase resulted from the creation of the research institutes under the Ministry of the Environment in 1994 and 1995. This intensity was even below the comparable developing-country average and less than half the corresponding Latin American average (Beintema and Pardey 2001).

Trends for agricultural R&D spending per capita and per economically active member of the agricultural population are consistent with trends for R&D spending relative to agricultural GDP (Figure 11.4). Agricultural R&D spending per capita declined slightly during 1971–96, from $5.1 per capita in 1971 to $4.2 in 1996. In contrast, agricultural R&D grew relative to the size of the agricultural workforce. In 1971, the country invested $37 in agricultural R&D for every agricultural worker; by 1996 the figure had grown to $45 per worker. This is not surprising. As

Figure 11.3 Colombia: Public agricultural R&D spending relative to AgGDP, 1971–96

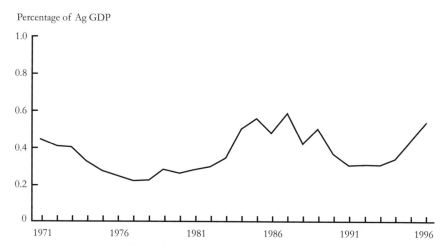

Percentage of Ag GDP

Sources: Expenditure data underlying Figure 11.2; AgGDP from World Bank 2001.

Figure 11.4 Colombia: Spending per capita and per economically active member of agricultural population, 1971–96

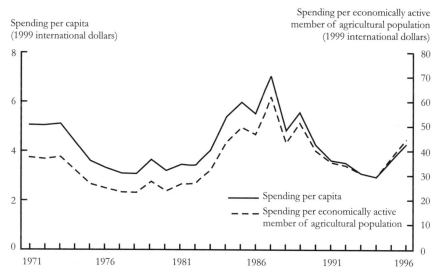

Spending per capita
(1999 international dollars)

Spending per economically active
member of agricultural population
(1999 international dollars)

Sources: Expenditure data underlying Figure 11.2; population and economically active member of agricultural population from FAO 2002.

in many developed and more-advanced developing countries, the share of farmers in Colombia's total population decreased as productivity in the agricultural sector and urbanization increased. In line with Colombia's relative level of research intensity, the country's levels of agricultural R&D spending per capita and per economically active agricultural worker were higher than the average for the developing world, but they lagged behind the levels of neighboring Latin American countries.

Private-Sector Research[13]

Hoechst, a German-based multinational company, initiated research activities in Colombia on agrochemical products and seeds in 1985 (and merged with Schering in 1997 to form Agrevo). Cargill, an American-based multinational, began locally testing introduced sorghum hybrids in 1987, but its Colombian research activities were taken over by Monsanto in 1998. Given recent mergers in the industry (and matters of confidentiality), complete information on the total number of researchers and spending could not be obtained from these companies. Nevertheless, the research activities conducted by the multinationals are small because they tend to outsource most of the research to CORPOICA and other agencies.

Falconi and Pardey (1993) estimated that in 1991 multinational companies accounted for only 2 percent of the country's total fte research staff. It seems the situation has changed little since then, with comparatively little private research—by either national or multinational firms—under way in Colombia. A notable exception is Floramerica, a Colombian flower grower and exporter. The company launched its own research program in 1982, and by 1996 it was spending $215,000 annually on R&D, slightly more than 1 percent of total public agricultural R&D spending.

Orientation of Agricultural R&D

In 1996, close to half the 948 fte researchers in the 22-agency sample reported by Beintema, Romano, and Pardey (2000) conducted crop research, and 21 percent did livestock research. The remaining scientific effort focused on forestry, fisheries, natural resources, and postharvest research. CORPOICA's research was almost equally divided between crops and livestock, but about a quarter of these activities were considered "multiprogrammatic," indicating an overlap between crop and livestock research or multidisciplinary research. Not surprisingly, the nonprofit institutions—dominated by the crop-producer associations—focused almost entirely on crop research, although CORPOICA undertook almost half the country's crop research in 1996.

Identifying the thematic focus of R&D is always difficult. More than one-quarter of the fte researchers in the Beintema, Romano, and Pardey (2000) study were reportedly engaged in yield-enhancing crop-improvement research in 1996, almost evenly split between breeding and pest- and disease-control research. Just over one-fifth of the researchers had a natural-resource focus, and only 3 percent dealt with postharvest issues.

Colombia has only a limited amount of "biotechnology" research under way, broadly conceived to encompass everything from basic tissue-culture techniques to technically demanding transgenic methods. Trigo et al. (2001) report that $5.8 million was spent on biotechnology R&D in Colombia in 1999, but $1.6 million of that total was spent by the international research center CIAT. The quantitative indicators included in the Trigo et al. study suggest the preponderance of this biotechnology research was comparatively low-end (but potentially valuable) micro-propagation and related plant- and cell-biology techniques. There was also some significant use of genetic marker techniques (most of which was probably done by CIAT) but very limited application of advanced genetic-engineering methods. Moreover, from 1987 to 2000, only 7 field trials for genetically modified material were conducted in Colombia (compared with 321 in Argentina and 247 in Brazil), and all these took place in 2000.

Impact of Public Agricultural Research

Several studies of the economic impact of agricultural R&D in Colombia—most based on the calculation of internal rates of return (IRR)—showed good performance for public investment in agriculture research (Table 11.7). For example, Scobie and Posada's (1977) study indicated that most of the benefits coming from rice research accrued to low-income consumers and rice producers (especially those with access to some form of irrigation). This study proved especially useful to ICA in demonstrating the commercial consequences of past research investments and in support of claims for further funding for researching other crops.

More recent aggregate studies by Romano (1987, 2000) include some information about the technological performance of the Colombian research system:

• The aggregate marginal IRR was 50 percent for research and 21 percent for extension, which compared favorably with the cost of capital in Colombia at that time (10 to 12 percent). The aggregate average external rate of return of 142 percent and the favorable benefit cost ratio of 14 to 1 confirmed that research and extension have been socially profitable public investments.

Table 11.7 Colombia: Ex post studies of the economic impact of public agricultural research

Crop	Internal rate of return (percent)	Study
Rice	58	Ardila 1973
Soybeans	79	Montes 1973
Wheat	12	Trujillo 1974
Barley	53	Jaramillo 1976
Oil palm	30	Aragon and Forero 1976
Potato	68	Peña 1976
Rice	87	Scobie and Posada 1977
Sugarcane	13	Vivas, Zuluaga, and Castro 1992
Sorghum	70	Romano, Bermeo, and Torregrosa 1994
Coffee (Variedad Colombia)	21–31	Farfán 1999

Source: Compiled by authors.

- Total factor productivity (TFP) in Colombia took off during the 1960s; growth accelerated during the 1970s but was followed by technological stagnation from 1980 to 1995. The estimated annual rate of growth in TFP from 1960 to 1995 was 1.5 percent, comparable to the rate of productivity growth reported for other countries (see, for example, Acquaye, Alston, and Pardey 2003).

- Since most agricultural research in Colombia was oriented toward the biological sciences, the technological development was more land-saving than labor-saving. (Romano 1987, p. 142)

Conclusion

Mainly as a result of the technical and financial assistance from the Rockefeller Foundation, agricultural research in Colombia received a substantial boost during the 1950s and 1960s, especially compared with many other countries in Latin America. However, during the 1990s, Colombia's economy fell into a crisis, resulting in a decline not only in government support for agricultural research but also, apparently, diminished private-sector funding for, and conduct of, R&D. The disposition of government funding has also changed. In the past, ICA received the lion's share of the government's allocations to agricultural research, but in recent years CORPOICA (the institutional successor of ICA) has received a smaller proportion, for which it competes with nonprofit organizations and international centers (CIAT and CIMMYT).

Thus the dominance of government agencies in the country's overall agricultural R&D effort has waned. Colombia's agricultural research system has evolved from a single public agency (ICA) to multiple agencies with diverse funding sources (including a reliance on various commodity levy schemes for part of the funds) and a variety of funding mechanisms (including a growth in competitive funding schemes and a diminution in block grants from the government). Taken together, these developments point to increasing institutional complexity in the conduct and funding of agricultural R&D in Colombia, but with no commensurate clear pattern of expanded funding support for research. Moreover, the proliferation of research funding agencies and providers has given rise to problems of overall coherence and coordination and, despite some policy initiatives intended to improve interagency linkages, success has been elusive.

There are signs the system is faltering, with research investment ratios that remain low by regional and international standards, a continuing lack of funds for training new generations of scientists (especially in light of the rapid rates of retirement noted above), limited capacity to innovate in the private sector, and few effectively functioning links between technology demanders and suppliers. Overriding all these problems is an ongoing civil war that has impeded the decentralization process and growth of farmer participation, and there are few indications that this situation will improve any time soon.

Abbreviations and Acronyms

ASOCAÑA	Asociación de Cultivadores de Caña de Azúcar de Colombia (Colombian Association of Sugar Producers)
ASOCOFLORES	Asociación Colombiana de Exportadores de Flores (Colombian Association of Flower Exporters)
ASOHORFRUCOL	Asociación de Cultivadores Hortalizas y Frutas de Colombia (Colombian Association of Horticultural and Fruit Producers)
CENIACUA	Centro de Investigaciones de la Acuicultura de Colombia (Colombian Research Center for Aquaculture)
CENICAFE	Centro Nacional de Investigaciones de Café (National Coffee Research Center)
CENICAÑA	Centro de Investigaciones de Caña de Colombia (Colombian Sugarcane Research Center)
CENIPALMA	Centro de Investigaciones en Palma de Aceite (Oilpalm Research Center)
CENIUVA	Centro de Investigación de Uva (Grape Research Center)

CEVIPAPA	Centro Virtual de Investigación de la Cadena Agroindustrial de la Papa (Virtual Center for Research in the Agroindustrial Chain of Potatoes)
CIAT	Centro Internacional de Agricultura Tropical (International Center for Tropical Agriculture)
CIMMYT	Centro Internacional de Mejoramiento de Maíz y Trigo (International Maize and Wheat Improvement Center)
COLCIENCIAS	Instituto Colombiano para el Desarrollo de la Ciencia y la Tecnología (Colombian Institute for Science and Technology Development)
CORPOICA	Corporación Colombiana de Investigación Agropecuaria (Colombian Corporation for Agricultural Research)
DIA	Dirección de Investigaciones Agropecuarias (Division of Agricultural Research)
FEDECACAO	Federación Nacional de Cacaoteros (National Federation of Cocoa Producers)
FEDECAFE	Federación Nacional de Cafeteros (National Federation of Coffee Producers)
FEDEPALMA	Federación de Cultivadoras de Palma de Aceite (Federation of Oilpalm Growers)
FEDEPAPA	Federación Colombiano de Productores de Papa (Colombian Federation of Potato Producers)
FEDERALGODON	Federación Nacional de Algodoneros (National Federation of Cotton Producers)
FEDERARROZ	Federación Nacional de Arroceros (National Federation of Rice Growers)
FENALCE	Federación Nacional de Cultivadores de Cereales (National Federation of Cereal Growers)
ICA	Instituto Colombiano Agropecuario (Colombian Agricultural Institute)
IDB	Inter-American Development Bank
IFPRI	International Food Policy Research Institute
INPA	Instituto Nacional de Pesca y Acuicultura (National Institute for Fisheries and Agriculture)

ISNAR   International Service for National Agricultural Research

MADR   Ministerio de Agricultura y Desarrollo Rural (Ministry of Agriculture and Rural Development)

OIE   Oficina de Investigaciones Especiales (Office of Special Research)

PRONATTA   Programa Nacional de Transferencia de Tecnología Agropecuaria (Program for the Transfer of Agricultural Technology)

UPOV   International Union for the Protection of New Varieties of Plants

Notes

This chapter is a summarized and updated version of *Agricultural R&D in Colombia: Policy, Investments, and Institutional Profile,* a report prepared by N. M. Beintema, L. Romano, and P. G. Pardey in 2000 as part of the Agricultural Science and Technology Indicators (ASTI) initiative. The authors thank Olympia Icochea for her valuable research assistance.

1. Producer organizations are also significant sources of agricultural R&D funds in some Central American countries, such as Costa Rica, Guatemala, and Honduras. In 1996, nonprofit organizations accounted for 45 percent of total agricultural R&D investments in these three countries, a percentage which was much higher than the share of nonprofit institutions in Colombia's total spending the same year. However, for these countries, research by nonprofit organizations is a much more recent phenomenon; most Colombian nonprofit organizations initiated their research activities several decades ago (Pardey and Beintema 2001).

2. Although CORPOICA was officially established in 1993, it did not initiate research until January 1, 1994. Public agricultural R&D agencies include government agencies, higher-education institutions, and nonprofit institutions. For additional information and other definitions used in this chapter, see the ASTI website at http://www.asti.cgiar.org.

3. In 1950, the office employed 2 Rockefeller scientists and 3 Colombian scientists; over the next 5 years these numbers grew significantly, to 11 Rockefeller and 40 Colombian scientists. Also, through fellowships granted by the Rockefeller Foundation, 30 Colombians received postgraduate training at U.S. universities from 1950 to 1955. Other Colombian nationals were sent to the Rockefeller Foundation program in Mexico for short-term training courses.

4. The objectives of this virtual center, named the Center for Research in the Agro-industrial Chain of Potatoes (CEVIPAPA), are to coordinate potato research, linking the input, on-farm, and postharvest aspects of potato production; to develop a technological information database; to evaluate existing technologies in Colombia and abroad; to identify methodologies for transferring technologies to small farmers; to support socioeconomic studies; and to cooperate with national and international research agencies. CEVIPAPA also disburses research funds obtained through the voluntary contributions of the potato farmers collected by FEDEPAPA. Because FEDEPAPA still conducts some of its own research (although this activity has decreased since the creation of CEVIPAPA), some of the research funds are channeled back from CEVIPAPA to FEDEPAPA.

5. The competitive scheme managed by COLCIENCIAS also experienced a decline in the total amount of funds available for distribution. Total funding for the 11 programs peaked in 1996; by 2000 it had declined to about the same level as in 1990. The program for the agricultural sector was about 4 billion pesos in 1996–97, declining to 600 million pesos in 2000. The available funds for 2001 increased slightly to 1 billion pesos—still well below the 1996–97 amount. This decline reflects the ongoing economic crisis as well as discontinuation of an IDB loan. A new loan was negotiated in 1996 and became operational in 1998.

6. MADR set up a special contract with CIAT to conduct research focusing on the oriental plains and research on fruits, grasses, rice, corn (in collaboration with CIMMYT), biotechnology, geographic information systems, production systems, and so on. This project ran from 1998 to 2003; a total of US$2 million of government funds were scheduled to be disbursed to CIAT each year. CIAT collaborates with CORPOICA on some of the research activities under this project, and in 2001 CORPOICA received about 5 million pesos for this joint work.

7. The financial data in this chapter were converted to 1999 international dollars by first deflating funds compiled in current local-currency units using a Colombia GDP deflator with the base year 1999, and then converting to U.S. dollars using a 1999 purchasing power parity (PPP) index from World Bank 2001. PPPs are synthetic exchange rates used to reflect the purchasing power of currencies, typically comparing prices across a broader range of goods and services than conventional exchange rates.

8. FEDEPAPA requested that the government impose a mandatory levy on potato production and sales but did not get approval for this levy. FEDEPAPA, however, has received some funds from the mandatory levy on fruits and horticultural products (the latter including potatoes).

9. This is similar to the residual claim that research has on most commodity check-off programs in the United States (Alston et al. 1996) but distinct from the levy funding of research in Australia under the Primary Industry and Energy Research and Development Act (1985 and 1989), under which all the funds must be used to support R&D (Alston et al. 1999).

10. Compiling expenditure data for higher-education agencies proved difficult. The data obtained often included only the direct research expenditures—such as the operational costs associated with university research or project funds received from external sources—rather than a comprehensive accounting of the costs, including salaries, rent, and utilities appropriately prorated to reflect the share of total faculty time spent on research. To redress these problems, an estimate of total expenditures for the higher-education sector was calculated using the average expenditures per researcher for government agencies and nonprofit institutions, scaled by the number of fte researchers employed by the higher-education institutions in our sample.

11. In 1996, these six nonprofit institutions accounted for 80 percent of the total research spending by the 11 nonprofit institutions.

12. In 2001, only 18 CORPOICA researchers were undertaking postgraduate studies, down from 39 in 1998 (CORPOICA, pers. comm., 2001).

13. Private participation in agricultural R&D is related to the appropriability of the revenue streams from the resulting technologies. The existence and effectiveness of intellectual property rights directly affects the extent of appropriablity. In 1996 Colombia acceded to plant varietal rights that are compatible with those of the International Union for Protection of New Varieties of Plants (UPOV) but does not currently allow for the patenting of plant varieties. Colombia is also a signatory to Decision 391 of the Andean Pact, which deems that material found in nature is a "discovery" and therefore not patentable.

References

Acosta, O. L., and M. Gómez. 1998. Programa nacional de ciencia y tecnología agropecuaria (National program for agricultural science and technology). *Colombia: Ciencia y Tecnología* 16 (2): 3–11.

Acquaye, A. K. A., J. M. Alston, and P. G. Pardey. 2003. Post-war productivity patterns in U.S. agriculture: Influences of aggregation procedures in a state-level analysis. *American Journal of Agricultural Economics* 85 (1): 59–80.

Alston, J. M., H. Lee, H. F. Carman, and W. Sutton, eds. 1996. *Mandated marketing programs for California commodities.* Giannini Foundation Information Series No. 96-1. Berkeley, Calif.: Giannini Foundation of Agricultural Economics.

Alston, J. M., M. S. Harris, J. D. Mullen, and P. G. Pardey. 1999. Agricultural R&D policy in Australia. Chapter 5 in *Paying for agricultural productivity,* ed. J. M. Alston, P. G. Pardey, and V. H. Smith. Baltimore: Johns Hopkins University Press.

Aragón, J., and F. Forero. 1976. Estudio socioeconómico de las inversiones realizadas en investigación y fomento de la palma africana en Colombia. *Revista ICA* 11 (3): 243–256.

Ardila, J. 1973. Rentabilidad social de las inversiones en investigaciones de arroz en Colombia. M.Sc. thesis. Programa de Guaduades, Universidad Nacional de Colombia, Bogotá.

Beintema, N. M., and P. G. Pardey. 2001. Recent developments in the conduct of Latin American agricultural research. Paper prepared for the International Conference on Agricultural Science and Technology, Beijing. November 7–9.

Beintema, N. M., L. Romano, and P. G. Pardey. 2000. *Agricultural R&D in Colombia: Policy, investments, and institutional profile.* Washington, D.C.: International Food Policy Research Institute and FONTAGRO.

Berdegue, J. A., and G. Escobar. 1999. Programa Nacional de Transferencia de Tecnología Agropecuaria (National Program for the Transfer of Agricultural Technology). PRONATTA, Ministry of Agriculture and Rural Development, Colombia, and International Network of Farming Systems Research Methodology, Santiago, Chile. Mimeo.

CORPOICA (Corporación Colombiana de Investigación Agropecuaria). N.d. The Corporación Colombiana de Investigación Agropecuaria CORPOICA: A new approach to agricultural research in Colombia. CORPOICA, Bogotá. Mimeo.

DNP–COLCIENCIAS (Departamento Nacional de Planeación and Instituto Colombiano para el Desarrollo de la Ciencia y la Tecnología). 2000. *Política nacional de ciencia y tecnología.* Documento CONPES No 3080. Bogotá: COLCIENCIAS.

Estrada, R. D., F. Holmann, and R. Posada. 2002. Farmer and industry funding of agricultural research in Colombia. Chapter 4 in *Agricultural research policy in an era of privatization,* ed. D. Byerlee and R. G. Echeverría. Wallingford, U.K.: CAB International.

El Espectador. 2002. Se desplomo la confianza. March 31.

Falconi, C. A., and P. G. Pardey. 1993. *Statistical brief on the national agricultural research system of Colombia.* Statistical Brief No. 6. The Hague: International Service for National Agricultural Research.

FAO (Food and Agriculture Organization of the United Nations). 2002. FAOSTAT database. http://faostat.fao.org/default.htm. Accessed August 13, 2002.

———. 2005. FAOSTAT database. http://faostat.fao.org/default.htm. Accessed September 2005.

Farfán, M. 1999. *Impacto económico de la investigación en café en Colombia: El caso de la variedad Colombia.* Documento CEDE 99-03. Bogotá: Centro de Estudios sobre el Desarrollo Económico, Universidad de Los Andes, Bogotá.

Hertford, R. 1996. El sistema nacional de tecnología y servicios agropecuarios de Colombia: Analisis y apoyo propuesto. Washington, D.C. Mimeo.

IMF (International Monetary Fund). *International financial statistics yearbook 2001.* Washington, D.C.: IMF.

Jaramillo, F. 1976. Evaluación económica de las inversiones en la investigación sobre el cultivo de la cebada. *ICA Boletín de Investigación* 42.

Machado, A. 2000. *La reactivacion agropecuaria una siembra incierta.* UN Periodico. No. 12 (July).

Montes, G. 1973. Evaluación de un programa de investigación agrícola: El caso de la soya. M.Sc. thesis, Universidad de Los Andes, Bogotá.

Pardey, P. G., and N. M. Beintema. 2001. *Slow magic: Agricultural R&D a century after Mendel.* IFPRI Food Policy Report. Washington, D.C.: International Food Policy Research Institute.

Peña, M. 1976. Evaluación económica de las inversiones estatales en investigación sobre el cultivo de la papa. Thesis, Universidad La Gran Colombia.

PRONATTA (Programa Nacional de Transferencia de Tecnología Agropecuaria). 2000. Informe de Gestión Consolidado Fondo Competitivo PRONATTA: Convocatorias 1995–98. Ministerio de Agricultura y Desarrollo Rural, Bogotá, Colombia. Mimeo.

Romano, L. 1987. Economic evaluation of the Colombian agricultural research system. Ph.D. diss., Oklahoma State University, Stillwater.

———. 2000. Integrated framework to analyze agricultural research impact. Poster at the 24th Congress of the International Association of Agricultural Economists, Berlin. August 13–19.

Romano, L., A. Bermeo, and M. Torregrosa. 1994. *Impacto socioeconómico de la investigación del ICA en el cultivo del sorgo.* Boletín Técnico. Bogotá: ICA.

Scobie, G., and R. Posada. 1977. *The impact of rice varieties in Latin America, with special emphasis on Colombia.* Series JE–01. Cali, Colombia: Centro Internacional de Agricultura Tropical.

El Tiempo. 2002. Deuda: Bola de nieve que amenaza con rodar. March 31.

Trigo, E. J., G. Traxler, C. Pray, and R. Echeverría. 2001. Agricultural biotechnology and rural development in Latin America and the Caribbean. Chapter 12 in *The future of food: Biotechnology markets and policies in an international setting,* ed. P. G. Pardey. Washington, D.C.: International Food Policy Research Institute.

Trujillo, C. 1974. Rendimiento económico de la investigación en trigo en Colombia. M.Sc. thesis, Programa de Guaduades, Universidad Nacional de Colombia, Bogotá.

UNCSTD (United Nations Commission on Science and Technology for Development), UNTAD (United Nations Conference on Trade and Development), and COLCIENCIAS (Instituto Colombiano para el Desarrollo de la Ciencia y la Tecnología). 1997. Productividad, innovación y desarrollo tecnológico en Colombia: Situación actual y políticas de fomento. COLCIENCIAS, Bogotá. Mimeo.

Vivas, L., J. Zuluaga, and H. Castro. 1992. *Las nuevas variedades de caña y su impacto económico en el sector azucarero del valle del cauca.* Cali, Colombia: Universidad del Valle.

Weersma-Haworth, T. 1984. Colombian case study. CGIAR impact study. Consultative Group on International Agricultural Research, Washington, D.C. Mimeo.

World Bank. 1983. *Staff appraisal report, Colombia: Agricultural research and extension project I.* Washington, D.C.

———. 1995. *Staff appraisal report, Colombia: Agricultural technology development project.* Washington, D.C.

———. 1999. Colombia agriculture technology development project. http://www.worldbank.org/pics/pid/co6868.txt. Accessed October 22, 1999.

———. 2001. *World development indicators 2001.* Washington, D.C. CD-ROM.

———. 2005. *World development indicators 2005.* Washington, D.C. CD-ROM.

Chapter 12

International Initiatives in Agricultural R&D: The Changing Fortunes of the CGIAR

Julian M. Alston, Steven Dehmer, and Philip G. Pardey

Introduction

Many believe that agricultural productivity growth, driven by research-induced technical change, is essential to long-run economic development. Consequently, a strategy of agriculture-led development has been a critical element in aid and economic-development policy around the world since World War II. An important component of this strategy has been the progressive development of the system of international agricultural research centers (IARCs) known as the Consultative Group on International Agricultural Research (CGIAR, or CG for short), in conjunction with and as a complement to the national agricultural research systems (NARSs) in developing countries.

When the CG was formed in 1971, 16 donors committed $20.7 million annually to found and foster research in four centers with headquarters in Mexico, the Philippines, Colombia, and Nigeria. In 2004, the CG spent about $425 million (including $19 million for so-called Challenge Programs), which it received from 63 members representing 22 industrial countries, 24 transitioning and developing countries, 13 international and regional organizations, and 4 foundations, supplemented by funds that totaled $16 million from Center-generated income and other sources. The CG now supports the work of 15 international agricultural research centers, with a combined total in 2004 of 1,063 internationally recruited staff and just over 6,700 locally recruited scientific and support staff.

The CG, which accounts for just 1.5 percent of global public spending on agricultural R&D (Pardey and Beintema 2001), has had a disproportionately large effect on improving productivity for large numbers of the world's farmers, increasing global food supplies, and lowering the cost of food for all the world's consumers. These results have come mainly from the release and widespread adoption of the yield-enhancing crop varieties bred by CG scientists, but also through R&D addressing pest, disease, and other production problems. The CG has also trained thousands of scientists and research staff and assembled one of the world's largest holdings of agricultural genetic resources.[1]

Despite the handsome and quite visible payoffs to past CG research, growth in funding for the CGIAR effectively stalled during most of the 1990s. Many fundamental considerations point to more, not less, international R&D. Growth in funding has resumed more recently, and total funding for the CG has increased by 5.5 percent per annum since 2000. Nevertheless, there are continuing grounds for concern about funding for the system.

The form and focus of CG funding have changed markedly, too. A rising share of the available funds is now earmarked for specific projects by donors (often with implicit or explicit requirements for tie-ins with donor-country institutions or scientists). And, in the past two decades, the CG has broadened its research horizons, moving away from its traditional focus on basic food crops to include environmental issues and other commodities, such as forest products and fish. Because this expanding agenda and the increased number of CG centers were not matched by commensurate increases in funding, CG breeding and crop-improvement work was scaled back, with inevitable implications for alleviating hunger worldwide.[2]

Institutional Beginnings

The seeds of the CGIAR were sown by private foundations. Beginning in the mid-1940s and accelerating through the 1950s, the Ford and Rockefeller foundations pioneered a series of bilateral, commodity-oriented cooperative research efforts that linked U.S. scientists and institutions with developing-country NARSs.[3] The first such venture was a cooperative program of the Mexican government and the Rockefeller Foundation, established in 1943 to conduct wheat research, which later evolved to become the International Maize and Wheat Improvement Center (CIMMYT). Another notable example was the rice research program at Los Baños, in the Philippines, that led the Rockefeller Foundation, in partnership with the Ford Foundation, to establish the International Rice Research Institute (IRRI) in 1960. Closely following these developments came the establishment of the International Institute of Tropical Agriculture (IITA) at Ibadan, Nigeria, in 1967, and Centro Internacional de Agricultura Tropical (CIAT) in Cali, Colombia, in 1968.

The further development of IARCs took place largely under the auspices of the CGIAR. The CGIAR is an informal organization providing oversight to a system of international research centers, a mechanism for collectively funding those centers, and a forum to discuss and affirm overall research-policy objectives.[4] Table 12.1 provides a chronology of major CGIAR systemwide activities. Developments regarding the CG (now also known as Future Harvest) centers themselves are briefly chronicled in the section that follows.

The Centers of the CGIAR, 1971–2005

The institutional development of the CG centers involved three main phases (Table 12.2).[5] In the first period, the four founding centers developed independently. The second phase took place in the decade that followed the formal establishment of the CGIAR in 1971. At that time, the CGIAR was relatively narrowly focused on what was perceived to be the main problem in developing countries: food deficits. The original mission statement read:

> To support research and technology that can potentially increase food production in food-deficit countries of the world. The research activities supported by the CGIAR are appropriately focused on food commodities which are widely consumed and collectively represent the majority of the food sources of the developing world and no major changes or additions are called for at this time. (CGIAR 1977, p. iv)

Norman Borlaug, Nobel laureate and founding director of CIMMYT's wheat program, reiterated this food-focused goal for the CGIAR in 1982:

> The mandates of the IARCs call for them to orient their research, training and technical assistance activities toward increasing the absolute availability of world food supplies, with particular emphasis on food production in the developing world. IARC research activities are to concentrate on those critical aspects of food production in the developing world that are not being adequately addressed elsewhere, which offer potential of widespread benefits of food security, either regionally or globally, and which address the problems of producers in low-income, food-deficit countries. (1982, p. 66)[6]

In keeping with this broad objective, seven centers were added that dealt with different issues, including different commodities, farming systems (agroecologies in

Table 12.1 Chronology of CGIAR and related events, 1940–2004

Year	Event
1940	Henry Wallace, U.S. vice president–elect, returns from an extended trip to Mexico and conveys the idea of a research-based "Green Revolution" to Raymond Fosdick, president of the Rockefeller Foundation.
1944–60	Norman Borlaug leads the wheat-improvement activities of the Cooperative Mexican Agricultural Program (OEE), a joint initiative by the Mexican Ministry of Agriculture and the Rockefeller Foundation.
1960	International Rice Research Institute (IRRI), established in Los Baños, the Philippines.
1966	International Maize and Wheat Improvement Center (CIMMYT) established in El Batan, Mexico.
1967	International Institute for Tropical Agriculture (IITA) established in Ibadan, Nigeria, and International Center for Tropical Agriculture (CIAT) in Cali, Colombia.
1969–71	Prefounding meetings for CGIAR held in Bellagio, Italy.
1971	First formal meeting of the Consultative Group for International Agricultural Research, presided over by Richard H. Demuth, director of the World Bank's Development Services Department and first CGIAR chair, in Washington, D.C., May 19, 1971.
	IRRI, CIMMYT, IITA, and CIAT begin receiving CGIAR support.
1974	Warren Baum becomes CGIAR chair.
1975	First developing-country members (Nigeria and Saudi Arabia) join CGIAR.
1977	First system review of the CGIAR.
1981	Second system review of the CGIAR.
1983	CGIAR begins conducting external management reviews.
	CGIAR begins conducting impact studies.
1984	S. Shahid Hussain becomes CGIAR chair.
1987	W. David Hopper becomes CGIAR chair.
1988	Review of TAC (Technical Advisory Committee) Secretariat conducted.
	Expansion inquiry initiated by the CGIAR.
1989	Canberra Declaration expands CGIAR's commitment to forestry and forest resources.
1990	Wilfried Thalwitz becomes CGIAR chair.
1991	Expansion of CGIAR through inclusion of natural resources centers begins.
	V. Rajagopalan becomes CGIAR chair.
1992	Ecoregional and systemwide programs introduced.
1993	Financial crisis (United States and other nations significantly cut funding).
	Chair commissions TAC restructuring study.
1994	Ismail Serageldin becomes CGIAR chair.
	ILCA and ILRAD merge to become ILRI.
	INIBAP folded into IPGRI.
1995	Ministerial-level meeting held in Lucerne, Switzerland. Lucerne Declaration reaffirms donor support to CGIAR; endorses focus on poverty, sustainability, and food security; and calls for broadened partnerships and increased attention to impact.
	CGIAR changes formula for allocation of World Bank resources.
	World Bank provides $20 million emergency financial support.
	Developing-country membership begins to increase significantly.
	UNEP becomes co-sponsor.
1997	CGIAR commissions third system review.
	Developing-country members outnumber industrialized-country members.
1998	Third system review of the CGIAR completed.
1999	CGIAR begins internal reform process, commissioning TAC to outline new vision and strategy.

Table 12.1 (continued)

Year	Event
2000	Ian Johnson becomes CGIAR chair.
	Consultative Council phased out.
	TAC presents and group endorses draft vision and strategy.
	UNEP withdraws from co-sponsor position.
2001	Science Partnership Committee, Oversight Committee, and Finance Committees dissolved.
	Interim Executive Council (Exco) established, followed by establishment of Exco and its Program Committee and Finance Committee.
	TAC dissolved; interim Science Council established.
	Phase 1 of Challenge Programs initiated.
	IFAD becomes co-sponsor.
2003	Three pilot Challenge Programs begin formal operations.
2004	ISNAR closed and elements incorporated as a division within IFPRI.
	CGIAR Science Council formed.

particular), and livestock diseases. These included the International Potato Center (CIP), the West Africa Rice Development Association (WARDA), the International Crops Research Institute for the Semi-Arid Tropics (ICRISAT), the International Laboratory for Research on Animal Diseases (ILRAD), the International Livestock Center for Africa (ILCA), the International Plant Genetic Resources Institute (IPGRI, previously IBPGR), and the International Center for Agricultural Research in the Dry Areas (ICARDA). In addition, two social science centers—IFPRI and the International Service for National Agricultural Research (ISNAR), which was closed in 2004 and now constitutes a division within IFPRI—were created and incorporated.[7]

This expanded group of 13 centers constituted the CGIAR throughout the 1980s. The system grew, and each center grew with it. Changes took place in the context of the most rapid growth of total spending experienced by the system, and a relatively simple and well-understood purpose. A culture developed in which research resources seemed abundant. At the same time, pressures were developing to extend the research agenda and place more emphasis on environmental sustainability, nutrition, income distribution, and poverty. Consequently, in the mid-1980s, the emphasis shifted. A new goals statement for the system was adopted in 1986, defined by the CGIAR's Technical Advisory Committee (TAC) Secretariat as follows:

> Through international agricultural research and related activities, to contribute to increasing sustainable food production in developing countries

Table 12.2 CGIAR-supported centers

Center	First year of CGIAR support	Foundation date	Location of headquarters	Commodities	Main areas of focus: Research activities	Main areas of focus: Region	2004 expenditures (million U.S. dollars)
International Rice Research Institute (IRRI)	1971	1960	Los Baños, Philippines	Rice	Rice-based ecosystems	World Asia	32.9
International Maize and Wheat Improvement Center (CIMMYT)	1971	1966	El Batan, Mexico	Wheat and maize		World	41.1
International Center for Tropical Agriculture (CIAT)	1971	1967	Cali, Colombia	*Phaseolus* beans and cassava	Tropical pastures Rice	World Lowland tropics Latin America	36.7
International Institute of Tropical Agriculture (IITA)	1971	1967	Ibadan, Nigeria	Cassava, cowpeas, maize, plantains and bananas, soybeans, and yams	Smallholder cropping and postharvest systems	World Dry, moist, and midaltitude savannas, and humid forests	42.6
International Crops Research Institute for the Semi-Arid Tropics (ICRISAT)	1972	1972	Patancheru, India	Sorghum, millet, pigeonpeas, chickpeas, and groundnuts	Farming systems	World Semi-arid tropics (Asia, Africa)	26.8
International Potato Center (CIP)	1973	1970	Lima, Peru	Potato, sweet potato, and other root crops		World	21.5

Center	Year	Year	Location	Research focus	Region	
International Laboratory for Research on Animal Diseases (ILRAD)[a]	1973	1973	Nairobi, Kenya	See ILRI		NA
International Livestock Center for Africa (ILCA)[a]	1974	1974	Addis Ababa, Ethiopia	See ILRI		NA
International Plant Genetic Resources Institute (IPGRI)[b]	1974	1974	Rome, Italy	Collection, conservation, evolution, and utilization of germplasm	World	32.0
Africa Rice Center (WARDA)[c]	1975	1971	Bouaké, Côte d'Ivoire	Rice	Sub-Saharan Africa	10.1
International Center for Agricultural Research in the Dry Areas (ICARDA)	1977	1977	Aleppo, Syria	Barley, lentils, faba beans Farming systems Wheat, kabali, and chickpeas	North Africa and Near East North Africa and Near East, world North Africa and Near East	24.6
International Service for National Agricultural Research (ISNAR)[d]	1980	1979	The Hague, Netherlands	Strengthen national agricultural research systems	World	2.4
International Food Policy Research Institute (IFPRI)	1980	1975	Washington, D.C., USA	Identify and analyze policies for sustainably meeting the food needs of the developing world	World, with primary emphasis on low-income countries and groups	31.4
World Agroforestry Centre[e]	1991	1977	Nairobi, Kenya	Agroforestry, multi-purpose trees	World	28.5

(continued)

Table 12.2 (continued)

Center	First year of CGIAR support	Foundation date	Location of headquarters	Commodity	Main focus Activities	Main focus Region	2004 expenditures (million U.S. dollars)
International Water Management Institute (IWMI)[f]	1991	1984	Colombo, Sri Lanka		Water and irrigation management	World	23.1
WorldFish Center[g]	1992	1977	Batu Maung, Malaysia		Sustainable aquatic-resource management	World	14.1
Center for International Forestry Research (CIFOR)	1993	1993	Bogor, Indonesia		Sustainable forestry management	World	15.1
ILRI, International Livestock Research Institute (ILRI)[h]	1995	1995	Nairobi, Kenya, and Addis Ababa, Ethiopia		Livestock production and animal health	World	31.7

Sources: Baum 1986; TAC 1987; CGIAR Secretariat, various years; and Web sites of respective centers.

Note: NA indicates not applicable.

[a] In 1995, ILRAD and ILCA were merged to form ILRI. ILCA did research on animal feed and production systems for cattle, sheep, and goats for sub-Saharan Africa.

[b] First established in 1974 as the International Board of Plant Genetic Resources (IBPGR). The Board was funded as a CG center but operated under the administration of the Food and Agriculture Organization of the United Nations (FAO), located at FAO headquarters in Rome. In 1993, IBPGR changed its name to IPGRI and was established as a self-administering CG center with headquarters in Rome. The International Network for the Improvement of Banana and Plantain (INIBAP) was established in Montpellier, France, in 1984. In 1992, INIBAP became a CG-sponsored center, but in 1994 INIBAP's functions were placed under the administration of IPGRI. INIBAP, however, continues to maintain its own board.

[c] Formerly known as the West Africa Rice Development Association. Originally located in Liberia, the organization moved to Bouaké, Côte d'Ivoire, in 1987, and has been working out of the IITA station in Cotonou, Benin, since January 2005 because of civil unrest in Côte d'Ivoire.

[d] Ceased operations in March 2004 and was reconstituted as a division within IFPRI in April 2004.

[e] Known as the International Centre for Research in Agroforestry (ICRAF) until 2002.

[f] Known as the International Irrigation Management Institute (IIMI) until 1998.

[g] Formerly known as the International Centre for Living Aquatic Resource Management (ICLARM); its headquarters were relocated from Metro Manila to Batu Maung, Malaysia, in 2001.

[h] ILRI became operational in January 1995 through a merger of ILRAD and ILCA. ILRAD research focused on livestock diseases (world) and tick-borne disease and trypanosomiasis (sub-Saharan Africa).

in such a way that the nutritional and general economic well-being of low-income people are improved. (TAC 1987, p. 219)

The third phase of the evolution of the CG system was instituted in 1990. At that time the establishment was extended to include five more centers, several of which had existed for a decade or more as independent operations.[8] The new CG centers included the World Agroforestry Centre (previously ICRAF), the International Water Management Institute (IWMI, previously IIMI), the WorldFish Center (previously ICLARM), the International Network for Improvement of Banana and Plantain (INIBAP, now closed as a stand-alone center and reconstituted as a networking organization incorporated into IPGRI), and the Center for International Forestry Research (CIFOR). Thus the mandate of the system was extended to include agroforestry, aquaculture, irrigation, and forestry. In the beginning of 1995, ILCA and ILRAD were merged to form the International Livestock Research Institute (ILRI), perhaps signaling the beginning of a fourth phase in the history of the CGIAR: an era of consolidation and contraction, as the organization was forced to economize in the face of resource constraints and slower growth. Notwithstanding the increasing fiscal constraints on the system, the next version of the CG mission statement—proposed by the third external review panel (CGIAR System Review Secretariat 1998, p. 11) and adopted at the October 1998 annual meeting—reaffirmed a broad agenda for the CG, which after minor subsequent revision read:

> To contribute to food security and poverty eradication in developing countries through research, partnerships, capacity building, and policy support, promoting sustainable agricultural development based on the environmentally sound management of natural resources. (CGIAR 2003a)

The latest version of the CG's mission statement is more outcome-oriented but still encompasses the broad agenda introduced in the 1990s. It now reads:

> To achieve sustainable food security and reduce poverty in developing countries through scientific research and research-related activities in the fields of agriculture, forestry, fisheries, policy, and environment. (CGIAR Science Council 2005b)

The essential story is one of mission creep, a broadening of the agenda—in line with the same trends in agricultural research agendas in rich-country NARSs—but without a commensurate increase in the amount of funding. In addition, in parallel with these developments, as described below, the cost of doing business rose, along with institutional complexity and the costs of seeking and allocating resources.

Funding Patterns of the CGIAR

While the CG system has captured the attention of the international agricultural R&D and aid communities through its scientific achievements and its pivotal role in the Green Revolution, it has spent only a small fraction of the global agricultural R&D investment. In 1995, the CG represented 1.5 percent of the nearly $22 billion (in 1993 prices) global public-sector investment in agricultural R&D and 1.0 percent of all public and private spending. Data on the evolution of CGIAR spending and the distribution of funds among the various centers are included in Appendix Table 12A.1. The data in the table represent expenditures from all funding sources in inflation-adjusted (1999 U.S. dollar) values. Figure 12.1 plots the nominal and real (that is, adjusted for inflation) values of total expenditures for the CGIAR.

The Evolution of Total Funding

The CG system began modestly. Between 1960 and 1964, of the institutes that would become the CG, only IRRI was operating as such. After an initial expenditure of $7.4 million in 1960, total spending rose to $1.3 million per year in 1965.[9] By 1970, the four founding centers—IRRI, CIMMYT, IITA, and CIAT—were allocated a total of $14.8 million annually. The progressive expansion of the number of centers, and the funding per center, during the next decade involved a 10-fold increase in nominal spending, to $141 million in 1980. During the 1980s, spending continued to grow, more than doubling in nominal terms to reach $305 million in 1990. The rate of growth had slowed but was still impressive. In the 1990s, however, although the number of centers grew—from 13 to 18 before contracting to the current 15—funding did not grow enough to maintain the level of spending per center, let alone sustain the growth rates. Since 2000, total funding has grown, but with a continuing trend toward support earmarked for specific projects and programs of research involving multiple centers and research providers outside the CG.

Figure 12.1 shows trends in the distribution of total CG system funding to the founding four centers, the nine added in the 1970s, and the 1990s expansion centers. In the early years of plenty, all the centers grew together, but they did not grow at the same rate. Funding allocated to the four founding centers has declined significantly. In 1971, these centers accounted for 100 percent of the allocation. By 1980, their share had slipped to 54 percent, and by 2004 it was down to 36 percent. During the stagnation of the 1990s, nine centers experienced a nominal decline in support, including the four original centers, CIP, ICRISAT, ILRI, ICARDA, and ISNAR. The centers being downgraded tended to be the larger centers. Among the pre-1990 centers, IPGRI grew the fastest, with its funding more

Figure 12.1 Nominal and real expenditures of CGIAR-supported centers

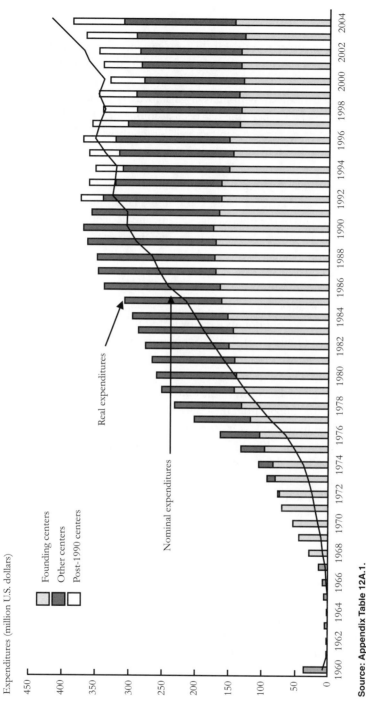

Expenditures (million U.S. dollars)

Founding centers
Other centers
Post-1990 centers

Real expenditures

Nominal expenditures

Source: Appendix Table 12A.1.

Notes: Pre-1972 expenditures represent those of precursor international research institutes. Data for IRRI are from 1960 onward, data for IITA are from 1965 onward, data from CIMMYT are from 1966 onward, and data for CIAT are from 1968 onward.

than doubling in just five years. Of the new entrants, the two forestry institutes showed the greatest gains. These broad trends indicate that, through both the addition of new centers and the allocation of funds among centers, the agenda of the CG shifted dramatically away from its original focus, especially in the 1990s.

Stagnant total CG spending has been accompanied by a shift in spending away from conducting research—intramurally or jointly with others—toward other activities. These other activities include hosting and managing research networks that facilitate research performed by others, some in conjunction with CG centers (Plucknett, Smith, and Özgediz 1990); rehabilitating seed stocks in war-ravaged countries like Rwanda, Afghanistan, and Cambodia; promoting zero-till systems in the wheat systems of the Indo-Ganges Plains; and developing smallholder milk-supply systems in Africa. Some of these initiatives entail technology-transfer activities that complement CG research; others involve a move into development efforts less directly related to research.

Changing Donor Roles

Over time, the number of donors has grown, and the pattern of support they provide has changed (Table 12.3). The U.S. government and U.S.-based foundations originally contributed two-thirds of the total. The support from foundations has declined steadily. The support from the U.S. government declined precipitously and relatively recently, especially in the mid-1990s (with some small reversal of this trend since 2000). Support from the Canadian government followed suit (although Canada doubled its previous year's contribution in 2003 and increased funding by another 60 percent in 2004). Taken together, in real terms the support from Canada and the United States in 2001 was equivalent to what they gave in 1977; and, even with the recent recovery, their combined funding in 2004 was still only 80 percent of that sustained during most of the 1980s and early 1990s. This North American withdrawal during the 1990s—a crucial event in the recent history of the CG—was offset to some degree by a substantial increase in Japanese support during that period. Japan's support has faltered in the past few years, however, as that country's economy has stalled, and it dropped by half in 2002.

In the beginning (using 1972 figures), the private foundations provided 49 percent of the total funding. European nations as a group provided 15 percent; the United States 18 percent; and the World Bank 6 percent. The picture is now very different. If the private foundations intended to provide seed money and eventually be displaced, they were successful. Their funding support has fallen in nominal terms and now constitutes less than 3 percent of the total. In 2004, European nations as a group (including multilateral support through the European Commission) provided $181 million, or 41.4 percent of the total. In the same year the World

Table 12.3 Donor contributions to the CGIAR

Donor	1972–75	1976–80	1981–85	1986–90	1991–95	1996–2000	2001–03	2004	Total	Present value[a]
Contribution (million 1999 U.S. dollars per year)										
European Union	18.4	44.0	47.2	79.0	86.9	89.9	90.4	115.8	2,195.6	3,190.9
Other European	2.3	6.8	11.3	20.0	25.1	30.3	24.3	27.7	577.3	785.2
Subtotal European	20.8	50.8	58.5	99.0	112.0	120.2	114.7	143.4	2,772.9	3,976.1
Japan	0.9	7.8	14.9	28.3	36.4	36.7	19.3	13.4	695.8	1,012.3
United States	19.2	45.7	75.3	76.3	59.7	40.2	49.0	50.3	1,759.9	2,976.6
Other	10.1	20.6	22.3	28.4	29.4	21.6	21.1	39.5	754.4	1,222.2
More-developed countries	51.0	124.9	171.1	232.0	237.5	218.7[b]	204.1	246.7	5,983.0	9,187.3
Less-developed countries	0.4	4.6	4.9	1.8	3.7	12.7	12.6	16.8	194.8	245.2
World Bank	7.0	19.2	31.5	41.3	47.4	45.6	45.9	47.3	1,137.3	1,663.9
Other international and regional organizations	10.2	32.3	50.6	47.5	47.4	41.4	43.7	49.1	1,317.0	2,099.6
Foundations	23.8	7.1	4.7	4.9	7.0	7.2	10.4	9.8	290.9	580.5
Other donors	0.0	0.0	4.0	9.9	6.4	13.2	23.0	37.5	273.6	270.2
Total	92.4	188.1	266.7	337.4	349.4	338.7	339.7	407.2	9,196.8	14,046.7
Percentage of total budget										
European Union	20.0	23.4	17.7	23.4	24.9	26.5	26.6	28.4	23.9	22.7
Other European	2.5	3.6	4.2	5.9	7.2	8.9	7.1	6.8	6.3	5.6
Subtotal European	22.5	27.0	21.9	29.4	32.0	35.5	33.8	35.2	30.2	28.3
Japan	1.0	4.1	5.6	8.4	10.4	10.8	5.7	3.3	7.6	7.2
United States	20.8	24.3	28.2	22.6	17.1	11.9	14.4	12.4	19.1	21.2
Other	10.9	11.0	8.4	8.4	8.4	6.4	6.2	9.7	8.2	8.7
More-developed countries	55.1	66.4	64.1	68.8	68.0	64.6	60.1	60.6	65.1	65.4
Less-developed countries	0.5	2.4	1.8	0.5	1.1	3.7	3.7	4.1	2.1	1.7
World Bank	7.6	10.2	11.8	12.2	13.6	13.5	13.5	11.6	12.4	11.8
Other international and regional organizations	11.0	17.2	19.0	14.1	13.6	12.2	12.9	12.0	14.3	14.9
Foundations	25.8	3.8	1.8	1.5	2.0	2.1	3.1	2.4	3.2	4.1
Other donors	0	0	1.5	2.9	1.8	3.9	6.8	9.2	3.0	1.9
Total	100	100	100	100	100	100	100	100	100	100

Sources: Compiled by authors from unpublished financial data obtained from the CG Secretariat (June 1998) and CGIAR Secretariat, various years.

[a]Calculated using a 4 percent interest rate.

[b]Includes multilateral funding from European countries via the European Union.

Bank provided $50 million (11.4 percent), the United States $54.2 million (12.4 percent), and Japan $14.4 million (3 percent of the total).[10] Through institutional and government aid programs, the developed countries as a group directly contributed $265.7 million, or 60.6 percent of the total allocation in 2004. Developing and transitional-country members provided $18.1 million (4.1 percent), with $11 million (60.1 percent) of this total coming from just five countries: Colombia, India, Mexico, Nigeria, and South Korea.

Donors have played an increasing role in influencing the allocation of the funds. Of course, donors should have *some* influence, but they are not the only stakeholders, and it cannot be assumed that donor interests necessarily coincide with systemwide objectives. Part of the CGIAR challenge is that its donors have specific objectives related to the geopolitical relevance of and distribution of benefits from its research.[11]

In the CG's early years, virtually all its funding came in the form of unrestricted support (wherein the funds were earmarked by center, and spending within a center was largely at the discretion of that center's management). This remained the dominant mode of funding for the CGIAR throughout the 1970s. Typically, new centers were fully funded with unrestricted support, and unrestricted funding for existing centers remained a significant share of their revenues throughout the 1970s and early 1980s. For example, in 1982 unrestricted funds as a share of the CG total averaged 84 percent, about 82 percent for the four founding centers and 87 percent for the newer centers.

After 1983, unrestricted funds declined steadily, to 44.5 percent of the total in 2003. This decline has two distinct phases. From 1983 to 1987, the unrestricted share fell, but total funding for the CG (in real, inflation-adjusted terms) continued to rise. For the period thereafter, both real funding and the unrestricted share declined, partly reflecting the fact that most of the new centers admitted to the CG in the 1990s joined with comparatively small amounts of unrestricted support (unlike those that joined during the 1970s). The corollary to the decline in the share of unrestricted funding is a rise in the share of funds earmarked for specific purposes.

The World Bank Role

The World Bank has played a pivotal role in many aspects of the CG that in some respects has gone beyond its role as a co-sponsor.[12] The chairman of the CG is chosen by the president of the World Bank, the CG's System Office (formerly the CG Secretariat) is located in the World Bank, many of the operational and staff costs incurred by the System Office are paid for by the Bank, and the Bank has provided a good deal of funding for the CG centers.[13] The Bank's support to the System Office and other noncenter activities such as systemwide reviews and CG committee work has averaged more than $6 million per year for the past five years. The Bank has also contributed funds as a donor. Its contribution rose from $1.26 million in 1972, to $45 million by 1997, jumping to $50.1 million in 1994 in response to a financial crisis in the system; it has remained at that level for all but two years since. Bank funding as a percentage of total CG center spending has increased for much of the CG history, from an average of 7.6 percent from 1972 through 1975 to 11.8 percent in 2004 (peaking at 15.4 percent in 1995).

The form, as well as the amount, of World Bank funding is of some consequence. From the inception of the CG until 1993, the Bank played the role of "donor of last resort." Through its review and endorsement of annual budget proposals for centers, the Consultative Group decided the desired overall pattern of funding for the system (or funding for the agreed agenda, in CG parlance), but individual donors remained free to make their final allocations to specific centers or specific projects within or across centers. Historically, the CG Secretariat played an active role in negotiating with donors to allocate core support across the system; nonetheless, funding for some centers fell short of the amounts deemed desirable. In all such cases the CG Secretariat would, as a matter of course, use Bank funds to fill in the funding gap, up to a limit of 25 percent of a center's approved program budget (with total Bank funding not to exceed 15 percent of the overall CG approved program).[14] Thus, centers that routinely secured less than their approved budget were insulated from these structural funding realities by the actions of the Bank. Although the Bank's funding practices maintained overall system priorities, the Bank had little chance to exercise its own funding preferences. From 1988 through the 1990s, the Bank was underwriting a growing share of the budgets of many centers (and a growing share of the CG's total budget). By 1992, every center sought Bank support. These CG developments (combined with internal pressures from within the Bank) prompted the Bank to exercise more discretion over the disbursement of funds from the late 1990s.[15]

The increasing tendency for the World Bank to earmark its support for particular areas of research (rather than leave decisions about allocation of funds to the discretion of the centers) was most evident after 2001. In 2003, only $15.95 million (or 37.1 percent of the agency's direct support to the centers) was in the form of general or core support, compared with $37.7 million (94.7 percent) in 2002. The remaining World Bank funds were directed toward global public goods research (39.5 percent), Systemwide Initiatives (4.1 percent), Challenge Programs (discussed in more detail below) (16.0 percent), and special allocations (3.3 percent).

The Broader Policy Context of Changes in the CGIAR

The decrease in support for the CG system in recent years may be better under-stood in the context of more general changes in development aid, global trends in public and private agricultural science investments, and other changes in national agricultural-research systems in less-developed countries, as well as some specific discussion of past CG research and its likely effects in the future.

Agricultural R&D as an Element of Development Aid

Since 1960, total official development assistance (ODA) from the Development Assistance Committee (DAC) countries, including both multilateral and bilateral assistance, grew in real terms to a peak of $71.1 billion (1999 prices) in 1992, dropping to $50.2 billion by 2001 (and increasing thereafter to $64.2 billion in 2003). There was no clear shift over time in the bilateral share of total ODA assis-tance: during the 1990s bilateral aid fluctuated around an average of 70 percent of total aid (Table 12.4).

Data on the sectoral orientation of aid are available for bilateral but not multi-lateral funds. In contemporary times, the agricultural component of bilateral assis-tance grew steadily, to peak at $4.9 billion in 1988, and declined to $2.1 billion in 2003. The data suggest a strong shift away from agriculture in aid-funding priori-ties. Agriculture's share of all bilateral aid fell from 15.2 percent in 1988 to 4.2 per-cent in 2003. The CG received a minuscule share of both total ODA (0.55 percent in 2003) and bilateral ODA (0.76 percent). However, from the 1970s to the mid-1980s, funding for the CGIAR grew more rapidly than overall ODA, so the share of CG funding in total ODA grew (to a peak of 0.76 percent in 1984). Since then, CG funding has moved more or less in line with total ODA, with the CG share fluctuating around an average of 0.58 percent in the 1990s and early 2000s. The CG share of total bilateral aid has followed a similar trend. In contrast, fund-ing for international agricultural R&D as a share of bilateral aid to agriculture grew from 4.2 percent in 1973 to 18.1 percent in 2001.

The pattern of aid funding and the CG share of that funding from the United States—historically the largest country donor to the CG—is worthy of note. Total ODA from the United States grew, albeit erratically, throughout the 1970s and 1980s, falling precipitously during the first half of the 1990s (from $13.4 billion, in 1999 prices, in 1992 to $7.1 billion in 1997) but recovering to $15.2 billion in 2003. U.S. bilateral aid followed the same general pattern. The agriculture compo-nent of U.S. bilateral aid peaked in 1980 (at $1.01 billion, or 24.7 percent of total bilateral aid), but, in keeping with global trends, U.S. aid priorities shifted away from agriculture thereafter (agricultural bilateral aid was only $0.2 billion in 2003, 1.4 percent of total U.S. bilateral aid).

Table 12.4 Context for aid to the CGIAR (amounts in million U.S. 1999 dollars)

| | Bilateral aid | | | | | | CGIAR total | CGIAR percentage | | | | |
| | ODA | | Amount | | Percentage to agriculture | | | Total ODA | Bilateral ODA | Bilateral Ag. ODA | U.S. ODA | U.S. bilateral |
Year	Total	U.S.	Total	U.S.	Total	U.S.						
1970	24,209	11,371	20,455	9,568	4.91	3.13	53.27	—	—	—	—	—
1975	34,718	10,899	25,692	7,704	11.13	14.31	131.64	0.36	0.48	4.36	0.26	0.37
1980	48,153	13,121	31,218	8,026	16.63	24.72	259.02	0.46	0.70	4.23	0.41	0.66
1985	40,912	13,378	30,148	11,641	15.93	12.67	306.99	0.73	1.00	6.26	0.64	0.74
1990	65,688	13,793	46,560	10,129	11.39	5.63	368.79	0.53	0.74	6.54	0.53	0.72
1995	62,756	7,865	43,219	5,994	9.82	8.23	360.86	0.56	0.81	8.27	0.55	0.72
2000	52,641	9,750	35,321	7,252	6.36	5.46	330.54	0.62	0.92	14.42	0.42	0.57
2003	64,152	15,152	46,249	13,550	4.22	1.36	364.79	0.55	0.76	18.11	0.34	0.38

Sources: Aid funding data from OECD 2005; CG funding data from Table 12.3.

The U.S. component of CG funding grew (in inflation-adjusted terms) during the 1970s and, also, though at an ever-slower rate, during the 1980s and early 1990s. It declined markedly from 1993 to 2001, increased significantly in 2002, and held steady thereafter. This trend was similar to that in the United States component of CG funding expressed as a share of bilateral U.S. aid to agriculture: that is, an increasing share of U.S. agricultural aid was directed to agricultural R&D from 1971 to 1992; this trend was strongly reversed from 1992 to 1995 but resumed thereafter (except in 2000). However, this general shift in U.S. agricultural aid priorities toward CG research was insufficient to offset the precipitous decline in overall and bilateral U.S. aid (through the early 2000s), and the result was a sharp decline in the U.S. contributions to the CG. Moreover, the very substantial shift of U.S. aid priorities away from agriculture, which first became noticeable in the early 1980s, meant that U.S. funding to the CG accounted for an ever-smaller share of total U.S. aid since then, despite CG research's commanding a larger share of U.S. aid to agriculture for most of these years.

Global Agricultural Science Policy

Today's external political, economic, and scientific environments are markedly different from those that gave rise to the CGIAR. In the late 1960s, the prospects of mass starvation throughout Asia and elsewhere had been averted, but the threat still loomed large in the minds of many policymakers.[16] National agricultural research systems throughout much of the developing world (especially Africa, Central America, and parts of Asia) were grossly underfunded, understaffed, and unprepared to lift agriculture by means of R&D-induced productivity growth. In the mid-1970s, agricultural research intensities (measuring investments in agricultural R&D as a percentage of agricultural gross domestic product) in the developing world averaged only 0.44 percent, compared with 1.53 percent among rich countries (Pardey and Beintema 2001). Most strikingly, between 1965 and 1970, *all* countries throughout Sub-Saharan Africa, the Asia and Pacific region (including China), and Latin America combined spent less on publicly performed agricultural R&D than the United States alone (Pardey, Roseboom, and Anderson 1991).

The CG was seen as an effective way of pooling resources to address the underinvestment problem and to locate research institutions throughout the developing world to redress the paucity of local research capacity. With comparatively few developing-country scientists trained to international caliber, most of the scientists staffing the CG centers were drawn from developed-country (often U.S.) universities. The invisible colleges that came with these staff served to stimulate the flow of knowledge from the first to the third world while providing the technical know-how to adapt and develop new technologies for developing-country (largely tropical) agriculture.

The rapid growth of the CG expenditures throughout the 1970s and early 1980s paralleled the growth in national research spending, especially in developing countries. Thereafter, the rate of growth of spending on agricultural research slowed in most countries, and in some countries spending even shrank (Pardey and Beintema 2001). CG spending has followed the same pattern, reflecting the slowdown in development aid spending (the source of most CG funds), among other factors.

In recent years, priorities for public agricultural research have also changed dramatically. The public research agenda has broadened. Public R&D funding—especially in the rich countries that account for nearly 90 percent of the CG's funding—has shifted toward research on postharvest handling, food processing and food safety, and environmental issues such as soil erosion and groundwater pollution; emphasis has shifted away from production agriculture. These adjustments reflect the increasing influence of nontraditional interest groups—environmentalists, food processors, and consumer lobbies—in the formulation of agricultural science policy, as well as the expanded research role of the private sector (Alston, Pardey, and Taylor 2001). In addition, some governments have pushed public funds toward more basic research, the benefits from which are more difficult for the private sector to appropriate, and away from applied research of more immediate consequence for industry (Alston, Pardey, and Smith 1999).

Donor funds directed toward both international and national agricultural R&D agencies (especially those in Africa) have reflected first-world concerns with the environment and agricultural aspects beyond the farm. Dalrymple (2004) and Gardner and Lesser (2003) have recently restated and reemphasized the "global" public-good rationale that spurred international collective action to fund agricultural R&D over three decades ago. Notwithstanding the fundamentally unchanged nature of these global public goods, donors increasingly seem to view agricultural R&D as a means of directly and rapidly tackling poverty problems rather than as an activity best suited to stimulating productivity and growth over the longer term, with poverty reduction brought about as a consequence of that growth.[17]

The organization and management of agricultural R&D has also been changing. The private sector is paying for and conducting an ever-larger share of agricultural research. In the developed countries, as many previously public roles have been privatized and university and other publicly performed research activities are becoming increasingly proprietary, the lines between private and public research are becoming blurred (Nottenburg, Pardey, and Wright 2002; Boettiger et al. 2004). Private R&D firms have increasingly been able to bid for publicly funded projects, some public research and technology transfer institutions have been explicitly privatized, and others (such as universities) have received a mandate to sell their research services to private firms. In addition, public agricultural-research facilities are being phased out in many countries, and management and employment structures have been altered (Alston, Pardey, and Smith 1999). These changes include the introduction and expansion of contestable funding arrangements among alternative, often public, research agencies (including the increased use of competitive grant processes); a shift away from long-term contracts toward shorter, fixed-term contracts for researchers; and expanded accountability and oversight procedures.

Similar changes have taken place in some developing countries as well, although the timing and specifics of the changes are different, and the private sector has generally played a smaller role as both a funder and performer of R&D (see the country case studies in this volume). Some countries (especially in Africa but also in Asia and Latin America) have seen a contraction in real public support for agricultural R&D. During the late 1980s and early 1990s, some of this reduction in domestic support was partly offset by an increase in donor funding for research, but in more recent years overall donor funding has declined, and spending priorities have shifted away from agriculture and agricultural R&D.

Intellectual Property Rights and Related Issues

The pace and focus of biological innovation in agriculture and related industries, who pays for R&D and how much, and the costs and benefits of the research all depend on the form of property protection afforded the results of specific R&D projects. Many countries are enacting or revising laws to protect biological material and the innovations and research processes surrounding that material. These national efforts are increasingly being shaped and circumscribed by international laws and conventions (Boettiger et al. 2004). These changes in property protection appear to be changing the roles of the public and private sectors with regard to the funding, performance, and dissemination of agricultural R&D, but because much else is changing too, the specific effects of changing property rights are not clear. Moreover, many of the practical implications of these property-rights policies remain unresolved, which makes it difficult to be definitive about their ultimate impact on the nature and rate of technical progress in agriculture.

Rapidly changing policy environments have resulted in some complicated problems for the operation and management of public (nonprofit) institutions such as the CGIAR (Nottenburg, Pardey, and Wright 2002). Advances in biotechnology that have been greatly reinforced by evolving intellectual property rights for agricultural research have increased the role of the private sector in research activities that used to be the exclusive domain of the public sector. Research outputs are being privatized, with stronger intellectual property rights protection. The traditional paradigm of the one-way flow of research output from public agencies to the private sector no longer holds (if, indeed, it ever did), and the acquisition of proprietary technologies from the private sector is an important consideration for the management of public institutions. Similarly, plant genetic resources, which were once considered a "common heritage of mankind," are increasingly subject to intellectual property protection through international agreements and national legislation (Binenbaum et al. 2003; Koo, Nottenburg, and Pardey 2004). Consequently, the intellectual property aspects of the germplasm held in CGIAR genebanks (and related information) pose major policy problems. Manifestations of these problems include concerns over biopiracy and arrangements for sharing benefits among those supplying and using new crop varieties, such as the provisions of the International Treaty for Plant Genetic Resources that came into force in June 2004.

The current trends in intellectual property protection may jeopardize the traditional role of the CG system, which has been based on the principle of free exchange of technologies and genetic materials. The centers face a new challenge: how to afford to give away germplasm while having to negotiate use rights for private-sector proprietary technologies with limited financial resources. Private-sector partners with the CG may insist on exclusive access arrangements to make it worth their while to invest substantially in development and marketing—contradicting the principle of open access. Unless the CG centers find ways to cope with these new circumstances, the effectiveness of international public institutions in benefiting the poor could be greatly diminished.

The CG system, like other agricultural research systems, appears to have seen a marked growth in administrative overhead in the past 20 years or so. Since a much higher proportion of funding is now received as project- or program-specific grants, rather than unrestricted funding, the role of overhead is perhaps more transparent than it once was, but it is also more important, as the system has become more top-heavy and bureaucratic and is beginning to deal with the growing complexities of intellectual property.

Funding mechanisms have evolved along with the CG system. In the early days, the funds were provided essentially unencumbered to centers, with minimal donor intervention. Over time, the system of funding has evolved to a much more elaborate and expensive process of donor–center bargaining over funding and activities—sometimes involving bilateral deals with donors, but increasingly involving multilateral arrangements with other CG centers, other research providers, and often several donor agencies in a consortium arrangement (Binenbaum and Pardey 2005). Thus rent-seeking by centers and the vested interest of donors have assumed greater importance, and the costs of negotiation and competition for funds have become ever greater. Compared with the original, albeit much smaller, CG system, the current setup involves much greater transactions costs and rent-seeking costs. At the same time, the quality of information in the system is probably lower and achieved at a greater cost, and there is reason to believe that resource-misallocation costs have risen.

Another issue that has relevance beyond the CG system is the (evolving) nature of the relationship between the international research system (and individual centers within that system) and other private and public agencies engaged in related scientific activity. Changes in international intellectual property regimes and modern biotechnology have added to the reasons for paying attention to these relationships (Binenbaum, Pardey, and Wright 2001). The nature of the relationship between an individual center and the national research system of the country in which it is located, and between that system and the research systems in other countries, influences the degree to which the center's work is redundant, synergistic, or complementary to the activities of others. An important question is, what is the comparative advantage of the CG system? In other words, if the CG system is designed to address international market failure, where is that failure most severe? It is there that the payoff for CG activities will be greatest.

Management and Allocation of Resources

Knowledge of the objectives and purpose of a research institution is critical for evaluating its achievements, setting priorities, and managing resources efficiently and effectively. The essential economic rationale for government involvement in science is market failure, in the sense that, left to itself, the private sector would do too little research, make the wrong mix of research investments from society's perspective, and charge the wrong price for the outputs from science. The arguments are particularly relevant in agriculture (for example, see Chapter 2 of this volume), and similar issues arise in considering international involvement and cooperation in agricultural R&D.

In modern economic parlance, the main problem is spillovers. Research results developed in one country (or part of a country) can be adapted and adopted elsewhere, often at little cost. Intellectual property rights provide inadequate protection for many types of agricultural technologies, even within a country. In addition, there is a market failure problem *among nations* that parallels the market failure among firms *within nations*. Each individual nation has diminished (inadequate) incentives to take action to rectify the *global* market failure in agricultural R&D. This is the prima facie case for international collective action in agricultural research. Alston (2002) provides a more extended discussion of these issues and summarizes empirical evidence on the importance of interstate and international agricultural research spillovers.

Spillovers lead to interconnected problems of appropriability and attribution, and thus in the assessment of returns to agricultural research (see Alston and Pardey 2001 and Pardey et al. 2004). A further set of difficulties arises when the goals of the investment are complex or unclear. Alston, Norton, and Pardey (1995) argued that research evaluators would do well to focus on a single objective—maximum net benefits—since multiple objectives require the specification of tradeoffs of net benefits, often against multiple, other, hard-to-measure objectives, and public-sector research is unlikely to be the best instrument for pursuing many objectives other than those associated with a market failure in research.[18] Even with a simple, single objective, evaluation is difficult.

Objectives of the CGIAR

The objectives of the CGIAR have always had a welfare or distributional element; they have not been focused simply on efficiency. Multiple goals are typical of public research agencies, even in rich countries. However, while motivated by a desire to alleviate poverty—as manifested most tangibly in hunger and mass starvation— the earlier incarnations of the CG system were much more clearly and narrowly focused on varietal (and associated crop-management) improvement for cereal grain and certain staple root crops. The more recent shifts toward adding environmental sustainability, improved nutrition, and poverty alleviation as explicit goals make the management and evaluation of the effort much more difficult. Consensus on the interpretation and achievement of such goals is elusive.

Perhaps more important is the fact that the CG system has been largely supported by the aid programs of the developed-country donors, not as a part of their agricultural science policy.[19] For instance, the USDA is the primary agency for U.S. agricultural R&D, but USAID is the primary agency for representing the United States in the CG system. Aid agencies cannot be expected to have the same perspective on science policy as science agencies; they are likely to pay much more attention to humanitarian and geopolitical objectives.

In addition to these complications, the "CG objective" has become more ephemeral with the rising importance of individual donors in determining the allocation of research resources. Donors may have primarily humanitarian reasons for being involved, but the nature of their involvement often reflects interests closer to home: for example, the Japanese government has taken particular interest in IRRI rice research. The U.S. and Australian governments have taken particular interest in CIMMYT wheat research—and these nations have numbered among the significant beneficiaries of the research they have supported.

Strategic Decisionmaking Processes

Strategic decisions within the CGIAR (including systemwide governance structures, the choice, location, and strategic orientation of the centers to include in the system, annual system and center-specific funding targets and strategies, and some scientific and key operational principles and practices) are made through a consultative, consensus-building process. This structure dates back to the early 1970s, when there were only four CG centers. At that time, just four donors accounted for 69 percent of the total CG funds; two of those donors (the Ford and Rockefeller foundations) had been instrumental in establishing research programs based on less-developed countries (LDCs) and precursor centers to the CG, and the main members of the Group were also well represented on the boards of each center.[20] Thus funding agencies, CG center boards, and other governance units within the CG had a focused and shared vision and a shared sense of how to achieve that vision. Hence, the costs of consultation were small.

As the size and scope of the CG grew (in terms of total funding, the number of members, and the number, location, and mandates of the CG centers), and the *formal* activities spread well beyond research (to include training, institutional development within LDCs, and science policy leadership), so too did the costs of consultation. To the annual general meeting (held in Washington, D.C., in October or November, and known as International Centers Week) a midterm meeting was added in 1979 (generally hosted by a developing country and held in May), and meetings of various standing, oversight, and partnership committees.

The growth in the scale and scope of the formal CG meetings provides a good indication of the growing costs of consultation. The first meeting of the CGIAR in 1971 had 58 participants, all of whom represented financial donors from the North (CGIAR System Review Secretariat 1998, p. 106). In 1987, International Centers Week (ICW) had 230 participants; by 1997 this number had grown to 480 and involved CG and non-CG center staff plus 54 member delegations. CG center delegations averaged 7.6 persons in 1997 (compared with 5.8 in 1987), noncenter delegations averaged 4.9 persons (2.2 in 1987), and member delegations averaged 2.6 (2.2 in 1987). Moreover, Centers Week grew to span two weeks, with numerous, generally back-to-back meetings in the week prior to ICW proper. Likewise, the midterm meeting grew from 155 participants in 1987 to 240 in 1997. Since 2000, efforts have been made to streamline CG decisionmaking processes. The last of the midterm meetings was held in May 2001, at which time the ICW was also scaled down to a one-week annual general meeting. Some of the CG's decisionmaking authority was devolved from the members at large to an executive council (although this council still seems unwieldy, with 22 members in 2003).[21]

Özgediz (1995) details the substantial work that has been done at the system level to evaluate CG research and provide information to TAC (one of the system's pivotal standing committees, now reconstituted as the Science Council), to donors, and to others that aid in setting priorities for R&D.[22] The amount and type of formal analysis used in this process is highly variable and to a large degree has reflected the proclivities of the TAC (now Science Council) chair. Little in the way of data or methods has carried over from one reporting cycle to the next. Thus, despite this long history of priority setting within the CG, it has yet to develop and maintain any systematic databases or analytical capacity designed to support priority-setting processes at the systemwide level.[23]

The CG has undergone three system reviews, in 1977, 1981, and 1998.[24] These reviews have made little use of formal evaluation techniques or quantitative analysis, and they have been expensive: the direct cost to the CG of the second review was around $450,000, and the 1988 review is thought to have cost about $1.5 million. The CG also undertook an impact study at the system level, carried out for a cost of $1.1 million between 1984 and 1986, which generated 24 CG study papers, a synthesis report in 1987, and several summary reports in 1988.[25] While providing a useful and reasonably comprehensive historical and contemporary account of CG activities, these studies were largely descriptive in nature. They stopped short of placing an economic value on the activities being evaluated. TAC has also prepared a series of reports (initially released at three-year intervals, later on a five-year cycle) on overall system priorities and strategies.[26]

The latest of these systemwide priority-setting exercises was a structured, but nonetheless largely consultative, multi-objective process that was tabled in December 2005 (CGIAR Science Council 2005a). The CG also has applied numerous review, assessment, and accountability procedures at the subsystem level, including more than 70 external management and program reviews of individual centers. These reviews are costly, and it is unclear what effect they have had on the conduct and performance of the centers in the light of the other significant and growing influences on each center's activities, notably the shift to project-based funding and the commensurate reduction in unrestricted funding.[27]

In addition, many centers engage in their own processes of periodic, internally commissioned external reviews, often involving in-depth peer review of the specifics of a center's planned or ongoing research. These various review requirements sometime require a substantial amount of quantitative research evaluation work within individual CG centers. Probably the most important and best-developed work along these lines is from CIMMYT. Scientists there have developed a global database on the resources that NARSs commit to wheat-breeding research and on the adoption of modern wheat varieties (including those developed at CIMMYT or based on CIMMYT-bred parental lines), and have undertaken a number of complementary adoption-cum-impact studies of specific aspects of CIMMYT work in various countries. Some of this more formal evaluation work has been used in setting research priorities within each center, but much has been motivated by a desire to shore up funding support.

Changing Use of Funds

Changes in the structure of the CG, the environment in which it operates, and its own modus operandi have had important implications for the efficiency with which resources are used, as well as for the total amount of funds available. The pervasive increase in external accountability demands placed by donors (and others) on the centers and the system, and the proliferation of more-specific reporting and review requirements associated with the shift to project funding mechanisms, have placed considerable additional transactions costs on the CG. These costs are difficult to document, but they include the costs of time spent by center management and, increasingly, scientists in preparing, revising, and submitting project proposals, as well as time spent briefing donors and preparing interim and final donor reports. In many cases the external reviews that donors require of special projects are also paid for with project funds.[28]

Even less visible, but nonetheless a rapidly increasing feature of much project funding, are the limitations on how project funding may be spent, including requirements to collaborate with or earmark project funds for donor-country institutions or scientists, irrespective of their advantages relative to other possible collaborators. All of these constraints directly affect research efficiencies and can add greatly to the cost of conducting research.

Several factors contributed to changes in actual (and changes in what would have been efficient) discretion over the allocation of CG funding. Certainly the longer-run trend toward more-restricted (mainly project-based, but increasingly programmatic) funding shifted resource-allocation decisions away from TAC, CG center directors, and CG scientists (arguably those best qualified to evaluate scientific opportunities and probabilities of research success) and toward individual (as distinct from collective) donor preferences. Indeed, the increased tendency of donors to earmark research funds to specific, well-defined research projects can be seen as cherry-picking among those centers, and research capacities within centers, that best align with the policy and, perhaps, commercial, interests of individual donors. However, a number of other factors were also influencing resource-allocation decisions and the configuration of the research itself. One was the changing (probably increasing) economies of scale and scope of R&D and reductions in some of the cost involved in longer-distance, multi-agency collaboration (as a result, for example, of easier travel and better information technologies). These economies might suggest less, not more, center-bound, programmatic research; although the rising transactions costs of conceiving, negotiating, and implementing multi-center collaborations would limit the efficient size of this type of R&D.

The shift from so-called unrestricted (or core) to more-restricted sources of support induced various institutional initiatives on the part of the CG centers. One such response was the formation of cross-center programs of research, intended to attract new funding sources to the CG, to revive the flagging interest among existing CG members, to shift the locus of decisionmaking closer to those most knowledgeable about scientific opportunities, to refocus CG research on longer-term research of broader global (or at least regional) significance, and also to respond to the fundamental economic forces pushing for an agglomeration of effort among CG centers. One manifestation of these institutional responses was the multi-center systemwide and ecoregional initiatives that were launched in the early 1990s. More recently, beginning around 2001, a series of time-bound, independently governed programs of research, dubbed Challenge Programs, were conceived. Three such programs (Water and Food, HarvestPlus, and Generation CP) were moving from their inception to operational phases by 2003.

Some evaluation and accountability is probably good (as is some engagement with donors), but, to achieve the potential benefits, assessment must contribute to setting research priorities and improving research efficiencies. The CG's costly review and reporting efforts have not provided sufficient substantive information to improve resource-allocation procedures. Relative to the early years, a much larger fraction of the total resources is spent on bureaucratic processes, rent-seeking within the system, and securing funds, leaving a smaller share to spend on research. In addition, the allocation of the residual funds among types of research has changed, with a much smaller share now going to the original CG agenda.

Changing Orientation of Research

In the early years, the CGIAR's focus was narrow. In the early 1970s, productivity improvement accounted for an estimated 74 percent of total CG spending, and rice, maize, and wheat together accounted for half of the total. Since then, the focus has broadened beyond staple grains and beyond productivity. With the addition of other centers dealing with other issues, it was natural that the share of CG research on staple grains should decline. The share of resources going to cereals (wheat, rice, maize, millet, barley, and sorghum) fell from 56 percent in the early 1970s to 37 percent in 2002. Similarly, research on the larger aggregate of crops (including roots and tubers, legumes, and bananas and plantains) declined in importance from 86 percent in the period 1972–76 to 71 percent in 2002. Livestock research has always constituted a much smaller share of the total than crops. Its share rose during the 1970s, remained around 20 percent during the 1980s, and fell to about 13 percent by 2002 (roughly the same share as when the CG was established).

By construction, these estimates allocate all CG expenditures to certain commodity areas, whether they involve basic, applied, adaptive R&D, or nonresearch activities. Another important perspective on CG spending is the share of R&D devoted directly to productivity-enhancing versus environmental or other resource-management (including "biodiversity") and policy-cum-institutional aspects.[29] The CG estimates that expenditures designed to enhance agricultural productivity declined from 74 percent of the total in the period 1972–76 to 34 percent in 2002, with the balance that year going to "strengthening NARSs" (23 percent) "protecting the environment" (18 percent), "improving polices" (15 percent), and "saving biodiversity" (10 percent) (CGIAR Science Council 2003b, p. 4).[30] Of course, some of these CG activities (involving an increasing amount of nonresearch activities, euphemistically dubbed "institutional strengthening") will be expressed eventually in crop and livestock production. But some of the change reflects the expanded mandates, including movements into social sciences, and more recent figures (after 1992) show a shift toward aquaculture and forestry.

The Payoff: Impacts of the CGIAR

On the face of it, CG spending appears to have been a very effective investment. The difficulty lies in determining the CG's true share of the achievements that many attribute entirely to the CG. How much could have been achieved without the interaction with the NARSs and previous work elsewhere? Partitioning results among institutions playing complementary or synergistic roles in science is problematic. The challenge is to determine the relevant counterfactual scenario: what would the world have been like if the CG had not existed and had not played the roles it has?

Nature of the Outputs

The CG system is a small part of the global effort in agricultural R&D, but within a relatively well-defined arena it is an important, if not the dominant, player. In developing fundamental genetic material to support the production of cereals and other crops in LDCs, the role of the CG has been central. The CG system provides materials that are adopted and adapted by NARSs. For instance, in 1986–90, Byerlee and Moya (1993) claimed that over 85 percent of wheat varieties released in LDCs were CIMMYT-derived, so that 70 percent of total wheat area in these countries was sown to CIMMYT-based germplasm in 1990. They also estimated that 43 percent of the total area planted to wheat in Australia, New Zealand, Italy (durum), South Africa, the United States, and western Canada was planted to germplasm with CIMMYT ancestry. In addition, improved rice varieties (many with CG elements in their pedigrees) were harvested on 74 percent of developing-country fields in 1991 (Byerlee 1994). In addition to their dominant role in developing wheat and rice varieties, for developed and less-developed countries alike, CG centers have played significant roles in developing genetic material for other crops (Evenson and Gollin 2003). And, apart from developing new varieties, the CG has collected and conserved a sizable share of the world's agricultural germplasm (Koo et al. 2004).

Genetic improvement of crops is only part of the picture. The CG system also has invested significantly in, and contributed to, the development and adaptation of improved agronomic and farming practices for LDCs. Livestock research has contributed to animal production and animal health—work that was until recently Africa-based but is now global. As well as providing information and technology for use by NARSs, the CG has helped improve the NARSs themselves through training and human capital development. These efforts have included the institutional work of ISNAR and the food-policy work of IFPRI. More recently the CG has contributed to a broader range of areas, including fish and forestry products, and placed more emphasis on environmental and resource issues. This shift represents a move away from the historical strength of the CG—developing productivity-enhancing technology that is widely applicable, with perhaps some modification to fit local conditions—to the pursuit of more site-specific results, with a range of objectives other than productivity.

Economic Evaluations of Agricultural Research in the CGIAR

A variety of studies have looked at various aspects of the research programs of the CG centers, including several formal research evaluation studies. Much of this work has been conducted within the CG system, looking at individual centers or programs, or systemwide, but some has been conducted by external agencies.

Economic approaches to research evaluation typically involve computing the streams of benefits implied by a simulation of what productivity, prices, and quantities produced and consumed might have been under a different pattern of research investments. Then the streams of changes in research benefits are compared with the associated streams of changes in research costs, using conventional capital-budgeting methods. The results are typically summarized as internal rates of return (the discount rate for future benefits and costs that equates the discounted present value of benefits to the present value of costs) or as benefit–cost ratios (the ratio of the discounted present value of benefits to the present value of costs). Public-sector agricultural research is regarded as a good investment if the computed rate of return exceeds the required rate of return for public investments (typically a real rate of less than 5 percent per annum), or if the benefit–cost ratio is greater than one.

In their statistical meta-analysis of these estimated rates of return, Alston et al. (2000a and b) explored the possible influence of differences among characteristics of the rate-of-return measure (for example, real versus nominal, and social versus private), the analyst (for example, self-evaluation versus external evaluation), the research (for example, crops versus livestock, developing- versus developed-country, basic versus applied), and the evaluation itself (for example, ex ante versus ex post, econometric or not, and type of lag structures used). In general the signal-to-noise ratio was low, so that it was hard to distinguish some of the effects, but others were statistically significant. There was no evidence that rates of return declined over time, or that the rate of return to environmentally oriented research would be as good as that to traditional areas of agricultural science, such as plant-variety improvement.

Table 12.5 summarizes the rate-of-return evidence for research carried out by the international agricultural research centers (IARCs).[31] A total of 62 observations—only 3.4 percent of the reported estimates in the meta-analysis—refer to IARC research. The average rate of return is 78 percent per annum, slightly higher than (but not statistically different from) the 73 percent average across all studies. All of the IARC evidence relates to crop research, with average rates of return for research on rice, potato, and wheat research identified in Table 12.5. The rates of return to other types of crop research conducted by the IARCs, is, on average, twice the average for rice research. However, reported rates of return range widely around the averages. The 142.3 percent average rate of return to other crop research is largely the consequence of one outlier observation that reports a rate of return of 1,490 percent per annum; deleting this outlier from the sample reduces the average rate of return to 30 percent per annum. Of the 62 IARC estimates, 6 (10 percent) of the estimates related to yield-enhancing research (compared with 42.5 percent of all the estimates); 18 (about 29 percent) related to crop-management research, and 30 estimates (48 percent) related to various other types of research.

Doing Well by Doing Good

Studies of the multicountry impacts of varietal-improvement research done in international centers have shown that a large share of the benefits accrues to the donor countries, a situation that Tribe (1991) referred to as "doing well by doing good."

Table 12.5 Summary of rates of return to agricultural R&D

Category	Number of observations	Rates of return (percent per annum)		
		Mean	Lowest observation	Highest observation
95 percent of sample[a]				
All observations	1,760	72.8	0.4	1,480
Research only	1,083	88.0	2.6	1,480
Research and extension	600	44.6	0.4	150
Extension only	77	79.4	1.3	350
IARC				
All observations	62	77.8	9.9	1,490
Rice	29	74.6	17.9	285
Potato	14	39.3	10.0	80
Wheat	6	43.3	16.0	54
Other	13	142.3	9.9	1,490

Source: Data files created and used by Alston et al. 2000a.
[a]Sample excludes the upper and lower 2.5 percent of the observations.

Beginning with John Brennan's work on the impacts in Australia of wheat varieties from the international wheat and maize research center CIMMYT (Brennan 1986, 1989), a number of studies have attempted to value the benefits to particular countries from research conducted at CG centers, in some cases comparing them against donor support provided by the countries in question.[32] In the first such study, Brennan (1986, 1989) reported that for the period 1973–84, Australia gained US$747 million in the form of cost savings to wheat producers as a result of having adopted CIMMYT-based wheat varieties. (He noted that Australia's annual contribution to CIMMYT was about US$340,000, while the average expenditure on wheat breeding in Australia had been about US$4–5 million per year.) On the basis of genetic parentage, he attributed two-thirds of the cost savings to CIMMYT per se, with the remaining one-third attributable to the inputs of Australian wheat breeders who used CIMMYT releases as parental lines.

Pardey et al. (1996) found that, depending on the genetic attribution rule used, the U.S. economy gained at least US$3.4 billion and up to US$14.6 billion between 1970 and 1993 from the use of improved wheat varieties developed by CIMMYT. In the same 23-year period, they found that the U.S. economy realized at least US$30 million and up to US$1 billion through the use of rice varieties developed by IRRI. These are large benefits relative to the U.S. support of CIMMYT and IRRI (US$131 million in present-value terms up to 1993), or even the total budget of the entire CGIAR system (around US$200–300 million per year in the

1980s and 1990s, but much less than that during the 1970s). They are likely to overstate the net U.S. benefits from IARC varieties in that they do not reflect price impacts.[33] For instance, Alston (2002) suggested that the effect of CIMMYT wheat varieties driving down the price of wheat would reduce the U.S. benefits from CIMMYT wheat varieties by $300–600 million in 2000 alone.

Criticisms of the CGIAR and the Green Revolution, and Some Responses

Although no one denies the significant contributions of the CGIAR to the Green Revolution, clearly some people are harmed by any large changes in technology, and the Green Revolution is surely no exception.[34] For instance, those farmers who cannot adopt the technology, but have to compete for resources and markets with those who do, are clearly worse off. So are those consumers who might not benefit from lower food prices but who experience lower water quality as a consequence of agricultural intensification.

Critics of the CG attach heavy weight to the negative aspects of agricultural innovations. Some of these critics have gone so far as to question the entire CG enterprise in the light of their perceptions of harm to the environment or to certain individuals or groups. Some of the criticisms are false, reflecting a misunderstanding of the facts or of the relevant counterfactual alternative, or an ideological position reflecting a bias against change. Others may be factually correct but overblown, owing to a lack of perspective: some negative impacts may be very large yet still be dwarfed by the enormous positive impacts that accompanied them. But some may be valid.

Recurring criticisms of the Green Revolution are that the technologies

- were inherently biased toward large farmers;

- were destructive of the environment, encompassing land degradation, air pollution, loss of water quality owing to salinization and runoff, and loss of natural habitats;

- replaced "natural" inputs and practices with "artificial" (less "organic" farming);

- encouraged globalization;

- increased farmers' dependency on manufactured inputs from the North;

- made production riskier and more vulnerable to climate and pests;

- increased the financial risks faced by farmers;

- displaced labor from agriculture;

- increased inequality;

- lacked a pro-poor focus, or at least outcome;

- worsened absolute poverty;

- bypassed farmers in poor or less-favored areas; and

- reduced biodiversity.

In short, it is claimed that CG technologies promoted unsustainable, high-input agricultural practices that may have raised crop yields but did so at the expense of the long-term economic and environmental sustainability of the agricultural system. In addition, genetic resource conservation and use practices of the CGIAR are said to have promoted the denigration of the biological base used in agriculture and led to biopiracy.

Most of these criticisms are not new, and many of them would apply with equal force to the application of modern agricultural technologies in rich countries as well. Clearly there have been some environmental and human-health consequences of the use of chemical fertilizers and pesticides, irrigation, and mechanization. Agricultural economists are guilty of having failed to quantify some of these effects, but it is also true that the effects are hard to quantify, and no one really knows what the physical impacts have been, let alone what they are worth.[35] Considering the conventional measures of private benefits and costs, which capture the main effects, however, the story is much clearer. Both farmers and consumers in less-developed countries have benefited enormously from the Green Revolution, and most assessors have judged that the benefits are to be measured on a different scale from the costs.

An appropriate assessment requires a clear understanding of what would have happened otherwise. In other words, what is the relevant counterfactual alternative? It certainly would not have been an option to preserve the conditions of the 1960s indefinitely. Many of the negative trends associated with the adoption of Green Revolution technologies would have been similar or worse without them. Would farmers seeking to survive using the old technologies have spared the environment? Would they have cleared more or less rain forest? Would they have farmed more or less intensively on fragile environments? What new technologies would have been developed instead? In many cases the answer is unclear or may be unfavorable to the critics of the Green Revolution.

A balanced consideration of the issues needs to account for all the effects that are quantitatively important. And it is also appropriate to take a broader perspective and incorporate other policies, recognizing that agricultural R&D policy is not the ideal instrument for pursuing social objectives other than economic efficiency and growth (Alston and Pardey 1996). In other words, it is perhaps the deficiencies of other policies that are to blame for some of the negative consequences of Green Revolution technologies, and not the CGIAR for having helped to make those technologies possible. Clearly it is important to take these criticisms seriously and debunk those that are without foundation; but it is also important to take action to address those that have merit—either through the revision of research priorities or, better, through the introduction of complementary policies to address the unwelcome side effects of otherwise beneficial technologies.

A misunderstanding of these arguments is reflected in the changing policies within the CGIAR over the past 30 years, and that misunderstanding has led to the broadening of the agenda and the incorporation of a wider range of interests and perspectives into CG decisionmaking processes. As noted above, the result has been negative consequences for the productivity of the system and, in turn, we suspect, for the resources being made available to it.

Conclusion

The rationale for government intervention in the private provision of agricultural R&D is market failure: individuals will underinvest, hoping to catch a free ride on the efforts of others. In an international context, countries play the roles of individuals to some extent (see Chapter 2). Any one country may underinvest in R&D if the results can be adopted and applied elsewhere so that the researcher will capture only a fraction of the benefits from investing in invention. In relation to R&D applicable to LDCs, both domestic and international market failures of these types have led to a large, persistent gap between the socially desirable rates of investment in agricultural R&D and actual investments.

The efficiency rationale for the CG system is to overcome, or at least to mitigate, the underinvestment problem. The humanitarian rationale is to help the food-poor. The CG as it exists today combines elements of these two rationales, with the effects of some self-serving motives of certain donors adding further complications. In order to be effective in achieving any of these objectives, the CG, given its relatively small resource base, should focus on the areas in which the market failures are greatest and where it has an advantage over public and private research in the NARSs.

In its first three decades, the CG system made its mark. Its primary focus was on cereal crops following the objectives of the preexisting centers. Even today, many of the more demonstrable results of the CG system are those identified most clearly with the first four centers. With the dramatic expansion of the CG, funding per center grew initially, but recently competition among centers for funds became more pronounced. CGIAR's total funding has become more uncertain in a number of ways. And of that total, a greater proportion is now provided in the less secure, and less flexible, form of restricted or project funding. Like the U.S. agricultural R&D system, the CG system is becoming more subject to earmarking by those who fund it. In addition, with expansion of the number of centers and the broadening mandate, the management of the CG system has progressively become more complex, top-heavy, administratively burdensome, and expensive, notwithstanding some recent attempts to streamline operations.

With the rise in the number of centers, the mandates of the system have changed, and the emphasis has shifted away from crop productivity toward objectives that have also risen in prominence in the national agricultural research systems of richer countries, emphasizing things such as sustainability, nutrition, and equitable income distribution at the expense of productivity. The comparative advantage of the CG does not appear to have been a criterion in recent decision-making. This situation may have been a consequence of the apparent abundance of research resources, which may have led to a perception that there was no opportunity cost to accommodating the newer political agendas in the system. This perception was clearly wrong. Similar patterns have been apparent in the agricultural R&D systems of the world more generally, perhaps for similar reasons. The consequence has been a reduction in the resources available for the more-traditional productivity-enhancing investments.

The CGIAR was brought into existence because of a perceived threat to world food supplies, and to build on the successful performance of IRRI and CIMMYT. Its purpose was to create additional, similar centers, mobilize funds for them, and provide a structure that would determine broad priorities, monitor performance, and allocate total funding in accordance with priorities and performance. Its early success was considerable, and the system (or parts thereof) remains a highly successful enterprise today, although some features of its evolution can be seen as undesirable. The key innovation of the CGIAR system was the development of IARCs, operating independently, governed by an independent board, and located in the ecology and social environment being served. There was great confidence in the ability of science to address the food-production problems of developing countries, and this confidence was justified quickly. The food research being undertaken required relatively little capital investment, so that the creation of new institutions was relatively cheap.

Over time, the CGIAR has misplaced its original, well-defined sense of purpose and to some extent has degraded its capacity to meet its original—and still relevant—objective: to stave off hunger by enhancing the capacity of the world's poor people to feed themselves, through research-induced improvements in agricultural productivity. This failure is in part an inevitable consequence of an important institutional attribute of the system: to be an element of international development efforts to reduce poverty, rather than a mechanism for providing multinational agricultural R&D investments as an international public good. The fundamental and main purpose and outcome are similar, but the priorities and effectiveness are different when the culture is one of providing welfare assistance rather than promoting economic efficiency. Moreover, over time, the priorities of the CGIAR have shifted in the same direction as the rich-country agendas for agricultural R&D— that is, toward "luxury" goods such as safer, higher-quality food and enhanced environmental amenities—which the poorest people of the world cannot afford to emphasize at the expense of the availability of food and the ability to pay for it. This change, too, is a reflection of a fundamental design flaw in the system: that its priorities are determined by donors—moreover, not by representatives of the science agencies of the donors—and that these priorities do not always accord with the fundamental purpose of the system.

It is time to rethink international approaches to agricultural R&D, because of both the changes that have taken place within the CG and the changing context in which it will have to operate. As noted in Chapter 2, rich-country NARSs are changing how they do business in ways that will have important implications for the technologies available to poorer countries. Poor-country NARSs will have to change what they do accordingly, and, clearly, so will the IARCs. The potential role of international cooperative ventures such as the CGIAR is likely to be even greater than in the past, but this change is coming at a time when the CG is losing ground.

To reenergize the CGIAR may require reengineering it. Such change could encompass a narrower constitution of the system, a different set of mandates, and different modes of operation, but it would retain the concept of multinational collective action—including charitable support from the richer countries—to provide agricultural R&D for poor countries. It is important to define clearly the limits of the role of the CGIAR and to understand the links between the CG and other institutions. Universities and other public elements of national agricultural research systems—and, perhaps, increasingly, private for-profit and private nonprofit enterprises such as the Danforth Plant Science Center or CAMBIA—can also play a greater role in light of changes in the science base for agriculture and intellectual property regimes.

The appendix to this chapter starts on page 350.

Appendix Table 12A.1 Expenditures by CGIAR-supported centers (million 1999 U.S. dollars)

Year	IRRI	IITA	CIMMYT	CIAT	CIP	ICRISAT	ILRI	WARDA
1960	36.13	0	0	0	0	0	0	0
1961	0.91	0	0	0	0	0	0	0
1962	2.05	0	0	0	0	0	0	0
1963	4.06	0	0	0	0	0	0	0
1964	2.59	0	0	0	0	0	0	0
1965	4.51	1.11	0	0	0	0	0	0
1966	4.86	1.50	2.18	0	0	0	0	0
1967	5.02	4.18	4.93	0	0	0	0	0
1968	9.62	10.46	7.05	0.82	0	0	0	0
1969	9.56	17.89	11.23	5.42	0	0	0	0
1970	10.51	16.01	18.42	8.34	0	0	0	0
1971	12.67	23.41	20.99	12.23	0	0	0	0
1972	14.78	21.13	21.78	14.72	1.65	1.32	0	0
1973	14.48	20.14	23.93	20.02	4.06	8.43	0	0
1974	22.58	20.78	21.56	17.48	6.35	10.89	2.95	1.36
1975	27.62	25.75	23.98	17.58	7.56	16.25	10.16	1.45
1976	30.50	27.60	27.14	17.38	11.75	18.28	22.34	2.23
1977	36.01	29.77	26.57	23.83	13.82	26.19	28.23	3.03
1978	34.31	37.87	30.29	28.29	12.71	30.74	33.49	4.13
1979	37.48	39.21	33.45	30.47	14.95	27.16	32.86	5.72
1980	38.70	35.35	33.72	31.86	14.93	26.51	35.16	6.35
1981	38.07	38.31	34.12	31.83	16.17	26.43	34.49	5.86
1982	39.85	43.22	32.36	34.21	15.79	31.02	30.84	8.22
1983	37.49	39.61	31.33	35.23	16.69	31.89	32.47	9.69
1984	39.53	40.89	36.49	35.28	17.25	31.00	34.90	8.63
1985	44.57	47.69	35.37	33.12	15.72	34.73	35.91	6.90
1986	41.49	50.67	37.87	33.86	22.87	44.02	40.61	9.66
1987	44.23	48.41	38.28	39.87	20.60	55.39	38.40	8.04
1988	40.47	49.39	43.32	38.28	23.19	46.27	42.13	7.12
1989	45.96	42.14	42.33	39.36	27.68	48.78	42.64	8.55
1990	50.52	43.83	39.94	39.63	26.55	47.34	45.04	10.10
1991	45.19	40.10	40.18	39.85	27.53	42.66	40.94	16.00
1992	47.53	40.66	38.42	36.68	24.79	37.55	37.47	11.55
1993	49.86	38.23	36.48	37.12	23.97	35.41	29.00	10.12
1994	43.64	36.87	31.64	38.29	24.44	32.29	26.07	9.49
1995	43.03	35.45	28.93	36.94	25.62	35.66	27.44	9.82
1996	41.92	38.94	31.67	38.54	27.29	32.54	27.12	10.26
1997	35.92	32.72	31.22	34.20	26.22	28.27	27.42	9.45
1998	35.51	29.83	32.67	33.98	22.01	22.12	28.10	10.04
1999	35.10	32.70	37.40	30.70	21.60	23.20	26.50	10.90
2000	31.93	29.48	38.20	28.89	19.78	22.82	25.95	9.21
2001	31.19	33.77	38.93	28.41	18.85	22.86	26.98	9.28
2002	31.58	30.83	39.05	30.54	18.16	23.36	26.00	9.27
2003	26.74	35.00	34.82	30.55	16.34	22.28	28.78	9.38
2004	30.55	39.55	38.16	34.07	19.96	24.88	29.43	9.38
1960–2004								
Total	1,310.82	1,270.46	1,176.38	1,067.91	606.86	968.51	949.83	251.18
Percent	13.2	12.8	11.8	10.7	6.1	9.7	9.5	2.5
PV total[a]	2,809.58	2,617.68	2,383.21	2,072.52	1,086.05	1,828.79	1,774.84	429.80
Percent	15.1	14.1	12.8	11.2	5.9	9.9	9.6	2.3

Sources: Authors' calculations based on unpublished financial data obtained from the CGIAR Secretariat (June 1998) and CGIAR Secretariat, various years.

Notes: Nominal U.S. dollar–denominated data were deflated with implicit GDP deflator (rebased from 1993 to 1999) obtained from World Bank 2003a. Data include all types of expenditures, specifically spending from unrestricted funds (for example, core funding) and earmarked support (for example, complementary, restricted core, and special project

IPGRI	ICARDA	IFPRI	ISNAR	ICLARM	ICRAF	IWMI	CIFOR	CGIAR total
0	0	0	0	0	0	0	0	36.13
0	0	0	0	0	0	0	0	0.91
0	0	0	0	0	0	0	0	2.05
0	0	0	0	0	0	0	0	4.06
0	0	0	0	0	0	0	0	2.59
0	0	0	0	0	0	0	0	5.62
0	0	0	0	0	0	0	0	8.54
0	0	0	0	0	0	0	0	14.13
0	0	0	0	0	0	0	0	27.95
0	0	0	0	0	0	0	0	44.10
0	0	0	0	0	0	0	0	53.27
0	0	0	0	0	0	0	0	69.31
0	0	0	0	0	0	0	0	75.38
0	0	0	0	0	0	0	0	91.05
0	0	0	0	0	0	0	0	103.95
1.28	0	0	0	0	0	0	0	131.64
2.27	3.41	0	0	0	0	0	0	162.92
2.93	10.97	0	0	0	0	0	0	201.35
3.73	16.55	0	0	0	0	0	0	232.10
4.75	21.23	3.86	0	0	0	0	0	251.16
5.60	24.11	4.51	2.21	0	0	0	0	259.02
6.00	26.54	5.34	2.71	0	0	0	0	265.87
4.89	24.86	6.21	4.61	0	0	0	0	276.08
6.88	31.22	7.55	6.26	0	0	0	0	286.31
6.17	30.66	8.63	6.31	0	0	0	0	295.75
6.42	30.97	8.96	6.62	0	0	0	0	306.99
7.00	30.38	9.95	8.53	0	0	0	0	336.92
6.92	31.92	8.10	7.56	0	0	0	0	347.72
8.16	30.48	10.97	8.23	0	0	0	0	348.01
9.45	30.73	13.94	11.65	0	0	0	0	363.20
9.02	28.12	15.07	13.63	0	0	0	0	368.79
9.42	25.70	15.71	12.61	0	0	0	0	355.87
14.03	23.47	15.26	12.17	6.96	14.88	10.40	0.00	371.83
15.17	23.55	13.88	11.53	7.98	15.34	9.88	2.67	360.18
17.78	24.76	14.29	11.45	7.09	18.22	9.60	5.24	351.15
20.93	24.98	14.73	12.28	7.58	17.94	10.04	9.50	360.86
20.91	24.30	16.97	11.73	9.01	18.22	10.66	10.14	370.21
20.11	28.35	18.59	10.68	8.73	22.80	10.35	10.89	355.93
22.01	23.94	18.87	10.04	10.55	21.41	9.33	11.26	341.67
20.40	22.80	20.10	9.70	12.40	21.80	8.80	12.70	346.80
21.06	22.92	20.76	8.03	10.19	20.27	8.72	12.34	330.54
22.10	20.38	21.52	7.75	12.53	22.86	10.91	12.05	340.37
24.21	22.98	21.47	8.42	11.63	20.61	19.57	11.06	348.74
26.28	24.33	24.60	11.88	14.39	25.44	21.35	12.63	364.79
29.71	22.84	29.15	2.23	13.09	26.46	21.45	14.02	384.94
375.57	707.44	369.01	218.82	132.13	266.26	161.07	124.50	9,956.76
3.8	7.1	3.7	2.2	1.3	2.7	1.6	1.3	100.0
559.34	1,259.04	548.98	346.38	163.61	333.14	198.39	150.40	18,561.76
3.0	6.8	3.0	1.9	0.9	1.8	1.1	0.8	100.0

funds) plus earned income, rundown of accumulated reserves, and so on. ILRI data include expenditures by ILRAD and ILCA, which were formed in 1973 and 1974, respectively, and merged operations in 1995. IPGRI data include expenditures by INIBAP beginning in 1992. See Table 12.2 for full names of centers.

[a]Calculated using a 4 percent interest rate.

Notes

The authors thank Nienke Beintema, Connie Chan-Kang, Jennifer Drew, Louise Letnes, Gordon MacNeil, the late Ravi Tadvalkar, and Shey Tata for their very able assistance in tracking down data and other information and helping to process it. Jock Anderson, Curtis Farrar, and Henry Shands offered valuable advice in preparing this chapter and its antecedents. This is a shortened, updated, and thoroughly revised version of a paper prepared for the study "U.S. Government Roles in International Cooperation on Energy Research, Development, Demonstration and Deployment," undertaken in 1999 for the Office of Science and Technology Policy, Executive Office of the President of the United States.

1. Koo et al. (2004) provide details of the more than 660,000 accessions currently conserved in 11 CG genebanks.

2. Many say that hunger is strictly a distribution problem, but, as Runge et al. point out, this "is akin to saying that if the rain fell evenly over the earth there would be no droughts. It may be true, but reality is unchanged, and wishing will not make it so. No mechanism exists—or is ever likely to—that massively redistributes food worldwide on the basis of need alone" (2003, p. 14). Moreover, the niggardliness of nature means that a global sufficiency of food today is no guarantee of the same in the future (Wright et al. 2006).

3. Baum (1986, pp. 5–6) and Culver and Hyde (2000) attribute the original idea of providing rich-country research assistance to developing-country agriculture to Henry A. Wallace, who founded the Pioneer Hi-Bred International Company in 1926, and served as U.S. secretary of agriculture from 1933 to 1939 and as vice president of the United States in the Roosevelt administration from 1940 to 1944. In 1940, before being sworn in as vice president, Wallace spent a month traveling through Mexico. Upon his return he met with Raymond Fosdick, president of the Rockefeller Foundation, and laid out his case for the foundation to invest in crop improvement research in Mexico: "The all-important thing was to expand the means of subsistence; that the corn of Mexico was only yielding 10 bushels to the acre; that the principal source of food among the Mexican masses was corn" (Culver and Hyde 2000, pp. 250–51). Perkins (1997, p. 106) also points to the pivotal role played by Wallace in seeding the Green Revolution.

4. The CGIAR is not a legal entity with a formal constitution. The only charter or terms-of-reference document that exists is its "Statement of Objectives, Composition, and Organizational Structure," approved when the CGIAR first met as such on May 19, 1971. The statement is reprinted in Baum (1986, 107–10).

5. More on the history of the CGIAR can be found in Baum 1986; Anderson, Herdt, and Scobie 1988; Gryseels and Anderson 1991; Anderson 1998; Alston and Pardey 1999; Anderson and Dalrymple 1999; and Farrar 2000.

6. David Chandler, the founding director general of IRRI, apparently shared the same view. Vernon Ruttan, the first economist to work for a CG center, quotes Chandler at a Saturday morning staff seminar during IRRI's early days as saying emphatically, "The purpose of this institute is not to do good science! . . . The purpose of this institute is to raise rice yields in Asia! . . . And raising rice yields in Asia may require that you do good science!" (2001, p. 26). W. David Hopper, chairman of the CGIAR from 1987 to 1990, shifted the emphasis from production to consumption and saw the CG's mission as increasing "the pile of rice on the plates of food-short consumers" (World Bank 2003a, p. 1).

7. Curtis Farrar (2000) provides an excellent history of the founding and first decade of IFPRI's operations and its controversial entry into the CGIAR. ISNAR ceased operation in March 2004. A new ISNAR Division, located in Addis Ababa, began within IFPRI the following month.

The new division focuses on institutional change, organization and management, and science policy issues facing agricultural research in developing countries.

8. Other centers that sought admission to the CG system—and were not successful—included ICIPE (insect physiology and ecology; founded in 1970, reconstituted in 1986), AVRDC (vegetable productivity and quality; founded in 1971), IFDC (fertilizer; founded in 1977), ITC (trypanosomiasis; founded in 1982), and IBSRAM (soil management; founded in 1985 and integrated with IWMI in April 2001).

9. The initial $7.4 million was spent mainly on capital items such as administration, research and housing facilities, research and field equipment, and the like. The 1961 commitment, largely used to meet operational expenses, was $190,000.

10. Table 12.3 also shows the cumulative CG contribution from 1972 to 2004: the total investment over 32 years was $9,196.8 billion, in 1999 prices, or $14,046.7 billion expressed in 1999 present-value terms.

11. Enlightened self-interest is an implicit, if not explicit, feature of the involvement of many countries in the international agricultural research system, and national interests in research aid imply some restrictions on where and how the aid is spent. For instance, the Jackson Report (Jackson 1984) recommended that the Australian development-cooperation program be focused squarely on the countries of the Asia and Pacific region that are important to Australia politically and economically. Economists and others have begun paying greater attention to the issue of "doing well by doing good" as an element of donor motivation in agricultural research (see, for example, Ryan 1987; Tribe 1991, 1994).

12. The Food and Agriculture Organization of the United Nations (FAO) and the United Nations Development Programme (UNDP) were the other founding co-sponsors of the CGIAR. The United Nations Environment Programme (UNEP) joined the system as a fourth co-sponsor in 1995 but withdrew in 2000. The International Fund for Agricultural Development (IFAD) became a co-sponsor in 2001. The co-sponsors lend legitimacy and an assurance of continuity to the CGIAR; they also finance core CGIAR functions (such as the System Office and Science Council operations) and forward nominations for key positions to the group (World Bank 2003b, Annex D, p. 15).

13. To date, all the CG chairs have been vice presidents of the World Bank. According to Anderson and Dalrymple (1999, p. 15) they commit between 2 and 10 percent of their time to CG activities, and are expected to act in the interests of the CGIAR, not the Bank. Thus, although the CG chair is a Bank official, another Bank staff member (usually the director of the Agriculture Department) is the official Bank representative to the CG. The Operations Evaluation Department review (World Bank 2003a, pp. 33, 58) addressed the potential conflict of interest inherent in these arrangements.

14. Of course, for some centers in some years, funding from the Bank exceeded the 25 percent target maximum, and for some years the Bank's overall contribution exceeded its 15 percent ceiling.

15. Anderson and Dalrymple (1999) document the key elements of this history and provide relevant details. Especially critical was the recognition that the CG was consuming a dominant share of the Bank's total grant resources (about 40 percent in 2002), for which a primary competitor was health issues such as HIV/AIDS. The World Bank Operations Evaluation Department report also makes mention of the open-ended nature of the Bank's commitment to the CGIAR, for which "no credible exit strategies have been designed" (World Bank 2003a, p. 33).

16. As an illustration of these generally held views, Schultz (1969, p. 301) reported on a two-page advertisement by Olin (a U.S. chemicals and basic materials company founded in 1892) in the July 1976 issue of the *Atlantic*, whose half-page heading read "Of the Billion People Who May Starve in 1976," followed by a paragraph stating: "The statisticians say that in ten years over a billion—not

a million, but a billion—people may be dying of hunger." These views were not confined to the popular press. The eminent ecologist Paul Ehrlich, in *The Population Bomb* (1968, p. xi), predicted that in the 1970s, "the world will undergo famines—hundreds of millions of people are going to starve to death in spite of any crash programs embarked upon now. At this late date nothing can prevent a substantial increase in the world death rate."

17. Those who advocate this role for research seem unaware of the long lags (typically decades) between committing funds to R&D and realizing a sizable share of the benefits from that commitment.

18. In this context, Alston, Norton, and Pardey (1995) argued for an inclusive concept of economic efficiency that refers to the achievement of the greatest net benefits for the society as a whole, taking a broad view of net benefits that encompasses nonmarket aspects of impacts (for example, on the environment), along with benefits revealed in market transactions.

19. Notably, almost all of the LDC representatives to the CG (mainly from members who joined during the 1990s) come from national food and agriculture agencies, not foreign-affairs or aid ministries.

20. Among the 11 sponsors that pledged their financial support to the CGIAR at the time of the group's second meeting in December 1971 (Baum 1986, p. 64), the four leading contributors were the Ford and Rockefeller foundations, the United States, and the World Bank.

21. By way of comparison, Monsanto Corporation, a U.S. agricultural products company with $4.94 billion in sales in fiscal year 2003, has nine board members.

22. In January 2001, TAC was replaced with an interim Science Council, which became fully formed in September 2003. The mission of the new Science Council is "to enhance and promote the quality, relevance and impact of science in the CGIAR, to advise the Group on strategic scientific issues of importance to its goals and to mobilize and harness the best of international science for addressing the goals of the international agricultural research community" (CGIAR Science Council 2005b).

23. Nor has the system developed a set of science indicators similar to those reported biannually by the U.S. National Science Foundation or on a regular basis by the OECD's Directorate for Science Technology and Industry.

24. The relevant reports are CGIAR 1977 and 1981, and CGIAR System Review Secretariat 1998.

25. Anderson, Herdt, and Scobie (1988) list the documents produced by the CGIAR impact study, and Alston and Pardey (1995) list other such CG studies.

26. These reports were released in 1973, 1976, 1979, 1986, 1992, and 1997.

27. Fuglie and Ruttan (1989) provide a mid-1980s estimate of about $200,000 per review, of which center staff time in preparing for the review accounts for 40 percent. A more contemporary estimate by Özgediz (1995) suggests the direct costs of a center review to be more like $300,000, to which must be added the considerable indirect costs of center staff time involved in preparing for the review. These indirect costs are hard to determine but may be around 75 percent of the estimated direct costs.

28. Most center directors now seem to spend much more (often an overwhelmingly large proportion) of their time in fund-raising activities rather than in managing the science being conducted in their centers.

29. The CG has used a number of classification schemes to report its research effort over time. Because centers have largely been left to themselves to decide what constitutes "productivity" or " biodiversity-saving" research, and so on, it is difficult to interpret the reported composition of CG research.

30. After 2002, the financial reports of the CG do not identify the "increasing productivity" orientation of center research.

31. Barrett (2003) reviewed evidence on the impact of the CG's natural-resource management research, while Gardner (2003) assessed the CG-related impact evidence more generally. See also Feldman's (2001) annotated bibliography of impact-assessment studies conducted in the CGIAR from 1970 to 1999. Table 12.5 also includes studies of CGIAR research done by investigators outside the CG.

32. Brennan (1986, 1989) and Brennan and Fox (1995) estimated the benefits from adopting CIMMYT wheat in Australia; Burnett et al. (1990) estimated the impacts of CIMMYT wheat in New Zealand; Brennan et al. (1997) dealt with IRRI impacts in Australia; Byerlee and Moya (1993) looked at the impacts of varietal spillovers in developing countries collectively; and Pardey et al. (1996) reviewed CIMMYT and IRRI impacts in the United States. More recently, Heisey, Lantican, and Dubin (2002) updated the Byerlee and Moya estimates of benefits to developing countries. Bofu et al. (1996) and Fonseca et al. (1996) estimated the benefits from adopting particular varieties of potatoes from CIP in China and Peru, respectively. Pardey et al. (1996) measured the U.S. benefits from adopting IRRI rice varieties. Brennan and Bantilan (1999) and Brennan et al. (2002) estimated the impacts on Australian producers and consumers resulting from varietal releases from ICRISAT and ICARDA for a range of crops. Some of the studies reported in Evenson and Gollin 2003 estimated the benefits to various countries from adopting material developed by CG centers, while other studies in the compilation documented adoption of CG releases without going as far as estimating the value of the benefits. Pardey et al. (2004) reported the benefits to Brazil from using improved varieties of upland rice, soybeans, and edible beans, highlighting the spillin benefits from bean varieties developed by CIAT and others.

33. Brennan (1986, 1989) noted this point but did not adjust his measures of benefits to Australia from CIMMYT. Most of the studies of this type have not accounted for the CG-induced changes in world prices. Notable exceptions are the studies by Brennan and Bantilan (1999) and Brennan et al. (2002) of the impacts on Australian agriculture of research from two other CG centers: ICRISAT and ICARDA. The main effects of these research-induced changes in prices are on the distribution of benefits between producers and consumers and thus among countries. They have little impact on the measures of global benefits.

34. Widely cited early critics of Green Revolution technologies include Griffin (1974), Lappé and Collins (1979), and Pearse (1980). Ruttan (2002) summarizes and evaluates some of these concerns.

35. Antle and Pingali (1994) measured the human-health and productivity effects of pesticide use, using survey data collected in two regions in the Philippines.

References

Alston J. M. 2002. Spillovers. *Australian Journal of Agricultural and Resource Economics* 46 (3): 315–346.

Alston, J. M., and P. G. Pardey. 1995. Research evaluation requirements in the CGIAR. International Food Policy Research Institute, Washington, D.C. Mimeo.

———. 1996. *Making science pay: The economics of agricultural R&D policy.* Washington, D.C.: American Enterprise Institute.

————. 1999. *International approaches to agricultural R&D: The CGIAR.* Paper prepared for Office of Science and Technology Policy, Executive Office of the President of the United States, Washington, D.C.

————. 2001. Attribution and other problems in assessing the returns to agricultural R&D. *Agricultural Economics* 25 (2–3): 141–152.

Alston, J. M., G. W. Norton, and P. G. Pardey. 1995. *Science under scarcity: Principles and practice for agricultural research evaluation and priority setting.* Ithaca, N.Y.: Cornell University Press. (Rept. 1998 CAB International).

Alston, J. M., P. G. Pardey, and V. H, Smith, eds. 1999. *Paying for agricultural productivity.* Baltimore: Johns Hopkins University Press.

Alston, J. M., P. G. Pardey, and M. J. Taylor, eds. 2001. *Agricultural science policy: Changing global agendas.* Baltimore: Johns Hopkins University Press.

Alston, J. M., M. C. Marra, P. G. Pardey, and T. J. Wyatt. 2000a. *A meta-analysis of rates of return to agricultural R&D: Ex pede Herculem?* IFPRI Research Report No. 113. Washington, D.C.: International Food Policy Research Institute.

————. 2000b. Research returns redux: A meta-analysis of the returns to agricultural R&D. *Australian Journal of Agricultural and Resource Economics* 44 (2): 185–215.

Anderson, J. R. 1998. Selected policy issues in international agricultural research: On striving for international public goods in an era of donor fatigue. *World Development* 26 (6): 1149–1162.

Anderson, J. R., and D. G. Dalrymple. 1999. *The World Bank, the grant program, and the CGIAR: A retrospective review.* Operations Evaluation Department Working Paper Series No. 1. Washington, D.C.: World Bank.

Anderson, J. R., R. W. Herdt, and G. M. Scobie. 1988. *Science and food: The CGIAR and its partners.* Washington, D.C.: World Bank.

Antle, J. M., and P. L. Pingali. 1994. Pesticides, productivity, and farmer health: A Philippine case study. *American Journal of Agricultural Economics* 76 (3): 418–430.

Barrett, C. 2003. *Natural resource management research in CGIAR: A meta-evaluation.* Operations Evaluation Department Thematic Research Paper. Washington, D.C.: World Bank.

Baum, W. C. 1986. *Partners against hunger: The Consultative Group for International Agricultural Research.* Washington, D.C.: World Bank.

Binenbaum, E., and P. G. Pardey. 2005. Collective action in plant breeding. Selected paper prepared for the American Agricultural Economics Association Annual Meeting, Providence, Rhode Island, July 24–27.

Binenbaum, E., P. G. Pardey, and B. D. Wright. 2001. Public–private R&D relationships: The Consultative Group on International Agricultural Research. *American Journal of Agricultural Economics* 83 (3): 748–753.

Binenbaum, E., C. Nottenburg, P. G. Pardey, B. D. Wright, and P. Zambrano. 2003. South–North trade, intellectual property jurisdictions, and freedom to operate in agricultural research on staple crops. *Economic Development and Cultural Change* 51 (2): 309–336.

Boettiger, S., G. Graff, P. G. Pardey, E. van Dusen, and B. D. Wright. 2004. Intellectual property rights for plant biotechnology: International aspects. In *Handbook of plant biotechnology,* ed. P. Christou and H. Klee. Chichester, U.K.: John Wiley and Sons.

Bofu, S., T. Weimning, W. Jimin, W. Chunlin, Y. Zhengui, W. Shengwu, and M. Huarte. 1996. Economic impact of CIP-24 in China. In *Case studies of the impact of CIP-related technologies,* ed. T. S. Walker and C. C. Crissman. Lima, Peru: International Potato Center.

Borlaug, N. 1982. Feeding mankind in the 1980s: The role of international agricultural research. In *Increasing agricultural productivity,* ed. T. J. Davis. Washington, D.C.: World Bank.

Brennan, J. P. 1986. Impact of wheat varieties from CIMMYT on Australian wheat production. *Agricultural Economics Bulletin No. 5.* Sydney: New South Wales Department of Agriculture.

———. 1989. Spillover effects of international agricultural research: CIMMYT-based semi-dwarf wheats in Australia. *Agricultural Economics* 3: 323–332.

Brennan, J. P., and M. C. S. Bantilan. 1999. *Impact of ICRISAT research on Australian agriculture.* Report prepared for Australian Centre for International Agricultural Research. Economic Research Report No. 1, Wagga Wagga, Australia: New South Wales Department of Agriculture.

Brennan, J. P., and P. N. Fox. 1995. *Impact of CIMMYT wheats in Australia: Evidence of international research spillovers.* Economics Research Report No. 1/95. Wagga Wagga, Australia: New South Wales Department of Agriculture.

Brennan, J. P., I. P. Singh, and L. G. Lewin. 1997. Identifying international rice research spillovers in New South Wales. *Agricultural Economics* 17 (1): 35–44.

Brennan, J. P., A. Aw-Hassan, K. J. Quade, and T. L. Nordblum. 2002. *Impact of ICARDA Research on Australian Agriculture.* Report prepared for Australian Centre for International Agricultural Research. Economic Research Report No. 11. Wagga Wagga, Australia: New South Wales Department of Agriculture.

Burnett, P. A., G. O. Edmeades, J. P. Brennan, H. A. Eagles, J. M. McEwan, and W. B. Griffin. 1990. CIMMYT contributions to wheat production in New Zealand. In *Proceedings of the Sixth Assembly of the Wheat Breeding Society of Australia.* Tamworth, Australia: Wheat Breeding Society of Australia.

Byerlee, D. 1994. *Modern varieties, productivity, and sustainability: Recent experience and emerging challenges.* Mexico City: International Maize and Wheat Improvement Center.

Byerlee, D., and P. Moya. 1993. *Impacts of international wheat breeding in the developing world, 1966–1990.* Mexico City: International Maize and Wheat Improvement Center.

CGIAR (Consultative Group on International Agricultural Research). 1977. *CGIAR report of the review committee.* Washington, D.C.: CGIAR.

————. 1981. *Second review of the CGIAR.* Washington, D.C.: CGIAR.

CGIAR Science Council. 2003a. Our mission. http://www.cgiar.org/who/index.html. Accessed April 20, 2003.

————. 2003b. *CGIAR financial report 2002.* Washington, D.C.: CGIAR System Office.

————. 2005a. *System priorities for the CGIAR, 2005–2015.* Rome: Science Council Secretariat.

————. 2005b. Our mission. http://www.sciencecouncil.cgiar.org/who.html. Accessed May 21, 2005.

CGIAR Secretariat. Various years. *CGIAR financial report.* Washington, D.C.: CGIAR Secretariat.

CGIAR System Review Secretariat. 1998. *The international research partnership for food security and sustainable agriculture.* Third system review of the Consultative Group on International Development. Washington, D.C.: World Bank.

Culver, J. C., and J. Hyde. 2000. *American dreamer: The life and times of Henry A. Wallace.* New York: W. W. Norton and Company.

Dalrymple, D. G. 2004. Impure public goods and agricultural research: Toward a blend of theory and practice. Washington, D.C.: United States Agency for International Development. Mimeo.

Ehrlich, P. 1968. *The population bomb.* New York: Ballantine Books.

Evenson, R. E., and D. Gollin. 2003. *Crop variety improvement and its effect on productivity: The impact of international agricultural research.* Wallingford, U.K.: CAB International.

Farrar, C. 2000. IFPRI's first 10 years. Washington, D.C.: International Food Policy Research Institute.

Feldman, M. P. 2001. Impact assessment studies conducted in the CGIAR, 1970–1999: An annotated bibliography. In *Milestones in impact assessment research in the CGIAR, 1970–1999,* ed. P. L. Pingali. Mexico City: Standing Panel on Impact Assessment, Technical Advisory Committee of the Consultative Group on International Agricultural Research.

Fonseca, C., R. Labarta, A. Mendoza, J. Landeo, and T. S. Walker. 1996. Economic impact of the high-yielding, late-blight-resistant variety Canchan-INIAA in Peru. In *Case studies of the impact of CIP-related technologies,* ed. T. S. Walker and C. C. Crissman. Lima, Peru: International Potato Center.

Fuglie, K., and V. W. Ruttan. 1989. Value of external reviews of research at the international agricultural research centers. *Agricultural Economics* 3: 365–380.

Gardner, B., 2003. *Global public goods from the CGIAR: Impact assessment.* Operations Evaluation Department Thematic Research Paper. Washington, D.C.: World Bank.

Gardner, B., and W. Lesser. 2003. International agricultural research as a global public good. *American Journal of Agricultural Economics.* 85 (3): 692–697.

Griffin, K. 1974. *The political economy of agrarian change: An essay on the Green Revolution.* Cambridge, Mass.: Harvard University Press.

Gryseels, G., and J. R. Anderson. 1991. International agricultural research. In *Agricultural research policy: International quantitative perspectives,* ed. P. G. Pardey, J. Roseboom, and J. R. Anderson. Cambridge: Cambridge University Press.

Heisey, P. W., M. A. Lantican, and H. J. Dubin. 2002. *Assessing the benefits of international wheat breeding research in the developing world: The global wheat impacts study, 1966–1997.* Mexico City: International Maize and Wheat Improvement Center.

Jackson, G. 1984. *Report of the Committee to Review the Australian Overseas Aid Program.* Canberra: Australian Government Publishing Service.

Koo, B., C. Nottenburg, and P. G. Pardey. 2004. Plants and intellectual property: An international appraisal. *Science* 306 (November): 1295–1297.

Koo, B., P. G. Pardey, and B. D. Wright with P. Bramel, D. Debouck, M. E. van Dusen, M. T. Jackson, N. K. Rao, B. Skovmand, S. Taba, and J. Valkoun. 2004. *Saving seeds: The economics of conserving crop genetic resources ex situ in the future harvest centers of the CGIAR.* Wallingford, U.K.: CAB International.

Lappé, F., and J. Collins. 1979. *Food first: Beyond the myth of scarcity.* Rev. ed. New York: Ballantine.

Nottenburg, C., P. G. Pardey, and B. D. Wright. 2002. Accessing other people's technology for nonprofit research. *Australian Journal of Agricultural and Resource Economics* 48 (3): 389–416.

OECD (Organisation for Economic Co-operation and Development). 2005. International Statistics online database (IDS/o). OECD Development Assistance Committee online (DAC/o). http://www1.oecd.org/dac/htm/online.htm. Accessed May 2005.

Özgediz, S. 1995. Strengthening evaluation in the CGIAR: Needs and options. Draft. Washington, D.C.: CGIAR Secretariat.

Pardey, P. G., and N. M. Beintema. 2001. *Slow magic: Agricultural R&D a century after Mendel.* IFPRI Food Policy Report. Washington, D.C.: International Food Policy Research Institute.

Pardey, P. G., J. Roseboom, and J. R. Anderson. 1991. Topical perspectives on national agricultural research. In *Agricultural research policy: International quantitative perspectives,* ed. P. G. Pardey, J. Roseboom, and J. R. Anderson. Cambridge: Cambridge University Press.

Pardey, P. G., J. M. Alston, J. E. Christian, and S. Fan. 1996. *Hidden harvest: U.S. benefits from international research aid.* IFPRI Food Policy Report. Washington, D.C.: International Food Policy Research Institute.

Pardey, P. G., J. M. Alston, C. Chan-Kang, E. Castello Magalhães, and S. A. Vosti. 2004. *Assessing and attributing the benefits from varietal improvement research in Brazil.* IFPRI Research Report No 136. Washington, D.C.: International Food Policy Research Institute.

Pearse, A. 1980. *Seeds of plenty, seeds of want: Social and economic implications of the Green Revolution.* Oxford: Clarendon Press.

Perkins, J. H. 1997. *Geopolitics and the Green Revolution: Wheat, genes, and the cold war.* Oxford: Oxford University Press.

Plucknett, D. L., N. J. H. Smith, and S. Özgediz. 1990. *Networking in international agricultural research.* Ithaca, N.Y.: Cornell University Press.

Runge, F. C., B. Senauer, P. G. Pardey, and M. W. Rosegrant. 2003. *Ending hunger in our lifetime: Food security and globalization.* Baltimore: Johns Hopkins University Press.

Ruttan, V. W. 2001. Imperialism and competition in anthropology, sociology, political science, and economics: A perspective on development economics. *Journal of Socio-Economics* 30: 15–29.

———. 2002. *Controversy about agricultural technology: Lessons from the Green Revolution.* Department of Applied Economics Staff Paper P02-15. St. Paul: University of Minnesota.

Ryan, J. G., ed. 1987. *Building on success: Agricultural research, technology and policy for development.* Canberra: Australian Centre for International Agricultural Research.

Schultz, T. W. 1969. What ails world agriculture? *Bulletin of the Atomic Scientists* (January 1968). Reprinted in V. W. Ruttan, A. D. Waldo, and J. P. Houck, *Agricultural policy in an affluent society.* New York: W. W. Norton and Company.

TAC (CGIAR Technical Advisory Committee Secretariat).1987. *CGIAR Priorities and future strategies: Documents relating to the review of CGIAR priorities and future strategies.* Rome: TAC.

Tribe, D. E. 1991. *Doing well by doing good.* Leichardt, New South Wales, and Parkville, Victoria: Pluto Press Australia and Crawford Fund for International Agricultural Research.

———. 1994. Feeding and greening the world. Wallingford, U.K., and Parkville, Victoria, Australia: CAB International and Crawford Fund for International Agricultural Research.

World Bank. 2003a. *The CGIAR at 31: An independent meta-evaluation of the consultative group on international agricultural research.* Vol. 1: Overview report. Washington, D.C.: World Bank, Operations Evaluation Department.

———. 2003b. *The CGIAR at 31: An independent meta-evaluation of the consultative group on international agricultural research.* Vol. 3: Annexes. Washington, D.C.: World Bank, Operations Evaluation Department.

Wright, B. D., P. G. Pardey, C. Nottenburg, and B. Koo. 2006. Agricultural innovation: Investments and incentives. In *Handbook of agricultural economics,* vol. 3, ed. R. E. Evenson, P. Pingali, and T. P. Schultz. Amsterdam: Elsevier.

Chapter 13

Synthesis of Themes and Policy Issues

Julian M. Alston, Philip G. Pardey, and Roley R. Piggott

T he developing world is not likely to benefit from rich-country agricultural research in the future as much as it has in the past, and so it will need to become more self-reliant in the provision of agricultural R&D. But even the richest countries continue to underinvest in certain types of agricultural R&D (Alston, Pardey, and Smith 1999). To add to the complexity of policymaking, changes are taking place in the technical and economic basis for agricultural R&D per se, as well as in the structure of the economy, such as decreasing trade barriers and changing consumer and producer demands. These problems of underinvestment and policy challenges are more acute in developing countries than in developed countries; and the task of correcting for the underinvestment in agricultural R&D is therefore even greater. But much has to be learned about what is wrong currently, and why, before effective remedies can be designed and put in place.

The research agenda of the world's richest countries is shifting away from the interests of the world's poorest people, such that developing countries that have relied on technological spillovers from the North will no longer be able to do so in the same ways or to the same extent. Moreover, excepting a handful of countries, the gains of developing countries in scientific and technological capacities have slowed from the pace achieved in the 1960s, 1970s, and into the 1980s, raising the prospect that a sizable number of developing countries may become technological orphans.

Concern that these changes were going unnoticed provided the motivation for this study of agricultural R&D policy in developing countries, as a companion to the previous volume covering richer countries (Alston, Pardey, and Smith 1999). The country coverage is broad and diverse enough to represent agricultural R&D

Table 13.1 Case-study NARSs at a glance

	Bangladesh	Brazil	China	Colombia
Date of inception of formal research	1928	Mid-1800s	1932	1879
Total expenditures[a]	1,275.7 (1995–2000 average, million taka)	1,417.5 (1996)	4,179.4 (2002)	166.7 (1996)
Agricultural research Intensity[b]	NA	1.7 (1996)	0.32 (1995–97 average)	0.53 (1996)
Total number of researchers[c]	3,185 (2001)	4,895 (1996, fte's)	29,920 (1999)	1,007.9 (1996, fte's)
Principal research agency	Bangladesh Agricultural Research Institute (BARI)	Brazilian Agricultural Research Corporation (Embrapa)	Chinese Academy of Agricultural Sciences (CAAS)	Colombian Corporation for Agricultural Research (CORPOICA)

Source: Compiled by authors from country case studies in this volume.

Notes: NA indicates not available.

[a]Unless otherwise indicated, expenditure totals are in international dollars (millions at 1999 prices).

[b]Measures the ratio of agricultural R&D spending to agricultural GDP in percentage terms.

[c]fte indicates full-time equivalent researchers.

in the developing world more generally. Key features of the NARSs in the case-study countries are summarized in Table 13.1, showing a wide range of variation in size of the NARSs, agricultural research intensities, and other details.

The mix and intensity of the problems faced varies across the case-study countries as one would expect, but they also share many common themes. Collectively, the case studies sound an alarm about the need for serious attention to developing-country agricultural R&D policy.

The Changing Context for Agricultural Research

The global environment in which agricultural research is conducted is changing. Borders are opening as a result of unilateral, bilateral, or multilateral trade policy reforms, and rules governing international trade in products and technologies are changing in consequence; consumer and producer demands for the products of agricultural science are evolving, and the structure of markets for farm products is shifting; and changes are also occurring in the nature of science itself and the legal and market institutions in which it operates.

India	Indonesia	Korea	South Africa	Zambia
Last quarter of 19th century	Early 1800s	1434	1910	1922
1,318 (1997–99 average)	278 (1998–99)	417.7 (2000)	232.2 (1999)	NA
0.32 (2001–3 average)	0.21 (2001–3 average)	1.82 (1999)	NA	NA
21,770 (1996–1998, 1992)	3,379 (2000)	9579 (2000)	906.7 (1999, fte's)	245.7 (2000, fte's)
Indian Agricultural Research Institute (IARI)	Agency for Agricultural Research and Development (AARD)	Rural Development Agency (RDA)	Agricultural Research Council (ARC)	Soils and Crops Research Branch (SCRB)

Market Context

The general trend toward the opening up of borders to trade in agricultural products has important implications for agricultural R&D policy. While progress on this front is much criticized for being too slow (and with some backsliding on the part of some countries), movements toward freer agricultural trade are expected to continue. The implication is that agricultural trading patterns will more closely reflect comparative advantage. An important implication for policymakers is that comparative advantage should guide R&D investments in developing countries more than it has in the past (see the Korea case study, for instance). However, it is not easy to judge comparative advantage and its implications for research priorities, not least because technological advancements, including innovations in transport and storage technologies, and other changes can alter comparative advantage in ways that are difficult to discern, and research lags can be long.

Consumer attitudes toward food products changed markedly during the late twentieth century. Particularly important have been the increasing demand for food safety and environmentally friendly food production. These might not yet be major considerations for some low-income countries, but they are likely to become so as incomes increase. They are certainly major considerations in some rich countries that import food products from the developing world.

Equally potent institutional changes are afoot regarding relationships among food production, wholesale, and retail operations. The structure of food marketing is changing rapidly throughout much of the developing world. Retail food sales are quickly becoming the prevailing mode of delivery to consumers, and supermarkets and self-service convenience stores are now dominant players in the agrifood economy (Reardon et al. 2003). Private food-quality standards and supply-chain management decisions made by food retailers are having increasingly pervasive and profound effects on commodity choice, quality, and timing of delivery by the farm-production sector. Taken together, these trends have important implications for on- and off-farm demands for technology, reshaping the incentives to innovate and changing the structure and likely sources of funds for the R&D required to develop and disseminate these technologies.

Spillovers of Scientific Knowledge and Technology

Agricultural science and technology spillovers are pervasive both within and among countries. Developing countries in particular have relied on the supply of basic science and certain agricultural technologies developed elsewhere, particularly in a few rich countries and the CGIAR. Spillovers extend beyond agricultural technologies that can be adapted to local conditions to include the underlying knowledge and scientific research. Intellectual property rights and other regulatory policies—including biosafety protocols, trading regimes, and specific regulatory restrictions on the movement of genetic material—influence the extent to which such spillovers are feasible or economic.

Variability in the agroecological basis of agriculture means that imported technologies often have to be adapted to local conditions before they can be used (as was usually the case with Green Revolution wheat and rice varieties). In some cases, imported technologies are also screened for biosafety reasons (note the fungus problem caused by imported maize seed in Zambia). Nevertheless, for some developing countries and for some types of technologies, the least-cost option has been, and will continue to be, to import and adapt technology. However, both the supply and demand for spillover technologies are changing.

On the demand side, some developing countries have expanded their own research capacity and shifted upstream, reducing their emphasis on adaptive R&D: examples include the largest developing countries, Brazil, China, and India. These countries have become a potential source of new technologies for the poorest and smallest countries, which will continue to emphasize adaptive research, relying on spillins of technology from other countries. On the other hand, the large, rich-country NARSs that have been the primary source of these spillins, in particular the United States, have progressively shifted away from the types of agricultural R&D that are most easily adapted and adopted by developing countries. And the same countries have also scaled back their support for the CGIAR and other IARCs that provide global public-good types of agricultural R&D.

Rich and poor countries alike will have to adapt their strategies to reflect continuing changes in the nature of agricultural R&D spillovers. Unless something else changes to compensate, the shifting balance of supply and demand for spillovers of agricultural technologies seems likely to leave many of the world's poorest countries as technological orphans; at particular risk are countries in tropical and subtropical regions. It will be a major challenge for the international community to establish an institutional framework that results in optimal investments in R&D by and for developing countries, given the nature and importance of international spillovers. The starting point is to understand them better: to recognize the forms that they take and determine how to measure them with greater precision.

Implications for the CGIAR
As discussed in Chapter 12, the CGIAR has evolved from its initial focus on enhancing the supply of staple food. The early CGIAR strategy was to adapt existing technologies, recognizing that developing countries lacked local capacity and the rich-country crop varieties were not directly applicable. In the context of an expanded set of priorities and stagnant overall funding, however, the CGIAR has progressively scaled back its support for productivity-enhancing research. Some have questioned whether that evolution has gone too far, especially in light of other changes in the source of productivity-enhancing agricultural technologies for the food-deficit countries. In particular, as the spillovers from rich-country agricultural R&D become less relevant, many developing countries will increasingly rely on IARCs to supply basic breeding materials or finished varieties of staple crops. It can be argued, therefore, that the CGIAR should return to the basic objective of enhancing the supply of staple food, especially in food-deficit countries—both by providing relevant technologies and by strengthening agricultural research capacity in these countries—while recognizing that the market, policy, and scientific contexts for R&D have changed dramatically over the past several decades so that a "business as before" strategy will not suffice.

Shifting National Policy Contexts
In addition to these common threads and global interdependencies, substantive local issues affect how local agricultural-research systems operate and the constraints they face. For example, in South Africa, amid the myriad changes associated with the collapse of apartheid, structural changes in science and technology policy have had an important influence on the NARS. Economy-wide structural change has been important in Zambia. Indonesia's 1998 change of government resulted in more-decentralized decisionmaking in all areas of government, including the financing and conduct of agricultural research. As a consequence, it is likely that agricultural

research in Indonesia will put more emphasis on farming systems and less on commodity-oriented research.

Some studies describe changes in the direction of research effort. In Bangladesh, for example, in response to a government policy to diversify away from cropping, crop research is receiving a declining share of agricultural research funds, with an increasing share going to livestock, forestry, and fisheries. The dualistic farming systems of Zambia and South Africa give rise to the question of whether the agricultural research system delivers as much for poor farmers as it does for large-scale commercial operators.

Research Funding Problems and Initiatives

Many of the problems facing agricultural research in the developing world relate to funding. Apart from the pervasive problem of simply not enough funding, in some places funding is also unreliable and highly variable from year to year. Initiatives to reduce these problems include policies designed to enhance the role of the private sector and innovations in funding mechanisms.

Pervasive Underfunding

Investment in agricultural research has high returns (see, for example, the meta-analysis of Alston et al. 2000, and the evidence in the chapters on Indonesia, India, and the CGIAR), and the case studies demonstrate that agricultural research has played a major role in helping to provide food for large and expanding populations (as in China, India, and Indonesia). But there is pervasive underfunding of agricultural research. In most of the case-study countries, the research intensity (agricultural research expenditure as a percentage of agricultural GDP) is less than the global average of around 1 percent (Pardey and Beintema 2001).

Underfunding of agricultural research is alarming for a number of reasons. Specific concerns include

- the continuing growth of populations, especially in the world's poorest countries;

- an increasingly scarce and deteriorating natural-resource base;

- the pervasive pockets of hunger and poverty that persist in developing countries, in many cases despite impressive national average-productivity increases; and

- the growing divergence between rich-country research agendas and the priorities of poor people.

Variability of Funding

The problem of temporal variability in the funding of agricultural R&D was emphasized in the Bangladesh case study, but it is a widespread problem that occurs for various reasons. Funding for agricultural R&D may have too much of a residual claim on scarce research dollars, as seems to be the case in Bangladesh. Donor funding varies in importance across the case-study countries, but is especially important throughout Sub-Saharan Africa; and it is subject to changing political circumstances within both the donor country and the recipient country. Variability may also result from major economic shocks, as occurred in Indonesia.

Whatever the reason, variability in research funding is problematic because of the long gestation period for new crop varieties and livestock breeds and the desirability of assuring long-term employment for scientists and other staff. Variability encourages an overemphasis on short-term projects or on projects with short lags between investment, outcomes, and adoption. It also discourages the specialization of scientists and other resources, even when it has a high payoff potential.

The solution to this problem has not been found yet, although the levy or check-off system used in some countries (e.g., Colombia) is a means of maintaining a flow of funds for agricultural R&D when other funding sources wane. The problem will become greater given the need for developing countries to become more self-reliant in agricultural R&D.

Funding Innovations

Some innovations in funding methods may have exacerbated the problems associated with insufficient funding or unreliable funding; others may have ameliorated them. The main traditional funding method has been block grants to research institutes, with little or no consideration of research priorities, research productivity, or research planning in general.

Unlike some developed countries, such as Australia or the Netherlands, developing countries make relatively little use of funding mechanisms such as commodity levies or check-offs. Countries that do use such methods of funding include Uruguay, Zambia, South Africa, Colombia, Brazil, and Indonesia. Indonesia has a long history of producer levies being used to fund research on plantation crops because of their capacity to generate profits for those segments of the industry supporting the research through enhanced exports.

In some countries, public research institutes or agencies have tried to self-fund some of their research activity by commercializing their research operations or outcomes (for example, India, Indonesia, and even some CG centers). China also does this, partly motivated by a public-policy desire that research institutes get in tune with market needs. This has had the unfortunate side effect of distracting attention away from agricultural research and toward unrelated commercial activities (for example, the sale of bottled mineral water).

Another potential source of funds is the commercialization of research outcomes, but this is critically dependent on an effective system of intellectual property rights (IPR). Many case-study countries do not have effective IPR; in others the system is embryonic or requires further development to enact, strengthen, or enforce laws. The lack of effective IPR hinders the participation of private entities in agricultural R&D, either as independent research providers or in partnership with public agencies. Even so, some successful private-public partnerships have been formed in India, Indonesia, and China. The India chapter provides an interesting example of innovative funding: the government offers matching funds for income generated by public research providers through commercialization of technology and services and contract research for the private sector.

Private Sector Involvement

The extent of private involvement in agricultural R&D varies across the case-study countries, but, in general, the private share of total research funding is small. In India, however, private-sector funding appears to have grown rapidly in recent years and now accounts for an estimated 11 percent of total agricultural research funding. The case studies indicate that greater private involvement in agricultural R&D is warranted; they also suggest ways to encourage it, including more effective IPR legislation, removal of unnecessary controls on direct foreign investment, greater transparency and stability in regulations that affect foreign investors, tax exemptions on research expenditures and venture capital, and more liberal policies on the importation of research equipment.

Around much of the developing world, realistically, one should not expect private funding for agricultural R&D to displace public funding to any great extent any time soon. Research to develop the technologies that are least appropriable (like new management methods and know-how) will continue to require public funding. Any expansion in the relative importance of private funding, or public–private partnerships in the provision of agricultural R&D, will be for technologies associated with inputs used in farming (such as chemicals, seeds, and machines), as has been the case in India, or with off-farm processes.

Most developing countries will continue to face a scenario with a negligible private-sector involvement in agricultural R&D and a scarce public-sector resource. The main policy choice for these countries will be how to make the best of those resources to capitalize on international spillovers and maximize payoffs.

Biotechnology

As explained in the India case study, modern biotechnology research raises a variety of new issues, particularly food and biosafety concerns and other issues arising from negative public perceptions of technology itself. Investment in agricultural biotechnology research across the case-study countries is uneven, and it is inhibited by inadequate legal and regulatory frameworks. Among the case-study countries, Brazil, China, and India are facilitating biotechnology research by strengthening intellectual property rights and putting in place a regulatory framework aimed at ensuring biosafety. In addition, these countries are making substantial public investments in agricultural biotechnology.

In rich countries, private firms have been active in biotechnology research because of the large potential payoffs from technologies developed for commercial field crops such as wheat, maize, cotton, and soybeans (James 2004). The same trend can be expected in parts of the agricultural sectors in developing countries, such as plantation crops in Indonesia and cotton in India. However, further public involvement will be required if biotechnology products are to be developed for subsistence farmers in developing countries and for specialty crop growers everywhere (Alston 2004).

Management Methods and Resource-Allocation Mechanisms

The case-study countries differ in details but share a number of common research-management issues, most notably staffing concerns and approaches to allocating research resources.

Staffing Issues

The case studies detail various staffing problems in government research agencies that lower the payoffs of research spending. The obligation to pay pensions to an expanding cohort of retirees is problematic in China; loss of research scientists to other national and international organizations is a concern in Bangladesh and South Africa; and insufficient integration of research scientists in India's NARS with regional and international research networks is troubling, especially given that modern science is blurring disciplinary boundaries. Insufficient promotion on the basis of research productivity (as opposed to seniority) seems to be a pervasive problem, although some countries (such as China) are moving to address this problem. Many case studies also report insufficient staff with Ph.D.s, loss of staff from public agricultural-research institutions because of noncompetitive salaries, low ratios of scientific to administrative staff, high ratios of salary to nonsalary expenditures such that scientists lack equipment and operating inputs, and isolation of scientific staff from scientific networks.

Some of these staffing issues, such as lack of recognition of performance, are deeply entrenched in the public sectors of these countries and will probably require a major change in public-sector management before they are overcome. Others, such as exposure of staff to scientific networks, may be more transient, given developments in communications technology.

Resource-Allocation Processes

In recent years, economists have developed formal models for the ex ante evaluation of research projects to assist decision makers in allocating research funds. These models are being used increasingly in more developed countries, but they seem not to be used on any systematic basis in the case-study countries (except as a condition of donor funding). Similarly, the allocation of research funds according to clearly articulated research priorities—as happens in many developed countries—is less common in the case-study countries. Notable exceptions are India, where there is now some movement in that direction, and Brazil's Embrapa, which is perhaps the greatest user of formalized benefit–cost approaches in research evaluation and priority setting.

Competitive research grants (grants given on the basis of the quality of the proposed project and the track record of the researchers, which are common in developed countries) are becoming more widespread in most of the case-study countries. These are generally seen as a mechanism that helps ensure value for money in the provision of research services, although they do have certain transactions costs and can involve rent-seeking costs, as detailed in the Brazil chapter (see also Alston, Pardey, and Smith 1999, pp. 25–26, and Alston and Pardey 1996, pp. 297–300).

Even in the developed countries, where competitive grants processes have been extensively employed, the efficiency gains have to be offset against the costs associated with the imperfections of the processes; the devil is in the details of the institutions and the market setting. For these kinds of reasons, it is not easy to generalize about the payoffs in practice from making research funds more contestable. In many developing countries where alternative research providers are limited, the potential benefits from making funds contestable nationally may not be large enough to justify the additional costs; opening up the process to nonnationals may be more useful.

Conclusion

The balance of global agricultural research investments is shifting in ways that will have important long-term consequences, especially for the world's poorest people. The primary reason is changes in the supply and demand for agricultural technologies in the world's richest countries, which have been the main producers of agricultural technologies. These countries will no longer provide the same levels of productivity-enhancing technologies, suitable for adaptation and adoption in food-deficit countries, as they did in the past. This trend has been compounded by a reduction of rich-country support for the international agricultural research system, which had already diverted its own attention away from productivity-enhancing technologies.

These changes mean that developing countries will have to become more self-reliant in the development of applicable agricultural technologies. To achieve complete self-reliance will be beyond the ability of many countries, especially given recent and ongoing structural changes in science and scientific institutions—in particular the rise of modern biotechnologies and other high-tech agriculture, and the associated roles of intellectual property. The largest developing countries—Brazil, China, and India—are making the transition, but they have yet to overcome the problem of chronic underinvestment in agricultural research, and they have many problems to address with respect to the effective management and efficient use of available resources.

The poorest of the poor will continue to rely on the supply of spillovers from other countries and from multinational efforts, but current international investments in productivity-enhancing research seem too small to fill the vacuum being created by the changes in rich-country research agendas. During the twentieth century, the world's poor countries were often slow to take advantage of the fruits of agricultural-science achievements in the rich countries; they began to adopt modern varieties and mechanical and chemical innovations, but only after a lag. One purpose of multinational initiatives was to shorten the lag and close the gap, and that goal was apparently being realized during the Green Revolution. But recent trends raise the specter of repeating the past: the return of a large and growing scientific and productivity gap, with attendant human problems. A rethinking of some national and multinational policies is required.

The issues are large-scale and long-term, and they demand serious attention, including further and more-specific analysis. Additional research policy analysis and evaluation will be required to support improved research policy formulation and priority setting. The benefits from effective policy research will come not only from increasing the agricultural R&D effort and making it more economically efficient but also from remedying harmful policies. Many developing countries lack the institutional capacity for social-science research oriented toward agricultural science and technology policy (Smith, Pardey, and Chan-Kang 2004). Like other types of agricultural R&D, policy-oriented research has to be locally adapted. A useful development in the case-study countries would be the establishment of domestic agricultural-research policy units to investigate and advise on a whole host of policy and practical issues concerning the NARSs, such as innovative funding methods, removal of constraints on private involvement in agricultural research, priority setting, workforce planning, incentive systems, and ex ante and ex post evaluation of research projects.

National governments in developing countries can also take some initiatives, as indicated by the analysis of case studies in this book, such as: (1) enhancing IPR and tailoring the institutional and policy details of IP to fit local circumstances; (2) increasing the total amount of government funding for their NARSs; (3) introducing institutional arrangements and incentives for private and joint public–private funding, such as matching grants and check-off funds; and (4) improving the processes by which agricultural research resources are administered and allocated. But such initiatives alone may not be sufficient. Another role for poor-country governments and others who care will be to remind rich people in developed countries that they can and should do more to help poor people in developing countries to feed themselves.

References

Alston, J. M. 2004. Horticultural biotechnology faces significant economic and market barriers. *California Agriculture* 58 (2): 80–88.

Alston, J. M., and P. G. Pardey. 1996. *Making science pay: The economics of agricultural R&D policy.* Washington, D.C.: American Enterprise Institute.

———. 1999. The economics of agricultural R&D policy. Chapter 2 in *Paying for agricultural productivity,* ed. J. M. Alston, P. G. Pardey, and V. H. Smith. Baltimore: Johns Hopkins University Press.

Alston, J. M., C. Chan-Kang, M. C. Marra, P. G. Pardey, and T. J. Wyatt. 2000. *A meta-analysis of the rates of return to agricultural R&D: Ex pede Herculem.* IFPRI Research Report No. 113. Washington, D.C.: International Food Policy Research Institute.

James, C. 2004. *Preview: Global status of commercialized biotech/GM crops: 2004.* ISAAA Brief No. 32-2004. Ithaca, N.Y.: International Service for the Acquisition of Agri-Biotech Applications.

Pardey, P. G., N. M. Beintema, S. Dehmer, and S. Wood. 2006. Agricultural research: A growing global divide? IFPRI Food Policy Report. Washington, D.C.: International Food Policy Research Institute (draft version).

Reardon, T., C. P. Timmer, C. B. Barrett, and J. A. Berdegué. 2003. The rise of supermarkets in Africa, Asia and Latin America. *American Journal of Agricultural Economics* 85 (5): 1140–1146.

Smith, V. H., P. G. Pardey, and C. Chan-Kang. 2004. The economics research industry. Chapter 2 in *What's economics worth? Valuing policy research,* ed. P. G. Pardey and V. H. Smith. Baltimore: Johns Hopkins University Press.

Contributors

Raisuddin Ahmed is research fellow emeritus and former director of the Market and Structural Studies Division at the International Food Policy Research Institute, Washington, D.C.

Julian M. Alston is a professor in the Department of Agricultural and Resource Economics at the University of California, Davis.

Flavio Avila is a researcher at the Empresa Brasileira de Pesquisa Agropecuária (Embrapa), Brasilia, Brazil.

Nienke M. Beintema is coordinator of the Agricultural Science and Technology Indicators Initiative at the International Food Policy Research Institute, based at Wageningen University, the Netherlands.

Derek Byerlee is a principal economist in the Agriculture and Rural Development Department of the World Bank, Washington, D.C.

Jung-Sup Choi is president of the Korea Rural Economic Institute, Seoul, Republic of Korea.

Steven Dehmer is a graduate student in the Department of Applied Economics at the University of Minnesota, St. Paul.

Howard Elliott is a former senior technical adviser to the Association for Strengthening Agricultural Research in Eastern and Central Africa (ASARECA) based in Entebbe, Uganda, under support provided to ASARECA by the U.S. Agency for International Development.

Shenggen Fan is a director of the Development Strategy and Governance Division of the International Food Policy Research Institute, Washington, D.C.

Keith O. Fuglie is the leader of the Impact Enhancement Division of the International Potato Center (CIP) and is based in Bogor, Indonesia.

Zahurul Karim recently retired as secretary to the Ministry of Livestock and Fisheries of the government of Bangladesh. Formerly he was the executive chair of the Bangladesh Agricultural Research Council (BARC).

Johann Kirsten is head of the Department of Agricultural Economics, Extension and Rural Development at the University of Pretoria, Pretoria, South Africa.

Hyunok Lee is a research economist in the Department of Agricultural and Resource Economics at the University of California, Davis.

Frikkie Liebenberg is an economist with the Agricultural Research Council in Pretoria, South Africa.

Suresh Pal is a senior scientist at the National Centre for Agricultural Economics and Policy Research (NCAP), New Delhi, India.

Philip G. Pardey is professor of science and technology policy in the Department of Applied Economics at the University of Minnesota, St. Paul, and director of the University of Minnesota Center for International Science and Technology Practice and Policy (InSTePP).

Paul T. Perrault is a former senior research officer at the International Service for National Agricultural Research, The Hague.

Roley R. Piggott is executive dean of the Faculty of Economics, Business and Law at the University of New England, Armidale, Australia.

Keming Qian is director of the Agricultural Trade Promotion Office of the Ministry of Agriculture, China, and former director general of the Institute of Agricultural Economics at the Chinese Academy of Agricultural Sciences (CAAS), Beijing.

Luis Romano is a consultant located in Bogotá, Colombia, and the former director of the planning office of the Instituto Colombiano Agropecuario (ICA).

Daniel A. Sumner is director of the University of California Agricultural Issues Center and Frank H. Buck, Jr. Professor in the Department of Agricultural and Resource Economics at the University of California, Davis.

Xiaobo Zhang is a research fellow in the Development Strategy and Governance Division of the International Food Policy Research Institute, Washington, D.C.

Index

Note: Page numbers for entries occurring in figures are suffixed by an *f*; those for entries in notes by an *n*, with the number of the note following; and those for entries in tables by a *t*.